Tales To Tickle Your Funny Bone
Touch Your Heart
and
Raise Your Hackles

Eldon G Lytle

THIS BOOK IS DEDICATED TO THE MEMORY
OF
F. WAYNE LYTLE and JUSTINE JONES LYTLE

REFER TO THE FOLLOWING MAP AS THE STORIES UNFOLD!

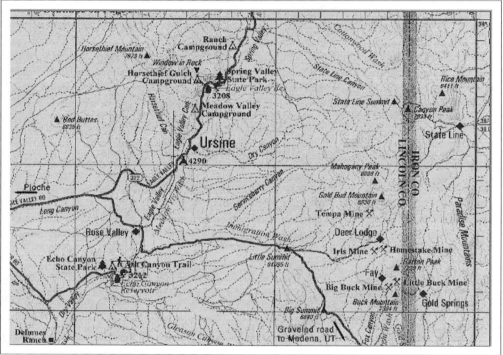

Elements of the story which `raise the hackles' of the author are signified graphically by the image of a denizen of the wilderness with hackles raised in response to distress, sometimes without further comment, to wit:

If you wish to become aware of potentially distressing `unpleasantries' which may offend your sensibilities or beliefs --- but perhaps make you a more informed or wiser person --- read these passages. Otherwise, skim or pass them by and search for stories which `tickle your funny bone,' or `touch your heart.'

Contents

Contents   vi

I   PREVIEW   **1**

1   STORY-TELLING AS A FAMILY TRADITION   **3**
  1.1   HOOP SNAKES   4
        Stubs   5
  1.2   BILLY JACK AND HIS RATTLESNAKE JUICE   6
        Meet Billy Jack   7
        Enter Snaggle Tooth   7
        The Potion Matures   7
        The Potion Works   8
        Winter Storage   8
        Enter Nellie Flatnose   8
        Super Kids   9
        Visit from Billy the Kid   9
        Testing for Descendants   9
  1.3   ALL OF THE BABIES ARE DYING!   10

2   BACKGROUND SETTING   **11**
  2.1   Close Call at the Dry Valley Sinkhole   14
        Quicksand Disaster   14
        Why Dry Valley is called *Dry Valley*   15
        Rose Valley Undergoing Degradation   16
        Logs from Days of Yore   17

3   THE LOG HOMES OF ROSE VALLEY   **21**
  3.1   Wayne's Log Home burns in Feb. 2010   21
  3.2   Farrel's Reply   24
  3.3   Age of the Log Sample   25
  3.4   Karen's Early Recollection of Freel's Log Home   25

4   A REVIEW OF FAMILY HISTORY   **27**
  4.1   The Pioneer Story   27
        The Nauvoo Expositor   27
        The Mormon Battallion   28
        The Gold Rush   29
  4.2   The Colonization Story   29
  4.3   John's Call to Carson-Valley   30
        The Utah War Story   30

4.4	'Profiteering'	31
	'Getting Gain' from One's Brethren	31
4.5	Of Wheat and Tares	31
	Vulnerability	32
	Orson Hyde Curses the Evildoers	33
4.6	Relevance to Lytle Family History	33
4.7	Outcome of the Utah War	33
4.8	Time for Story Telling	34
4.9	The *Wild West* Experience Continues – Utah's Dixie	34
	The St. George Temple Story	35
4.10	The Charles-Margaret Story	36
	Back to the Dry Valley Sink	37
4.11	The Moodyville Story	37
4.12	Shifting Church Policy	38
	Jacob Hamblin	39
	A Story of Dollars and Sense	40
	Mexican Hit Men	41
	Charles Constructs a Single Gauge Railroad	42
	Execution of Charles' Will	42
5	**CHARLES MAKES A U-TURN**	**45**
5.1	Hackles Galore	45
5.2	Life in Eagle Valley	46
5.3	The Lower-Muddy Mission Call	46
	Clearing away Historical Debris	47
5.4	Testing for Crookedness	47
5.5	Collateral Damages of the Utah War	49
5.6	Charles' Negative Ruling	50
	Separatism Supplants Communion	50
5.7	Pertinent Consequences	51
5.8	Analysis	51
	No Water Fit to Drink	52
5.9	Question of Identity	52
5.10	Dominos	53
5.11	More Dominos	53
5.12	Subsequent Lifestyle	53
5.13	Final Note on the Charles Lytle Story	54
6	**MARY'S STORY**	**55**
6.1	The Government Legislates Religion	55
6.2	Freel and Mary Jensen Are Wed	56
6.3	Mary Tells Her Own Story	56
	Family Origins in Denmark	56
	Becoming a Second Wife	56
	Events Subsequent to Edmunds-Tucker	56
6.4	Teaching in Nevada	58
6.5	Milton and Teenie Are Married	58
6.6	Freel and Mary Are Married	59
6.7	The Log Homes Are Built	59
6.8	Gladys and Wayne	59
6.9	Freel and Mary Are Both Non-Mormon	60
	Jack Daniels and Orange Aid	60

6.10 Grandma Bronc Buster   61
6.11 Grandma's Politics   61
6.12 Grandma Attends Church   61

7   JUSTINE — WAYNE MAKES HIS OWN U-TURN   63
7.1 Personal History of Justine Jones Lytle   63
     School in Enterprise   63
     School in Rose Valley   63
     Work at the Ranch   64
     Recreation   64
     Sick with Quinsy   64
     Marriage and Subsequent Events   65
     Family Illness   65
     Close Call in Reno   65
     The Move to Vegas   66
     Farrel's Trombone   66
     Eldon Plays Grandpa Jones   66
     Noel's Shortcut   66
     Professor Cuddles   67
     Larry Learns to Drive   67
     Karen's Talent for Singing   67
7.2 The Seth Jones Family Comes to Rose Valley   67
7.3 Wayne's Baptism   67
7.4 Orderville   69

II BEYOND BILLIE JACK IN THE RED NOTEBOOK   73

8   MORE TALES FROM THE NOTEBOOK   75
8.1 Review and Preview   76
     The Moaning Bush   76
     An Unfaithful Wife   76
     Tikapoo's Curious Demise   76
8.2 The Chinese Herbal Cure   77
8.3 The Bed-Bug Cure   77

9   PEOPLE IN THE VALLEYS AND HOW THEY DIED   79
9.1 Haswell Lytle   79
9.2 Pat Devlin   79
9.3 Samuel Lytle   80
9.4 Jay Damron   81
9.5 Epha Francis   82
9.6 Elmer Hammond   82
9.7 Barbara Adair   82
9.8 Bill Brown   83
9.9 Mining Tragedies   84
9.10 An Electrocution   84
9.11 Mike Lytle   85

10 JUSTINE IS STRICKEN WITH ALZHEIMER'S   89
10.1 Onset   89
     Headaches   89

Persistent Decline 90
Recognition Fails 91
Last Travels 91
The Struggle Ends 91

11 LOU — A KIND LADY   **93**
11.1 Henry Diefendorf 93
11.2 Invitation from Lou 94
11.3 A Range Cow Pays a Visit 95
11.4 Flash Flood and Aftermath 95
11.5 Pine Nuts 96
11.6 The Fate of 'Humandung' 96
11.7 Hired Gun 96
11.8 A Failed Robbery 96
11.9 Runaway Team 97
11.10 Pack Rat Problems 97
11.11 Innocence 98
11.12 Turning the Train Around 98
11.13 Rose Valley Stop-Over 98
11.14 Modena 99
11.15 A Good Cowboy 99
11.16 Mules 100
11.17 Caruso in State Line 100
11.18 Snowshoe Freight Service 100
11.19 Henry's Homestead 101
11.20 Raffety Steals Away Lou 102
11.21 Henry Works for Jim Hollinger 102
11.22 Progress at the Homestead 102
11.23 The Threesome 103
11.24 The Access Challenge 104
11.25 Wildlife Friends and Foes 105
11.26 Time to Get Out 105
11.27 Subscripts 105

12 RADIONIC HEALING   **107**

13 FRANK HAMBIN AND FAMILY   **109**
13.1 On to New Climes 109
13.2 The Virtues of a Bad Man 109
13.3 Travel Chores 110
13.4 Arizona 110
13.5 Dave, the Navajo 111
13.6 Learning from a Master Cowhand 111
13.7 'Bustin' a Maverick 112
13.8 Dave's Sister Lily 113

14 THE MINE   **115**
14.1 The Lucky Boy Gold Mine 115
14.2 Mining the Vein 115
14.3 The Tunnels 116
14.4 The 'Not-So-Lucky" Boy 116

15 TEACHERS I HAVE KNOWN 117

15.1 Miss Dalton 117
15.2 Laura Stephan 118
15.3 Virginia Delmue 118
15.4 Maude Frazier 119
15.5 Phoebe and Amy 119
15.6 Mr. Brinley 120
    Movie Making in Condor Canyon 120
    Class of the County 121
    Assembling a Skeleton 121
    A Boxing Match 121
15.7 Seth Jones 122
15.8 Karl Myers 122
15.9 School in Panaca 123
15.10 Attending BAC 123
15.11 Walking the Girls Home 123
15.12 Mixing Majors 124
15.13 On to Boston 124
15.14 Teachers at the Conservatory 124
15.15 Attending Concerts 125
15.16 Testing out Well 126
15.17 A Blind Date 126
15.18 And All That Jazz! 126
15.19 Other Experiences 126
15.20 Visit from a Boston Friend 127
15.21 Editing the BAC Newspaper 127
15.22 Debating Successes 128
15.23 Good Lord! Don't Marry That One! 128
15.24 Towards a Career in Education 128
15.25 A Heartless Professor 128

16 PLANTING SEEDS 131

16.1 School Days 132

17 MEMORIES 135

17.1 Thanksgiving Feast 135
17.2 Freel, Freight, and Whiskey 135
17.3 Preston, Nevada 136
17.4 Uncle Jeb and his Model T 138
17.5 Thunderbabies 140
17.6 End of the Coco Story 141

18 SO YA THINK YOU'D LIKE TO BE A COWBOY 143

18.1 Some FreeHand Verse 143

19 THINGS KIDS SAY 147

19.1 Sweet Memory 147
19.2 Overheard from a Six-Year Old 147
19.3 Overheard from a Seven-Year Old 147
19.4 Rose Valley School 148

20 EARLY DAY REMEMBRANCES 149

20.1 Fear of the Dark 149
20.2 Grandma's Foot Warmers 149
20.3 A Perfect Christmas 150
20.4 Hauling Hay 150
20.5 Aunt Maggie 150
20.6 Battling Snow and Mud 151

21 DEER AND OTHER HUNTING STORIES   **153**
21.1 My First Deer 153
21.2 Scratchy Balks 154
21.3 Double Success 154
21.4 Eldon's Big Buck 155
    Don DaGrade's Recollection 155
21.5 Cougar Encounters 156
21.6 Cougar Warning 157
21.7 Baby Rattle Snake Juice 157
21.8 Rushing in Where Wise Men Fear to Tread 157
21.9 The Midnight Breakfast 159
    Hunting Ox Valley and Ophir Basin 159
    Plan for the Hunt 160
    Resetting the Alarm 160
    Rex Springs into Action 160
    Twelve O'clock and All Is Well! 160
21.10 An All-night Conversation 161
    Wounded and Exhausted Hunters 161
    Something Strange Afoot 161
21.11 Firefight in a Frying Pan 162
    Cartridge Management 162
    A Pocket Full of Pine Nuts 163
    The Barrage 163
    Problem Analysis 163
21.12 The Family Hunt at Reeses 164
    A Wind-Swept Night 164
    The Wind Dies Down 165
    The Hunt Begins 165
    Shots are Fired 165
    Buck Fever Again Manifests 165
    The Carry 166
    Getting Out 166
    Post-Hunt Review 167
21.13 Reflections 167

22 COW, HORSE, DOG, AND RABBIT STORIES   **169**
22.1 Sheep and Flooding 169
22.2 A Skittish Team 169
22.3 Will's Black and White Team 170
22.4 Queen's Triumph 170
22.5 An Ice Statue 171
22.6 Old Blaze 171
22.7 Saving Lunch 171
22.8 Old Snap 172
22.9 A Chemical Hazard 172

22.10 Maud and Rocks 172
22.11 Katie 173
22.12 A One-Man Cow 174
22.13 The Banyon Cow 174
22.14 Horse-Cow Games 176
22.15 Cotton Tails and Owls 176
22.16 Jack Rabbits and Snakes 176
22.17 Old Jack 177
22.18 Scamp 177
22.19 Pup Dog 178
22.20 Scratchy and Whirlwind 179

23 IT   **181**

24 WAYNE'S DIARY, 1986-1987   **183**
24.1 Rose Valley 183
24.2 Alamo 201

25 SILVER STRANDS AMONG THE GOLD   **213**
25.1 Marginal Land 213
25.2 An 'onery' Team 214
25.3 Rose Valley Elementary 214
25.4 Thunderstorms 215
25.5 Kid Horses 216
25.6 Old Snap 216
25.7 Bully and Babe 217
25.8 Enter the Opposite Sex 217
25.9 Enter Justine 217
25.10 Range Management 218
25.11 Husband Management 218
25.12 Wayne Meets Piano 218
25.13 Recess Activities 219
25.14 Specific Teachers 219
25.15 Enter the Model T 220
25.16 Doing 'Body Work" ' 220
25.17 Tragedy in Utah 220
25.18 Under the Spreading Chestnut Tree 220
25.19 Twenty Below 221
25.20 Balancing Act 221
25.21 Going on the Road 221
25.22 Other High Schools 222
25.23 Venturing Forth 222
25.24 Slim Sandwiches and a Drunken Beatuy 223
25.25 Upgrading to the Model A 223
25.26 Wayne and Justine 224
25.27 Working for Wages 224
25.28 Attending BAC 225
25.29 Debating and Other Activities 225
25.30 Walking the Girls Home 226
25.31 The Costs of Dating 226
25.32 Potato-Picking Date 227
25.33 Drag Racing 227

25.34 An Update of Girl Friends 227
25.35 Heading for Boston 228
    Adventures of the Road 228
    Car Problems 229
25.36 The Conservatory 230
    Getting Accustomed to City Life 230
    Studies at the Conservatory 230
    The Hill Family 231
    Meet the Sea 231
    Great Performances 231
    Sundry Details 232
25.37 No Horns 233
25.38 The Road Home 233
25.39 Home Again 233
25.40 Death of Boyd Jones 234
25.41 The Great Depression 235
25.42 Creeping towards Marriage 235
25.43 Marriage at the Temple 235
25.44 Raising Turkeys 236
25.45 Eldon is Born 237
25.46 Off to Reno 238
25.47 Teaching in Preston 238
25.48 Justine Teaches Values to a Wino 239
25.49 Noel is Born 240
25.50 The Insatiable Desire to Hunt Deer 240
25.51 Reeses 241
25.52 Eldon's First Deer 241
25.53 Missing Old Blue 241

26 Still More Threads in the Fabric   **243**
26.1 Power and Water 243
26.2 Julene is 'born 244
26.3 Larry is Born 244
26.4 Kids at the Wheel 244
26.5 U.N.R. 244
26.6 Getting a Masters Degree 245
26.7 Getting a C- 245
26.8 Battery Acid 245
26.9 The Buy of the Day 246
26.10 Word War II 246
26.11 Setbacks 246
26.12 Misrepresentation 247
26.13 Below-Par Merchandise 247
26.14 Band Teacher 247
26.15 A Rotten Ladder 248
26.16 Mike Is Killed 248
26.17 Digging for Quicksilver 249
26.18 Jim Signs on at the Power Company 249
26.19 Jim is Electrocuted 249
26.20 Freel Injury and Death 250
26.21 The Ranch is Sold 250
26.22 Teaching in Pioche 250

26.23 Looking South 250
26.24 Off to a Good Start 251
26.25 Wayne Tells a "Flewsie" to Take a Hike 251
26.26 Traffic Problems 251
26.27 No Church Vacation 252
26.28 Larry's Mission and Marriage 252
26.29 Educational Challenges 253
26.30 Experiences in Las Vegas 253
26.31 An Agent for New York Life 254
26.32 Mary Passes Away 255
26.33 Church Assignments 255
26.34 Back to Rose Valley 256
26.35 Wayne's Poetic Response 257

27 CARS I HAVE KNOWN AND DRIVEN   **259**
27.1 First Generation 259
    First Model T 259
    Other Model Ts 260
    Chevys 260
    Still More Model Ts 262
    Dodges and Fords 262
    'Slob' Trouble 263
    Coverups 263
    An Oldsmobile 264
    A Dodge as Tractor 264
    A Chrysler 265
    Ford V8 265
    Model B Ford Pickup 265
    The Black Chevy Sedan 265
    The Chevy Half-Ton and Ford 'Lemon' 266
27.2 The Great Lincoln Highway 267
    Troubles Pile Up 267
    No Left Turn 268
27.3 48 Ford 4-Door Sedan 269
27.4 The 'Silver Streak.' 270
27.5 Lurch 270
    Grandpa Jones' Big Truck 272
    '58 V8 Ford Sedan 272
    '58 4 Door Sedan 273
    'Up' is 'Down' in the Great Basin 273
    The Willys and Whippet 274
    'Power' Steering 274
    The 58 Ford in Vegas 274
    The '49 Dodge 275
    The '64 Ford 275
    The Pontiac 6 275
    The Oldsmobile 6 276
    Ford Escort Doesn't Match to the Subaru 276
    Grandpa Jones' Really Big Truck 276
27.6 Stanton and Alwyn 276
27.7 Master List - Cars I've Driven or Owned Over the Years 277

28 LDS CHURCH ASSIGNMENTS HELD BY WAYNE LYTLE **279**
28.1 Early Music Assignments 279
28.2 Priesthood Group Leader 280
28.3 Ward Chorister 280
28.4 Temple Worker 280
28.5 Home Teaching 281
28.6 Special Temple Experience 281

III   NATIVE AMERICAN TALES **283**

29 FIRST ENCOUNTER **285**
29.1 Initial Encounter 285
29.2 Southern Paiutes 286
29.3 LaVan Becomes Paiute 286
    The Adoption 286
    Indians Removed to Moapa 287
    The Integrity of Paiute Culture 288
29.4 The Snake Clan 288
29.5 Indian Artifacts 290
29.6 Axle Grease or Craftmanship 290

30 PAUL MAMEGOENA **293**
30.1 Ottawa Indian Artist 293
30.2 Chicago 293
30.3 Paul Returns to Art 293
30.4 Attempts to Restore Paul's Work in Spring Valley . . 294
30.5 Current Status of Paul's George Washington Rock Art . 295
30.6 Word from Paul to the Milletts 295
30.7 Paul Becomes a 'Bohemian' Artist of Fame 295
30.8 Paul Sketches a Famous Portrait 297
30.9 Honors Won and Lessons Given 297
30.10 Humble Quarters 297
30.11 Paul Becomes an Outcast 297
30.12 A Poem in Paul's Honor 298
30.13 Postlude 298
30.14 Tepee Lost 298
30.15 Sure Cure 299

IV THE STORY-TELLING CONTINUES **301**

31 THE WEST-SIDE CATTLE COMPANY **303**
31.1 More Roots of the Red Notebook 303
31.2 The Roundup 305
31.3 Rat Splatter 306
31.4 The Evening Watch 307
31.5 Rolling Your Own 308
31.6 Freel Forgoes 'Days O' Work' 308
31.7 The Strawberry Roan 309

32 THE ADVENT OF THE WILDLIFE POLICE **311**

32.1 Invasion from the South 311
32.2 Replenishing the Meat Supply 311
32.3 Atomic Survivor 312
32.4 Restocking the County Larder 312
32.5 Lurch Rescues the Warden 312
32.6 Treading the Line 313
32.7 Feeling Like a Paiute 314

33 DOUBLE-BARREL POWER   **315**
33.1 Freel's Weapon of Choice 315
     Cooper Hawks 315
     Protecting Grandma's Current Bushes 316
     The Stable Shot 316
     Solving the Beaver Problem 317
     More Skunks 318
     The Turkey Massacre 318
     Turkeys 318
     Old Cluck 319
     Kid Stuff 319

34 FISHING   **321**
34.1 The Fiercest Bite We Ever Had 322
34.2 German Browns 322
34.3 Rose Valley's Fishing Bonanza 323

35 OTHER TALES OF THE RISING GENERATION   **325**
35.1 Karen Nearly Drowns 325
35.2 Blood and Hair 327
35.3 On Throwing Stones 327
35.4 Age Gap 327
35.5 Recovering Montezuma's Gold 328
     Establishing a 'Base Camp' 329
     Raising the Ladder 329
     Breaching the Plug 330
     Aftermath 330
35.6 Rose Valley Playground 332
     Dugouts 332
     Big Pharma 333
35.7 Desperado Country 333
     Encounter with a Cougar 333
     Running a Trap Line 334

36 THE WAR IN THE PACIFIC COMES TO ROSE VALLEY   **335**
36.1 Meet Don Wilson 335
     Quick Draw 335
     Don's War Chest 335
     A Potential for Trouble 336
36.2 Punchin' Cows with Don 336
     A Mustang in Training 336
     The Horse Race 337
     Rites of Passage 337
     Crows Have Armor 338

36.3 Disappearance of Don Wilson 338
36.4 War Again Comes to Rose Valley 338
    Meet Jerry Barber 339
    The Ultimate Sacrifice 339

37 THE OSHINSKYS   **341**
37.1 Living Apart 341
37.2 Place of Residence 342
37.3 The Oshinskys' Pickup 342
37.4 Nowhere to Call 'Home' 343
37.5 Aged Tenants in an Ancient Cabin 344
37.6 Life at Diefendorf's 344
37.7 History Repeats 345

38 DORAN AND CAROLYN'S KIDDY STORIES   **347**
38.1 BOUNCE 347
38.2 MOUSE IN THE HOUSE 351

39 COWBOY VERSE INSPIRED BY THE NOTEBOOK   **357**
39.1 Old Blue: A Hunter's Tale 357
39.2 Tikapoo: A Campfire Story 363

40 MELANCHOLY   **367**

V OTHER PERSONAL HISTORIES   **369**

41 JOHN LYTLE   **371**
41.1 Youth and marriage 371
41.2 Farm at Far West Missouri 372
41.3 Events at Far West 372
    Caring for Joseph's Horse 372
    Driven out by a Mob 372
    Heavenly Cavalry 373
41.4 Removal to Commerce/Nauvoo 373
41.5 Nauvoo Days 373
41.6 Exodus to the Rocky Mountains 374
    Term as Bishop 374
    Call to Carson Valley 374
41.7 The Call to Dixie 374
    Building the St. George Temple 375
41.8 Summary 375

42 CHARLES LYTLE   **377**
42.1 A Kindly Host 378
    Charles' Home as a Stage Stop 378
    A Boarding House for Teachers 378
42.2 Charles as a Father and Businessman 378
42.3 Mining Connections 378
42.4 Food Storage Program 379

43 FREELAND H. LYTLE   **381**
43.1 Early Years 382

   43.2 Working at Delamar 382

   43.3 Mary and Tina Marry Cowboys 383

   43.4 The Rose Valley Ranch 383

   43.5 Gladys and Wayne Are Born 384

   43.6 Freel is Injured 384

   43.7 Wayne's Memories of Freel 384

   43.8 The Question of Freel's Middle Name 385

   43.9 Addendum — The 'Religious' Heifer 387

   43.10 Brother! 387

44 MARY GLADYS LYTLE — WAYNE'S SISTER   **389**

   44.1 Birth and Childhood 389

       Stove Quarrel 389

       Teachers 390

       Self-Transport to School 390

       Getting a Nickname 391

   44.2 Teen Years 391

       Blacky and the Piano 391

   44.3 The BAC Year 392

   44.4 Off to Boston 392

       The Hill Family 393

       Landlubers at Sea 394

   44.5 Illness 394

   44.6 Marriage 394

   44.7 Karen's Birth and Jim's Injury 395

   44.8 Hazards of Quicksilver 396

   44.9 Community Service 396

   44.10 Pionionette 396

   44.11 Shooting 397

   44.12 Jim is Killed 397

   44.13 Dan Platt 398

   44.14 Working for a Living 398

   44.15 Being a Grandmother 398

   44.16 Gladys and Pete Are Married 399

   44.17 Move to Panaca 400

45 WILLIAM CRESFIELD MOODY   **401**

   45.1 Early Years 402

   45.2 Conversion to Mormonism 402

   45.3 Marriages and Missions 402

   45.4 Called to Dixie 402

   45.5 Service in Eagle Valley 403

   45.6 Dry Valley and Moodyville 403

   45.7 Wood Cutter 404

   45.8 Paiutes and Ranching at Deseret 404

   45.9 Flight towards Mexico 404

   45.10 Settling in Arizona 404

   45.11 Spiritual Gifts 405

   45.12 Declining Years 405

**46 HARRIET HENSON MOODY — FIRST WIFE OF WILLIAM
   AND MOTHER OF MARGARET**   **407**

46.1 Marriage to William 407
46.2 Conversion 407
     Gathering to Zion 408
     Affluence 408
     Call to Dixie 408
     Call to Eagle Valley 408

47 MARGARET JOSEPHINE MOODY LYTLE   **409**
47.1 Conversion to Mormonism 410
47.2 Trek to Salt Lake City 410
     Days of Hunger 410
     Financial Setback 410
47.3 Colonizing Dixie 410
47.4 Margaret Meets Charles Lytle 411
     Margaret vs. Charles 411
47.5 Life in Dry Valley 412
     Milk for the Baby 412
     Mexican Killers 412
47.6 The Cattle Business 413

Appendices   **415**

Appendices   **417**
     MORMONS OF THE MUDDY MISSION 417
.A   Early Settlement 417
.B   US Army Reconnaisance 417
.C   Muddy Mission Founded 418
.D   St. Thomas Founded 419
.E   Dangling Questions 419
.F   West Point 420
.G   New St. Joseph 420
.H   Muddy Mission Terminates 420
.I   The Muddy River Mission — Additional Detail 421
     MANAGEMENT OF MATERIAL THINGS 424
.J   'Oxymormons' 424
.K   Zion/Mammon Ambivalence 424
.L   Promoting What Is 'Good for Business' 426
     Potential for Abuse of Authority 426
.M   Do As I Say, Not As I Do 426
.N   Charles As an Eye-Witness To Change 427
.O   An Incongruous Mission 'Call' 427
.P   The Evidence 428
.Q   Knowing When To Say NO! 429

Part I

PREVIEW

Chapter 1

STORY-TELLING AS A FAMILY TRADITION

When Freel (43) and Mary (63) showed up in local towns with eggs, milk, butter and sweet corn to sell, their customers knew that the merchandise was first rate but that the stories with which Freel would entertain them were the true value. His son, Wayne, took up the tradition with great enthusiasm and has passed it on to his posterity --- thus this book.

The Paiute would likely say that when Wayne and Justine Lytle died, the pussy willows along the creek slumped to earth in mourning, the road runner visiting in their yard sat stunned as though transfixed by some gigantic *hoop snake* (1.1), and the Man's Head, a prominent geological feature overseeing Rose Valley (next page), bowed in homage.

In truth, although Justine had been smitten with Alzheimer's while in her late sixties (10), Wayne had enjoyed fine health in his 'golden' years until the fallout from Yucca Flat at long last kindled cancer and he had no rattlesnake juice (1.2) to counter the curse of the Feds. Their passing left a void which could not be filled. Thus, the discovery among Wayne's belongings of several dog-eared notebooks filled with his distinctive penmanship — one of them with a red cover — caused considerable excitement among those whose lives were intermingled with his tales and narratives. Inside were stories about the people, animals, and places which had given substance to his childhood, youth, fatherhood, professional years and the evils of old age which had ravaged his sweetheart, our mother, with Alzheimer's.

The style of Wayne's writing is captivating; much of it flowing from reality to fantasy, prose to poetry, with as much ease as the yarns of Mark Twain or the narratives of Homer. The blend is so natural and persistent that the reader is challenged to decide what is real and what is not. Many of us were there as observers or participants and still we argue about the fantasy or truth of this one or that one. Perhaps, when Wayne laid down his pen, he was not certain either.

Figure 1.1: Rose Valley's Distinctive *Man's Head* Rock Formation

> *Yarns and tall tales were the stuff of Wayne's growing up and the substance of his appeal to many with whom he bantered during the course of everyday life. It was a family tradition. Whenever his father Freel showed up in local towns with eggs, milk, butter, and sweet corn to sell, his customers knew that the merchandise he peddled was first rate but that the stories which he told were the best value.*

To illustrate where this is going and kindle a foretaste of what survived Freel in his oral traditions and Wayne in his writings — and now propagates among his posterity as a legacy — let us first listen to Freel detailing the matter of Rose Valley's 'hoop snakes' and their ultimate tragic demise.

1.1 HOOP SNAKES

According to Grandpa Freel, hoop snakes were remarkable creatures which inhabited the region when the pioneer settlers first arrived, but disappeared soon thereafter. I first heard of them when Grandpa made good on his promise to tell a story for every swath of corn rows that we hoed plus 25 cents. It went like this . . .

"Did I already tell you about Ol' Hook Jaw, the rainbow monster of Lake Tahoe?" "Yes," Grandpa, "they caught him and mounted him on a board over the lake picture in the bar, but a Nevada zephyr[1] worked him loose and he flopped back into the lake and got away . . . Tell us a new one. Tell us about the strangest thing you ever saw right here in Rose Valley."

---

[1] Whirl wind or, in a dry area, 'dust devil.'

"The strangest? Well that would have to be the *hoop snakes*. They appear to have become extinct ... haven't seen one for years, but I can remember them it as plain as yesterday when they rolled down the slope at the bottom of the meadow to water in the evening."

"What do you mean – *rolled*?"

"Well, hoop snakes were really long and nimble and fast like you wouldn't believe. They were smart critters, and roamed in groups hunting rabbits and other varmints. They'd work together, like coyotes, corner an animal, focus on it until it was hypnotized and swallow it down in a flash. Even coyotes and badgers knew better than to trespass on hoop snake territory!"

"But what about the *rolling*?"

> "Well, they was really smart. They'd slither as far as the top of the ridge, grab their tails in their mouths and come bouncing down the slope like so many wagon wheels busted loose and headed for bottom. Just at the right instant, they'd let go of their tails and plop their heads into the creek for a drink. Then they'd crawl back up into the brush to spend the night and rest for the next day's hunt."
>
> "I remember one time we were pitching hay down there and saw about fifty of them come rolling in at once. They kicked up dust and made the brush fly like a stampede of horses! Strangest thing I ever saw in Rose Valley. No question!"

Stubs

"Why don't we see them any more, Grandpa?" "Well, that's another strange story. One year they kind of vanished, and when a naturalist professor fellow came by checking the wildlife, we told him how all the hoop snakes had disappeared. That feller wandered around a day or two down on the ridge investigating. On his way out he said he wasn't sure, but he thought they had all starved to death. He said he couldn't prove it, but the evidence pointed in that direction. He reported finding hoop snake skulls scattered around in the area with just a stub of the snake attached to them."

"Why just stubs?"

"He theorized that when they got really, really hungry, and went into a roll, their tails started tasting mighty good and they just ate themselves up until they was nothing left but stubs."

"Stranger still, this fellow gathered from a close study of the eye sockets in those skulls, that hoop snakes had a special way of seeing things."

"What did he mean by that?" Grandpa.

"Well, he said he thought that for them critters images connected up in a kind of hoop to match the roll."

After hearing the story, I made several hikes down to Hoopsnake Ridge, but never did find so much as a single 'stub'. I even considered practicing a few 'rolls' to test out the looped image scenario, but luckily thought better of it! (Eldon)

Figure 1.2: Hoop Snake perspective.

Figure 1.3: Human Perspective

Figure 1.4: Nothing Left but Stubs!

We've now had an opportunity to hear Freel expound 'truths' about local wildlife which one can scarcely imagine. It turns out, however, that when it came to storytelling, father and son shared the same gene. If you think Freel's 'hoop snakes were 'far out,' try on for size the following tale from Wayne's *Red Notebook* about the extraordinary properties of the Billy Jack's *magic snake medicine*. Place names and settings are actual settings identifiable on the introductory map on *Page iv*.

1.2   BILLY JACK AND HIS RATTLESNAKE JUICE

One day along came Nellie Flatnose, a young squaw from the Flatnose tribe, quite tall, strong and beautiful, with long black hair. Billy immediately took a shine to her, she rolled her eyes his way, and before long, they were married. In due time, she had a most perfect male child and they named him Billy Running Water. Before too long, a daughter was born to them, the most beautiful female child ever seen. They named her Pretty Bird Nellie Jack.

Meet Billy Jack

BILLY JACK was just an ordinary man; about 5 ft. 10 inches, 170 lbs. and well built. That frame of his was connected by muscles, with very little fat in between. His favorite occupation was riding his medium sized horse, "Red" and serving as cowboy for the local ranchers. He could pitch hay, hoe weeds, milk cows, feed cows and pigs and anything else that might bring him board and room and a few dollars. One day he rode old Red up Serviceberry Canyon, shot a deer, skinned it, cooled it out, boned it, and wrapped the meat in his slicker, behind the saddle, where it would attract little attention. He rolled the hide up and decided to carry it in close to Eagle Valley and stretch it, then tan it. As he was riding down Serviceberry Canyon, he saw a rattlesnake crawl into a hole in some rocks. Old Red shied at it. For some reason, he unrolled the hide, found a long, small, dry pole and hung the hide over the hole. Quicker that he could count, strike, strike, strike, a half dozen rattlesnakes struck that rawhide.

Enter Snaggle Tooth

The last one was a big snake and his fang hung in the hide and when Billy pulled the hide away, there was that snake dangling and writhing, trying to get loose. Bill suspended the hide in the air with the snake still dangling, got two other sticks and gingerly lifted the snake away from the hide. The snake promptly got loose and crawled back into the hole. The venom on that hide was concentrated in a small area and Billy Jack had an idea. He got some serviceberries, choke cherries, some squaw bush berries, pinenuts, put them on top of the venom which showed amber white on the hide, put in a few wild strawberries and rolled the whole lot with the hide and hid the hide between two tree branches. That mixture might develop into some real good scent for his traps the next winter. He rode on down the canyon and home by the Eagle Valley Trail.

The Potion Matures

In about a week he was back to look for cattle and to check on the deer hide, which was still there. It was smelling pretty ripe, but he unrolled it and out came a serviceberry. Without thinking, he tasted that berry and WOW! He almost lost his breath, tingled from head to toe and felt three feet taller. As he rode along, a big log had fallen across the trail. He dismounted and moved that log with no trouble. A large rock was in the way and without thinking, he moved it. Old Red seemed to have a piece of gravel in one hind foot and he picked up the horse's whole hind end and removed the gravel. He was feeling good and was stronger than two men. On the way home, some cows he was driving started acting up. He rode close to a long horned steer, bailed off and threw that steer flat on the ground. When he let the steer up, there was no more trouble. Red started tiring, so Billy Jack got off and left the reins on the saddle horn, Red followed the cows down the trail and Billy kept them in line from the side. He arrived at the ranch in good time, put the cows in a corral, unsaddled Red, did the chores and reported in for supper. Ed remarked that he'd never seen Billy Jack or any other man eat that much that fast. Billy jack managed to get some sleep, but was up early and got everything done before breakfast. Again, he ate like he had never done before. Ed sent him back into the same area on a new horse, to look for more cattle. He had stashed the deer hide in the same tree, but this time he had a small jar, gathered all the berries and venom that was still there and put it in the jar. He tasted another berry and he had the same experience. WOW! On the way home, the horse tired. He actually took that horse on one shoulder and drove the cows himself. Near Eagle Valley he go back on the horse as he normally would do.

The Potion Works

He hid the jar where no one would find it and as soon as possible, went back to the same area, shot another deer skinned it and held the hide near the snake den. The snakes all took a strike at it, with old snaggle tooth getting hung up again. Billy Jack released the snake and let him go again. The hide was wrapped with the same kind of berries and pine nuts next to the venom. In a few days, Billy Jack was back with another jar. In the meantime, he worked so well and got so much done, that Ed raised his pay a dollar a day. During the next week, he went to a dance in Pioche and really danced up a storm with the ladies. One of the miners really got teed off and asked Billy Jack to step outside. Out they went, with a crowd following. The miner took one swing at Billy, missed and Billy picked the guy up by the nape of his neck and the seat of his pants then hung him up on a nearby telegraph pole. When Billy said, "Anybody else want to try me?" Nobody did. They went back to the dance shaking their heads. He learned to dance carefully with the ladies, so that he didn't squeeze them too hard.

Winter Storage

The next time Billy Jack went back to replenish his supply, a big male cougar climbed into a tree and as Billy and his horse rode under the tree, out jumped the cougar. Billy was completely surprised, as was the horse, which jumped twenty feet. Billy grabbed that cougar around the neck with both hands and squeezed as only he could do. The animal gradually loosed its hold on the man and horse and became glassy eyed. Billy dumped it on the ground and dismounted. The lion slowly got its breath back and as soon as it was able took off at full speed. Billy wiped a little blood off one arm, rubbed some black mud on the horse's wounds and went on his way, getting another deer and getting another snake strike on the hide. He was getting enough "medicine" to last through the winter. One more trip, "medicine" in 4 jars, which he carefully stashed, each in a separate place, and he was set for the winter. Around the ranch, Ed kept putting more of the work onto Billy Jack but Billy didn't mind. He couldn't sleep well if he wasn't tired. He built new fences, new mangers and hauled and chopped cords of wood. Ed's place became a showpiece for the whole area. Every rancher wished he could find a man like Billy Jack. Some of the single women set their hats for Billy, but he wouldn't nibble.

Enter Nellie Flatnose

Then, one day along came Nellie Flatnose, a young squaw from the Flatnose tribe, quite tall, strong and beautiful, with long black hair. Billy immediately took a shine to her, she rolled her eyes his way, and before long, they were married. In due time, she had a most perfect male child and they named him Billy Running Water. Before too long, a daughter was born to them, the most beautiful female child ever seen. They named her Pretty Bird Nellie Jack. All this time, Billy Jack was daily taking little tastes of his medicine and during the summer time, would go back to

Serviceberry and replenish his supply. On one trip to Serviceberry, he noticed that where two canyons converged, there was a beautiful spot for a home, with quaking aspens and pines in the background. He brought Nellie and the two children to see and they thought it was beautiful. On that trip, he showed them his medicine and how he gathered it. Nellie wanted to cook and eat Snaggle Tooth but Billy wouldn't let her. He was afraid to let her and the children taste his "medicine."

Super Kids

The house was built with logs from quaking aspens, junipers and pinion pines. Another son Jackson Teel and another daughter, Deer Bear, were born. Billy Jack fed his family by trapping, working occasionally for Ed at the ranch, by keeping a milk cow and raising a few cattle. The children grew and soon Billy Running Water was a strong lad. One day, while Billy was gone, Nellie got the scare of her life. She looked out the cabin door and there was little Billy face to face with a large lynx cat. She froze with fear and didn't say a word. Quicker than the eye could move, that child dived for the large cat's neck and choked it down with both hands. When the cat was limp, he let go and as Nellie ran to get her child, the cat came to its senses and dashed away. "Mommy, I didn't want to kill it," he said. She was proud of that boy. He was a chip off the old block. On another day, she looked toward the corral and there was little Pretty Bird in the corral with an untamed horse. Nellie watched as that child patted that horse on its front legs, then on its nose and led it around with a little rope she had. Those two, the child and the horse, became perfect friends and little Pretty Bird was soon on its back, riding it, as only a little girl could do.

Visit from Billy the Kid

Another day, while Nellie and her children were alone, two men came riding up the canyon and dismounted. Nellie left the children in the cabin and greeted them. They were on their way to State Line and wanted to rest their horses and themselves. Nellie offered them food, which they accepted and brought the four children out. The kids immediately became less shy and soon were playing games with the younger man. He gave each one a shiny marble. All were waving good-bye as the men saddled up and went on their way. Weeks later she learned that the men were Billy the Kid and Ben Jesher, and they had held up the stage station in State Line, taking considerable money. She told Billy Jack that to her and the kids, they seemed just like common people.

Testing for Descendants

As time passed by the children grew older and needed to be enrolled in school. Billy Jack and Nellie moved to State Line, where Pretty Bird and little Billy were entered in school, to be taught by Kate Flinspach. As soon as school was out in the spring, back to Serviceberry they went. Billy jack visited the snake den as soon as berries were ready, and the snakes performed as usual. Those four children grew into as fine and handsome young people as were in the whole territory. They married well and if you see an unusually handsome, dark-eyed person nowadays, you'll know he's a descendant of Billy Jack and Nellie Flatnose. If you get a chance, ask them if they know about the "miracle snake medicine." If he's descended from Billy Jack, he'll know.

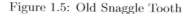

Figure 1.5: Old Snaggle Tooth

1.3   ALL OF THE BABIES ARE DYING!

"Wayne! What can we do?" Justine cried out it distress. As she sobbed uncontrollably, Wayne held her for comfort and asked, "About what, Justine?" "All the babies are dying . . . all of the bablies are dying . . . and there's nothing that we can do about it! "We'll put extra wood on the stove, feed them, and put them to bed." They'll go to sleep and everything will be fine."

"It won't help! It won't help! They will all die and there's no one but God who can save them."

Suddenly it occurred to Wayne what was going on. Justine's mind, ridden with the rot of Alzheimer's had transported Justine backwards in time to the devastating diphtheria epidemic of her youth when she had personally witnessed the suffering and death of countless children, having held some of them in her own frail arms as they gasped in vain for the breathe to sustain their lives.

It would be hours before Justine stopped wringing her hands and returned once again to the bliss of forgetfulness . . . which summarily punished her with the inability to recognize either her own husband or children. (Chapter 10)

Chapter 2

BACKGROUND SETTING

An inverse attraction between man and the harshness of his environment makes the most sense but man seems to be senseless in this regard.
– Source Unknown

Freel and Mary together with his son Wayne and his wife Justine made their home in the high desert of southeastern Nevada, an area where temperatures alternate between -60F and 120F, where winds alternate between mild and variable to hurricane force — where for six months running not a drop of rain falls only to be followed by a deluge which washes away miles of railroad track and changes the entire drainage channel as far south as water can run in a sinkhole.

Figure 2.1: Union Pacific in Caliente

To visit the area, travel north from Las Vegas on Highway 93 until you reach ⟸ Caliente, Nevada. The Union Pacific transits this once booming railroad town where mountains of freight were loaded and unloaded by Freel and his fellow teamsters, untold millions in gold and silver bars were transported from local mining camps for

delivery to parts unknown, and entire herds of range cattle were crowded into cattle
cars for export to the stockyards of California, a goodly number of them having been
provided by Wayne, Freel, and their partners in the *West Side Cattle Company* (See
Chapter 31).

Figure 2.2: Approaching the town of Panaca

Travel north some twenty miles to Panaca[1] situated in Meadow Valley, a community first settled by Mormon pioneers from Utah's Dixie in 1864, who mistakenly
assumed they were colonizing the western boundaries of Utah.

Figure 2.3: Cathedral Gorge State Park

If nature's sculptures in the clay formations of ancient lake beds and water caves
fascinate you, turn left upon exiting Panaca Valley and visit *Cathedral Gorge*, one
of three Nevada State Parks in the area.

---

[1]This terms is allegedly an English adaptation of the Paiute term 'Panaker,' meaning *silver*.

Next, continue upgrade to Pioche in a northerly direction. Pioche is a mining town of historical renown which boasted the death of scores of men from gun-shot wounds before the first natural death occurred there. World War II, however, represents the last 'boom' experienced by Pioche, which has narrowly escaped 'ghost-town status' more recently by virtue of it's tenuous hold on the title of 'County Seat' and an influx of retirees from regions south. The old elementary school where Wayne taught for many years, and from which I graduated at some point in the dim past still stands but has been condemned by authorities as 'unsafe' — which must be true because there lingers in the recesses of my mind to this day the certain prospect of getting my 'butt kicked' by Emrys Jones, Principal, if I misbehave in a notable way(Chapter 21.3). The same lack of 'safety' lurked within in the now locked doors of Thompson's old Movie Theatre, where 'cut-ups' were 'given the boot' if their disorderly conduct elicited complaints from the audience.

Figure 2.4: Mainstreet Pioche

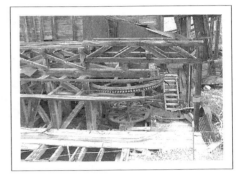

Figure 2.5: Pioche Tramway head

Now travel eastward from Pioche at the Echo Dam State Park turnoff situated on the lower east side of town. Traverse the flat below Pioche and turn right at the Echo Dam marker.

Some five miles later the alfalfa fields of *Dry Valley* (make a note of this name) point the way north to Echo Dam itself, an earthen structure erected squarely atop a sinkhole capable of siphoning water out of the dam at more rapid rates than that of the stream feeding it.[2]

> The dam is located in precisely the same area where I was nearly drug to death by a horse tripped up by the sinkhole's quicksand during a cattle roundup in 1954. I'll detour briefly at this point to relate this story for two reasons:
>
> - First, for the purpose of putting to rest once and for all the fiction that pumping further down the valley from deep below the valley floor is to blame for the loss of water from Echo Dam.
>
> - Second, because the main thread of our story takes several twists around this Dry Valley.

---

[2]See http://www.parks.nv.gov/ec.htmforanofficialdescriptionofparkfacilities.

Figure 2.6: Echo Dam Turnoff - The Feds flaunt their ubiquitous presence. The Federal government has staked out a claim to some 90% of the land in Nevada.

2.1   Close Call at the Dry Valley Sinkhole

On one occasion, the Delmues had advised Freel that cattle with his brand were ranging in Dry Valley, whose confines were dangerous for cattle due to residual cyanide (22.9) awash from the old mill situated there (4.11). Someone else was using our good saddle, so I saddled up Scratchy with an army-surplus model which was serviceable but flimsy compared to standard roping saddles. Mike Lytle (9.11) and I rode together the approximately three-mile stretch leading through what is now called 'Echo Canyon' to the upper reaches of Dry Valley.

There, we split up, Mike taking the east side of the creek channel and I taking the west side, which was land owned by Freel. Within approximately one-half mile, I glimpsed several cows with Freel's brand exit the tall brush alining the channel and dash into the wash. Scratchy flanked them in a flash and turned them up the channel towards Rose Valley at a fast clip.

Quicksand Disaster

Without prior warning — there was no visible water in the channel — Scratchy's front feet lost contact with any supporting surface, sucking her up to the neck into quicksand! Her momentum sent her head over heads and I found myself making brutal contact with the debris cluttering the creek bottom. As luck would have it, Scratchy's forefeet had neither been broken nor seriously injured, but the shock of the flip-flop and fall had rattled her to the point of terror. She struggled to her feet and moved violently away from me, only to discover that we were still attached by a stirrup – the flimsy enclosure of which had allowed my left foot to pass through and lodge there.

Thereupon, Scratchy took off up the creek bed dragging me through quicksand, over rocks, and through brush at a rapid clip. There appeared to be no remedy. My fate seemed sealed, like that of HasWell Lytle before me (Chapter 9.1). Mike had disappeared and calls for help found no ears to fall upon.

Finally, bruised, battered, bleeding, and nearly unconscious from repeated impact with rocks and other debris, an opportunity for escape suddenly presented itself! Scratchy dashed up a opening in the creek bank in an effort to avoid the occasional patches of quicksand which continued to plague her in the channel proper. At the edge of the breach a large sage bush presented a sizable trunk as it entered the ground. This I seized and held on to with every ounce of strength remaining. While the force of Scratchy's momentum nearly pulled my leg from its socket, the poor construction of the stirrup was the first to yield, and I found myself stretched up the bank but delivered from a certain and hideous demise in the channel traversing the Dry Valley Sinkhole!

Why Dry Valley is called *Dry Valley*

S UBSEQUENT to that experience I enjoyed improved insight into why Dry Valley was called *Dry Valley*. Except for brief periods of heavy spring runoffs or flooding, waters flowing through Echo Canyon submerge in the sands and gravel at the head of the Valley. This precludes the possibility of dams and canals to exploit the water for irrigation. Pioneer settler William Moody had discovered this the hard way when called by Mormon authorities to settle Dry Valley in 1867-68 (45.6). Later, Charles Lytle (William's son-in-law) became owner of considerable land at the head of the Valley in the vicinity of where Echo Dam now sits, some of which he bequeathed to Freel along with his Rose Valley ranch (4.12). Never, however, given that irrigation dams and canals were ruled out by the sinkhole, did Freel contemplate agricultural development there. **Dubious honor though it may be, the author is likely the only person living or dead who can 'boast' of having been drug by a horse through the sinkhole which routinely reduces Echo Dam to a mud hole by summer's end!**

Figure 2.7: Echo Dam – April

Figure 2.8: Echo Dam – Mid June

Rose Valley Undergoing Degradation

CONTINUING UP-CANYON from Echo Dam, Rose Valley comes into view with its array of meadows, fields, pastures, corrals, etc. In the recent years the wetlands appearing in the photo have been destroyed and its principle meadow allowed to revert to wire grass by interests who, given that there is absolutely no indication of any agenda on their part to develop the valley for agricultural or grazing purposes, are buying up ranches in the area piecemeal with the apparent intent of pumping their underground water reserves to Clark County.

Figure 2.9: Rose Valley of years past. The wetlands pictured no longer exist.

Following the narrow, paved road up the east side of the Rose Valley, one reaches a bridge. Turn right and follow the asphalt up the canyon past Montezuma's gold (Chapter 35.5) to URSINE (the US Postal designation for *Eagle Valley*), or turn left on the dirt road crossing the head of the Valley to visit the log homes constructed by Freel and Sam as a brother-brother project in 1910 after Charles first provided Freel with ranch land in Rose Valley.

Figure 2.10: Wayne's log home

Figure 2.11: Freel's log home

Logs from Days of Yore

The logs in these homes had been transported into the Valleys by wagon, having in still earlier times been harvested high in the mountain chain to the east which

Figure 2.12: Gladys and Wayne at home in 1912

Figure 2.13: Home in 1983

divides Nevada from Utah. (See Chapter 3.3)

A S OF THIS DATE, Wayne's house no longer exists, having burned to the ground (Chapter 3) when the local power monopoly[a] celebrated the home's 100th birthday by cutting off power to it in mid-winter 2010 — despite forewarning by the author — forcing the unemployed renter to use wood for heating in a dormant and, as it turned out, clogged chimney system. The County fire department showed up in FEMA fashion with fire suits, sirens, and flashing lights — but once on site, simply stood around and watched it burn, having no contingency plan for fighting fires in the Valleys.

[a]The so-called *Lincoln County Power District*.

PERHAPS THE BEST WAY to visualize the broader scenario enfold is to envision the proverbial box which encloses yet another, and another, and so on. In the following chapter we observe Freel-Mary and Wayne-Justine within the context of their rustic log homes. The included exchange of letters between Larry and Farrel at the time of fire brings a broader perspective to these homes and their history. The story also provides background for the tradition of story-telling which forms the central theme of this book.

3

THE LOG HOMES OF ROSE VALLEY

The Rose Valley house burned down today so I thought while it was on my mind I would tell the story for posterity. This is a bedtime story unlike any other.[a]

---

[a]The renter had lost her job as the depression struck the area. When she could't pay her bill, Lincoln County Power District disregarded a caution by the author and pulled the plug on her in mid winter, forcing the use of an old, apparently clogged chimney. The fire consumed logs which had been scientifically dated to some forty years before Columbus (3.2). **Such is the money-driven insanity now sweeping the country from 'sea to shining sea,' bringing its very survival as a nation into question.**

3.1 Wayne's Log Home burns in Feb. 2010

On Mar 10, 2009, at 12:25 AM, Larry Lytle wrote: *Between 1901 and 1910 the creek in Rose Valley flooded three times to the extent that the creek channel changed from the west side of the valley to the center of the valley. In February 1910 most of the houses from Eagle Valley to south of Caliente were washed away. 20+ miles of railroad were washed out down Caliente canyon. Logandale and Overton were washed away by the flood.*

Severe hardship followed because of the winter weather and loss of rail service, (Overton got drinking water by rail [5.8]) In Rose Valley Freel (our grandfather) and Sam Lytle (brother) were newly married and starting their families. Gladys, Freel

Figure 3.1:   The County fiddles while a national treasure burns.

and Mary Lytle's first child, was born in a tent in 1910. On February 25, 1911 Freeland Wayne (our father) was born in Freel's house. The log walls were up and a tarp was used for a roof.

To build their houses Freel and Sam dismantled a log boarding house at the Pope Mine near Fay, a good sized mining town near Deer Lodge (Hackett's ranch). The logs were Ponderosa pine logs cut in Water Canyon where the canyon heads up near Government Peak above Deer Lodge. (There is a grove of young trees starting again in Water Canyon and still a small stand of Ponderosa trees in Ox Valley). They put a set of wagon axles in the front and back to carry a few logs and transported them to Rose valley using horse teams. Sam was an engineer and mechanic, while Freel was the cowboy farmer. The road up the East bench of Rose Valley to Modena was built by them at that time to get the logs into the valley more easily. Prior to that the road went up the bottom of Immigration Canyon. They then constructed a pit with a walkway above to set the logs on and then cut the logs lengthwise with a two-man saw, one man on a walkway above and the other below. It took them all winter to finish the sawing. The two houses were constructed during 1911-1912. (Since the original logs had been 16" thick, the half thickness 8" logs were entirely adequate walls for a log house. When the logs were reassembled they each had a home, the twin of the other.) Sam Lytle died from flu and pneumonia 28 March 1916. His ranch property and home were purchased from his widow, Margaret Conway, by Freel and his brother, Les. Freel got the home, which much later became Wayne's home.

In 1952-53 the bedroom addition was added to the back of Wayne's house. I remember the carpenter working. He was our

Uncle Stanton Jones, Grandma Justine's brother. In 1973 Mom (Larry's wife, Sandra) and I moved a house trailer to Rose Valley to completely remodel the house in preparation for Wayne and Justine's return. As I remodeled it, I found the logs numbered A1, A2 A3, etc for one wall and B1, B2, B3, etc. for the adjoining wall. Old painted bedsheets had been used for interior wall covering as well as old newspaper. One newspaper was from State Line, Utah --- just over the hill from Fay and Deer Lodge --- and described the successful suicide of a Confederate Captain. ``He cut his throat with a large butcher knife and made it from one side clear to the other" ... Back when men were men!!

Wayne and Justine slept in the 'north bedroom' (with the north door open a crack year-round). The boys slept in the northeast room. My bed was the bottom bunk, Noel above me and Farrel and Eldon in the center double bed. Julene had her own room with all of her dolls. On cold mornings we would all rush to the fuel oil stove in the living room and fight for our place to get a little warmth. Most of us were branded by the hot grate of the stove on our hind ends many times. Wayne would build a fire under the car engine to warm it up for the trip to the school in Pioche. First, he had to milk the cows and check on Freel and Mary. Eldon and Noel would put chains on the Ford if it had snowed. Then they would go to school and I would stay home with mom and my wagon and Teddy. (Shar has the Teddybear.)

I remember at least two times when floods went through the house. One time was when we had gone to Disney Land right after it opened in 1955. There was only the Submarine, Castle and Roads of the Future rides open. We were so glad to get out of California! We came home to a washed-out road and 6" of mud through the house. The house had one other fire. When I remodeled it, the northeast wall in the kitchen was burned and the roof and rafters had been replaced. The wood kitchen stove had caused a fire at one time. One other time it almost burned. My brothers loved to set old tires on fire and roll them down the Sandhill. One night they were especially ambitious and drug a tire up on the Mans' Head and set it on fire. They kicked it off and it lit on the roll, jumped the fence and fell flat on it's side on the roof burning brightly. (All of this always happened at night when mom and dad were to meetings.) Somehow they got off of the Man's Head down the Sandhill over the fence and on the roof before everything burned up. Tires burn and burn and burn and they are difficult to put out. Sock fights in the dark were a favorite and of course nobody had socks for school the next morning.

In 1959 when I was 10 we moved to Las Vegas where Dad began teaching school. Talk about culture shock! We used to run out of the house in Rose Valley every time we heard a car come down the hill because it happened so rarely. We traveled back and forth (through Moapa) to visit Grandma Mary (Grandpa Freel had died by then) and deer hunt. The deer stories that were told in the Rose Valley house would fill volumes ... and a few of them were even true!

3.2   Farrel's Reply

Dear Larry,

Writing the story of the Rose Valley house is an excellent idea. I've gone through it and corrected the things that I know about. After our siblings add some more to the story (and you probably will too, when you read it again) please send it out again in a final edition.

I don't know whether I told you about this or not but it adds some interesting detail about the logs that are in both houses. When Eldon cut out a section of log to enlarge a window in his house (originally Freel's house) there was a large piece of log left. I brought it home because one could see a lot of tree rings. I was interested in extracting climate information from tree rings (dendrochronology is the term for studying tree rings) and had read a couple of books about it. I have always been meaning to cut a cross section from the log and polish it to make them visible but never got around to it which turned out to be a good thing.

Last summer the dendrochronology group from the University of Nevada in Reno (Prof. Scotty Strahan is the leader) was camped at Horse Thief Gulch campground and met Andrew Porter (a nephew). Prof. Strahan and Kurt Solander were there to take cores from pinyon and ponderosa to add to their collection. They have enough data, from these two species to date tree rings, accurate to one year, back in time for 600 years and they are working up to 1000 years. After talking to them for a while, Andrew sent them down to meet us. Since I had read the books I knew enough about it to converse intelligently on the subject and we had a wonderful time for a couple of hours. As they left I remembered the Rose Valley log section in the garage and offered it to them. They accepted it like I had given them gold.

A couple of months later a package arrived that contained a polished cross section from the log. Since they knew the growth pattern of the tree rings in this general area, i. e. periods of wet years produced wide rings, drought produced narrow rings--in one place so narrow that it takes a magnifying glass to see that there are two--and in another place no ring separation at all which means that there was no rain at all, they found the same pattern on the Rose Valley log and could write a date by each ring or missing ring. Dr. Strahan wrote with a very fine pencil the date every 100 years all the way back to the core which started in 1462, thirty years before Columbus. The tree could be a bit older than that since we don't know how far up the tree the section came from.

3.3 Age of the Log Sample

The full cross section, about six inches thick, is mounted on a nice board and will go up on our wall as soon as I find the studs to mount it to (it's heavy). The whole piece with its intriguing ring pattern is a thing of beauty! (Farrel)

THE LOG SAMPLE was taken when the author enlarged the left-most window of Freel's home as seen in the photo. Days prior to enlarging the window, the author had assembled an outdoor basketball standard for his grandson, Seth Lytle. Included with the kit was an instruction sheet, detailing the steps required to assemble it. At one point — at that juncture where the upper and lower extensions of the pole were to be connected by jamming one into the other — was a warning which read: CAUTION! THIS STEP IS IRREVERSIBLE! As I raised the roaring Steele chain saw to cut away the cross section of the logs in question, there flashed before me that warning. Any mistakes that I had made in measuring the new window and cutting the 8-inch thick logs for a fit would be just that: IRREVERSIBLE!

3.4 Karen's Early Recollection of Freel's Log Home

All the cooking was done in the old wood stove. There was a temperature indicator on the oven, but it took some doing to keep it regulated. But Grandma and my mother could bake wonderful bread and pies and cakes and never burn them. There was a reservoir on the side of the stove to heat water. We bathed once a week in the galvanized wash tub. The tub was brought into the living room, filled with hot water from the reservoir and the stove, and you tucked your knees up to your chin so that you could fit into the tub. Everyone used the same water, although Grandma would add hot water from the tea kettle to warm it up after each use. You were fortunate if you got the first bath, and didn't have to bathe in everyone else's dirt. And of course, we used chamber pots and an out house. Toilet paper was too expensive to buy so we used pages from the Old Sears and Montgomery Ward catalogs for toilet paper. I still remember how scratchy it was.

How excited everyone was when we finally got electricity! My father had some experience with electricity, so he wired the house for my grandparents. Then we could have electric lights, running water in the house, a refrigerator, and a radio. I remember my father and grandfather shushing us kids while they listened anxiously to the news reports after the United States entered World War II.

Later they divided a bedroom and installed a bathroom. And my grandmother acquired an electric stove and a washing machine. Of course all those things didn't come a once because there still wasn't a lot of money. But it certainly made life easier for my mother and grandmother.

Chapter **4**

A REVIEW OF FAMILY HISTORY

``We come from Mormon country, but we're just *Jack Mormons.*[a] Real Mormons
have horns, but us Jack Mormons just have bumps. See, you can feel one of
my bumps right here." Sure enough, Frankie Hill could feel a bump!
–Mike Lytle.[b]

[a]A term used in reference to persons of Mormon heritage who are either inactive in the
Church's programs or unorthodox in their beliefs.
[b]Quote from Wayne's *The Red Notebook.*

4.1   The Pioneer Story

As we remove the wrapping from the present story box, we find our two 100-year old
log houses enveloped in yet another story trove, whose threads and themes establish
a link from the western reaches of the United States in Nevada and Utah, to the
banks of the Mississippi at the city of Nauvoo, Illinois. John Lytle, Charles' father
and Freel's grandfather, was the very blacksmith who took his sledge hammer to
the press of the *Nauvaoo Expositor,* reduced it to scrap metal and threw it into a
pool of water in Nauvoo, Illinois.

The Nauvoo Expositor

The paper in question was viewed by local residents as a 'libelous rag' dedicated
to stirring up anti-Mormon sentiment in Illinois in order to drive them out and

neutralize their influence as a voting block. Joseph Smith had been libeled by it along with other associates, whereupon the City Council decided that its license and term of service had played out. Joseph Smith, the founder of the Mormon Faith and other associates were arrested and jailed for the destruction of the press, leading directly to the murder of both Joseph and his brother Hyrum at Carthage, Illinois, shortly thereafter.[1]

The Expositor, however, had succeeded in its agenda, for the governor of the state issued orders against the Mormons, which forced them to abandon the beautiful and prosperous city which they had erected on the banks of the Mississippi and to either migrate westward or be slaughtered in Illinois as they had been in Missouri.

> *Charles Lytle,* Freel's father and Wayne's grandfather, had been born in 1846 at Des Moine, Iowa, while his family was en route to the Rocky Mountains. This area at that time was still essentially open territory, except for the occasional intrusions of Mexican miners intent on exploiting its gold and silver resources. Brigham Young — colonizer par excellence — immediately claimed the territory for the exiles and named it the *State of Deseret.*

Pioneer Heritage

The Mormon Battallion

While en route to the Valley of the Great Salt Lake, recruiters for the U.S army intercepted the pioneers and requested formation of a 500-man battalion to engage the Mexicans, sweetening their request with the guarantee of payment of substantive wages to the participant soldiers. Owing to their destitution, the sectarians assented at the prospect of an income, formed the battalion from fathers and sons surviving the violence of Missouri and Illinois, and continued their march westward, with the battalion taking a round-about route to California as a contingent of the U.S. Army and from thence back into the Rocky Mountain area as purported civilians of the *State of Deseret*, which, ironically, in concert with their own march, had now been incorporated into the *US of A.*

---

[1]See http://en.wikipedia.org/wiki/Nauvoo_Expositor.

The Gold Rush

The main body of immigrants reached their destination in the Valley of the Great Salt Lake by July 24, established a government for themselves, issued a currency, and devised a phonetic alphabet for use in their educational system. Separation from the 'Union,' however, was to be short-lived. As if the necessity of rapidly settling the territory weren't sufficient challenge for Brigham, gold was discovered in California, and before the sectarians could catch their breath, an army of gold diggers swarmed across the plains and into *The State of Deseret* in 1849.

Gold-rush emblems.

4.2   The Colonization Story

Upon arrival in the area, Brigham Young immediately launched a program of settlement which saw carefully selected groups of skilled laborers building towns from Cedar City and Dixie in the south, to Carson Valley at the base of the Sierra Nevada in the west, to the fertile regions of Sonora in northern Mexico.

Counter-atrocities in Missouri and Utah

The master plan was to establish a national reserve for the exiles which was self-sufficient and beyond the reach of 'extermination' orders, and violent persecution. (Virtually an entire community of Mormons had been corralled and killed in Missouri at Haun's Mill in 1838 by a murderous mob — an atrocity which ultimately played itself out during the *Utah War* in the counter-massacre of *Gentiles* at *Mountain Meadows* west of Cedar City in 1857[5.5], some seventy miles east of Eagle Valley, where Charles was destined to settle and Freel — Wayne's father — was born.)

The author's birth place, Cedar City – adjacent to rich lodes of iron ore – was the 'iron' mission. Dixie, situated on the Virgin River to the south, was a 'cotton' mission, as were regions of the Muddy River in the remote southwest which served as resupply and rest stations for the growing numbers of Mormon emigrants disembarking in San Diego from origins in Europe and traveling up the Colorado by boat to its confluence with the Muddy and thence by wagon northward to Salt Lake City.

4.3   John's Call to Carson-Valley

In 1856, after serving as a bishop for 11 years in Salt Lake City, John Lytle was
called on a mission with his family to settle Carson Valley, a grueling journey across
the Salt Flats and down the Humboldt to drainages flowing from the Sierra Nevada.
There they established themselves near Mormon Station in Washoe Valley in a
cabin, fenced, plowed, planted, and undertook development of irrigated fields and
orchards. Charles Lytle (Freel's father) accompanied the family, having reached the
age of 12 years by that time.

> WHILE THE MODERN READER may look upon such an undertaking as pure
> drudgery, nothing could be further than the truth for most pioneer set-
> tlers. For them, there was in fact the same exhilaration in breaking new ground,
> building dams to water crops planted in rich soils for the first time, and watch-
> ing them grow to maturity as that experienced by a team of mountain climbers
> conquering a peak for the first time. Their lives were difficult and fraught with
> danger but by no means unrewarding!

The Utah War Story

Bigoted politicians in Washington, however, still intent on 'subjugating' the Mormons, passed laws, culminating in the Edmonds-Tucker act — which made polygamous marriage a felony — and dispatched an army of 2,500 men under General
Johnston to occupy Deseret and facilitate enforcement of this law.

Thus, no sooner was the John Lytle family settled in the shadows of the Sierra
Nevada, than a messenger arrived with orders from Brigham Young to return to
Salt Lake and take up arms against the invading army. John Lytle complied, sold
his newly developed properties for a 'ruinous' price, and returned to Salt Lake to
become a combatant in the so-called *Utah War*. What was *ruinous* for the departing settlers was that non-Mormon locals essentially 'land-jumped' (cf. 'claim-jump')
the improvements made by those who left, paid only a small portion of their true
value, or signed purchase agreements which were subsequently broken.

4.4 'Profiteering'

To what extent Mormons also benefited from the take-over remains unclear. The worse case scenario is that the gentiles who enriched themselves outwardly from the evacuation order may have formed private arrangements with departing Mormons to share the profits deriving from the severely-skewed 'buyers' market. This form of theft, i.e., via money-driven networks operating undercover, is the most radical manifestation of an age-old problem which has plagued many societies. It entails schemes of one kind or another to 'profiteer,' or 'get gain' by dispossessing people of their property through manipulation, 'pawn brokering,' 'scalping,' outright theft, or even murder.[2]

'Getting Gain' from One's Brethren

A study of Mormon history reveals that a recurrent problem faced by Joseph Smith, the movement's founder, was the inclination of some Mormons, both leaders and lay members, to 'profiteer' at the expense of other Mormons. This had happened at Kirtland, Ohio, and later in Missouri, when certain members having 'inside' information rushed into the area which Joseph had designated as the target for the 'upbuilding of Zion,' bought up lands at cheap prices from the locals of the area, and then proceeded to resell them to their Mormon brethren at elevated prices when they arrived seeking lands upon which to settle.

> **This story repeated itself in Nauvoo on such a scale as to result in a public statement by Joseph that the Church in its present state of corruption could offer salvation to no one — that individuals should look to the Lord for mercy on *Judgment Day* based upon the merits of their own good works:**
>
> *Pres. Smith rose; read the 14th Chap. of Ezekiel — Said the Lord had declared by the prophet that the people should each one stand for himself and depend on no man or men in that state of corruption of the Jewish Church —that righteous persons could only deliver their own souls — applied it to the present state of the Church of Latter Day Saints — Said if the people departed from the Lord, they must fall —that they were depending on the prophet hence were darkened in their minds from neglect of themselves ...* [a]
>
> ---
> [a]Ehat & Cook, editors. *The Words of Joseph Smith*, (Grandin Book Company:Orem, Utah, 1991), p. 120.

4.5 Of Wheat and Tares

The thinking of persons like John Lytle was in *Zion* mode, i.e., they considered properties which they had developed to belong to the Lord, who had simply made them temporary stewards. Thus, removal from one area to another merely entailed a change of stewardship rather than considerations of *gaining* or *losing* anything other than spiritual blessings. At Carson Valley, however, the properties in question were

---

[2]Think of Cain and Abel.

hijacked by persons with no intention of consecrating their use to the upbuilding of Zion.

The theology pertaining to such matters dates back to Biblical times, when Jesus of Nazareth had emphasized the foolishness of attempting to serve God and Mammon simultaneously. **There had been an update to this issue by Joseph Smith for Mormons in 1831-32 which placed it in the context of their communities:**

> Nevertheless, in your temporal things you shall be equal, and this not grudgingly, otherwise the abundance of the manifestations of the Spirit shall be withheld.(D&C 70:14)

> For verily I say unto you, the time has come, and is now at hand; and behold and lo, it must needs to that there be an organization of my people, both in this place [Kirtland] and in the land of Zion [Missouri] *...for a permanent and everlasting establishment and order unto my church* ...that you may be equal in the bonds of heavenly things, yea, and earthly things also, for the obtaining of heavenly things. *For if ye are not equal in earthly things ye cannot be equal in obtaining heavenly things* ... (D&C 68:4-6)

What faithful zionists often failed to take into consideration, however, was that — as in Kirtland, Missouri, and Illinois — within several years of their arrival in Deseret, *Zion* had been overrun by *gentiles* (non-Mormons) and pseudo-Mormons, while their economy had become increasingly capitalistic with slippage toward crass mammonism (as in mining camps, for example).[3] To put it mildly, the motives of not few 'brethren' were no longer purely 'zionist.' In new testament terms, one might say that developments beyond their control had sowed 'tares' in Zion which were beginning to present problems for the wheat. Expressed in more sinister terms there were now wolves among the sheep intent upon sating themselves with the flesh thereof.

Vulnerability

The profiteering which took place in Carson Valley, therefore, upon the recall of the colony to Utah, was essentially old news to John Lytle, who had witnessed similar depredations before and no doubt anticipated repetition of the pattern. In fact, the broad program of colonization in process, which frequently entailed repeated relocation of families from one area to another, presented a continuing opportunity and temptation for profiteering at the expense of zionists called upon to `pull up stakes' and settle elsewhere.

---

[3]See *APPENDIX: MANAGING MATERIAL THINGS*

Profiteering in Carson Valley

Orson Hyde Curses the Evildoers

Orson Hyde, a general authority of the Church, who had been 'mill-jacked' out of a saw-mill at the base of the Sierra Nevada worth approximately $10,000 in gold, countered five years later by pronouncing a malediction from the pulpit of the Utah Legislature upon those far-flung valleys, the substance of which was that the curse of God should be upon the region until the inhabitants of the area established a just and righteous society.[4]

4.6   Relevance to Lytle Family History

Why have we devoted space to this unpleasant subject? Simply because it lies at the center of developments in the history of the Lytle family and their moral values. In particular:

> CHARLES, both as a youngster in Carson Valley and later as a businessman himself, observing the slippage from zionism in progress, learned to carefully examine the motives and integrity of those around him, be they 'Mormon' or non-Mormon, leader or layman — especially where large amounts of money were at stake. Our story makes contact with this theme anew as it touches upon Charles and the family in subsequent chapters.

> WE CLOSE THIS SUBJECT FOR NOW by noting that a *profiteer* is the psychological antithesis of Wayne and Justine Lytle — to whom this book is dedicated — who routinely gifted to those less fortunate than themselves either monies or goods beyond that for which they had legitimate need.

4.7   Outcome of the Utah War

Meanwhile, Mormon partisans intercepted and destroyed Johnston's supply wagons, while winter was reducing his army to starving and disease-ridden men, thus exacting

---

[4]http://www.nevadaweb.com/nevadaca/curse.html

losses upon the hapless invaders before any shots were fired. Depending upon the version one wishes to believe, either (1) Brigham responded to overtures of peace and guaranteed safe conduct into the Valley, where the army was granted permission to establish a fort and take refuge from the hellish weather, or (2) Johnston prevailed and forced the Mormons into subjugation.

The latter version sounds like Johnston trying to appear triumphant to his superiors while the first suggests the Mormon take on the outcome. Militarily, Brigham could have easily exterminated Johnston's army had he chosen to do so, but wisely desisted, knowing from past experience in Missouri and Illinois that the next army dispatched to subjugate and/or exterminate the sectarians would be multiplied by a factor of ten. Since the subject of Mormon-Washington relations is far beyond the scope of this book, we make no further comment except in relation to the issue of plural marriage, which does directly impact our story (see, e.g., Chapters 7.4 and 6.3).

Armies Multiplied

4.8   Time for Story Telling

A T THIS JUNCTURE, we peal off the current layer of Lytle family history and expose the next. First, however, we observe that the endless days and nights spent between Nauvoo and the Rockies, followed by the round trip to Carson Valley and back for virtually countless miles, no doubt provided more than ample opportunity for telling family stories and spinning yarns which improved from one recitation to the next. While square-dancing no doubt did have its place in making life livable during those heart-rending times, the stories told between dances no doubt had equally important entertainment value. The tales exchanged at John Lytle's campfire, whose pedigree extended across the Atlantic to the banter of gatherings in Ireland, were no doubt embellished as adroitly with reality and fantasy as with the zigs and zags from mirth to ire manifest in the 'Irish' of his posterity.

4.9   The *Wild West* Experience Continues – Utah's Dixie

John Lytle, never one to confuse setback for defeat, responded next to a call in 1861 by Brigham Young to the Dixie mission, whereupon he again packed up his family, disposed of belongings in such a way as to minimize losses, and removed to what was then generally viewed as the most 'Godforsaken' mission in Deseret. There he joined the settlers struggling to survive while taming the Virgin River for irrigation purposes.

> ``It may be a Virgin at its source, but it's a dirty whore by the time it reaches Dixie,'' was a commonly voiced point of view.

Initially the colonizers lived in dugouts carved in the red sandstone of the region. In time, however, the settlers prevailed, built homes of brick and adobe and, if history has it right, actually managed to cultivate cotton and grow silk worms in Utah's Dixie.

The St. George Temple Story

WORD CAME DOWN from Salt Lake in 1871 that a temple was to be erected in St. George, similar to the one which had been erected in Illinois and subsequently burned by mobs. The location selected by Brigham Young turned out to be seasonally boggy.

Dixie sand stone bluffs

To solve this problem, lava and sandstone were quarried from the surrounding mesa and pile-driven into the foundation area with a canon dating back to Napoleon when he invaded Moscow.[5] It was a grueling task but the structure slowly took shape and was eventually dedicated for use — before the temple in Salt Lake. John Lytle and those of his boys yet at his table[6] or visiting their father assisted in the construction, and the blocks of stone from which it was built likely bear the marks of their hammers and chisels.

---

[5] http://www.mormonwiki.com/St._George_Utah_Temple
[6] Charles had married in 1869 and moved to Nevada.

The St. George Temple

4.10   The Charles-Margaret Story

A moment of reflection reminds us that Charles Lytle had been driving and managing teams of horses and oxen since the age of ten, when he no doubt drove his father's team a goodly part of the way across the Salt Flats and along the Humboldt River in the 1000 mile+ round-trip trek between Salt Lake and Carson Valley during the Utah War (4.3).

It comes as no surprise, therefore, that in 1869, at the age of twenty-three Charles, emerges as the owner of a freight line (cf. trucking company).[a] This business required itinerancy between northern and southern parts of the territory, including Salt Lake City, Filmore, Cedar City, St. George, and parts in between (47.4). Family histories have it that Charles met his wife, Margaret Moody, in St. George, whereupon they travelled to Salt Lake for marriage there in the *Endowment House* (a structure used to perform Mormon marriages and other sacred ordinances before either the Salt Lake or St. George Temples were complete).

---

[a]John Franklin Moody, Chapter I, p. 401.

Back to the Dry Valley Sink

Charles initial contact with Margaret may have been either in some St. George social setting, or through her father, who having managed to survive a severe financial reversal[7], had served Church missions in St. George (1863), Eagle Valley (1866), and Dry Valley (1868?), where he ultimately succeeded in winning the contract to construct a large quartz mill (the very same Valley just south of Rose Valley whose sinkhole nearly did the author in (2.1)) to process the silver ores being mined at Pioche by the Meadow Valley Mining Co.[8] and freighted into the Valley by wagon for processing. If Charles had by then extended his freight line into southern Nevada, he may have made direct contact with William Moody in the Panaca|Pioche|Eagle-Valley|Spring-Valley|Dry-Valley area and subsequently been introduced to Margaret as a business associate at the Moody family residence in St. George (47). Suffice it to say that the particulars of their meeting are shrouded in the dust of colonization, freighting, construction, and plural wives/homes in progress during that period.

Freight teams in Pioche.

4.11   The Moodyville Story

History records that the small settlement to which Charles and Margaret soon moved after their marriage in 1869[9] was in Dry Valley and named 'Moodyville' for its

---

[7]A substantial sum was lost when wheat in storage for resale had spoiled.

[8]From a silver lode discovered by Paiutes and staked out by Jacob Hamblin in 1864 which exploded into a 'boom' town by 1869.

[9]With the driving of the golden spike at Promontory Summit, Utah, on 10 May 1869, the early pioneering period of the Mormons came to an end. (See Eugene E. Campbell, *Establishing Zion:*

founder, Margaret's father. Although it had first been established in response to a mission settlement call (45.6), it was soon home to a population involved in the Pioche mining boom. The town's population reputedly consisted of less than a hundred persons, most of whom were involved in constructing the Pioche|Dry-Valley mill or otherwise servicing the construction and/or operation of it.

Oddly enough, it appears that *Dry Valley* was selected as the site for the mill because it proffered the nearest source of abundant *water* to the Pioche diggings — not a flowing stream of water in Dry Valley itself, of course, but a copious underground supply accessible by virtue of its proximity to the surface. A well was sunk at the mill site from which water was obtained for its operations.[10]

After initially carting water to Moodyville from the stone-bottomed channel of Rose Valley (Echo) canyon, one or more domestic wells were apparently dug to service the little settlement, which was situated near the exit of the Flatnose wash, an area which is a mile or more northeast of the site where the mill was later built and in close proximity to the water-laden sands where the author nearly met his Maker (2.1) *and* where Echo Dam was subsequently built.

> Being enveloped by air currents flowing from the north-end canyons interfacing it with Rose Valley and Flatnose, this particular site appears to be the only area in Dry Valley potentially capable of producing fruit, a fact which serves to confirm its prior settlement as an independent agricultural community separate from the mill area proper.[a]
>
> ---
> [a]Temperatures in Dry Valley to the south of the former Moodyville are *substantially colder*. Similarly, the most successful orchards in both Rose Valley and Eagle Valley were located respectively in the air currents issuing from their north-end canyons.

Despite the foresight invested in situating Moodyville, and despite an expansive area of rich land in the vicinity, a repeat of irrigation programs which had been successful in Rose Valley and Spring Valley was not possible ... the sink adjacent to it made short shrift of the waters exiting the canyon. Lacking agricultural resources for the support of families in the community, they were ultimately forced to relocate as milling operations across the Valley later dwindled and came to a standstill.

4.12   Shifting Church Policy

The enthusiastic participation of Mormons in the Pioche mining bonanza signaled an essential turnabout of the Church's initial policy towards mining. Brigham Young had initially forbidden that his settlers join the gold rush or undertake mining operations, recognizing that the luster of gold and silver may quickly become a serious distraction from their fundamental zionist objectives. However, with the steady flow of gentiles into Deseret and a growing capitalist economy on the upswing, Church leaders found themselves jammed between the proverbial 'rock and a hard place:' Either maintain the prohibition on mining and continue an exclusive concentration

---

The Mormon Church in the American West, 1847-1869 (Salt Lake City: Signature Books, 1988)

[10]See http://www.robertwynn.com/PiocheH.htm: "Pioche History Profile." Sources referenced: *Bancroft, Vol. 25 26; Davis, History of Nevada, Vol. 2; Ralph Andrews, Historic Hires of the West; Elbert Edwards, 200 Years in Nevada.*

on agriculture while gentiles exploited the mineral resources of Deseret for themselves — or get into the game and garner as much of it as possible to advance their
own agenda.

Jacob Hamblin

Brigham Young opted for the latter. Thus, by the 1864, when Paiutes in Meadow
Valley presented Jacob Hamblin with a sample of rich silver ore gathered nearby,[11]
Brigham actually ordered Erastus Snow from St. George to Meadow Valley with a
company of men, who organized a new mining district with new rules to represent
Church interests. It was, in fact, Mormons who transported a 5-stamp mill from
Hiko to Bullionville in Panaca Valley and launched it for Raymond & Ely in competition with Meadow Valley Mining Companys' Dry-Valley mill, constructed under
contract with William Moody, whose labor pool consisted largely of the destitute
settlers of the Church's Dry Valley mission living in Moodyville (45.6). The district
was reportedly abandoned by some Gentiles after work had already been done on
the *Panaca*, the original discovery ledge — the presence of so many Mormons made
the place distasteful to them.[12]

Jacob Hamblin – Stakes out First Pioche Silver Lode

The purpose in spelling out these details is to emphasize the degree and speed
with which zionism ceded ground to capitalism among Mormons at large following
the gold rush. The relevance of this trend will soon confront us head on as we pursue
the Charles Lytle story (5).

---

[11] "Some friendly Indians showed him the location of high grade silver ore. **The town of
Pioche, Nevada, a town not far from the southwestern Utah border, was established
when in 1864 William Hamblin staked his claim there. He did not move his family
there because of the wickedness of the area.** In 1872 one mine produced a record of 36 bars
of silver worth $6,000 in three days." http://members.cox.net/leavittfamilies/H_Wm%20Hayes%
20Hamblin.htm

[12] See http://www.robertwynn.com/PiocheH.htm.

A Story of Dollars and Sense

One version of events has it that Charles moved to Moodyville because his father-in-law, William Crestfield Moody, was kind enough to offer him a job. The fact of the matter appears to be that Charles had business aplenty where he was[a] *but*, being *more affluent* than his father-in-law following the Moody family's failed investment in wheat (4.10; 47.2) and call to the Dixie mission (47.3), responded to the need to lend William's son George a hand by providing freighting services (most likely at bargain rates) to transport materials required for construction of the mill and, subsequent to its construction, to transport both wood for its operation[b] as well as ores from Pioche for processing together with the materials required to keep the mill in operation. **What is certain is that Charles, by virtue of his freight line, was prospering financially far beyond what a working wage could have possibly provided *and* in-laws surrounding him were prospering as well.**(45.6)

---

[a]The demand for freighting services between Salt Lake, Cedar City, Dixie and settlements in between was in a steep climb as capitalism steadily displaced zionism as the prevalent economic order. See *APPENDIX: MANAGING MATERIAL THINGS* .1.

[b]William Moody also obtained the contract to provide the wood to fire the mill's engine.

Left – Echo Dam Embankment
Center – Dry Valley Wash Where Author Was Drug by Horse
Wash Far Side – Road in Moodyville Area
Two Miles Down Valley – Mill and Harriet Henson Home

Wood for the Mill's Engine

Mexican Hit Men

Margaret's life history (47.5) includes an account of how Charles' residence in Moodyville had been singled out by Mexican killers — most likely 'hit men' employed by Raymond & Ely[13] — who, after approaching Charles' home there after dark while Charles was away, had a falling out among themselves and rode off without doing 'the job' — whether to rob the Company payroll or Charles' savings or simply to kill him as a key figure in Meadow Valley Mining Company's operations, we do not know.

A NOTHER INDICATOR that Charles had accumulated substantial capital during his tenure in Dry Valley is that when many Mormons drifted away from the area after discovering that it was in Nevada in 1870,[a] Charles had cash on hand in gold and silver not only to pay Nevada taxes but also to buy up properties in Eagle Valley (specifically, the Chamberlain holdings), launch a cattle business, and eventually build an imposing home there for Margaret.

[a]Nevada assessed the settlers back taxes payable only in gold or silver.

Eagle Valley Mainstreet – Charles Lytle Era

---

[13]Pioche history reports numerous shoot-outs by hired guns as the competing companies vied for possession of silver-bearing lodes. The town's infamous *boot hill* is reportedly graced with the bodies of dozens of gun-fighters imported for battle by competing interests.

Charles Constructs a Single Gauge Railroad

Yet another aspect of Charles business dealings reported by his son Freel (Wayne's father) was his successful bid for the construction of a single-gauge railroad which was instrumental in transporting ores from some point north in the Bristol-Silver|Jack-Rabbit region to the Pioche area. That he acquired other properties with mining potential east of the Valleys is beyond question as well --- Freel reported that Charles had traded one of those properties (`The Home Stake Mine') for Rose Valley in its entirety, plus a substantial slice of real estate in northern Dry Valley. (42)

Execution of Charles' Will

Charles died in 1907, thus preceding Margaret in death. Freel and his siblings came into titular possession of their ranches in Rose Valley and Eagle Valley in 1910 when Margaret decided to parcel out their holdings to the children before her death. They were given the choice of receiving their portions either in cash or in land.

Sam Lytle

Freel elected to take his in land, as did Les and Noma — hence the three-way division of Rose Valley, each with an attendant acreage in Dry Valley. Others chose land in Eagle Valley. Sam elected to receive his inheritance in cash, whereupon Freel invited him to join forces in developing his Rose Valley Ranch. It was Sam, in fact, who provided the carpentry skills used in the construction of the log homes previously described (3) as well as the frame home in which Les, their brother lived on his ranch adjacent to Freel's in Rose Valley.

Rose Valley divided three ways (February view): Noma — far side; Les — Middle; Freel —near side. Right to Left — Serviceberry, Government Peak, and Tobe along mountain chain in distance. State Line situated (not visible) at base of Government Peak on far (Utah) side. See *Page iv* for map.

Chapter **5**

CHARLES MAKES A U-TURN

Charles as a young man had observed profiteering maneuvers in progress at Carson Valley, and apparently learned to carefully examine the motives and integrity of those around him, be they `Mormon' or non-Mormon, leader or layman --- especially where substantial sums of money were to be made or lost.
— Chapter 4.4

5.1 Hackles Galore

Author's Note: This chapter is pretty much HACKLES and more HACKLES. The purpose for its inclusion is to explore the reasons for Charles Lytle's retreat from Church activity, which, so far as Wayne and Justine are concerned, entails navigating the twists and turns which initially brought them together as non-Mormon (Wayne) versus Mormon (Justine).

The substance of the chapter is that Charles recoiled and rejected the Church as hopelessly corrupt when his bishop called him to `pull up stakes' in Eagle Valley and settle in a mission which was in fact defunct. Charles apparently read the incongruous call as an attempt to hijack his freight line and other assets for use by Church-related profiteering interests promoting an import/export operation from Callville at the junction of the Muddy and Colorado rivers.

If you prefer to limit yoursef to stories which *Tickle Your Funny Bone* or *Warm* ⟸ *Your Heart,* read the section directly below and then skip to the next chapter. On the other hand, if you are interested in an unwhitewashed account of the realities of life confronted by Lytle-family pioneers in Meadow Valley, be brave and forge ahead.

> FOR ADDITIONAL DETAIL AND COMMENTARY ON THE BUSINESS ETHICS OF
> THE ERA AND POSSIBLE CORPORATE ENTITIES IN POSITION TO PROFIT FROM
> CHARLES' BOGUS MISSION CALL, SEE *APPENDIX: MANAGEMENT OF THE
> MATERIAL WORLD* (.I)

5.2   Life in Eagle Valley

As Charles' involvement in the Dry Valley operation wound down, he purchased the
Chamberlain Ranch in Eagle Valley, moved his family there, acquired a cattle herd
which included some 500 herefords, and built a large, comfortable home. Meanwhile,
his freight line appears to have continued operations and become an increasingly
valuable asset. Relative to this period of his life, Freeland Lytle, who worked as a
teamster himself before becoming a rancher (17.2), used to tell this anecdote about
his father, Charles:

> Every year the Lytles took their turn at boarding the school teacher in their home. One
> of the teachers took a dislike to the pipe that Charles smoked, and wasn't shy about
> telling him so. She was always after him for smoking that   smelly old pipe.'
> One day she came in and found him asleep in front of the fire place with the pipe in
> his mouth. Sneaking over to the fire place, she scooped up a little soot and blackened
> his face with it. When he found out, he knew right away who'd done it. He could hear
> her laughing up in her room. She walked around with a smirk on her face for several
> days, but he didn't say anything. But he bided his time, and one day he came in to
> find that she'd washed and dried her long stockings, and they were all rolled up in
> little balls in a basket sitting by the fire place. He fetched a spoon and filled up the
> stockings with soot from the fire place.
> She took the stockings up to her room and never noticed. The next morning she put
> them on and went to school and still never caught on. But when she took them off
> that night, you should have heard her yell! You could hear her all over the house. Her
> feet and legs were all black! She never said anything more about his pipe. (Karen
> ---Pages from the *Charles Lytle Family Book*)

5.3   The Lower-Muddy Mission Call

A large question mark, however, settles over the family record as the story unfolds in
the Eagle Valley area at this time. Freel (Charles' son) reports that *the* bishop (iden-
tity unknown) approached Charles and issued a call for him to pull up stakes and

remove to the Lower-Muddy (River) Mission[1] (See *APPENDIX: MUDDY RIVER MISSION* .I). Thereupon, according to Freel, Charlie looked him straight in the eye and said: "My wagon will be the first AFTER yours, Bishop." When the Bishop noted that he wouldn't be going himself, Charlie averred, that if that were the case, he would NOT be going either.

Clearing away Historical Debris

A cloying orthodoxy — which the founder of Mormonism, Joseph Smith, so vehemently hated — now stands squarely in the way of understanding both what Charles did on this occasion and why he did it. To sort out the facts surrounding this event it is necessary to 'hew away more than a hundred years of encrusting *vilifications* and thick layerings of *iconographic* pigments, masks ultimately false to the entire cast.'[2]

- The *vilifications* are that Charles simply became imbued with the wickedness of Pioche's mining environment, lost the Spirit, and became disobedient.

- The *iconographic pigment* encrusting the picture is the deeply entrenched notion that Mormon-conceived operations of the period and in this area were uniformly 'zion'- oriented, 'above board,' and devoid of profiteering (4.4).

In hewing both away, we find a Charles who had stood faithfully in 'zion mode' beside his father and family both in Carson Valley and at Dixie under the most trying circumstances (*and* at the side of his father-in-law at the Dry Valley Mission) — while looking with jaundiced eye at the under-handed practices which, having infiltrated the Church at Kirtland and Nauvoo, subsequently slithered across the plains with the pioneers and resumed operations openly in Deseret until they provoked Orson Hyde to call forth the curse of God upon them in Carson Valley (Chapter 4.5).

> To acknowledge and speak of such practices was not taboo in the Lytle family. Charles and Freel referred to persons (Mormon or non-Mormon) who placed wealth above decency in business dealings as *swindlers* and *cheats*, men so *crooked* that they would have to be *screwed into the ground* when they died. The author recalls Freel's advice about dealing with one local who cultivated a large orchard and sold apples: "Take your own containers and pick your own apples; buy his pre-picked apples and you'll get bushels decked out with beauties on top and rotten ones in the bottom."

5.4 Testing for Crookedness

Charles' strategy in testing the Bishop himself for commitment to the same call was likely his way of determining whether the call was issuing from the 'zion' or the

---

[1]To arrive at this mission, Charles would first make his way to the Muddy River in the Moapa area and thence south along that river on its downward sweep through the desert to its confluence with the Colorado River.

[2]Lance S. Owens, "Joseph Smith and Kabbalah: The Occult Connection." *Dialogue: A Journal of Mormon Thought, Vol. 27, No. 3, Fall 1994*, pp. 117-194.

'mammon' side of the Church's ambivalence at the time[3]. He was, as previously emphasized, well acquainted with both, based on what he had personally witnessed in connection with his father and father-in-law's experiences and the distinctly non-zionist trends he saw unfolding among Mormons as he operated his freight line from north to south and east to west *and* participated in a mining boom (Pioche) facilitated by both Mormon labor and leadership (4.12).

$\Longrightarrow$ **Judging by Charles reaction, it appears that the Bishop's answer was for him confirmation that the motivation behind the call was to either 'jump' his freight line outright or get its services for free by issuing a *mission* call.**

Recall once more that Charles had witnessed his own family transit from prosperity to destitution as John Lytle was called successively both to and from the Carson Valley Mission and ultimately to Dixie, where their very survival was in jeopardy. As late as 1869, in fact, Charles had visited his betrothed (Margaret Moody), only to find her living in a dug-out in St. George, while cocky neighbors scoffed at them and flaunted their possessions in typical profiteering mode (47.3).

Again, *judging by Charles reaction to the Bishop in question,* one can easily imagine Charles in a quandary about those who had moved into their home and taken possession of their land when they were sent south from Salt Lake to serve settlement missions, and whether there were private connections between those issuing the calls and the 'move-ins.'

Meanwhile, Charles had also apparently learned that, following the wholesale release and exodus of settlers from the Muddy Mission in 1869-70[a], the only surviving component of the plan driving the Lower Muddy operation was to sustain a port on the Colorado accessible by steamboat to service corporate interests endeavoring to import/export commodities to/from California[b]. Transport in that category matched up with his own speciality, which entailed the use of heavy wagons drawn by oxen (47.4) or large draft animals to move 'freight' as opposed to the stages and carriages required for the transport of emigrants.

---
[a]*Appendix: MUDDY RIVER* .H
[b]Study *Appendix: MANAGEMENT OF THE MATERIAL WORLD* .I.

IN THE CASE OF CHARLES LYTLE, an established freighting outfit, if it could be gotten in 'zion' mode (i.e., for nothing), translated into huge savings for any profiteering group, plus the possible option of passing Charles' cattle ranch and other holdings on to others, not as titled property for which full and equitable payment must be made, but as a consecrated 'stewardship' available for assignment to others for little or nothing once he accepted the *mission* call.[a]

---
[a]Charles 'temple' marriage (performed at the 'Endowment House' in Salk Lake) entailed the consecration of one's all to the upbuilding of 'zion' but, needless to say, not to 'mammon.'

---

[3]See *Appendix:MANAGEMENT OF THE MATERIAL WORLD* .I and Chapter 4.5

Doubtless, Charles had also received news of Orderville (7.4), a new colony in southern Utah settled primarily by destitute refugees from failed zionist settlements on the Muddy River in Nevada.[4]

If Charles did in fact entertain such thoughts when he declined the call to a failed settlement mission, he was, of course, simply evading a highly irregular maneuver with `SWINDLE' written all over it. There was, however, still another complicating factor at the time potentially even more sinister. While we hesitate to speak of it, any consideration of Charles response to the Bishop's call and the history of the Lytle family in Meadow Valley would be incomplete without mention of it.

5.5 Collateral Damages of the Utah War

A heavy cloud had suspended itself over the leadership of the LDS Church at the time of the *Mountain Meadow Massacre* in 1857 — a byproduct of the Utah War (4.3) which had not as yet fully dissipated at the time Charles executed his 'U-Turn' with the Church. In words purporting to be those of John D. Lee himself[5]:

> . . . there was a reign of terror in Utah [including Meadow Valley[6]], at the time, and many a man had been 'put out of the way,' on short notice, for disobedience, and I had made some narrow escapes.[7]

Given that Lee's alleged account represents fact, it appears that an oath of secrecy[8] had been administered to all having knowledge relating to the massacre or having personally abetted or participated in it, which included not a few brethren in the Cedar, City/St. George area[9] — **the principle source of Church leadership and settlers in the Meadow Valley area soon thereafter in 1864 (Panaca) and 1866 (Eagle Valley).**

---

[4]Purely as a matter of speculation, it is interesting to consider the possibility that had Charles actually removed to the Lower Muddy, he would likely have crossed paths with Grandma Great (Adair)(7.4) and/or family in their flight from the Muddy Mission to Orderville for survival.

[5]John D. Lee was made 'scapegoat' for all who participated in the massacre, being the only man of the many responsible who was ultimately, charged, prosecuted, tried, and executed for the ritual killings.

[6]It wasn't until 1870 that Meadow Valley shifted to Nevada jurisdiction.

[7]John D. Lee, *Confessions of John D. Lee* as dictated to Wm. W. Bishop, Attorney at Law, Pioche, Nevada, May 17, 1877 and published by Bryan, Brand Co., Publishers, St. Louis, Mo.

[8]Euphemism for 'secret combination'[4.4].

[9]The Jacob Hamblin family, for example, heard the shooting and commotion at Mountain Meadows from his nearby ranch, but allegedly had no part it personally, save, perhaps, translating for the Indians who did. (John D. Lee, *Confessions.*)

THIS MEANT, in effect, that Charles was placed in a position where he had to sort through the particulars of what by all accounts was a *fraudulent* mission call, while knowing full well that the authority issuing the call may have been actively shielding himself at the time from arrest and prosecution.

Site of Mountain Meadow Massacre, some 70 miles west of Eagle Valley
John D. Lee was singly tried and executed for the massacre in 1874, 27 years after the fact.

5.6   Charles' Negative Ruling

It should come as no surprise, therefore, that not only did Charles NOT remove to the Lower Muddy, but never again --- to the author's knowledge --- did he participate in Church activities or attend any of its meetings. So far as the exact date of his alienation, history records that active settlement of the Lower Muddy River Mission extended from 1865 to 1870(see *APPENDIX:MUDDY MISSION* .I.) His marriage in the Endowment House was in 1869, at which time he was obviously still active and in good standing with the Church. After their marriage, Charles and Margaret moved to Dry Valley, Moodyville, Nevada (where his first son, Edwin Lytle, was born in 1870). Directly thereafter, he moved to Eagle Valley, which appears to place them under the presiding authority of Church officials in Meadow Valley at the time the *call* was attempted.

Separatism Supplants Communion

Charles had been an active Mormon his entire life, from the Valley of the Great Salt Lake, to Carson Valley, back, and subsequently to Dixie. When he married Margaret in the endowment house he had made a commitment to the Eternal Marriage of Mormonism and swore allegiance to the Law of Consecration . . .

Still, subsequent to the *Muddy Mission call,* Charles irrevocably cut off any further connection with the Church. It is a matter of record that when the active bishop requested permission to baptize his children in Eagle Valley some eight+ years latter, there was a wall between them. Charlie fired back — "You can if you can catch 'em."[10] Thereupon Margaret tried to force the issue, but Charles intervened, instructing her that baptism must be their own decision, not hers.

5.7 Pertinent Consequences

Freel, Wayne's father, chose not to be baptized and later married Mary Jensen, whose mother had forced upon her the same decision in the wake their bitter, poverty-ridden experience following the breakup of the family by the Edmunds-Tucker anti-polygamy Act. (Mary's story is spelled out in Chapter 6.)

5.8 Analysis

> **Given his past history of compliance and faithfulness, what had so re-pulsed Charles that he reacted in this manner? Why did he not sim-ply decline the call while otherwise remaining active in the Church?**

Lacking indicators to the contrary, the most probable explanation for Charles' sudden, irreversible disaffection with the Church as an institution was two-fold:

1. As formerly suggested, Charles had either satisfied himself or been informed privately that underlying the 'call' to the by then failed[11] Muddy Mission was a scheme to 'jump' his freight line, cattle ranch, and other holdings as a step in advancing the commercial objectives cooked up by profiteers targeting the Lower Muddy for import/export via the Colorado.[12] He may have perceived in the person facing him the ultimate 'TARE' among the mixed growth of his present *Piochified* environment (4.12) — the frontman[13] for Mormon profi-teers driven by greed and greed alone ...and *possibly* implicated as well in the Mountain Meadow killings (4.4).

---

[10]Freel's account.

[11]Insofar as legitimate zionist settlement was concerned, it was 'all over' at the Lower Muddy Mission as of Brigham's visit in 1870. The settlers had been released and gathered at Orderville or returned to the sites from which they had been called. Only commercial objectives remained active.

[12]That freighting services were a key element in commercial objectives for the Lower Muddy is witnessed by the fact that a railroad spur was later constructed to the site.

[13]The Bishop in question, possibly unaware of background circumstances, may have merely been following instructions.

At the shoreline, looking north across the schoolhouse; inset, the front steps and a water filled building

Remains of St. Thomas on the Lower Muddy.

2. The climate on the Muddy River at its union with the Colorado was too harsh for year-round settlement, especially for a growing family of young children. Thus, with respect to Margaret and the children, the call heinously placed them in the EXPENDABLE category and would almost certainly have eventuated in the death of one or more of them.

No Water Fit to Drink

It is a matter of record, that many Mormon families previously sent there simply could not endure the deadly environment of the Lower Muddy, becoming ill and covered with sores after drinking the waters in the area, and ultimately perished or fled — just as the Paiutes transported to the reservation in that area (29.3) in former times who had returned via Indian Peak or Cedar City (and ultimately to Eagle Valley) with word of their horrendous experience. To determine whether his 'cotton' settlements at the juncture of the Muddy and the Colorado could survive, Brigham Young personally visited them in March 1870 and, having witnessed conditions there himself, released them to settle elsewhere. That fall, a flood wiped out the new Muddy village of West Point (Appendix .I) and survivors were reassigned to Orderville, Utah (7.4).

5.9   Question of Identity

THE ULTIMATE QUESTION staring us in the face, of course, is: **Who WAS this Bishop who informed Charles that he would not be going to the Muddy Mission himself?**   The answer, obviously, is an easy target for disclosure. The author, however, finds the answer too close to home for comfort . . . and therefore deems it prudent to break off that aspect of Charles' story without further inquiry or comment.

INSOFAR AS CHARLES' REACTION is concerned, one can only say that there is nothing equivalent to (1) flip-flops in fundamental church policies and doctrine and/or (2) the discovery of corruption in leadership (**Chapter** 4.4) more calculated to interminably disaffect its members — especially in view of the Mormon scriptural injunctions:

- **"To trust no one to be your teacher nor your minister, except he be a man of God, walking in his ways and keeping his commandments."** [a]

- **". . . all you that are desirous to follow the voice of the good shepherd, come ye out from the wicked, and be ye separate, and touch not their unclean things."** [b]

---

[a]Book of Mormon, Mosiah 23:14.
[b]Book of Mormon, Alma 5:57-61.

5.10   Dominos

Whether Charles was or was not an intended victim who took decisive measures to remove himself and his family from profiteering prospect lists and preserve their lives, the fact remains that the ill-advised 'mission call' in question was to effect the lives of Charles' children and their posterity for the indeterminate future.

Indeed, his personal reaction may not have been the full extent of its consequences. History records that the participation of Eagle Valley's entire male membership in Church activities essentially 'dried up' in subsequent years. As Charles had occasion to discuss his disheartening experience with associates, there looms the possibility, at least, of a 'domino effect' extending into other families as well.

5.11   More Dominos

MOREOVER, so far as the central theme of our story is concerned, according to Freel's account, it was that incident which placed Wayne and Justine together initially as non-Mormon versus Mormon . . . and, incidentally, those mere bumps on Mike Lytle's head rather than fully-formed horns which Frankie Hill expected to find there!(See *Introductory* quote to Chapter 4.)

5.12   Subsequent Lifestyle

Charles' behavior in subsequent years indicates that he had come to hold precisely the same opinion of the Church in his generation that Joseph Smith had voiced relative to the situation in Nauvoo (4.4), namely, that in its present mode of operation, righteous persons must 'deliver their own souls' — that the Church as an institution could not truly hold out the promise of salvation to anyone. In a word, from that perspective, it all came down to God's judgment with respect to one's personal conduct. Accordingly, reports of Charles lifestyle uniformly depict him as a cordial, generous man who loved people, extending a hand of fellowship to Indian (42.4) and White Man alike while remaining aloof from the Church.

5.13   Final Note on the Charles Lytle Story

In corrupt LDS circles, profiteering attempts targeting other members, when foiled, are typically followed up with libelous counter charges which attempt to discredit and shift responsibility to the intended victims. **This process is often facilitated by naive, uninformed individuals who hold to the fantasy that 'all is well in Zion,'[14] ergo the victim must be at fault.**

In the author's experience, common countercharges are 'infidelity (to the Church),' 'apostasy,' 'theft of the property involved,' and/or wickedness entailing God's punishment in the form of 'suffering the gall of bitterness,' 'mental illness,' the proclivity to be a 'hermit,' and so on. In Charles case, it has been suggested by his own descendants that he took to drinking, carousing, and other 'cowboy/miner' practices, thus leading to his inactivity. **Such charges are entirely and completely unfounded**, which — as detailed directly above and in his personal history (Chapter 42) — his unwavering Christian lifestyle effectively refute!

> It is the author's personal opinion that, lacking Charles gift of discernment and refusal to be victimized, his family would have perished on the *Altar of Mammon* at the Lower Muddy — which means, in effect, that we shall always remain in his debt. AT ANY RATE, IT IS WELL PAST TIME FOR HIS DEFAMATION TO CEASE!

---

[14]2 Nephi 28:21.

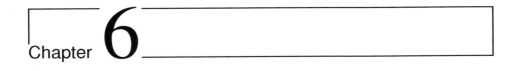

Chapter 6

MARY'S STORY

There was nothing like a swig of cool whisky to top off a hard day's work and no one seemed the wiser, that is until Mary caught a whiff of it on his breath. Thereupon, she launched a search, discovered the bottle in its hiding place, marched with it into the kitchen, deftly popped the cork and began to pour *Jack Daniels* down the sink.

6.1 The Government Legislates Religion

In those [pioneer] days, young ladies were often recruited in Salt Lake by emissaries from the settlements to teach school in the local schools. Most were Mormon or had Mormon affiliations and most found husbands in the area. One of these young ladies was Mary Jensen. After meeting Freel, they corresponded and eventually married. Mary's family had been a victim of the Edmunds-Tucker Act which readily passed congress, *Abraham, Isaac, Jacob and the Constitution be damned!*[1] Her father had been presented the choice of deserting all but one of his plural wives and the children issuing therefrom or go to prison for an unspecified number of years.

For Mormons and non-Mormons alike who may have wondered who the (in)famous Edmunds and Tucker were, their portraits are now readily available on the internet. Rumor has it that they too had horns of a tusk-like variety, but managed to conceal them by growing beards!

---

[1] Plural marriage had been an integral component of Biblical law since the Abrahamic era and is still an aspect of many religions the world over. The First Amendment to the U.S. Constitution states specifically: **"Congress shall make no law respecting an establishment of religion, or prohibiting the free exercise thereof; or abridging the freedom of speech, or of the press; or the right of the people peaceably to assemble, and to petition the Government for a redress of grievances."**

> M ARY'S MOTHER had been one of the wives caught up in the polygamy
> debacle. She harbored a bitterness for the Church, ceased to be an active
> Mormon and forbad her children to join. The *Story* from her side depicts a
> young mother and her 'orphaned' children eking out an existence as best they
> could until she remarried.

6.2   Freel and Mary Jensen Are Wed

Mary Ann Jensen and her sister Teena Jensen came from Utah to Nevada to teach
rural school — Mary in Clover Valley and Tenna in Eagle Valley. While Mary was
visiting Teena in Eagle Valley, she met Freel, who was working as a cowboy after
finishing his work as teamster in Delamar, and they fell in love. Mary said, *"My
gosh, he was almost thirty years old. All those cowboys were the same. They didn't
have gumption enough to get out and find a woman. They would just sit and wait
for a teacher to come in, then they'd try to marry her."*

We now listen intently as Mary tells her own story in her own words.

6.3   Mary Tells Her Own Story

Family Origins in Denmark

My mother, Ellen Christina Benson, was born in Schleswig Holstein Denmark, Nov.
15, about 1854.(Wonsbeck, Haderslev, Denmark, 22 Nov1850?) She had four brothers: Paul, Christian, Ludwig, and Jeppe; and two sisters: Mette Marie and Mary.
Paul and Christian came to Chicago shortly after the big Chicago fire. Paul invested
in a clothing store, was married and had four children: George, Ella, Walter, and
Mildred. Christian was a partner in an import fish business and went to Europe in
a freight ship two times a year to purchase fish. He was also married and had two
children: Anna and Alfred.

Becoming a Second Wife

My mother, Ellen Christina, also decided to come to Chicago where her brothers
were, and had a millinery shop there. Soren Madsen was sent on an LDS mission
to Chicago, converted my mother to the church, became engaged to her and asked
her to come to Salt lake City to be married. But before she was able to come he
became engaged to another girl, but mother was married to Madsen as second wife
(19 Oct 1874). A son, Joseph Christian Madsen, was born on July 31, 1875.

Events Subsequent to Edmunds-Tucker

As plural marriages ceased to be allowed in the Church, my mother (eventually)
married Burre Jensen and moved to Monroe, Utah. Five children were born to
them: Paul Ludwig, Johanna Marie, Mary Anna, Katrina Christina, and Martha
Julene. We had a nice home with an orchard and berry bushes. But in the early
days there was but very little work to be had, and it was hard to make a living.

My father was a carpenter and was hired by Smith Parker to build a house for the family. He made a payment on a small log house and ranch and moved us there. The nearest "town" was Box Creek about one mile from our ranch. But as there was no more work to be found there, my father went to Park City and was employed as a carpenter there. But he had previously had attacks and was found dead of a heart failure. (February 1895 near Park City, Utah)

Mother had a few cattle, but knew very little about taking care of them. And she raised chickens and sold eggs by the crate of 30 dozen in Koosharem about 15 miles from where we lived. We received 7 or 8 cents a dozen for them. I remember one time when we couldn't sell them and had to take them back home. We had a "White House" cook book and looked up all of the recipes that used eggs.

That kind of life was very hard on mother who had been raised in a different kind of life. But we kids didn't mind as we always had enough to eat and had ways of entertaining ourselves. We skated on the ice on the soles of our shoes and went swimming in the ditch. And Paul made a sleigh that could be pulled by a horse and we really went sleigh riding. Paul put shelves on the outside of the house and we gathered up all the broken dishes and everything that we could find and played "keeping house!"

Mother's brother, Paul Benson, and his wife decided to come to Utah to see his sisters in Manti and Grass Valley. But his wife wouldn't come any farther than Manti, as they would have to come by team from Richfield to Grass Valley. When Uncle Paul came in the door he said to Mamma, "Kenna du mae, kenna du mae?" Do you know me? Uncle bought a new spring wagon for the boys. They had a small team: Ship, a lazy bay, and Nellie, a runaway brown. They were used as work or riding horses. We had to walk a mile to go to school at Box Creek, and when there was snow on the ground our feet would get very cold. But we loved our teacher, Miss McCarthy from Monroe.

But as ranching was too hard for our mother, she sold the ranch and bought a home in Koosharem about 12 miles from Grass Valley, and we enrolled in the school there. There were 75 or 80 pupils and two teachers. We were graded by the books in reading. As there was very little money, Mother decided to take the team and wagon and go and try to sell some goods. (dry goods, cloth etc.) There was some mining being done in Blue Valley (Giles, Handsville and Junction) So, with Hannah or myself to drive the team, we went there to sell merchandise and did quite well. Later we went without her.

Paul got a job from Shedrick Nicewonger to ride on the Fish Lake Range to brand calves and look after his cattle. He received calves in payment. Wages with board and room were about $15 a month. But calves were selling for 7 or 8 a head.

Paul made arrangements with Nicewonger to run a dairy at Fish Lake. He had one large living room and one small log cabin where we made and stored the cheese on shelves from floor to ceiling. Paul hired a boy to help us, drove the cows off from the range, "broke" them to milk, and left Teenie and I and Frank to milk the cows and make the cheese.

We had an oblong cheese vat and a galvanized cheese hoop open on both ends, with cloth inside, into which we put the curd. We had a bench with pole lever, outside, where the cheese were pressed. In the evening they were put into cheese cloth jackets and pressed until morning when they were ready to put on the shelves, but had to be turned over every day.

Cheese rennet and coloring were purchased in liquid form. And if we were out of the rennet we could make it from a calve's stomach lining. The cheese were shipped to Salt lake City and we always had a market for them. When the cowboys happened along to stay over night, Teenie and I would go to bed in one corner, blow out the light and the boys would go to bed in the other corner. Joe rounded up some wild horses on the range and went along with them on a freight train to Chicago, where they were sold. He visited our uncles and their families, Paul and Christian Benson.

When we were through school in Koosharem, our mother made arrangements for a scholarship for Hannah and I in the Wasatch Academy in Mt. Pleasant. But mother died from inflammatory rheumatism on July 2, 1901. Hannah was married to John Peterson that fall.

6.4   Teaching in Nevada

Teenie and I went to school at the Wasatch Academy. The next summer Teenie and I went to get work at a boarding house. Teenie went to school at the Collegiate Institute and finished 3rd grade. That fall we went back to the Wasatch Academy for the final year of high school. At that time the educational course included normal training and practice teaching. Teenie sent for her grade standing to the Institute at Salt Lake and was valedictorian of the class. We went back to Salt Lake City and worked that summer, and inquired at the employment agency for teachering positions. Lyman Woods at the agency was looking for a teacher who could play well enough on the piano to accompany school songs, etc. As I could play well enough for that, I signed a contract to teach in Clover Valley, and Teenie signed a contract to teach in Eagle Valley. I also played the auto harp and harmonica. We came on the train to Caliente and by team driven mail stage to Pioche. We stayed over night at the Price Hotel, and then went to Eagle Valley on another horse powered mail stage.

We were informed that the Charles Lytles would board the teacher and we stayed there two weeks. But Charles Lytle had died in July and Mrs. Margaret Lytle and Maggie went on a vacation trip to California. I went to Clover Valley to teach and Teenie went to stay with Bob Hammonds. There were about fourteen pupils in Eagle Valley, beginners to 8th grade; and twelve in Clover Valley school. We had a Christmas program which was to be followed by a dance. But the fiddlers had started to celebrate before the dance and weren't able to play. So I substituted on the harmonica and had the dance anyway.

6.5   Milton and Teenie Are Married

Milton escorted Teenie "around" and Freel came to Clover Valley to see me. It was said that the Eagle Valley boys and the Spring Valley boys waited for the teachers to come in before they would get married! Milton and Teenie were married in August 1908 by Bishop Neils Peterson. They were married in our mother's sister's home, Metta Marie Provstguard in Manti, Utah. Milton built a house on one of his father's fields across the creek from Ursine (Eagle Valley). There, three of their children were born: Sarah Frances died from pneumonia at the age of 1 year and is buried at the Hammond cemetery at Eagle Valley.

6.6 Freel and Mary Are Married

Freeland Henson Lytle and Mary Ann Jensen were married on December 11, 1908. We were also married in the Provstguard home by Bishop Neils Peterson. We went on a honeymoon to Long Beach, California, for 3 weeks: returned to Eagle Valley and lived with Freel's mother, Margaret Lytle, and sister, Maggie, for about a month. Then we bought two tents and moved to Rose Valley. There Mary Gladys was born on August 13, 1909, weighing in at 3 and 1/2 lbs. It rained so hard that the tent, bed and everything else was wet or damp. We had Mrs. Craw, grandmother of all the Craws, staying with us to help, and as Les and Ellen were in Idaho on vacation, she advised us to move into their house for a week.

Freel made a frame house "as soon as possible", consisting of living room, bed room and kitchen and we moved there. Freel's youngest brother, Sam, was living at Fay and was an engineer in the mines. But the mines closed down and they decided to move to Rose Valley, as the ranch was then owned by his mother.

6.7 The Log Homes Are Built

Sam and Freel purchased a log boarding house from the mine owners at Fay, and they hauled the logs to Rose Valley in winter weather and piled them up. (When I looked out one day Wayne was on top of them.) They then built a frame, placed the logs on it, and sawed them lengthwise with a rip saw, and as Sam was a carpenter, they built the two log houses now owned by Mrs. Freel Lytle and Wayne Lytle (Chapter 3).

Milton Hammond decided to find a new location for his family, and as Paul lived in Sevier County, Utah, he decided to go there. So he loaded up a covered wagon. It took 7 days to reach our destination. Wayne was 2 years old, Gladys 3. When we went on the train to Manti to see Auntie and Uncle Provstguard, Wayne said, "I want to go back to the wagon." Milton purchased an uncultivated farm 8 miles from Gunnison, Utah. It is now a modern farm on which they still live.

Freel and I came back to Rose Valley and lived there for 50 years. Freeland Henson Lytle died (of a heart attack) in the Caliente Hospital, June 17, 1958. (Mary Jensen Lytle died in the Caliente Hospital, June 24, 1965. (of complications due to a stroke) She was buried by the side of her husband June 29, 1965, in the Lytle Cemetery at Eagle Valley.)

6.8 Gladys and Wayne

Mary Gladys Lytle was born August 13, 1909. Freeland Wayne Lytle was born February 25, 1911. Gladys and Wayne were raised on the Rose valley ranch. When they were small I would put Wayne in front of the saddle and ride horseback up to Eagle Valley to visit my sister, Teenie Hammond and family. The horses were never gentle and one day when I was coming home, Prince shied and jumped across the road in front of Devlin's house. Wayne said, "Dod, didn't he dump a long ways!" They had dances and social gatherings in the Eagle Valley Hall. Freel would harness and hook the team up to the buggy, drive up, put the little folks on the stage platform to sleep, and dance until after midnight.

As we had but very few cattle when we first moved to Rose Valley, Freel did a lot of riding on the range for his mother and his brother Ed. One year he rode so late in the spring that the grain he had planted dried up because it hadn't been watered, and he didn't ride so much after that happened. Wayne had to help with the work on the ranch at an early age and learned to drive team and ride a horse. Gladys also learned to ride and would ride to the pasture for the cows. Slim was a tall horse and Freel's mother once said she looked like a peanut sitting up there!

They went to school and finished the 8th grade in Rose Valley. There were seven students: Grace and John Devlin, Lena, Leah and Mike (Leslie) Lytle, and Gladys and Wayne all cousins. One of he teachers, Laura Steffan, played the piano very well, and Gladys took piano lessons from her beginning at the age of 7.

After graduating from the 8th grade at Rose Valley, Gladys, Wayne, and Leslie "Mike" went to Eagle Valley for the first two years of high school. The following year they went to Panaca for the Junior year, and graduated from Cedar City. An accomplished musician, Carl Meyers, came through Rose Valley looking for a place that was "high and dry," and stayed there for a year.

Wayne and Mike enrolled for violin lessons and Gladys studied and practiced piano. The following year Freel bought an old Buick touring car from Will Warren of Eagle Valley, and they drove to Boston, Massachusetts and entered the New England Conservatory of Music. Wayne and Leslie studied violin and Gladys had piano lessons. At the end of the year they drove home in an old Flint car.

6.9   Freel and Mary Are Both Non-Mormon

So ... when Wayne and Gladys were born to Freel and Mary, neither parent was an active Mormon, despite their Mormon heritage. My recollection of their life style, however, is that Mary's principles were strictly Mormon and more than adequate to counter the rough-tough, freighter-cowboy-miner influences to which Freel was constantly exposed. Thus, so far as his 'tall tales' where concerned, an effective filter kept content within proper Christian limits. To my recollection, Mary's closest approach to profanity was a zesty "OH FHAAAAAAA!" uttered with a resounding stomp of her right foot on the floor. (Eldon)

Jack Daniels and Orange Aid

On one occasion Freel found it necessary to leave the Valley long enough to do business with associates elsewhere. A friend, expressed his appreciation by gifting a bottle of *Jack Daniels* whiskey to Freel. Knowing that Mary had a strong aversion to alcohol, upon his return, Freel stashed it in the cool-room adjacent to the kitchen. It seemed things were working out well. There was nothing like a swig of cool whisky to top off a hard day's work and no one seemed the wiser, that is until Mary caught a whiff of it on his breath. Thereupon, she launched a search, discovered the bottle in its hiding place, marched with it into the kitchen, deftly popped the cork and began to pour *Jack Daniels* down the sink.

Freel was heart sick, but what could be done ... other than remind her that she herself regularly stashed a bottle of *Orange Aid* soda pop in there and routinely mixed it with cold water to refresh herself. "TAIN'T THE SAME AND YOU KNOW IT!" So that was the end of *Jack Daniels*. He later confided to me that he reckoned *Orange Aid* was Grandma's only vice! (Eldon)

6.10 Grandma Bronc Buster

Freel recalled that one day Wayne came in bawling because the horse had bucked him off. He was only a little fellow and he felt pretty bad. Grandma said, "Well, we'll see about that!" She went out and strapped on some spurs, caught the horse, and climbed aboard. Whap! She slapped him with the reins and raked him with the spurs! You should have seen that horse jump! But she never turned a hair. Every time he'd jump, she'd slap him with the reins and rake him with the spurs. Whap! Whap! First one side and then the other. Finally, that horse was so tired he could hardly move. Then she got down and handed the reins to Wayne. "There! Now you can ride him." (Karen)

6.11 Grandma's Politics

When Wayne taught school in Pioche, Freel found it necessary to bring in a hired man to help him feed and manage the cattle. There was an old bunk house out under the locust trees bordering the chicken yard fence for hired help. One balding red-headed fellow (we'll call him *Joe*, for short) worked for Freel several winters running. His performance was acceptable, but he was always spouting communist dogma at mealtime. It was hard to tell whether he was serious or just teasing Grandma — he'd discovered that she hated 'commies' with a vengeance. He barely escaped getting walloped with her cast iron frying pan a time or too. Then one year Joe didn't show up at the appointed time ... but a couple of FBI agents did, just to check him out, they said. Joe it seems, was indeed a registered member of the communist party. (Eldon)

6.12 Grandma Attends Church

AFTER FREEL DIED, Mary moved to Pioche and took up residence just down the street from the Horlachers. Sue Horlacher and Maime Campbell matter-of-factly stopped by to invite Mary to Church. Mary readily assented and attended regularly until her death. In her case the adage seemed to fit: *You can push Mormons out of the Church, but you can't squeeze the Gospel out of Mormons.*

Chapter **7**

JUSTINE — WAYNE MAKES HIS OWN U-TURN

Wayne was seldom there and I danced with many boys, which was the custom then. I had dates with Kenneth, Leland, Keith, LaMar and others. One time when Wayne did get there for a dance, he happened to ask LaMar what he was doing and LaMar said, "I'm trying to take your girl away from you." He almost did ...

— Justine

7.1 Personal History of Justine Jones Lytle

I was born in Enterprise, Utah on October 1, 1914 and we lived at the ranch, one mile from Enterprise. It was a dry farm with one little spring that gave us water for the house. Pop built a concrete holding tank near the house and another at the corral. With the tank near the house, we could raise a small garden and have a small orchard. When I was about four years old, we all had the influenza except Pop, and we were very ill. My dad took care of us and succeeded in getting a nurse to help out. When we were ill, we became so weak that Pop said we sounded like little birds squeaking when we talked.

School in Enterprise

When I started to school, we had to walk the mile to Enterprise. My dad was a teacher and I went on foot to school with him. He always trotted and I insisted upon trotting with him. My side would ache so badly that it felt as if it would burst. When the snow got too deep, sometimes we would go to school on a horse.

School in Rose Valley

In about 1924 Pop got the position of teaching school in Rose Valley. We all moved, Dad, Mamma, Alwyn, Boyd, Stanton and I, along with two work horses and one Jersey milk cow. Rose Valley was fun. There were ledges and hills to climb, and there was a boy there named Wayne. The bigger kids never did go off and leave me, even if I was "too little." We lived in Rose Valley for two winters and I played lots

63

of tag with Wayne, and even let him hold my hands once in a while. He was older and bigger and went to the one room high school in Eagle Valley, with J. Harold Brinley as the teacher.

Work at the Ranch

When we moved back to Enterprise, my father planted a lot of dry land wheat and even bought 40 acres watered from the canal. We used to haul hay from that 40 acres in the night. Pop would tell us stories all the way home on the hay wagon. When the wheat was ripe, I had to help with the header because they needed one more hand and Stanton had asthma and hay fever so bad that he couldn't go near grain. Besides that, I had to cook because Mamma wasn't well — and we usually didn't have much to cook. I can remember washing dishes way into the night, and I had to go outside for the water and heat on the wood-burning stove.

Recreation

We didn't work all the time. Pop got a little gray mare and I used to ride her when I had a chance. After it rained, I would get her to go fast, pull back on the reins and she would slide, which was much fun. One day she slid and fell on me. Mamma found out about it and made me promise to quit riding the mare. Regretfully, I minded Mama and rode no more. The boys used to have a 22 rifle. I didn't like to shoot it, and they would give bullets to me to get me to shoot. Soon I had more bullets than they had and traded bullets for some pretty important favors. The chief recreation in Enterprise was dancing and as I became a teenager, I loved to dance. Of course Wayne was seldom there and I danced with many boys, which was the custom then. I had dates with Kenneth, Leland, Keith, LaMar and others. One time when Wayne did get there for a dance, he happened to ask LaMar what he was doing and LaMar said, "I'm trying to take your girl away from you." (He almost did.)

Sick with Quinsy

When I was a junior in high school, we had a lot of snow, it rained on it and froze, and I got wet every day going to school. I came down with a cold which developed into quinsy and I almost died. When I was well enough to write, I dropped a note to Wayne and he came right over in spite of the terrible roads. We went together quite steady after that. When we got engaged, he didn't have enough money to buy a ring.

Marriage Photo – St. George Temple

Marriage and Subsequent Events

We were married on November 15, 1933 in the St. George Temple, even though Mother's health was poor. Grandma Adair, especially, encouraged me to get married. I had lived in fear of my mother's dying for several years and was becoming very nervous. She died when our second son, Eldon, was a year old. After we were married, we went to Los Angeles for a short honeymoon, and then lived in Rose Valley for three depression years.

Family Illness

Then Wayne took me and the boys to Reno during the bitter winter of 1936-37, went to one semester at the University of Nevada, taught two years in Preston, Nevada, then started teaching in Pioche. While Wayne was going to school in Reno in 1937, the two boys became very ill, and then I became ill and the three of us had to stay in that little apartment for two months.(15.25)

Close Call in Reno

When spring came and the boys and I finally were better, Wayne went to Winnemucca by train with the University band. He played tuba. I got Sister Pendleton to tend the boys and walked to the station to meet Wayne. As I got near the station, a man came from out of the dark, seized my arm in an iron grip and said, "Keep your mouth shut and keep walking." I was too horrified to do anything but what he said. After we had gone about a block, George Pendleton just happened to step out of a bar, saw me and the man and started for us. The man promptly disappeared and George said, "You little fool, don't let me catch you alone down here again." I was green, green, green, but learned a big lesson that night.

The Move to Vegas

After teaching in Preston, Wayne taught elementary school in Pioche for several years, then in Rose Valley for three years during World War Two, then back to Pioche for several more years. I became completely fed-up with moving from Rose Valley to Pioche and back again and finally said, "I'll move one more time and that's it." We moved to Las Vegas in August, 1958. After fifteen busy and happy years in Las Vegas, I suggested that we move once more and in January, 1974 we moved back to Rose Valley. After Wayne retired from teaching, there wasn't really anything to keep us in Las Vegas and besides, the children and grandchildren would rather visit us in Rose Valley.

Farrel's Trombone

In thinking back, I can remember when Farrel used to play trombone solos in Lincoln County High School band program and Prof would accompany the solos on the piano. During pauses in the solos, Farrel would take the slide off the horn, empty the water out of it, then put it back on in time to go on with the solo. We became so nervous about this that we urged him to take the horn to the shop and solder the spit valve. He did and warped the slide so badly that we had to get another trombone for him.

Eldon Plays Grandpa Jones

When Eldon was just old enough to talk, Grandpa Jones came to see us in Preston driving a new truck. Eldon was so impressed with Grandpa and the new truck that in all of his play, he was Grandpa Jones. One day while the Whitlocks were visiting us, Eldon tripped over a rocker and fell. He said, "Oops, Grandpa Jones fall down." Brother Whitlock chuckled about that for days.

Noel's Shortcut

When Noel was old enough to drive, he practically lived in the car. One evening, in order to go from Mary Hansen's to Gladys's house, where we lived, he went up the street to Joe Bleak's, over past Cole's and down past the grade school, claiming all the time that this was shorter than going past the L.D.S. Church which was straight through. Now, when we want to visit San Francisco, we get Noel to take us. We can depend upon his driving and he does follow the shortest route.

Professor Cuddles

Julene loved animals. One of the strangest pets she ever had was "Professor Cuddles," a small, non-poisonous snake that lived in a small cage in Robert Moss's seventh grade room in Pioche. I'll never understand how she could let that snake cuddle under her chin. Old Blaze, the sorrel horse, was a special pet of Julene's, and was very careful never to hurt her or friends, or to go off and leave them like he would another person.

Larry Learns to Drive

Larry also likes cars. It was a great day in Las Vegas when he was old enough to apply for a driver's license. He and Wayne went to the Driver's License Division, Larry passed his tests, and that night borrowed the car and took his girl for a ride. It must have been quite a sight to see a dozen girls from the Las Vegas High School Rhythmettes going to Seminary with Larry in the old pick-up.

Karen's Talent for Singing

Karen grew normally but reached a stage when she seemed to be all arms and legs and knees and elbows. To see Karen in pigtails sitting in an easy chair was quite a sight. As she grew older, Karen had such a sweet singing voice that we would get tears in our eyes when she would sing.

> I think that our children and Karen are special and want them to know that we love them and that life would be nothing without them.

> END OF JUSTINE'S PERSONAL STORY

7.2 The Seth Jones Family Comes to Rose Valley

When Seth Jones and family came to Rose Valley from Enterpise, Utah, they were all orthodox Mormons. Seth had been hired to teach in Rose Valley. Wayne recounts the fateful day when, while milking a cow, looked up to see a *VISION OF LOVELINESS* come tripping down to the corral with Seth and Freel. This fair maiden was Justine, Seth's daughter. Wayne's life changed decisively at that point. When the day arrived that he asked Seth for his daughter's hand in marriage, Seth replied that he could think of no other young man that he would rather have as a son in law, but he had to become a Mormon and marry her in the St. George Temple. (For the story replete with 'hackles' delving into the non-Mormon past of Freel Lytle and his son Wayne, see Chapter 5, *Charles Makes a U-Turn*.)

7.3 Wayne's Baptism

Wayne readily complied by preparing himself for baptism and received the enthusiastic consent and blessing of Freel and Mary. It turned out that Justine's Grandma Adair ('Grandma Great') had been a polygamous wife hailing from Orderville, Utah,

Figure 7.1: Children of Wayne and Justine, Left to Right: Larry Lytle, Julene Lytle, Noel Lytle, Eldon Lytle, Farrel Lytle

Figure 7.2: Corral area in Rose Valley where Wayne first met Justine

many of whose settlers had lived the highest order of the Mormon Faith after 'dancing with death' on the Lower Muddy. (See *APPENDIX:THE MUDDER RIVER MISSION.*)

Figure 7.3: Site of Orderville, Utah, where Grandma Adair lived the highest order of the Mormon Faith.

7.4 Orderville

In Orderville, we make contact with another connection to the Lytle family story, especially as it relates to Charles Lytle (5) and *Grandma Great*, Justine's grandmother. Orderville was established at the direction of Latter-day Saint leader Brigham Young in 1870 specifically to live the United Order, a voluntary form of communalism defined by Joseph Smith.

> **Orderville was settled primarily by destitute refugees from failed settlements on the Muddy River in Nevada. The extreme poverty of these settlers likely contributed significantly to their devotion to the principles of the United Order.[a]**

---

[a] en.wikipedia.org/wiki/Orderville,_Utah

Well I remember Grandma Great! She had a fierce work ethic which she instilled in her own children and grandchildren. A schedule was laid out first thing every morning and there was no going to bed until it was finished. And no cheating . . . every stitch sowed on Sunday would be removed with your *nose* on Judgment Day!

Her skills included those of *midwife*, a calling which which brought a constant barrage of joys and sorrows. To Grandma Great, there was nothing so exhilarating as the cry of a newborn child, nor so heart-wrenching as to watch helplessly as a mother's life was lost in the throes of childbirth. Hence Wayne's invariant celebration of *Mother's Day*, as also his constant devotion to Justine during her long struggle with Alzheimer's, and service to other aged mothers who had gambled their lives to *provide a safe haven for children coming into a wild and cruel world*.

GRANDMA ADAIR was 'fearsome,' to be sure, and I hated it when she hugged and kissed me — because she had whiskers! (Or so it seemed.) So, when Wayne and Justine's children were born, they were born to Mormon parents on the Jones side and quasi-Mormon grandparents on the Lytle side. Just the same, their genealogy linked to polygamous marriages on both branches of a pedigree whose women had given their all to raise up a *righteous generation!*

To emulate Wayne's style in *The Redbook*, I now insert two poems honoring motherhood. The first bemoans the separation of mothers from their children in modern times; the second depicts the sacrifice of a mother's life for that of her newborn child.

WHY?

The telegrams arrived at night, Trailing sorrow in their wake:

COME SEE MOTHER ON FIRST FLIGHT. DON'T DELAY. MAY BE TOO LATE!

Mother dieing? You forget. Years don't pardon anyone. That you forgot, you now regret --- Did Mother once forget her sons?

``In my eighty seven years I've seen my share of life go by, Years of sweet and bitter tears, I've learned so many ways to cry ...In this age when wide we roam, Why must a lonely mother die To bring her scattered children home?''

And then she added with a sigh ``Now you're here, I want to live! Redeem the years we've spent apart! I have a world of love to give ...Painful burden of my heart.''

We stared in silence at the floor Within the darkness of the room. The nurse, impatient at the door, Insisted that we leave her soon . . .
(Eldon)

Mothers Day Flowers

MOTHERS' DAY GIFT

Please accept my humble gift! The fruit of passion, yes, but love;
And that almighty Power which blessed Our purpose with a
sacred kiss. Receive this soft and fragile flesh This blood,
and bone, and sinew sired In holiness before our God Who it
with mortal breath inspired ...

To us this day is born a son! Who kissed the color from my lips And
in exquisite pain has sipped The bitter-sweet of mortal bliss.
Accept this last, this final gift The magic fabric of my womb
In ransom paid for caustic tears To etch these verses on my
tomb!

--- Eldon

Part II

BEYOND BILLIE JACK IN THE RED NOTEBOOK

Chapter 8

MORE TALES FROM THE NOTEBOOK

Fawn had led Tikapoo to the spot where Ike found him, buried him, and had traveled east in order to come into Eagle Valley from another direction. By the time Ike had gotten Tikapoo to Eagle Valley Fawn was gone, evidently following the tribe to northern Nevada where she could find a younger husband.

Figure 8.1: Spring Valley Canyon near Tikapoo's intended grave.

8.1   Review and Preview

Having savored at the outset the flavor of Wayne's writing in his story of Billy Jack and the magic snake juice (1.2), *and* having traced their history from Nauvoo, Illinois, to Pioche, Nevada, and toured its adjacent 'story country,' we are now prepared to delve further into the *Red Notebook.* We begin with Wayne's brief account of Tikapoo and his sojourn in Eagle Valley.

The Moaning Bush

Ike Mathis was riding his horse north from Eagle Valley, up the Spring Valley Canyon and had gone about two miles, when without warning, the horse gave a mighty jump sideways, almost dumping Ike. The subject of the horse's fright was a pile of brush. Ike started investigating and heard groans coming from that pile of brush. He moved some brush and there lay Tikapoo, flat on his back in a little depression, with a large stone on his chest, a bowl of water and some pemmican near his head. Ike moved the rock, and with help, Tikapoo crawled out of the little depression and sat down. After a short time Ike got him on his feet, put him on the horse and led the horse to Eagle Valley.

An Unfaithful Wife

For convenience, young Fawn had married Tikapoo, evidently in order to care for him, and the rest of the tribe had left them by themselves in Spring Valley, in Tikapoo's tent. Fawn had led Tikapoo to the spot where Ike found him, buried him, and had traveled east in order to come into Eagle Valley from another direction. By the time Ike had gotten Tikapoo to Eagle Valley Fawn was gone, evidently following the tribe to northern Nevada where she could find a younger husband.

Tikapoo's Curious Demise

AFTER A DAY OR TWO with food and water, Tikapoo was on his feet again. Somebody hauled his wickiup from Spring Valley and he pitched it near Eagle Valley at the mouth of the Back Canyon. He was able to get around and people gave him food and a few articles of clothing. One evening some of the local boys were visiting with him. The moon came up in the east. Tkiapoo pointed at the moon and said, "When moon get right here, pointing straight up, Tkiapoo Yaiquay." The boys protested, saying "No, no Tikapoo you are strong. You are not ready to die." He assured them that he would and the boys quit arguing and went to bed. But sure enough, the next morning he was dead! He was buried near the site of his camp at the mouth of the canyon that still bears his name.

Aunt Maggie said, "The old boy evidently rolled over in his sleep and burned to death in his own fire." [1]

8.2 The Chinese Herbal Cure

It seems that Gladys suffered from various maladies and when American medicine failed to provide any answers, she surveyed literature advertising herbal remedies from abroad. An ad in a health magazine featured a program of treatments based on ancient Chinese herbal tradition. The benefits represented as deriving from this program appeared to address most of her own health problems, so she ordered the treatment kit. It made its way by 'slow boat from China' to California and thence by railroad to Caliente. Eventually it arrived in Rose Valley, courtesy of the local post office.

Upon removing its multiple layers of packaging, she peered into a box containing more than a dozen little paper bags carefully numbered for daily use. The instructions crudely printed in a nondescript blend of Chinese and English instructed that the herbs assembled in each bag were for a single day and were be brewed up as a tea and consumed with her regular meals for that day.

Gladys launched the treatment program according to the specified protocol, beginning with the extraction from the box of the day's packaged herbs, the brewing, and the drinking of the tea at meal time. There was no immediate change in her health, but after about a week, her condition did strike her as having improved.

Wayne remained skeptical, noting that the herbs didn't appear to be exotic or special — just collections of nondescript bark, twigs, and rolled leaves. Moreover, he couldn't observe any real improvement in Gladys' condition. So ... he and Mike put their heads together and contrived an experiment. They ventured forth onto the local ridges, collected an assortment of herbs offered by the area, *added a few rabbit droppings and deer berries* for good measure, and carefully packaged them in the Chinese way. These they carefully numbered to extend the treatment period and slipped them to the box.

The home-made supplementals didn't capture Gladys' attention and so she took them in stride without noticing that the originals had all been used up. Gladys was pleased with the overall result, having dutifully brewed up and consumed the entire lot, foreign and domestic. Wayne and Mike, who were pleased that Gladys was pleased, kept their silence and life in Rose Valley moved forward.(Eldon)

8.3 The Bed-Bug Cure

Bed bugs were a constant menace in the early days. These loathsome parasites, crawled in from 'who knows where,' up the legs of beds and set up housekeeping in mattresses. At night, they would stealthily exit their nests in the mattress, attach themselves to any exposed body parts, and depart only when bloated with the blood of their victims. Aside from their potential for spreading other diseases, bed bugs left distinctive red spots on the skin where they penetrated and sated themselves.

---

[1]This version of events does not 'add up,' since death by fire would hardly be a matter of conjecture. For a recitation, cowboy-verse version of this story, see **Chapter** 39.2.

An ad in a magazine captured Wayne's eye. It was brief but to the point. "SURE-FIRE BED BUG KILLER. ONLY ONE DOLLAR! MONEY BACK GUARANTEE." A single dollar was far less expensive than the containers of sulfur fitted to bed legs which were normally used to trap bed bugs en route to the mattress above. Wayne promptly placed his order. (1ex)

A small box arrived within a matter of weeks from the bed-bug company. Inside were two numbered blocks of wood and a single line of instructions: PLACE BED BUG ON BLOCK 1. SMASH BED BUG WITH BLOCK 2!

Chapter 9

PEOPLE IN THE VALLEYS AND HOW THEY DIED

All I can remember about Sam is how dressed-up he looked lying in his coffin here in their house in Rose Valley. Sam also built the lumber house for Uncle Les and Aunt Ellen. Nelson Bleak ... made other repairs in that house not too long ago. Nelson said those corners were square, the floors and ceilings level and the walls straight.

9.1 Haswell Lytle

Haswell was Charley's cousin. (Charles Lytle, Freel's father). He spent time at Eagle Valley and worked at various jobs around the ranch, then went on to Timber Mountain, east of Caliente to work for Charley in a logging operation there. Charley made the remark, "You can take two half broke horses and make a team out of 'em in logging work." After a few days of work Haswell took the running gear of his wagon, with his team, up the mountain to get a log. The team spooked, started running, Haswell got a foot caught and they dragged him for at least a mile through the brush and rocks. It was said that when the team finally stopped, the flesh had all been torn off Haswell's rib cage. He was buried in the Lytle cemetery in Eagle Valley, where his grave can be seen to this day.

9.2 Pat Devlin

Pat married Aunt Noma Lytle and they settled on their ranch in Rose Valley. Pat, of necessity, did keep a gun around the house, but was very careful not to let his children handle it. He gave each a course in gun handling. When Pat was younger,

Figure 9.1: Original stage/wagon stop-over area with Devlin home in background and Rose Valley Elementary in Foreground.

he became expert in handling a six shooter and could twirl one on a finger and "palm" it with great dexterity. Pat had been known to inhabit saloons and drink quite liberally. One day, he was demonstrating his skill with a six shooter while drinking in a saloon, and accidentally shot and killed a man, a complete stranger to Pat. After that, one never saw a six shooter or revolver around the Devlin Ranch.(15.3)

9.3   Samuel Lytle

Sam was the youngest son of the Charles and Margaret (Moody) Lytle family. He was an active and mechanically gifted man, an expert carpenter. He told his youngest sister, Maggie, "Someday they'll invent a wagon that will go fifteen, miles an hour." Maggie replied, "They might invent one that will run up hill, but they'll never get it down." Sam married Maggie Conway and they had three children: Charles, Adel and Fred. Adel is the only one living — Adel *Burton*.

Sam and Freel, his next older brother, worked together and had much in common. They bought the large log house at the Pope Mine near Deer Lodge, hauled the logs to Rose Valley on the frames of their wagons, lifted the logs by derrick onto an overhead scaffold and split them lengthwise with a two man rip saw. One man stood on the log, with the other underneath. When finished, there were enough logs for two houses, the same size and design as the one purchased. Every log was numbered and lettered so that it would fit as in the original. (In recent years, the interior of Sam's house — now my house — was rebuilt. The numbers were still on each log.)

Sam secured a job as engine man at Gold Springs, his main assignment being to keep the large, one cylinder diesel running. Everything in the mill was powered from the shaft run by this engine. Sam discovered that water was required in a chamber at the side of the engine, to keep it running. About an hour after Sam went off shift, the engine would stop. The foreman would ask Sam how to keep the engine running. Sam's reply was, "Make me Master Mechanic and it will run 24 hours around the clock." They refused to do that and trouble with the engine continued. A spy was even hid in the rafters to spy, but Sam got a long pole and rousted him out. I don't know how it ever did turn out.

> JIMMY INDIAN had a great liking for Sam. On one occasion, Sam went to Salt Lake City and upon returning he said, "Jimmy they've invented a new paint and we can paint you white." That was Jimmy's greatest wish to be white. He said, "Sam, the next time you go to Salt Lake, buy a can of that paint for me." Sam said, "You bet, Jimmy, I'll get it."

Sam bought a one "lunger" Diesel engine for the well in Rose Valley, built a redwood tank above his home and watered the yard. He planted vegetables, including cantaloupe. On one occasion, he had been to Pioche and had bought a dozen cantaloupe from a peddler. Upon arriving home, he saw his mother and Maggie approaching on horses. He quickly took a half dozen cantaloupe and scattered them among his vines. After he had visited awhile with his mother and Maggie he said, "Let me check my cantaloupe." He promptly returned with two or three and they were amazed. Maggie said, "Our cantaloupe are still small." Sam said, "Oh, things grow fast on this well water."

Sam's grandsons, Robert and Sam came here to Rose Valley a year or two ago. Their Grandmother had told them that their Grandfather had died from injuring himself building Freel's house. But that was not true. She had rancor in her soul because of something. The truth was, Sam caught a bad cold working on his machinery early in the spring and kept exposing himself until he caught pneumonia. Freel's house had been finished for months. Sam died of that pneumonia, which could not be cured at that time. His grandson, Sam, said, "I believe that. I myself get pneumonia very easily."

> ALL I CAN REMEMBER ABOUT SAM is how dressed-up he looked lying in his coffin here in their house in Rose Valley. (Sam's house was the house Wayne and Justine lived in, but recently burned[3.1]). Sam also built the lumber house for Uncle Les and Aunt Ellen. Nelson Bleak added interior living and made other repairs in that house not too long ago. Nelson said those corners were square, the floors and ceilings level and the walls straight. (That house was recently razed after Harvey Whittemore bought the McCrosky brothers interests in Rose Valley.)

9.4 Jay Damron

Milton Damron and Amy Lytle Damron had two children, Jay and Myrtle, now Bliss. Both Jay and Myrtle were outstanding and attractive people. Jay was especially gifted in mechanics. He could "fix" anything and make it run. On one occasion, there was a funeral in Eagle Valley and my mother was worried about Papa's ability to drive in the "traffic" to the graveyard. There must have been 30 Model T's there. So Jay was enlisted to drive our car. His parents could ride with Billy and Maggie Warren. Jay did a good job for us. When Jay was about 18 or 19, during the cold weather he got busy fixing Henry Hammond's Model T. He caught cold, didn't stay indoors and developed pneumonia. Dr. McGregor came from St. George, but couldn't help any. He sedated Jay with morphine, but Jay soon died. What a tragedy! Everyone was torn with grief. Uncle Milt cried for two months afterwards.

9.5   Epha Francis

Epha lived with the family at their home in Spring Valley. On May 15, 1917, she contracted acute appendicitis. A freak storm, with about 18 inches of snow, had hit, and it was impossible to take Epha out. She died at their home in Spring Valley, I believe.

9.6   Elmer Hammond

Elmer, son of Joe and Zina Hammond, grew up in Eagle Valley and was a very attractive young man with outgoing personality. He married Beth Truman of Enterprise and they had a son, DeLoyd. I believe they had made plans to live in another area. Elmer was helping his Uncle Henry saw winter wood with a motor driven circular saw, when the saw broke off the shaft and headed for Elmer. He tried to protect himself with an arm, which the saw promptly lopped off. Those present said it seemed the saw was bound for Elmer. It literally split the front of his body open. He was rushed to Salt Lake City, but soon died in a hospital there.

9.7   Barbara Adair

Barbara was with a group of young people from Pioche who went rabbit hunting, using a model A Ford coupe. Sue Lloyd stood on one running board, holding a gun. Barbara was on the other running board without a gun. Sue's gun discharged accidentally, striking Barbara in the back. She became a paraplegic at that moment. After much hospitalization and surgery, Barbara was placed in a wheelchair. She finished high school, fell in love with Kent Rollins and they were married. Two children, Shauna and Erick, were born to this marriage. Barbara kept house and raised them with Kent's help. One of her anxious moments was seeing little Erick in the middle of the road near their home in Pioche. She solved the problem by calling the sheriff, who came and brought her son to her. They moved to Las Vegas, where Barbara became involved in painting and in art shows. More occasional surgery was required, but she went on bravely. Kent was strong enough to carry Barbara from the car to the church, from the car into a store or into a wheelchair and to stores and art shows. Erick went on a mission and I believe both he and Shauna are now married. Barbara's condition gradually deteriorated and, after surgeries and hospitalizations, she died as a result of the injury. She was a relatively young woman at the time of her death. Barbara was Justine's first cousin, Israel and Louella Adair's daughter.

9.8 Bill Brown

Bill was a bachelor who moved here from the mid west, I believe. His first job was as a miner in Pioche and then in the Deer Lodge area. Bill's great ambition was to "strike it rich" on his own. He found "colors" of gold and silver on a location near Deer Lodge, staked out a claim or two, and set to work on his own. He would pitch hay or do any odd jobs long enough to support him, then back to work on his mine. Bill built a little lumber cabin near the Hackett residence at Deer Lodge and lived there.

A S HE GREW OLDER, Bill's health began to fail. I heard him make the statement, "When old 'number one' here gets to the point where I can't take care of myself, I'll end it quick!

Bill Brown's house at Deer Lodge

One day, while at his mine, Bill's nose started to bleed and it was still bleeding when he reached his cabin. He was taken to a doctor, who informed him that he had dangerous high blood pressure and had to drastically change his living habits. Bill tried, but the nosebleeds came again. He "ended it quickly" by putting a 22 rifle in his mouth and pulling the trigger. When the Hacketts found him, proper authorities were notified and funeral services were arranged. I believe his body was shipped out for interment.

While Mike, Jack (Jack Lytle was a 2nd or 3rd cousin of Mike and Wayne.) and I were mining at Deer Lodge Justine, Farrel as a baby, and I were living at the "teacherage" near Hacketts' home. When school started, we moved into Bill Brown's cabin to live for a short time before moving back to Rose Valley. At the end of the first day, Justine met me at the door of the cabin. Somebody had thrown dirt over Bill's blood on the floor and Justine had swept the dirt off the blood. Guess who cleaned it up! I did.

Hacketts' home at Deer Lodge

9.9   Mining Tragedies

THE *FREE* FAMILY of Panaca, got a lease on the Salt Lake Pioche mine, near the highway leading south from Pioche, and indeed did "strike it rich." They were mining carbonates of high mineral content, hired several men, and were doing very well. One morning in the summer after an evening thunderstorm, as the skip started down the shaft, an explosion and fire erupted, killing four men. Those killed were Mason Price, Jimmy Wheeler, Ronnow Lee, and Lathe Mathews. The state mining engineer said that the rain had wet the used carbide that was thrown into a can near the shaft, the gas had blown into the shaft and this caused the explosion.

An around-the-clock operation was being conducted at the Number One mine in Pioche. At near the end of one shift, a foreman took three men into a drift to investigate a missed shot. One of the men evidently picked into it and all four were killed at that location. George 'Red' Lees was one of them. To all experienced miners, a missed shot was a treacherous situation.

9.10   An Electrocution

Jim Lees was a miner and among other mines, worked at the Little Buck mine in the Gold Springs area. He met my sister Gladys Lytle of Rose Valley and they were married in December 1934. After being married for a year or two, Jim developed sciatic rheumatism and could no longer work as a miner.

Jim and Gladys

Karen was born and they lived with Gladys' parents (Freel and Mary) in Rose Valley. Jim went to doctors, even to a specialist in California, who told him that he would never recover and would be lame and bent over for the rest of his life. Jim was a strong man and did much work on the ranch, at other jobs and especially digging for quick silver. Gladys started massaging Jim's back and leg every night, being very 'religious' about it, and Jim gradually got over it. He recovered so well that he got a job with the Lincoln County Power District, built a house in Pioche and bought a new Ford car. Jim was very active in civic activities in Pioche, helping to improve and place lights around the Pioche ballpark. One day, while working on a high voltage line in Caselton, Jim climbed a pole to make repairs on the 'hot' line. Gene Mcleod threw a supposedly cloth tape up to Jim, the wind caught the tape, draping it over the hot line and over Jim's body. Jim dropped to the ground and didn't live 24 hours after the accident.

9.11   Mike Lytle

Mike was my first cousin, son of Uncle Les (Freel's brother). In the springtime of about 1950, Mike and I were driving around in the Deer Lodge area. We came to the Iris shaft and decided to go down. We lighted our carbide lights and went down the ladder about 100 ft. to the bottom of the shaft. We had to drop about 7 or 8 feet from the end of the ladder. Soon we noticed that our lights were burning more dimly, meaning much carbon dioxide. Mike helped me to the ladder, then I reached down and helped him up and we climbed out. About three years later, Everest Hackett and Dutch Hall stopped near the Iris shaft. Everest wanted to go down and out into the drift to see if a heifer that was missing had fallen into the 'glory hole.' Everest started down and Dutch said, "That might not be safe. Come out and let's not go down." So they didn't.

Not too long after, Mike, Howard McCrosky, and Farrel Lytle went to the Iris shaft, where Mike wanted to get some good pipe to be used at the corners of the fence around the Rose Valley transformer station. They wired a pulley to a tree limb above the shaft, threaded a heavy rope through it and Mike went down the ladder without the rope. About halfway down, the ladder broke and Mike fell to the bottom. One of the boys rushed down to Hackett's home nearby at Deer Lodge and Helen Hackett came to Rose Valley. Somebody rushed to Pioche to get Dr. Gemmell and also to request a rescue team from the Combined Metals. After reaching the location, Dr. Gemmell could not force himself to go down that shaft on a rope. The rescue team and Everest Hackett put Mike on a short stretcher and guided the pad as the stretcher was lifted out on ropes.

While Helen went to Pioche to get help, Everest gathered up all the rope that he had and came to the shaft with us. Howard and Farrel lowered Everest at the end of a rope to the bottom. He found Mike groaning, but unconscious. He moved him so that debris from the shaft would not fall on him and covered him with a blanket, trying to make him comfortable. Then because of his fear of carbon dioxide in the shaft, Howard and I lifted him back out, about 150 ft. A man on the end of a rope is very heavy. We were young and strong, but it was all that we could do to pull him up. When the mine rescue team arrived, they looked at the shaft and grown men turned pale. One man was finally brave enough to go down and Everest went down again. Together they tied Mike to the stiff stretcher and the crew above began pulling him up. The shaft did not go straight down, it slanted along the vein of ore that had been followed down into the rock. So it was necessary that someone be pulled up along with the stretcher to keep from banging against the sides and keep the ropes free. Again, Everest volunteered to do it. At the time he was in his 60s, tough as nails and an incredibly brave man. Days later he still could not move his arms very well from hanging at the end of a rope for so long.

About half way down there was a drift across the shaft and rails from a mine car track extended across the shaft. The ropes to Everest and the stretcher had to be pulled up through it all at the same time. I spent the afternoon at the end of a rope swinging back and forth to keep the ropes free. As Dad remembers, Mike kept asking for a drink from the pump the hand pump in front of the Les Lytle home that had such cool, sweet water and he died about the time he reached the top. (Added by Farrel.)

(Now back to Wayne:) "I was right at the head of the shaft helping guide the stretcher. As Mike neared the top he said, "I want a drink from the pump." Then he died right at that point. Dr. Gemmell checked him out on the level area near the shaft, shook his head and didn't get into the ambulance that took Mike to Pioche. I knew that the ambulance had become a hearse, but didn't say so. In Rose Valley I picked up Aunt Ellen and Mike's wife, Mary, taking them to Pioche. On the way,

Mary kept saying how Mike would recover and everything would go on as before. I knew better, but didn't say anything. When we walked into the hospital, Dr. Gemmell came out and told us that Mike was dead. **What a needless way to lose a bosom friend!**

Mike and Wayne

Chapter 10

JUSTINE IS STRICKEN WITH ALZHEIMER'S

"What am I gonna do? Wayne has left me and I don't know this other man who is living in the house ..."
—Justine after losing recognition of husband and family.

10.1   Onset

Justine had worked while we lived in Las Vegas at Cornet on 5th, became a secretary for George Tate, an architect, and worked at W.T. Grant Department Store. She always stayed busy with the Mia Maids and home and kids.

Headaches

It started with headaches. She had had quite frequent headaches all her life — "Jones headaches" — but during the last two years we worked in the St. George Temple, the headaches became more severe. We went to Dr. McGregor in St. George and he prescribed various drugs, among them being Hydergene, but none seemed to help much. Loss of memory began to set in and President Bowler had to release us from the temple work. Before being released, we were referred to the Salt Lake Clinic, where Justine was given a battery of tests, with Dr. Crockett at first being in charge, then when she was sent to the LDS Hospital, Dr. Wirthlin became our doctor. After a battery of tests, a cat scan among them, Dr. Wirthlin called me aside and said that their verdict was Alzheimer's disease. As an after thought he said, "May I express my sympathy?"

Persistent Decline

Gradual mental deterioration had already set in and trying to guess what she would do next was a puzzle. On one occasion she took my purse with a 500-hundred dollar check in it and hid it. My first impulse was to blame somebody else. Rex and Patty White had visited us and my first impulse was that Patty had gotten it, but I did not accuse her and just waited. Eventually the purse showed up in a most unlikely place. Larry, Sandra and family were visiting and my car keys disappeared. The kids and I looked into and under everything, but no keys. Larry took a number from the car, went to Caliente and had a key made, but it wouldn't fit. They went back to Alamo and my only solution seemed to be to hire the car towed to Caliente where a key could be made.

> THE NEXT MORNING, as one last resort, I got on my knees and prayed about the keys. A flash came into my mind, showing the keys in a chest of drawers in the bedroom. Low and behold, there they were under some pillowcases. The kids had looked there but hadn't seen them, covered as they were. **Prayers, even about everyday physical things, can be answered!**

I had an extra pair of keys made and hung them underneath the car. We went back to the temple a few times, but it became a very traumatic experience for Justine, so we gave it up. When she could still talk she said, "Wayne, what am I gonna do?

Fifty Years Plus

When it came to making bread, Justine would forget about ingredients already put in, so I started mixing the ingredients together and let her knead the bread. One day, after it was all ready for her to mix, she said, "mix it yourself smarty." I mixed it and managed to get things fairly well together, but I am not a "kneader." After it was baked, I gave a loaf to Rula, Eldon and family and Rula complimented me on the fine "french bread.". It was not supposed to be french bread, and that was the last of the homemade bread at our house.

Recognition Fails

On another occasion, Karen and family were here, with Gladys along. After they had visited awhile, Justine lost her composure and ordered them out of our house. Of course they left, rather shaken. She got to the point where eating was difficult for her and I began feeding her, which I still do. She has a good appetite and sleeps well. Her speech has become incoherent and she lets loose with shouts and vocal outbursts that strain the ears. At times, I'm sure she is trying to communicate and when we can't understand, it makes her angry, thus bringing on the outburst. We went to church together for months, but getting her to the car and into the chapel became more and more difficult. I borrowed a wheel chair, but I soon stopped taking her to church. Vocal outbursts became too frequent. One of the saddest things I do is go to church and leave her home. She really wants to go but her condition will not allow it.

Last Travels

Awareness of family comes and goes. She really does not seem aware of little Luke Scott, Larry's and Sandy's youngest. She gets upset with too much activity by the little ones. Seganne Molan, a registered nurse, comes in three times per week to help give her a good thorough bath. She wears a diaper, and infection sets in so very quickly and easily, unless she gets a thorough washing quite frequently. Deterioration comes quite rapidly. For example, one day she will be walking quite readily, with assistance. Then the next day walking is very difficult. We went by plane to Seattle and San Francisco, then by plane to Toronto during the summer of 1985. I'm glad we did. A plane trip this summer would be impossible. On one of our long plane trips last summer, she made up her mind that she was going to walk out of that plane in flight. Luckily, she was held down by the seat belt and could do nothing but fuss, which I was able to keep in hand. I ordered her a wheel chair at Toronto Airport and a young man pushed it for me. He just waved our custom's statement at the officials and we went through customs like a breeze! May 16, Friday. Just today Justine said, "Oh, don't worry, I'll do the dishes!"

The Struggle Ends

(A continuation of Justine's story from another notebook.) Justine, of course, always gave an assignment her very best, but her memory started slipping and her general mental condition deteriorated. I got a wheel chair for her and got a hospital bed someplace. For quite a length of time, she sat in the wheel chair and ate as I fed her at the table. Then, I had to feed her, sitting up in bed. She was hospitalized in Caliente two or three times. I figured that I would get more help in caring for her if we moved to Alamo. So Larry bought a trailer house with our money and we moved to Alamo. I had figured right. We got good help in Alamo, both from Larry's family and from the Alamo Ward Relief Society. There were more here than in Pioche or Rose Valley. Her lungs filled up once more and Larry and I rushed her to Caliente in his van, but she died of pneumonia just a few hours after we got her to the hospital in Caliente (Nevada). The date was August 28, 1990 at 2PM. She was a wonderful wife and mother.

``Wayne gave constant, unselfish care to Justine for 15 years. He is truly a saint!''(Manetta). *The theme of the following poem centers on the spiritual growth flowing from the pain with which Divine Providence may inflict upon us.* (Compare Wayne's reponse at Chapter 26.35)

THE FLESHY TABLES OF THE HEART

Literal the Hand of God
It wrote before
For Moses
For a king
The Hand Invisible now writes again,
For me --
I feel it groping in

A chisel grates,
Chills
Reverberating
Shock my hollow ruddy cage of bone.
Splinters tingle,
Spattering my ribs and spine
With spears of flint ---
Stubborn Bleeding Stone!

How You pound!
Breathless, I await the blows
The firm veneer
The brittle granite crystals

Streaming
Trinckle down.

How exquisite!
How sublime, the flow,
The pulse of fleshing tables In my veins.

Whet on stone
The chisel pauses,
Then descends in pulp
Slicing characters
Resplendent - Jagged - And profound -

The lines appear
Alive
New and everlasting fountains
Throbbing silhouettes of Law.

Lord,
Behold!
My sobs already have become a sigh ...

Chapter **11**

LOU — A KIND LADY

As autumn wore on, word circulated among the men, "There's a new girl down in crib number four. She's a young blonde and a dandy!" This created a good deal of activity and waiting for a turn among the men. Henry thought he'd check it out but Lou intercepted him. She said, "Don't go droolin' around there. I'm woman enough for you." He followed her advice . . .

11.1   Henry Diefendorf

Henry walked around a bend in the trees and there it was, State Line! It was a warm, May day, the road had been dusty and heavily traveled by teams and Henry was dusty and tired. As he walked into State Line, he noticed a small stream, laid down his small pack, and washed his face and hands in the water. He was soon dry and started looking at the sights.' There was Smithson's Hotel, Store and Restaurant, Flinspach's meat market, Brown's Saloon, Kirkpatrick's Saloon, swelling houses and that was about it. Henry was staring into the store window, wondering how he might eat, when a kind lady spoke to him and offered him two dollars.

Henry accepted and in his somewhat broken English (Henry was a recent immigrant from Germany), promised to pay it back. The lady was very gracious and said she knew he would. She said, "You can always find me with the rest of the girls down there in the draw. My name is Lou." She motioned to four or five little stone houses a hundred yards away. Henry later knew them as the cribs.' He was sorry that his first acquaintance was a prostitute, but of one thing he was sure. She had a heart of gold.

A box of crackers, some cheese, a can of sardines and he had his first meal. He found a sheltered place to camp near a ledge on the nearby mountain, and set out to rustle a job at the Johnny Mine. As he walked the mile and a half to the mine, a mountain loomed quite large to the west. He soon discovered that the mountains were named Government Peak and Mahogany Mountain. After speaking with a foreman at the Johnny Mine, he was told to report for work on the swing shift in two days. After a night's sleep and some more crackers, cheese and sardines, Henry struck out and explored the region. He found the Ophir Mine two miles beyond the Johnny and high upon a ridge that led from Government Peak. In another area just south of the Ophir was the Robert's Mine. Each had its own ore-refining mill, with five stamps at the Johnny and the Robert's Mills and ten stamps at the Ophir Mill.

Figure 11.1: A Kind Lady

A steady stream of teams was going and coming from the south summit towards Deer Lodge, bringing logs to the sawmill which was just at the west edge of town. It was a bustling place and Henry was about to become a part of it. As he walked into town that evening, a boy of about ten and a girl of about eight were busy carrying water to a garden near their home. Upon asking, he found that their mother had saved a few pea seeds and had brought them with her for many miles. The peas were planted and were starting to sprout, thanks to the loving care of the youthful gardeners. The children, Rex and Betty, had also transplanted two cottonwood trees and were watering those. Henry helped them carry one load of water. A few days later, he walked past their garden after work and found them busily pulling up sagebrush and piling it around the plants as a fence. Henry helped them for a few minutes doing that.

11.2   Invitation from Lou

Henry had gone to work on the three hundred-foot level of the Johnny, which was a gold mine. His boss was Ulorey Sargent, a nervous man, but kind in his way. His motto was, "Don't take chances. Be sure it's safe." Henry was given a "muck stick" [shovel] and was young and strong. He moved a lot of ore for his dollar and a half a day. Later, he learned to handle the drills and was paid two dollars a day. On his first payday he took the two dollars to Lou. She graciously accepted it and invited him in. He never lacked for female companionship while in State Line. He often said to himself, "As soon as I can afford it, I'm gonna take her out of that crib' and give her a better life."

Figure 11.2: Young Henry Diefendorf

11.3 A Range Cow Pays a Visit

As summer came on, Rex and Betty's peas grew and bore pods. The two cottonwood trees did well also. One day near the end of June, their mother said, "Tomorrow we'll eat the peas." The children could hardly get to sleep because of the excitement over the peas. But sleep they did and when they awoke at daybreak, a range cow had come down the canyon and had eaten all the peas and the trees. Poor heartbroken children!

11.4 Flash Flood and Aftermath

Government Peak is just over 9,000 feet in elevation and as July came on, heavy thunderstorms moved in, sometimes stopping movement of wagons and teams. One July day a flash flood swept through town, washing out the roads, but missing most of the houses. Poor Lou and the other girls in the gulch got the worst of it. Henry helped Lou shovel the mud out of her little house, got fresh water when available and washed the floor and the walls. Lou had to wash mud out of most of her clothing and her bedding. Henry had dragged pinion pine logs off the mountain, purchased a little lumber and had one room roofed over. Lou stayed with him for three days, but she was too independent and too ambitious to stay out of her house for long. Besides, she didn't make any money when away from home. On one of his trips to the mountains, Henry brought some good, strong mahogany sticks back with him. He bent them while green and formed them into the shape of snowshoes. Young Freel Lytle occasionally came over the divide from Deer Lodge in a one-horse cart loaded with beef for Flinspachs' Meat Market. Henry got Freel to bring a strip of green cowhide on his next trip and finished building his snowshoes. He hung them up out of the storm and checked them from time to time. Henry paid for an occasional visit to Lou. She always treated him like a special person. He thought it wouldn't be too hard to fall in love with Lou, if he could just get her out of that environment and set up a decent home for her.

11.5   Pine Nuts

Henry had been working for several months when he got his first 20 dollar gold piece in his pay envelope. He thought and thought and finally hid it under a board in the floor near his stove. As fall came on, people started gathering pinion nuts in the nearby hills. Henry picked as many as possible and hung them in a seamless bag from the ceiling. One day, he saw an Indian wagon stopped near Smithson's store. He watched as Smithson traded canned goods for 300 pounds of pinion nuts. Henry wondered what Smithson would ever do with them. After all, one could eat only so many pine nuts.

11.6   The Fate of 'Humandung'

School started about October first and about 20 children attended in grades one through eight. Mr. Handy started out as teacher. One day he kept the boys after school and made an announcement, "Whoever placed the human dung on the toilet seat will please remove it at once!" "Human dung?" The kids had never heard the term before and the children named Mr. Handy behind his back, "Humandung." He had to resign and Mrs. Roberts took over for the major portion of the year that was left. "Humandung" left town.

11.7   Hired Gun

Mr. Wedge, who had a wife in State Line, had two claims right in the middle of the Ophir group. He wanted 10,000-dillars for the claims and the Ophir Company kept trying to buy them for a song. One night while Henry was in the Babcock's saloon, Mr. Wedge and a stranger started arguing very loudly. The stranger called Mr. Wedge an obscene name and Wedge rushed out the door saying, "I'll do it, I'll do it." He came back with his rifle in a few minutes. The stranger stepped from behind the door and shot Wedge in the back. The "hired gun" was freed on a self-defense plea. The Ophir got Wedge's claims for a song.' Wedge was buried in a shallow grave in the "Eternal Hills." His wife left town.

11.8   A Failed Robbery

It was a beautiful autumn season. Many teams hauling all sorts of food, hardware and dry goods came and left. Henry stored some canned food and flour and beans. During the autumn, Nat Gardner came with a whole wagonload of fresh apples, pears and pomegranate from Utah's Dixie. Nat sold every apple, pear and pomegranate and left State Line with fifty dollars in his wallet. Before reaching the Little Meadows two masked men on horses stepped from behind a tree, held a six shooter on Nat and relieved him of his wallet and the 50-dollars, with one of the men putting it in his coat pocket. Nat waited until they had mounted up, grabbed his rifle from beside the seat and fired a shot over their heads. In a matter of minutes Nat had the coat with the wallet in it and commanded, "You take off down that road as fast as your horses will run or the buzzards will be pickin' your bones." They left and Nat saw them no more, he being one coat ahead after the exchange.

A S AUTUMN WORE ON, word circulated among the men, "There's a new girl down in crib number four. She's a young blonde and dandy!" This created a good deal of activity and waiting for a turn among the men. Henry thought he'd check it out but Lou intercepted him. She said, "Don't go droolin' around there. I'm woman enough for you." He followed her advice.

11.9   Runaway Team

One day Freel Lytle was driving a stage and four from Modena to State Line, with four passengers. He stopped at Little Meadows to change horses and the stable hand put a pair of good horses on wheel and a pair of broncos on lead. Passengers were loaded and Freel clucked at the teams. The broncos jumped out at a full run and the wheel horses had to go along. There was a large fenced enclosure and Freel circled them around the enclosure twice and headed them out the gate and uphill the next time around. He soon had them under control and went on to State Line. When he unloaded his passengers at State Line a young lady said, "I hope you do that the next time I ride with you." "Not if I can help it." was Freel's reply.

Figure 11.3: A pack rat steals Henry's Gold

11.10   Pack Rat Problems

As Henry continued to work, he acquired another 20-dollar gold piece and hid it under the floor with the other. When he got another gold piece. He pulled up the board and the other two were gone! Who could have taken them? He looked at everybody with suspicion and even spoke to Rex and Betty. They had not been in his house and had seen nobody enter it. Henry brooded and didn't even work with his usual energy. After about a week had gone by, he was sitting in his house one night with a coal oil lantern lighted, when he heard a rustling and tapping. A *wood rat, pack rat* or *trade rat,* whatever name it might be called, crept slowly along the floor, wary of danger. When Henry saw it, the rat had one of his gold pieces, dropped it and scurried away, only to come back with the other gold piece. Henry scooped them up and was so thankful that he didn't even try to kill the rat. If he could save up a total of ten gold pieces, he was going to try to buy a team and wagon, the one most expensive desire he had. The gold pieces were hidden where not even a rat could find them after that.

11.11   Innocence

Bobbie and Debbie Bean were about 10 and 8 respectively. Their parents' house was not too far from the "cribs." One day the two children wandered down by the Cribs, caught the attention of Sally in No. 3 crib and she gave each of them a piece of candy. They were tickled and went home eating it. Their mother asked them where they got it and when they told her she became angry and forbade them to ever go there again. A week or two passed and they wandered down that way again, only to get more candy. When they came back eating that, their mother flew into a rage and promised them a sound thrashing if they went down again. When she had calmed down, the children said, "Mamma, do you know her?" Their Mother said, "of course not!" Bobbie said, "That's funny. She said she knew Daddy." Daddy didn't know it yet, but that was a very poor evening for him to come home.

11.12   Turning the Train Around

As the railroad advanced from north to south, it carried a large construction crew along. Men with teams, plows, scrapers went on ahead. Blasting powder had to be used in some of the worst places. The surveyors who laid it all out were skilled engineers, indeed. Right behind the locomotive was supply cars. Ed Hall remembered carrying, at age 15, 85-pound wooden kegs of rail spikes to the end of the rails. When his carry became 300 yards, the engine and the units would be moved forward, and his carry would gradually lengthen again. It was told that as the unit came to Modena, many people came with teams and wagons and on foot to see the mighty "Iron Horse." The locomotive was sitting on the tracks, quietly chuffing. The engineer stuck his head out and yelled, "All who hain't got a tree close better head for the hills. I'm gonna turn around." He blew the whistle and put out some good strong chuffs. People fell over each other and some teams even ran away. When all had settled down again, there sat the locomotive in the same spot while the engineer laughed his head off. Modena became an important freight depot, with many wagons with singles, wagons with four, and wagons with sixes loading and departing.

11.13   Rose Valley Stop-Over

Note: Those headed west took the "road through the hills" across the state line, through Rose Valley and on to Pioche. The freighters and passengers left their names written in wagon grease on the white cliffs in Rose Valley. The railroad tracks washed out because of floods down Rainbow Canyon below Caliente a number of times. Each time it bankrupted the company, which had to be cleared through court before another company could be formed and the track rebuilt on a higher roadbed. For forty years Modena was the end of the line and the freight was hauled by teams through Rose Valley. In the canyon on the west side of the Big Summit, the tracks left by the steel wagon wheel treads are still engraved in stone along the bottom of the canyon.)

Figure 11.4: Justine's Mother – Clarissa Hoyt Adair Johns

11.14 Modena

A good spring was found within two miles and supplied plenty of water for the railroad tower as well as for the residents. The Lund family set up a General Merchandise Store and A.W. Peak set up another general Merchandise Store. It is said that in those days a well-stocked store carried 200 items in contrast to the 200,000 items in today's well-stocked store. A weather bureau was set up in Modena, with a family in residence and cards were mailed daily to surrounding locations, predicting the weather. (*This weather station is still working and the Modena record has the longest time depth of any in the area, over 100 years. Farrel*) Clarissa Adair, a teenager then, later Justine's mother, became housekeeper at the weather station. One day during a summer thunderstorm, she was upstairs cleaning. A ball of lightning came in through one open window, passed the fear stricken girl, and exited through another open window. For the rest of her life, she lived in stark fear of lightning storms.

11.15 A Good Cowboy

Milt Damron rode his horse into Modena one day and stopped at the rail station. The station manager asked for Milt's help. He had bought a saddle horse for his daughter, but every time one of them entered the corral, the horse would lay his ears back, bare his teeth and chase them out of the corral. Milt said he'd take a try at it. He simply got his bridle and saddle, walked into the corral, bridled the horse, saddled it and rode out the gate. The station man said to his wife, "He's either a good cowboy or a damned fool." Milt was a good cowboy and the horse became gentle with his owners. The "free ride" was over.

11.16   Mules

Babcock Brothers ran freight wagons and stage service into State Line and return to Modena. On one occasion, a heavy freight wagon pulled by six horses got into trouble and rolled over north of Little Meadows, on a particularly difficult grade. Placing a span of mules in the middle of the six animal team solved the problem. At a signal from the driver, one mule would jump the pull chain and both would pull at a right angle to the general direction of the other two teams. This would keep the wagon on track and as soon as the danger was passed the one mule would jump back over the chain and go on as before. When bullion was ready to ship, little was said, but an armed guard would sit beside the driver, with other passengers as usual. No bullion was ever stolen.

11.17   Caruso in State Line

Sam Lytle came into town with an odd "contraption." He called it a phonograph. It had round, black cylinders which would turn when powered by a small spring motor, a needle would follow a groove on the cylinder, a large horn reached out from the machine, and when Sam started it up, there was the voice of Caruso! It was set up in the Smithson's store and people came and went all day to listen to the marvelous machine. Another black disc even had the voice of Jenny Lind on it. Sam said Thomas Edison had invented it. Would wonders never cease? On one occasion, Sam predicted that a machine without horses would be invented that would go 15 miles per hour. They all knew he was crazy on that one and several said as much.

11.18   Snowshoe Freight Service

At about the middle of December, the weather was unusually warm. Then one afternoon, a huge cloud with lightning, thunder, rain and hail came straight over Government Peak. Before people knew what was upon them, the wind wheeled to the north, the rain and hail turned to snow and what had begun as a spring like day turned suddenly into winter, with a full-blown blizzard. By the next morning, there were three feet of snow, with higher drifts. Within 24 hours, teams and wagons began to move slowly, but three days later the snow came again, and fears were realized. State Line was snowbound! As luck would have it, Lou had been expecting a bottle of stomach medicine from Dr. Campbell in Pioche and it hadn't arrived. She felt that she would almost perish without it, so Henry got out the snowshoes, put on some warm clothing and headed for Modena. He made it to Little Meadows, the first day, stayed in the stage station, then on to Modena the second day.

He got beans, flour, sugar and Lou's medicine, which was waiting in the post office. He also got one piece of hard candy for every child in town. After four days, he was back, Lou had her medicine and the children were happy. There were four teams in town and Smithson's ran out of grain for them. He discovered that horses would eat pine nuts in a pinch and slowly fed them what nuts he had left. The thermometer dropped to forty below for a few nights and everybody used all the clothing and bedding they had. Henry even chopped some limbs off nearby trees and dragged them in using his snowshoes. After 20 days, the January thaw came and things started moving again. Everyone mentally made note of what he would do differently if snowed in again.

11.19 Henry's Homestead

Logs had piled up on the Deer Lodge side of the mountain and needed moving to the sawmill. Three dollars a day was offered for axemen and laborers, so Henry tried logging for awhile. Soon Henry went back to the Johnny for two fifty per day. He was slowly getting enough money to buy a team. When spring came, Henry borrowed a horse and rode past Government Peak and into Serviceberry Canyon. There in a broad area of the canyon was where he wanted to live. He made up his mind to file for a homestead when he had a team, more money and time to get to Pioche. In the meantime, he hung on at the mine and saved his money. The next winter was milder and the town wasn't snowed in again, although everyone had made provision better than ever before. Then that spring, Henry got his chancel A man who claimed to be in hard circumstances offered his team, wagon and harness for 10 gold pieces. Henry had 12 gold pieces and bought the outfit for 10, having 2 left over.

Figure 11.5: Henry at the Homestead

11.20   Raffety Steals Away Lou

As summer came, Henry determined to quit the mine and strike out on his own.
Things were gradually slowing down in the mine. He even asked Lou to go with
him but Charley Raffety, with a team of matched dapple grays and a surrey with
a fringe on top, took her right out from under Henry's nose. Besides, Raffety had
a Spanish American War pension. They drove away toward Modena. Somebody
reported that Raffety had a house and a small homestead in the mountains to the
south. Henry went west, up the canyon toward Spring Valley and soon discovered
what was wrong with his "bargain" team. One of the horses balked. But of all the
men in the area, Henry was the one with patience enough to handle a balky horse.
After hours he made it over the summit and headed down hill toward Spring Valley.
Even the balky horse would go down the mountain. He arrived at Jim Hollinger's
ranch at about sundown. Jim was at home and told Henry to unhook and unharness
his team and put them in the corral and feed them. Then Jim invited him to supper.
Jim had some fresh baked sourdough bread, potatoes and gravy and ham. He had
a pot of good coffee.

11.21   Henry Works for Jim Hollinger

Jim, being a bachelor, and Henry, being a bachelor, gave them things in common.
After spending the night, Jim offered Henry a job, which Henry readily accepted.
Henry would get a dollar and a half a day and food and lodging. His team could
earn their keep, especially when haying time came around in about a month. There
were acres and acres of native wild hay. Jim had purchased a red durham bull and
was excited about introducing this new breed of cattle into the area. The crossbred
and inbred herefords common to the ranchers could range in the hills and outrun a
deer, but they were lightweight cattle. Many of them were brockle-faced and what
was lacking in weight many times were made up in horns. There were a few jerseys
mixed up in the lot, which made them wilder and thinner, but some gave more milk.
Jim had gentled a few of the larger cows and milked them. He made butter and
cheese that was hauled over the mountain to State Line and to Pioche. Left over
milk and curd was fed to pigs and chickens. Henry fit right into the routine and was
soon milking, feeding pigs and chickens, irrigating, fixing fence and all the myriad
chores that go with a ranch. Jim didn't run any cows on the open range, so Henry
did not have to become a cowboy.

11.22   Progress at the Homestead

Henry took two days off around the Fourth of July, put a bed roll and a little
grub on his better horse and went up to Serviceberry Canyon. **Things looked
good, with the quaking aspens in full foliage, a good stream of water and
about two acres of native grass.** That two acres could be enlarged to about
five, when some of the brush were grubbed. He made up his mind. That was where
he would homestead! It looked good and besides, it was only about four miles over
the mountain to Raffety's place and Lou. As soon as the chance came along, he
went to Pioche and started the necessary steps to homestead 160 acres.

Figure 11.6: Cabin structure at the Homestead

ASPENS

Quaking aspens in the summer Stammer at the patient sky; In their nervous shade the flutter, Mutter silly reasons why

They shudder, shiver, shimmer, tremble, When it's so hot and not a care Disturbs their timid, leafy rustle, Senseless in its strict despair.

Quaking aspens in the autumn Kindle in their limbs a fire, A self-sown shroud of immolation, To appease impending ire.

Aspens scintillate in winter, Icy ghosts against the snow, Who not a stutter, whisper utter, In their palpitating woe.

That fall, after Jim's hay was all in, Henry took both horses, riding one and leading the other which was loaded with a pack. Upon arriving he went to work with axe and saw, cutting some of the best quaking aspens and dragging them to a little point, where he would build his house and to a level area, where he would make a corral. By the time snow fell, he had a usable cabin, a pole corral, with a good pole gate and had grubbed two acres of brush. He had a little spring on the hill behind his cabin and enough water in the main creek to water his land if he managed it right.

11.23 The Threesome

One day he rode the good horse over the mountain and found Lou and Raffety comfortably settled in a neat little cabin, with about five acres of grass hay and pasture. They were glad to see him and before he left, he found that Raffety drove to Modena every Thursday and Lou usually stayed at home. Whenever Henry was at his home in Serviceberry Canyon, Thursday was spent visiting Lou. He loved that woman. However, after spending a month at his place during the next spring, he had to go back and work for wages, taking his team with him. The little stream of water was carefully ditched so it would water his four acres even in his absence.

Figure 11.7: Mountain pass midway between the Raffety and the Diefendorf homesteads. A time shift would put you face to face with Henry at this very spot every Thursday on his way to visit Lou.

11.24   The Access Challenge

As soon as Jim's hay was up, he bought a mowing machine and dump rake and picked his way as best he could with his wagon toward Serviceberry canyon. **Try as he would, he had to leave the wagon, take his machines apart and carry them by pack horse over the mountain to his home.** Several trips were needed, but he did cut his hay, rake it and drag it to his stack yard on a pole "sled" he made himself. He got 3 tons of good wild hay.

A wild idea struck him. He could winter there with his team! On the next trip out, he bought flour, sugar and canned goods, as well as 200 lbs. of oats. He dug a hole under his cabin and stored the perishable goods there, away from frost. He would try to get some fresh meat with his 40-82 rifle, veritably a small cannon. Much to his dismay, a hard winter set in and he and team were snowed in. Hay and oats were carefully rationed to the horses, as were canned goods and other food to himself.

11.25 Wildlife Friends and Foes

One cold winter day he looked out and a large buck deer came hobbling to his stack yard. He opened the gate and hid quietly and the deer went to his stack and started eating. He left a bucket of water, which it promptly drank, and he had another boarder. The deer had evidently been shot, but with food, water and a bed, it recovered gradually. Another day he looked out. His horses and the buck deer were looking up the canyon, evidently much alarmed. To his surprise, a large, thin cougar came straight toward his corrals. The 40-82 was a godsend. He got himself a cougar hide that day. He had seen people use ashes in a pit to tan cowhides, so he tanned the cougar hide. It turned out quite well, even though he didn't have a young squaw to chew it. It was impossible to ride over the mountain, so he went weeks without seeing Lou. The January thaw moderated conditions considerably and the old buck deer left. He never did get really gentle and Henry didn't try to touch him. The next time he saw the deer, it had lost both horns and came in to spend one more night at the haystack, which was getting perilously low. His horses were picking some brush and leaves, he learned to trap rabbits, and he was getting by.

11.26 Time to Get Out

Then, near the first of March it started snowing, snowed for three days and when it finished, there were five feet of new snow. But the weather warmed and the snow settled quite fast and within a week he could travel, if he picked his way carefully. He got on one horse and got out! He was out of hay and out of grub.

End of the story about Lou, Henry and Charley.

11.27 Subscripts

These thoughts were at the bottom of this page of the Red Note Book. *Were they ideas for future stories?*

- Those sour dough biscuits tasted awfully good!

- The machines of destruction.

- One vivid memory.

- Serviceberry was not the place for Ericka.

- At long last, he had Lou for his very own.

POSTSCRIPT

Henry did eventually get Lou. They are buried side by side in the Modena cemetery. To make the story short, after Charley died Henry moved in with Lou (her working name was Tempa). They lived on Charley's ranch for many years and when Lou became old and sick --- fifteen years older than Henry --- they moved to Modena. When she died Henry buried her at Modena where he eventually joined her. Charley is buried in the cemetery at Fay, all alone. "Love's longest wait" paid off for Henry in the end. (Manetta)

Chapter 12

RADIONIC HEALING

She finally just took the machine off the shelf And very carefully then treated herself.

Radionic Healing – have you ever heard of this? It will fix you, no matter how you're feeling. The machine was brought in by our Aunt Bessie. She got it to give treatments to cousin Tessy. Tessy had bunions and aches and a little gout. She had ailments and pains beyond all get out.

Aunt Bessie would take a thing and point. She could cover the whole page, even every joint. It had a most extraordinary book There were ailments on any page where you might look. A little bobbin would go round and round.

Some said it could even find things in the ground; One day old Uncle Ben went kind of crazy, To put it mildly he was a little hazy. Aunt Bessie got the number for cranial nerves She kept hunting, even in the reserves.

Ah, that was it, red blood corpuscles. He was having trouble with his sphincter muscles, After two or three hours of regular pulsing, We could all tell that the ailment he was repulsing. The next day he felt at least as good as new, Did all his chores and ate breakfast, too.

Then poor Aunt Bessie got terribly sick, For all the rest of us the machine wouldn't tick. We dosed her and rubbed her like all get out, Oh alas! alas! she had to sit and just wear it out. Arthritis, Bursitis, Bell's Paralysis, Berger's Parathesia, Cancer, carbuncle, cataract, neuralgia, acute amnesia.

Without a machine like that we just couldn't do. It keeps the whole family — except Bessie — feeling like new. She finally just took the machine off the shelf And very carefully then treated herself.

Figure 12.1: Auntie Bessie's machine.

Chapter 13

FRANK HAMBIN AND FAMILY

Frank never admitted anything, but where was he when he pretended to be hunting a lost mine with Bill? Where did he get that beautiful, new buckskin saddle horse? Where did he buy that new blue print store dress? Where did the money come from? The old horse thief! But, all she had ever said was, "Frank, you pull that one agin' and I'll tell the kids!"

"Good boy, Ken!" These words from Dad helped at the end of another long day. Kenwell Hambin was driver and headman, with able assistance from his mother during the day. Just after dark, Dad always joined the family which included, Sarah, 11, Jody 8, Elburn 6, Mother and Ken aged thirteen and headman. A proclamation issued in Utah Territory bore the words: **$250 reward. Wanted for horse thievery. Frank Hambin, description follows...**

13.1 On to New Climes

Frank Hambin and wife, Katie, deemed it advisable to leave Nevada and head for Arizona Territory until the thing sort of blew over. Too, that $1,100 hidden deep in Frank's pocket gained from the sale of horses might build itself considerably in Arizona Territory. Ken, who was old enough to catch at least part of the reason for moving asked simply, Dad why don't ya stay, and tell'em ya didn't do it? Why she ever defended that rough swearin, sometimes thieving and rugged old bear of a husband, Katie never knew. Frank never admitted anything, but where was he when he pretended to be hunting a lost mine with Bill? Where did he get that beautiful, new buckskin saddle horse? Where did he buy that new blue print store dress? Where did the money come from? The old horse thief! But all she had ever said was, "Frank, you pull that one agin' and I'll tell the kids!"

13.2 The Virtues of a Bad Man

That held him for awhile. She'd do it too for stealing horses. But what else would the old scoundrel do? Ah well, life with him did have its good points. He always worked hard at something. There was always food. They had nice kids. He loved her and the children, too. In fact he had said many times, "Katie where'd I ever find such a wonderful woman and such fine kids. Doggone I love ya' all. By George, I'd do anything fer ya. By golly I'd even —-." "Yes, Frank, I love you too. I'm glad we're headin south instead of north at this time of the year." Now there were things to be done. "Sarah, take the bucket and bring some water from the barrel. Jody and Elburn git some wood. Ken, are you helpin' Dad?" The warm southern Nevada November day was crowding quickly into darkness. A cool wind rustled through the mesquite and shadscale. A good fire and plenty of bedding were needed. For a week now, three in a bed hadn't made the bedding too heavy. "I'll be glad when we get to Las Vegas," Frank exclaimed. "The horses need more'n grain besides this desert brush an alkali. Ole Poky ain't doin like he should, Ole Shines gitting pore an Ole Buck don't carry me like he used to. They need a good drink, too." Dad quickly slipped hobbles onto Buck's front feet. "Won't Poky and Shines run away dad?" "Naw, they won't leave the wagon fur. This's new country to them as well as us," son. "Come an git yer beans and sourdough."

13.3   Travel Chores

Mother could do wonders even around an open fire. There was always something extra to surprise and tickle the palate. When supper was done Mother ordered simply, "Sarah, wash the dishes, Jody you help. Elburn git Dad to undress ya fer bed, an you hadn't better wet it anymore. Ken you try and watch him just once. I can't wash bedding at every water hole." All were soon bedded for the night and snoring soundly, all except Mother. A coyote howled drearily over the wasteland. Mother's thoughts drifted back. The ensuing days of desert travel and hardship were taken in stride by these hardy pioneers. Father joined his family and rode upon the wagon after crossing the River. Often and sometimes both he and Jody rode Old Buck near the wagon.

13.4   Arizona

Arizona was different. The warm Phoenix sun shone with welcome to people who were used to Eastern Nevada's cold blasts. Ken bronzed like a veteran. Even the three months of school he was forced to endure didn't make him any paler. That was the last formal schooling he was to see. Besides he could read and write better than Dad already and just about as well as Mother. He was with Dad every possible moment hauling freight with team and wagon. Horse trading didn't go so well with Dad when Ken was along. On one occasion when a deal with "boot" thrown in was just to be closed, the other man questioned, "Are ye shore this horse don't balk mister?" Before Dad could say a word, Ken chipped in, "I've seen him balk on a loaded wagon on a chilly mornin', course not often." That eliminated the "boot" and Dad had to talk fast to make an even trade. The trade later proved to be a horse that would balk on an empty wagon on a morning not quite so chilly. Dad drove in a strange silence all the way home. After they reached home, Dad blurted out at supper, "If this kid could only keep his mouth shut!" "But Dad, I only told the truth," said Ken. "Yeah, the truth,but — " "That should be the right thing to do," said mother with finality. "I always tell the truf," chimed in little Elburn. "So do I," came from Sarah and Jody simultaneously. Nobody could hear what Dad said as he left the table but it sounded like, "A man has to be crooked to keep even around this bunch." Sarah, Jody, and even little Elburn all enjoyed school. Ken was a good boy at school but his thoughts were far away. David was the best pal he had. Dave was an Indian boy, pure Navajo. He was just a year older than Ken but just a half inch taller and no heavier. He didn't seem to catch half of what went on at school, but outside what he didn't know about cows and deer and trapping wild animals would be hard to imagine.

13.5   Dave, the Navajo

One Saturday and Sunday they went clear to Lost Canyon after deer. All Dave had was an old 22 and Ken didn't have a gun. They sighted a bunch of deer a half mile off and Ken wanted to go after them at once. Dave said simply, Follow me. A dozen times Ken felt like standing up straight and going after the deer his own way, but a warning hand from Dave halted him. Besides, he had nothing to kill a deer with. Just at the time Ken had decided the deer had long since gone. Dave carefully raised his old 22 pulled the trigger and a beautiful four point buck dropped dead not more that twenty yards away. Never again did Ken have an impulse to do a thing his own way when in the wilds with Dave. Dave's father was one of the few Navajos who ran cattle. Ken could not have been truly friendly with a sheepman's son. He liked cattle. He had learned a good deal about cattle already from his friend "Hy" in Nevada.

13.6   Learning from a Master Cowhand

Dave's father, called "Pete" for short taught Ken much more. Ken, riding Old Buck, went with Pete and Dave as often as possible. He could never figure how Pete knew in advance just how to handle a bunch of cattle. On some occasions a bunch would start "acting up" and Ken would be ready to tear after them on a moment's notice. Pete would apparently pay absolutely no attention to such "critters" at some times. Invariably they would stop running and work into an open place so that the riders could look them over at will.

On other occasions, upon sighting a bunch that acted just exactly the same Pete would be after them at once. They's got it in their necks, he'd say and before the ornery beasts could find heavy scrub their pursuers would be around them. Pete always had a good Indian rawhide rope ready at such times. He made Ken a gift of a handsome new rawhide and taught Ken much about throwing an open loop with a back slack and toss without swinging it over his head as so many did. Ken was eager to bulldog and brand a calf all on his own. One day, as Dave was looking at a bunch about a mile away, Ken and Pete came upon a cow with a husky, near ten month old bull calf. Ken took after the calf and with luck and Old Buck's aid, caught the calf squarely by the neck and one front foot. Pete caught it quickly by the hind feet and Ken jumped off to get the fire ready. When Ken pulled out his jackknife, Pete smiled faintly and handed Ken a knife with a blade keener than he had ever seen. Better for calf, use this, grunted Pete. Ken did a really good job at marking and branding that calf. Pete himself said, "Good job!" and never left the saddle. All finished and Ken deftly let the big weaner up. But instead of running at once to its mother, it came for Ken, intent on revenge. Nothing offered protection except a tiny piion tree and round this tore Ken with the calf in hot pursuit. On the fifth round the exhausted Ken turned upon the beast and threw his arms around its neck. Both boy and calf went down and after a struggle, the calf left abruptly to go to its bawling mother. Ken was dusty, perspiring and with all the pride taken out of him, gathered up his rawhide and branding iron and clambered aboard Old Buck just a bit white and shaky. It was only than that he noticed Pete's laughter. The bronzed old redskin was making the hills echo with a whoop and a laugh more resounding than Ken had ever heard an Indian make. Ken caught the mirth of it and laughed good naturedly. When Dave came up and heard the story, he laughed a little and said, "I learn one day, too." Next time a big calf was roped, Ken had Old Buck mighty close and was in the saddle before the animal could find his whereabouts.

13.7   'Bustin' a Maverick

On another summer day, high in the mountains, Pete, Dave and Ken were riding along each with his own thoughts, when there was a rush from the timber and a maverick bull came charging for them with head lowered. Each horse scrambled desperately and escaped the first onrush. Upon the return charge, Pete's rawhide noose settled squarely over the bull's neck and before the animal knew what had happened, it had been "busted" just as squarely as any critter had ever been. An animal was "busted" by suddenly slackening the rope and galloping about it. Then as its feet tangled in the rope, Pete urged his horse straight away from it, leaving it helpless upon the ground. Before Ken and Dave had time to gather their wits, Pete was off and quickly batted the bull's horns off with a club. While Ken was still appalled by the spurting blood and Pete's apparent coolness, this master of the rope had turned the animal loose. Ken astounded urged, "Gee, aren't ya even gonna brand that big long ear?" "I don't know if he is mine," Pete said simply.

That gave Ken a glimpse of absolute honesty that added to his resolve to always do the right think. The thought came to his mind, "What would Dad have done?" He didn't need to answer his own question. A steep trail down a rough slope detracted his thoughts.

13.8 Dave's Sister Lily

Dave had a sister, Lily, who was just younger than Ken. To Ken, whose girl acquaintances could be counted on the fingers of one hand, Lily was a pretty girl. Her skin wasn't as dark as Dave's or Pete's and the way she braided her hair gave her an intelligent, friendly look. She practically never spoke to Ken, but when she did look at him he caught a lively something that made him wish he could see more of her. One day while her mother was busy, he succeeded in getting Lily to ride Old Buck while he led the horse. After not more than a hundred yards, he could see that she probably could lead horses for him. When she learned to ride she wouldn't say, but Ken could see that she sat a horse as well as her brother. After a short time Ken said, "Here you take the reins." But Lily just shook her head and refused. They crossed the freight road and there was Dad, driving along with a big load of hay. "Hey son, whose yer friend? By the way paddle home an' help me unload this hay." Lily blushed and hung her head and Ken hurried back to their hogan. She vaulted off Old Buck and hurried inside, to be greeted by a volley in Navajo from her mother. That night at suppertime Dad remarked casually, "Say son, whose that little squaw I saw ya sparkin' with this afternoon?" "Oh, that's Lily, Dave's sister." "Looks a little dark 't me," was Dad's rejoinder. "I'll bet she's a nice girl," mother broke in. "She never says anything," Ken said. "That's the way with them squaws. Never say a word. I'll bet her Maw looks like a sack a' oats." "She's fat but she's purty nice," defended Ken. "Oh, this girl don't mean nothin' to ya anyhow, does she Ken?" — this from mother. "Oh, no, nothing a'tall," Ken answered quickly, but a deep blush sped quickly from his neck upward. "Keep friends with the boy but fergit that little squaw. No good'll come of it," counseled Dad. "How come you know so much bout squaws?" put in Mother. "Pass the bread," was all Dad had to say to this, and Ken noticed that he was a little red too.

Chapter 14

THE MINE

We mined and sorted 50 tons of ore and shipped it to a mill in northern Utah. Each one of the company received $85 as his share of that carload of ore. Being in depression times, we were glad to get even that amount.

14.1   The Lucky Boy Gold Mine

One day Everest Hackett stopped at our house in Rose Valley and said, "Freel, if you want to go in on a gold mine, I have found one." My Dad said, "Sure, Everest, I would like to take a try at it." Everest said, "It shouldn't cost much — we can pick up most of the tools we need at some of those old abandoned claims up around Deer Lodge. Next, Everest spoke to uncle les Lytle and to Uncle Milt Damron and an informal gold mining company was born. My dad, Freel, was the least experienced of the four, but could do a lot of work. Everest had spent one year at the Colorado School of Mines and had done much mining around his home at Deer Lodge. Uncle Milt had worked for years as a miner. Uncle Les had worked for wages as a miner for a year or two. After formally locating the property and staking out a claim, 1500 ft. Long and 500 ft. wide, the location notice was filed at the Recorder's office in Pioche and the "Lucky Boy" mine was born.

14.2   Mining the Vein

There usually was a month during the last of February and into March when ranch work was slow, the snow usually had melted down and time was available for work on the "Lucky Boy." Powder, fuse and blasting caps had to be purchased, but the cost was divided among the four and was not much. They started by making a "drift," which became a tunnel, following a gold-bearing ledge about 18 inches wide. The ore was sorted from the waste and each dumped separately. A panning outfit was always on hand, consisting of a mortar, a cast iron jug and a pestle, a cast iron shaft about 14 in. long, with one end larger. Rock could be broken up in the jug or mortar panned in a pan consisting of one half of a small frying pan. It really was exciting for us kids to see the "colors" that Uncle Milt could pan out, as well as Uncle Les and Everest, and eventually my Dad and Mike and I. Uncle Milt very carefully took the gold from the pan by pouring quick silver on it. The gold would immediately dissolve into the quick silver. Uncle Milt eventually took that quick silver to a jeweler and had a gold ring made for his daughter, Myrtle. The ring had a local garnet stone on it.

14.3   The Tunnels

After the tunnel had been driven into the hillside a hundred feet or more, we would drill a "round" usually ten holes, load them with powder, with a cap connected to fuse about in the center of the charge. After lighting the fuses, rush out, count the shots to be sure all had gone off, then go home and wait over night for the powder smoke to clear out. Next morning we hurried into the tunnel to see what new and rich ore might have been reached by the previous day's round. Another drift and tunnel were eventually started, so that it could under cut a wider and richer ledge that Uncle Milt had found. Uncle Milt measured and figured and we all drilled and shoveled and worked for what seemed like ages. Finally, one evening Uncle Milt said, "This round should tap that ledge. It'll be about fifty feet below the outcropping on the surface and should show us what we've got." So we drilled deeper that usual, loaded the holes, set them off and went home.

14.4   The 'Not-So-Lucky" Boy

Next morning I was first in the tunnel with my carbide light and Uncle Milt was right behind. Where we had set off that round was a profusion of crystals of all colors and sizes. I said, "Uncle Milt, isn't it beautiful?" He said, "Oh horse manure," and left the scene. We had blasted into a fault and the rich, gold bearing ledge did not reach that depth. Uncle Milt said, "This damned country will do it to you every time." So, we had to go back to work on the smaller seam that we had been following. We mined and sorted 50 tons of ore and shipped it to a mill in northern Utah. Each one of the company received $85 as his share of that carload of ore. Being in depression times, we were glad to get even that amount. Another carload was shipped in another season, with about the same return. There are still a few tons of ore piled on the dump of that old "Lucky Boy" mine. Someone else has "jumped" it and has given it a new name, under its new ownership.

Chapter 15

TEACHERS I HAVE KNOWN

One day as she was beating John on the shoulders with a ruler, the ruler broke, with one part flying across the small room. She couldn't see where the part landed, and every time she had a chance she would look for it. We kids knew where it was, but we didn't tell her.

Early School Bus for Spring Valley Children

15.1   Miss Dalton

Miss Dalton was the first teacher I ever had. She came from Minnesota and taught us well in that little one room frame "school house" in Rose Valley thrown up hastily by our parents. My Dad said, "They train their teachers right in Minnesota." I remember one incident clearly, even though I started before turning age five. Gladys told me that I had come home from school, leaving my desk in a mess and teacher was pretty mad about it. I must have gotten there early and cleaned it up, because I remember no more about it.

117

The students were Mike, Lena, Leah, John Devlin, Gladys, Grace Devlin and I. We were all brothers, sisters and cousins. Using a ball and bat, we played "rounders" in which game the ball was rolled in front of the runner, to get him out. We also played "hopscotch" and climbed many ledges. "Run sheep run" was also popular.

Miss Dalton stayed two years and married George Adair at the end of her second year. George was drafted into World War I and she went back to Minnesota to wait it out. I remember how handsome George looked in his khaki uniform with the rolled leggings. Upon his return, they went to California, where they had one son, I believe. George became a successful cement contractor and outlived her by many years. A poster of World War I was nailed to our schoolhouse. It depicted two or three German soldiers with spike helmets, impaling a child on a tree with a bayonet. Those soldiers inspired hate in me.

Figure 15.1: 1st Grade Photo - John Devlin, Leah, Lena, Gladys, Mike, Wayne (all Lytles)

15.2   Laura Stephan

Our next teacher was Laura Stephan, from San Bernardino, California. A teachers' agency mailed pictures and resumes for young women seeking employment. Laura was chosen and a contract drawn up. I remember well the school board meeting, which we all attended. The School Board was Uncle Pat Devlin, Uncle Les and my dad, Freel. After the contract was filled out and signed, Aunt Nome Devlin jokingly wrote in pencil on the bottom "and Murray." Murray Devlin was twenty one and eligible. Laura Stephan came and fell in love with Harry Devlin, their seventeen year old. She *got him*, too.

Laura could play the piano, so an old piano was secured from somewhere and Mother started Gladys and me on after school piano lessons. Laura was paid 50 an hour for the lessons and gave us a full hour. That was too much for me and I begged to quit, which I did. Gladys stayed with it and has always out-played me on the piano. One or two of the other girls also took piano lessons. After Laura and Harry were married, they settled in her hometown, San Bernardino, where Harry became a successful cement contractor, and they raised three sons, I believe. The name Devlin is still known in the San Bernardino area.

15.3   Virginia Delmue

Then came Virginia Delmue, wife of Joe Delmue. She was the one who wielded the ruler with the least provocation. Especially did she pick on John Devlin, who was older that I. She came to school many times as tight as a fiddle string and the least little thing would set her off, in John's case his failure to be quick with a response to questions about his studies. One day she was beating John on the shoulders with a ruler, the ruler broke, with one part flying across the small room. She couldn't see where the part landed, and every time she had a chance she would look for it. We kids knew where it was, but we didn't tell her. One day she just touched me on the back with the ruler as I was standing, writing on the blackboard...

> I JUMPED ABOUT THREE FEET and started bawling. It showed how tense she kept all of us. Uncle Ed and Aunt Emmie Lytle sent their brain-damaged daughter, Fannie, to Rose Valley to go to school with Virginia Delmue. That was a mistake, because Fannie soon became a target for the ruler. After a month or so, Fannie was withdrawn from school, with no explanation. John Devlin told me that as eighth grade graduation came near, he made up his mind that if she didn't graduate him, he was going to run up to her, kick both her shins, then run out the school house door and leave home. Fortunately, she graduated him.

Each fall, our fathers would each haul a load of juniper (cedar) wood. As each of us boys grew large enough, we were given the job of chopping the wood and starting a fire before school started. At the end of a month or two, we would get a check from Lincoln County for three or four dollars; a reward for which we were very proud.

15.4   Maude Frazier

For many years, Maude Frazier, spinster from Las Vegas, was Deputy Superintendent. She used to drive a one-seated Overland car and visit our school once in the fall and once in the spring. Achievement tests were administered in the spring. We enjoyed taking those tests and scored well on them; evidence that we were well taught in the "three R's". Maude Frazier later became Superintendent of Schools for Clark County. Next came Majorie Cross, from the Los Angeles area. She and Lawrence Laycook, a migrant cowboy from Texas, developed quite a romance but were never married. After leaving here, Lawrence wrote a letter to my Dad explaining, "Marge and I agreed to disagree."

15.5   Phoebe and Amy

Next came Phoebe West. She told the story about the teacher who sent a note home, near winter saying, "Suzie smells, bathe her." Back came the reply, "Suzie ain't no rose. Don't smell her. Larn her." Miss West fell into Suzie's category, I fear, about mid winter. She developed a crush on Murray Devlin, who was still unmarried, and tried her best to get him, but Murray wouldn't cooperate. She became so upset that she quit before a year was out and went back to Los Angeles. Amy Devlin Mathews stepped in to complete Phoebe West's term. Amy was a good teacher. Gladys, Mike and I graduated from the eighth grade with Amy as teacher.

Wayne Graduates

15.6   Mr. Brinley

In our ninth grade year, Mr. Brinley became our teacher in the Eagle Valley High School. He opened new vistas in learning as fast as we could grasp them. He really was an outstanding teacher. His student body the first year, about the fall of 1924, consisted of Lorraine Hollinger, Lydia Hollinger, Mabel Hammond, Wayne Lytle, Gladys Lytle and John Leslie (Mike) Lytle. I remember that on one occasion he asked for my algebra assignment and I said I had been too busy and too tired to get it. He said, "Wayne Lytle, you're lazy!" I was never unprepared again. On another occasion, I had written a short story and stood to read it. In about the second sentence, I passed out from stage fright and fell on the floor. He revived me and when I gained a little composure, had me read my story.

Movie Making in Condor Canyon

After school had been in session for most of the year, the whole six of us got into Uncle Les' Model T Ford, sluffed school and went to Condor Canyon to watch the filming of a motion picture, silent film, of course. Upon reaching the Delmue Ranch we parked the Ford, "commandeered" a railroad handcar parked near the tracks and went coasting down Condor Canyon. After a mile or two, we came around a bend at a good clip and came face to face with a huge locomotive. Luckily, we had taken a cedar post along and were able to brake our handcar to a stop, lift it off the tracks and watch proceedings.

Filming was in progress and we observed our first illustration of fakery in the movies. A small cheese cloth and plaster of Paris dam had been built, with a small bridge just below it. The big engine chugged to a stop at the edge of a large railroad bridge, the female star got out of the train, stepped gingerly to the edge of the "chasm", just as a flood of water was released from a tank onto the tiny, fake set up. The tiny bridge washed out, the whole thing being in line with the camera, which was focused on the large bridge, with the tiny bridge in perfect alignment. When we returned to school the next day, Mr. Brinley, made a big fuss and insisted that we bring written excuses from our parents. I think he secretly wished that he had been invited.

Class of the County

J. Harold Brinley had been fired from the High School in Panaca because he flunked a trustee's son. He vowed that with just six of us he could take more prizes at the Lincoln County Fair than the high school in Panaca did. We did just that. We took first place, in short story, public speaking, zoology drawings, one act play and other things. As a group of six kids, we really "got with it." We even took the one act play, "Betsy's Boarder" to Alamo in Henry Hammond's Model T. Poor Henry, his Ford was over loaded and on the way back we had flat tires, arriving in Pioche just at sun up. We ate breakfast in Wing's Restaurant in Pioche. I had eaten salt pork all my life and was amazed that the ham Wing served was not salty.

During the year we put on two or three programs in the Eagle Valley town hall, in which we attended school. At these programs we would "crank up" two or three freezers full of ice cream and sell it at 10 cents per cone and raise money to buy gasoline for the trip to Alamo or otherwise. We needed a piano, so Lorraine Hollinger, Mike and I borrowed Lorraine's father Sam's team and wagon, went to Spring Valley and hauled a piano down from the Spring Valley elementary school which was no longer in use. Gladys was the only one who could play the piano and we did sing songs like *Long Ago, Santa Lucia, My Old Kentucky Home, etc.* Mr. Brinley made sure that we got training in everything that could be provided.

Assembling a Skeleton

In our study of human anatomy, a skeleton was needed. So he found out where an Indian grave yard was located and we proceeded, as a student body, to the cemetery (north and west of Dwyer's housenow Eagle Valley Resort) and dug up the skeleton of a full grown man and a rather small boy, with a cracked skull. My father told of a time when one of the Indian children fell into the irrigation ditch that ran near the Indian village. Before a parent could reach the scene, the other children became excited and started throwing rocks at the boy in the stream as he rolled in the current. When he was pulled out, he was dead and was buried in the Indian cemetery. We evidently dug up his skeleton.

A Boxing Match

During the second year, our student body increased to twelve, with Nellie Dwyer, Edgar Hammond, Mary Fogliani, George Fogliani, Dora Fogliani, and Martha Hollinger and Zelma Hollinger coming in as Freshmen. Victor Cottino and Leo Hall came in during the winter. The best-organized game we could play was volleyball. A set of boxing gloves was secured during the second year and we boys boxed. Vick could knock me on my pratt every time. George was the best boxer in the group and we thought he couldn't be bested. We begged Mr. Brinley to put on the gloves with George, but he wouldn't. Then one day Gladys circulated a note through school, saying, "Mr. Brinley is chicken." When Mr. Brinley intercepted the note, he flushed and at recess agreed to box with George. We were amazed. George couldn't touch him! So far as we were concerned, he excelled in everything. He bought the first Chrysler car to come in our area.

During his third year in Eagle Valley, a gasoline lantern exploded in his home, severely burning him. Dr. Hastings in Pioche treated him effectively, insisting that he eat beefsteak, which he had never eaten. He recovered completely and later went on to Las Vegas to become principal of the Las Vegas High School, then assistant Superintendent in charge of personnel as well as Bishop of the Las Vegas Ward for a few years.

Harold Brinley was most influential in getting me to move to Las Vegas for my last ten years of teaching. We were always going to have a reunion of those Eagle Valley classes, but Mr. Brinley was killed in a private plane accident near Las Vegas before we could stage that get-together. He had retired from the school system before his death. Mr. Brinley always emphasized a college education for all of us. He also preached Mormonism when he got the chance. Lorraine, Lydia and Mabel were Mormons. Gladys, Mike and I were not. I have been a Mormon since 1933. Gladys has been a Mormon for just a few years.

15.7   Seth Jones

As we went to high school in Eagle Valley, Seth Jones came to be teacher in Rose Valley. Of course, Justine was one of his children. The first time I saw her, she was wearing a white dress and was running through Uncle Les' corral. She looked like an angel to me. From that meeting came many developments. We were married in the St. George Temple when Justine was 19 and I was 22 on November 15, 1933. While Seth, Clarissa and family were living here in Rose Valley, a Mr. Sprague and another man from Cedar City drove into Rose Valley in a Model T truck, loaded with three new Baldwin pianos. My father bought one, the Monarch, Seth bought one, the Ellington, and the High School in Eagle Valley bought the Hamilton. All three were player pianos and we children just loved to put a roll into the piano and pump away. "Repazz Band" was my favorite. We have the Ellington in our home today. The roll players became inoperative and had to be removed. After Seth and family spent two years in Rose Valley they moved back to Enterprise where I went many times to visit Justine.

15.8   Karl Myers

Next, enter Karl Myers. He was a man about my size, not particularly attention getting, and came walking down the hill into Rose Valley and knocked on the door at Uncle Les' house. He announced that he wanted to "teach violin and piano to the children and chop wood." He wanted board and room in exchange for his teaching and wood chopping. Uncle Les and Aunt Ellen took him up on his offer and Mike, Ezie , Gladys, Myrtle Damron and I became his pupils. He said he was a graduate of the Petrograd Conservatory in Russia. We had no reason not to believe him. He spoke somewhat broken English. We discovered later that he wanted to stay out of any town because of a drinking problem. There were pianos in each home, each of us ordered a Sears Roebuck $12.49 violin, complete with case and bow, and our musical instruction began. Karl Myers had had little practice in teaching young people. Rather than starting on fundamentals, we did "Stabat Mater" by Rossini and the "Hungarian Dances" by Brahms, among other difficult compositions. Especially on the violin, this was way over our heads.

15.9 School in Panaca

In the meantime, the third year of High School in Panaca was not very productive. I do remember that in Panaca, the basketball team was outstanding, with John Dorrel, Ted Deck, Grant Lee, Reeves Liston and Jay Mathews among the top players. Cecil Baker was coach. Mr. Price was principal and I can remember Miss Ohman, Hr. Hammond and Dorothy Ronnow as teachers. Mr. Poulsen was band teacher and played baritone horn. Miss Ohman's English class was first for us every morning. After we had gathered in her room for class, Clemons Walker would start begging her to let him go out on the back step and smoke. At first she would refuse, but before the period was over, Clem would always get his smoke. Gladys and I went to BAC High School in Cedar City for our senior year of high school and Mike went to West High School in Salt Lake City. Among our teachers were Parley Dalley, chemistry and math, Ira N. Hayward, English and drama, Roy Halverson, band and orchestra, William H."Pa" Manning vocal and opera, Glo Robinson, biology, Tuff Linford coach, Mr. Wood, history. It was a good year. We boarded with Mr. And Mr. William Corry and son, Earl.

15.10 Attending BAC

The next year 1928-29, Gladys, Mike and I attended Branch Agricultural College (BAC) Junior College in Cedar City with Ray Oberhausley as director. It was an outstanding year. One high graduate said to me, "College is a cinch. It's just a rehash of what you had in high school." How wrong he was! I was thrilled to find out how many wonderful subjects were offered. I enrolled in 21 quarter hours besides trying out for the debating team, playing baritone horn in band and violin in the orchestra, also a few weeks in the chorus. Gladys took a similar course, but her health wouldn't let her continue. I scheduled my time to the minute, studying until the library closed at 10 pm every school night.

15.11 Walking the Girls Home

Friday evening was the night of the school dance and I took full advantage of that. One night I went to the dance alone and succeeded in walking home with three girls, one at a time starting the project at 11:30. Mildred Farnsworth was the first to say how tired she was. I said, "May I walk you home?" She said, "Yes." And away we went. As soon as I bid her good night, I ran back to the dance. Edith Warren was the next to complain of being tired and I walked home with her, then back to the dance on the dead run. Last, I danced with Margaret Pryor, Justine's cousin. That was the last dance and of course I asked to walk home with her. She lived a mile and a half from the school and it started snowing. When we reached her home she dared not ask me in, but cried on my shoulder. It snowed harder and harder, we both got wetter and wetter and I really was a sodden "Romeo" when I reached my apartment. Anyhow, some kind of record established! Which I did not publish.

15.12   Mixing Majors

Ira N. Hayward gave us a stiff course in Freshman English, and a thesis with anno-
tated bibliography to write during the spring quarter. With information available
in the library, I proved that the atom could not be split. In sociology class, Jack
Smith bet Flo Robinson that Cedar City had a population of 3,000. I believe, Jack
shared the box of candy with us.

As spring came on, Parley Dalley called me in for a conference, and advised me
to change my course from Chemical Engineering. He said that my major interest
seemed to be in the arts and in literature. I accepted his advice but had already gone
through, Trigonometry, Analytical Geometry, Calculus and Chemistry. Calculus
seemed to be a real challenge to the reasoning process and it did make sense.

I got on the debating team and after beating Dixie College we debated at Snow
College and Ricks College in Salt Lake City, where we lost. We thought because the
judges were two coeds called in off the sidewalk. I got a small part in a school play
and traveled with the troupe to Panquitch, Kanab, Beaver and Minersvillea real
nice trip. I received good grades, second on the honor roll, first to Winnell Dolley,
then to Lilliam Adams. I consoled myself in that they didn't debate or take part
in a play. All in all, the first year of college was a real success for me. Incidentally,
BAC had its first football team during the fall of 1928. (Now BAC is Southern Utah
University (SUU).)

15.13   On to Boston

In the meantime, Karl Myers was busily teaching Mike, Ezie, Gladys and me. He
said, "They are cheniuses," which was a great overstatement. He urged us to go
to Boston, to the New England Conservatory. The school had gained fame as the
"Boston Conservatory" but he was right in recommending the New England Conservatory to us. Some people had capitalized on the fame of the "Boston Conservatory"
and had set up an upper flat school that principally took money from young people
who didn't know better. We received a catalog from the New England Conservatory
and studied it with enthusiasm. I particularly remember the page about "living in
a great city." During the last of August, 1929, Mike, Gladys and I were in the 1924
four cylinder Buick that our fathers had purchased from Billy Warren and on our
way to Boston. We had muddy road from Rose Valley to Cedar City, then gravel
road from Cedar City to Salt Lake City. On the gravel, Mike stepped it up to 40
MPH and we discovered that the boot in one front tire made the car "gallop." Of
course, changing a non-booted tire from the rear remedied that. The rims did not
come off, and tires had to be changed while the wheel remained on the car. I have
written a separate account of our many problems with the '24 Buick and of our
selling it for $20 soon after reaching Boston. (See stories in *Cars I have owned*[27].)

15.14   Teachers at the Conservatory

We found the Conservatory, after having to rent a battery to make the Buick functional, and each of us enrolled for about fifteen semester hours of college credit.
First of all, we took piano lessons and our teacher was Gregory Mason, of the great
Mason family of Boston. We were given an individual test on piano and each of
us was graded "Elementary Beginner." This really was not accurate for Gladys,

because she could play hymns, etc. and was praised by Mr. Mason for her performance. Mr. Reasoner was our violin teacher, with his per lesson fees being rather low on the scale. The $12.49 Sears violin outfits had to go and Mike bought one Stanley violin and Gladys and I together bought one Stanley violin at the price of $150 each. These violins had been made from wood collected by a member of the "Stanley Steamer" family and were fair in quality. Especially, Mike's violin had a fine tone. Our harmony teacher was Mr. Curry and our solfeggio teacher was Mr. Lenom, who spoke more French than English in class and kept us confused part of the time. Our English Literature teacher was Dr. Smeath. We found out the next year that Mr. Reasoner had been letting us get away with faulty position in holding the violin. G. W. Chadwick was Director of the Institution and had made significant contribution to the music world with his compositions. He was an elderly, kind man who had to walk heavily on a cane. Wallace Goodrich was assistant Director and was not kind. I listened to him *roast* the orchestra in rehearsal, which seemed to be uncalled for. Mr Lenom sticks in my memory, because of his language and eccentricities, which included wearing a large, black scarf around his neck, tied in a bow. One day a girl and I were standing in a hallway. Mr. Chadwick tottered along on his cane, another professor walked abnormally and had an eye twitch, Mr. Lenom came trotting along, with bow tie flowing at the sides, another hobbled by. The girl remarked, "They don't have to be crazy to teach here but it sure helps."

Wayne, Gladys, and Mike at the Conservatory

15.15 Attending Concerts

The Conservatory boasted Gainsborough Hall, nearly acoustically perfect, with a huge pipe organ. One day I went into the Hall during study period, and listened to a Russian woman violinist play Mozart's concerto in D major. It seemed that the beautiful sounds were coming from the heavens. It was a truly outstanding performance. Mr. Reasoner said, "You don't hear fiddlin' like that everyday boy." I agreed with him.

We had an opportunity to hear Rachmaninoff in concert, but I couldn't get anyone else to go with me in the evening. Instead, we all went to the RKO Theatre and heard "Rubinoff and his magic violin"— second rate to say the most about it. I wish I had gone to hear Rachmaninoff all by myself. One day, in harmony class, Mr. Curry accused me of copying from Gladys. It just happened that our minds ran in the same channel. I made sure our compositions were different after that. What Mr. Curry didn't notice was that Billy Hill copied Gladys' harmony nearly every day. Billy played in Les Brown's orchestra at night and had little time to do his own. The harmony book, written by Mr. Chadwick, ended all pieces with I,IV,I,V,I chord progression.

15.16   Testing out Well

San Roma was pianist and composer in residence. It was a real privilege to hear him perform. Every time Mr. Lenom was absent from class, Mr. Tuttle, a senior, filled in for him. We learned much on those days. Mr. Lenom tested us by taking each alone and having him beat out a single line piece, reciting the notes in syllables and in pitch if possible; a taxing experience. Regular tests were given in a huge hall, with occupants in every other seat. One standard test was given all Freshmen, all Sophomores, etc. We passed each testing!

15.17   A Blind Date

Mike and Kay Hill went together steadily and they thought that I should have a girl friend. Kay got a date for me with a girl who went to the same high school. We met at Child's Restaurant on Huntington Ave. She was a good-looking girl, but she smoked a cigarette in a long holder, fashionable I suppose. We had nothing in common and it was a dull evening. The date didn't last longer than dinner at the restaurant. She got on a streetcar and went her way. I got on another car and went my way. So much for dating for me in Boston.

15.18   And All That Jazz!

The professors at the Conservatory said, that jazz was evil and would ruin the musicianship of anyone who played it. It seems that most of them were against improvisation, a skill that should be encouraged early in a child's education. The professors evidently didn't know that there was a jazz band beyond compare that rehearsed in the basement of the building. I heard an excellent concert by a German Brass Band made up of Conservatory students. The lead trumpet player was a husky girl. Mr. Curry had composed, published and had performed, a full orchestral composition. I asked him if it sounded in concert as it had to him on paper and he said, "Certainly." We had the privilege of seeing Hamlet performed in one of the five balcony theatres in Boston by the Fritz Lieber Shakespearean Troupe. It really was impressive especially when viewed from the fifth balcony, which we could best afford.

15.19   Other Experiences

The winter went all too soon and the time approached when we must return home. We found a Flint "boxed in" sedan, got it for a reasonable price and had a car with hydraulic brakes! The only fault was that it had never been driven on a gravel road and as soon as we reached gravel roads in Wyoming the tires blew one after another. Salt Lake City was the only place that size tire could be found.

But to get back to Boston. Kay Hill took us in her Model A Ford runabout to see the BAA Marathon. The crowds of cars and people were immense, and as we were trying to get out of the jam, Kay ran into the rear end of a car in front of her. Not much damage was done, but Gladys had a swollen nose and face. Mike gave the other motorist $15 to forget about it.

As the time approached for us to leave, Kay was determined to come with us. Her mother and father were dead set against it and Mike really didn't want her to come. He knew it wouldn't work. It would be difficult to get a maid in Rose Valley. If I remember right, it took 19 days for us to drive to Boston. We came back in 7 days, by driving far into the night. Forty-five miles per hour was our speed. Many cars passed us, but before the day was over, we passed them all. While we were in Boston, the Hill family invited the three of us: Mike, Gladys and me, to go with them to their Grandma's Island in Casco Bay. We drove to Portland, bought a ticket on a boat and sailed out to the island. Several passengers were on the boat and when we reached open water and the boat started pitching and tipped over all our chairs. Mike, who was clinging to a rail at the side said, "Don't look now, but a woman's hanging onto my leg." Things soon righted and we reached the island. Their relative, who lived by fishing, got his boat and took Mike, Frank, Gladys and me fishing. We didn't catch much, but found out how rough and foggy it really was. Mike said, "Turn off the motor." He did and it was so rough that one side of the boat would ship a little water, then over it would tip and ship water on the other side. Gladys got deathly sick and we had to go in. For the short time we were there we learned that they lived a different life.

15.20   Visit from a Boston Friend

Years later, Kay Hill was on her way to a church convention in California and came to Rose Valley to see us all. She had married Putnam, as pre-arranged and had one son. Her husband was vice president of the Cuticura Soap Company and they had traveled much; had even dined with royalty. But Kay made herself right at home around the kitchen table in Mother's kitchen. While she was outside near the corrals, Eldon came rattling along in the old pickup, backed up to a road bank, unloaded his horse, put it away and parked the pickup. She said, "I would give anything if my boy could do that." Eldon showed her a rattlesnake he had killed. She said, "If you find another, bring it in alive."

15.21   Editing the BAC Newspaper

After the two semesters at the New England Conservatory, the fall of 1930 found the three of back at BAC. I was chosen as editor of the school newspaper, "The Student" and received some sound advice from Ira N. Hayward in journalism. "Do not editorialize in the articles you put on the from page. The editorial page is there for a purpose." Mr. Hayward had a keen mind and a keen sense of humor. After Rachel Petty stumbled and rolled down the stairs in Old Main, My Hayward said to her, "Rachel, they haven't repealed the law of gravity, yet." The Rollo brothers ran the newspaper office and it is from them that we learned about "Journalistic profanity." The show Front Page is typical. Fred Foster was assistant editor and we would write poetry to keep "canned stuff" out of our paper. We were just going to press when the Girls' Dormitory on campus burned. We jerked the front page, against the Rollo Brothers wishes and came out with a huge headline and article, GIRLS' DORMITORY BURNS! An amusing aside has to do with one young girl picking up some of the letters scattered about after the fire. She opened one, read a few lines and said at the top of her voice, "Don't anybody read any of these letters!"

15.22   Debating Successes

The second year was another debating year. Rex Harris, Zola Smith, Laverne Gentry and I won a medal by beating Dixie in a key contest. Later, I won a medal by being classed the most outstanding extemporaneous speaker in a contest at Dixie College. I'll mention Roy Halverson again. When an opportunity arose, he would take a few of us in his Model A Ford, get some wieners and marshmallows and he'd drive up Cedar Canyon. We'd build a fire, he'd get out his violin and play for us out there in the beautiful mountains. It was really a choice experience to be invited on one of those outings. Just about as true art as one could find.

15.23   Good Lord! Don't Marry That One!

I had been going with Lillis Jones, but during the second year that ended. On one occasion I had brought Lillis to Rose Valley. She was an outgoing and bossy person. While she was over here, my Dad got me aside and said, "Good Lord, son don't marry that one." Justine and I managed to keep the fires burning, even though she dated other boys and I dated other girls. I just couldn't find another as appealing as she was.

15.24   Towards a Career in Education

Mike and I graduated from BAC at the end of spring quarter, 1931. Gladys had had too much illness and didn't graduate, I believe. The fall quarter of 1931 found me back at BAC, but that was really a waste. I needed upper division credit and couldn't get it there. They made me yearbook editor, but at the end of fall quarter I dropped out. The Great Depression was too severe.

15.25   A Heartless Professor

After getting married and trying various things, the second semester in 1937 found me at the University of Nevada in Reno, majoring in Education courses, so that I could qualify for a Provisional Teacher's certificate. I can remember Professor Hall, Dean of Education, who was a good teacher. He had authored a book, "The Question in Education." Miss Reubsam was a poor teacher, in my estimation. Professor Harwood was a good teacher, but heartless. After traveling to Reno in below zero weather in the great "Winter of 37," my wife and children got sick. I missed a class here and a class there. One day Mr. Harwood asked me to stay after class and said, "Get in or get out." I could have bawled. He could have cared less. I also went to Summer School that year and did qualify for a Provisional Certificate and began teaching grades 5-8 in Preston, Nevada. I taught in Preston for two years, then on to Pioche, for a total of 15 years. After a break during World War II, I taught in the little one room "shack" in Rose Valley.

The old Rose Valley school house shortly before demolition.

Chapter 16

PLANTING SEEDS

I planted some seeds; They grew where they fell. Some fell among choking weeds; Others grew strong and well.

I planted some seeds; They grew where they fell. Some fell among choking weeds; Others grew strong and well. All needed care and love; And life giving rain from above. The harvest was sweet, wonderful; Many ate and enjoyed to the full. I planted some thoughts; They stayed where they fell. I hope my thinking was mild; As befits the mind of a child.

Rose Valley School Class, 1946.

Wayne, Farrel, Eldon, Marilyn, Kent, Noel, John (Buddy)
3 PhDs and 2 Masters degrees[1]

I hope by my having been here; Some child will think straight and clear. We will be rewarded from above; For all our thoughts of charity and love. I planted some deeds; I hope they did well. For

---

[1] Rose Valley school class in 1946. Back, Wayne (teacher) and Farrel Middle, Eldon, Marian and Kent. Front, Noel and John (Buddy). All cousins, all Lytles. Farrel, Eldon and Noel are the children of Wayne and Justine Jones. Kent, Marian and Buddy are the children of Jack and Alice Jones. Justine and Alice were cousins, thus the children were double cousins.

what reason performed; With some none could tell. As you go through life; Look ahead and also look back. Try to keep right and straight; And stay on the proper track ...

16.1   School Days

Wayne invited each student separately to his desk to give an account of his/her studies and be quizzed. More advanced students often assisted by tutoring their classmates. At recess time, Wayne, joined in the recreation, which typically consisted of softball, basketball, touch football, or 'kick back.' A rocky dirt field located adjacent to the school provided ample area for exercise. The 'restroom' consisted of an old two-holer situated at some distance to the rear of the building.

> THE SINGLE ROOM was heated by an fuel-oil stove installed front-corner, south end. Since the walls were planks without insulation, on cold days, when the stove was fully fired up, the heat softened the varnish on the front row of desks. Meanwhile, drinking water in the opposite corner would freeze.

- Wayne organized field activities designed to teach and provide practical experience. The project which first comes to mine was that of designing and constructing a barometer. For this, we made a trip to Dry Valley to the old stamp mill located there. During its heyday, large quantities of quicksilver were used to absorb the gold and silver present in the sludge produced by crushing ore shipments from Pioche and mixing the powder with water. Not a little quicksilver was too *quick* for the rivets at the bottom of its tanks, and escaped into the clay strata underlying the mill. We dug around until we found enough quicksilver to service a barometer.[2] Once a tube was primed with quicksilver, and fastened to a open beaker of water, the quicksilver would rise and fall in the tube. Eventually, we managed to calibrate the tube with markings which reflected atmospheric pressure. In the meantime, Wayne was teaching us how one aspect of weather forecasting was based on readings of atmosphere pressure. Our forecasts weren't too far off the mark ...

- Then there was the physics project which involved little cargo boats and floating them in calibrated bowls. The task was to weigh the boats when loaded lightly, moderately, and heavily, and measure the amount of water which they displaced, taking special note of the critical level at which the boats would sink. We learned (hopefully, I'm remembering this right) that "an object floating or emerged in water is buoyed up by a force equal to the weight of the water displaced," and that shipyards had to keep this principle in mind when loading ships with diverse displacement specs.

- The school 'library' consisted of a standing bookshelf against the side wall. Wayne furnished it with an array of books ranging from science and math, to easy reading and the writings of famous authors. *Wild Animals I Have Known* was among my favorites.

---

[2]During the summer of 1965, Eldon and Joe Wilkin recovered approximately twenty flasks of quicksilver at this old mill site.

- We also had a period dedicated to music, which normally consisted of singing songs now regarded as 'oldies.' *Annie Laurie* and *The Church in the Wildwood* resounded in the vicinity of the old school. You can hear them still if you have pure pitch and an ear for melodies that never die.

Each spring, standard tests were administered to monitor student aptitudes and achievements. If we didn't score at least two levels above norm for our age, we considered ourselves failures.(Eldon)

MEMORIES

All of life is memory except for the one brief instance we call the present.

17.1 Thanksgiving Feast

When we lived in Rose Valley, one year we had a prosperous and memorable Thanksgiving Feast. First of all, we had a 50 lb. turkey that we had raised. Around the turkey we had a dozen good fat chickens. Around the chickens we had two dozen mallard ducks. Around the ducks we had four dozen fat valley quail. All were roasted, stuffed with Grandma's delicious homemade dressing. A little hummingbird was atop a good pinewood stick, in the middle of the whole circle. When that table was ready, we all ate with great enthusiasm and had a very special Thanksgiving day!

17.2 Freel, Freight, and Whiskey

Just after the turn of the century, driving freight wagons was a common and often a very dull occupation. Sometime the boredom of a trip was changed when a barrel of whiskey would spring a leak. The barrel would of necessity have to be shifted so as not damage other goods, and a smell would be added to the dust. Upon arrival at its destination, the bill of lading would be marked "leakage" to explain the missing contents. On one occasion a vital shipment of parts for the ore mill at Delamar, Nevada was overdue. My father (Freel), who held a position as teamster for the superintendent, was dispatched in a buckboard to possibly find the cause of the delay. After driving many miles over the rough, dusty road, Father came upon the group of teamsters. To use his words, "One of the wagons had a barrel of whiskey aboard and the teamster had made his own leak by hammering a hoop loose and then making a hole with a horseshoe nail. They were drinking the whiskey out of a bucket and were all drunker than hoot owls. I threw the most necessary light part on the buckboard and told those guys to straighten up and get on into town. They got there the next day, bleary eyed and pretty quiet. The freight was in good shape, but on the bill of lading for the barrel of whiskey was scrawled one word, leakage'."

17.3   Preston, Nevada

Justine and I entered Preston on a late afternoon near the end of August, 1937. I had a contract to teach grades 5 thru 8, with the annual salary of $1,125 written on it. Justine had Farrel and Eldon seated on her lap. The person we saw was a boy in his early teens. I asked him where Peterson's lived. He giggled and went on his way. The next person we saw was a girl, also an early teenager. To the same question she answered "Yes" and went on her way. I said, "If this is a sample of my student body, I'm in trouble." But they were not representative of the student body. Everyone else was working and the Jensen boy and the Bradley girl were the only ones in sight. We were told later, "Their parents were too old to have children when they were born." I had been working with my brother-in-law, Jim Lees all summer and he said one day in Ely, "Wayne, put down your halo and come have a bottle of beer with me, just for old times sake." Foolishly, I did and eyes and ears were taking it all in. By the way, I never did like beer. A few days later, when we were unloading Grandpa Jones' big three ton truck at the teacherage and prospective students were all gathered around to help, watch and listen, Eldon proudly announced, "My daddy drinks beer." Just a perfect introduction to a Mormon community. I taught the four upper grades and Alice Spencer from Idaho, taught grades one through four. A majority of my students were: Buddy Jones, Enid Jones, Helen Gardner, Jane Gardner, Amos Gardner, Neal Jensen, Marion Arnoldsen, Caryl Arnoldsen, Junior Peterson, Dale Peterson, Anna Madsen, Virginia Whitlock, Christy Hermansen, Betty Hermansen, Sylvia Cates, and Jimmy Nielsen.

First School Class, Preston 1937

Felton Hickman (later band director at the University of Nevada) had been my predecessor and he had a small band, which I kept going. During the first year I rehearsed the band, gave concerts and drilled them in marching without instruments, accompanied by a drummer and led by a majorette. We aimed at taking the marching group to The Heldorado in Las Vegas and the PTA ladies made an attractive quilt to be auctioned at a dollar a chance, with thirty chances sold. I won the quilt on the first drawing and promptly put the quilt back on auction. The next winner did the same, as did the next and so on. We earned enough money on that quilt to take about fifteen marchers to Las Vegas, stay all night and return. Jack Whitlock drove the school bus for us. Marilda Whitlock was paid by the Federal Government to run a recreation program in the town. She involved everybody in softball, basketball, tennis and all sorts of games and activities, suitable for indoors and outdoors. There was a usable town hall of sorts. She even blended her Federal program into MIA. She was activity director there. Partly because of her influence, we became active in the Preston Ward, I as chorister and Justine in the MIA. I later became a teacher in the Sunday School, also. Christian Jensen was our Bishop. He was a kind man, but he also smoked occasionally, which we all knew. He said that a good menthol cigarette would "cut his asthma loose." One evening the Stake Presidency from Ely had come to Preston for a meeting. They arrived early and were sitting in their car waiting in the dark. A man came walking up the street smoking a cigarette, flipped it away and unlocked the Chapel. It was Bishop Jensen! Within two weeks, Carl Madsen was our new Bishop.

We decided to put on a play, so a group of us adults began preparing it, under Sister Whitlock's direction. Mr. Jones was asked by Alice Spencer to take a part. He said, "I couldn't go on the stage in that chapel unless I had a good stiff jolt of whiskey first." Alice promised him the whiskey and sure enough, on the night of the play, she produced a fifth of whiskey from her purse. He took a stiff shot and the play went on. After school had been going for sometime, in geography class we spoke of the Ruth pit, which was just 35 miles distance. Helen Gardner, an eighth grader, said that she had never seen the pit. I said, "For heaven's sake Helen, one of these days I'll put you in that pickup and we'll go see the pit." She fluttered her eyes and said, "That will be wonderful." I changed the subject. Felton Hickman had been accused of being too friendly with an eighth grade girl. I didn't fall into the trap. Justine and I were good friends with Hyrum and Mirilda Whitlock. They were older than we were but that didn't matter. Hy and I went deer hunting together a few times, but didn't get any deer.

DURING OUR SECOND YEAR THERE, the Whitlock house caught fire. She went screaming into a burning room and I went after her. She was reaching up and feeling along a timber. I felt where she was reaching and found a twenty dollar bill. I gave it to her and she agreed to come out of the burning room. The house was a complete loss. The Gardner home had burned during the first year we were there. Of course, there was no fire department.

During the second year we were there, Mrs. Peterson accused Justine of flirting with her high school age son, Van. Justine got hopping mad. I heard that at Pioche I could get a whopping $1,340. So, after two good years in Preston, we were off to Pioche, where we had a home nearby in Rose Valley. In Pioche, our Ward activities continued right on.

WHILE IN PRESTON, I spoke in Sacrament meeting a few times. One Sunday, another young man and I filled a speaking assignment in Lund, just five miles distance. The subject of my speech was the *Word of Wisdom.*[a] I proposed that the *Beneficial Life* ad that was always on the back page of the *Improvement Era*[b] should be moved inside the front cover and the back page devoted to pertinent fact concerning the Word of Wisdom. I still think it was a good idea, but of course it didn't happen.[c]

---

[a]The LDS policy of promoting one's health by abstaining from alcohol, tobacco, and drug-based beverages.

[b]Official organ of the LDS Church during Wayne's years of Church service.

[c]Perhaps Wayne's message had more impact than he realized. Not many years hence the insurance ad was repositioned and the back page featured a monthly message entitled "Virtue Is It's Own Reward."

During the first year, I was visited by the Deputy Superintendent of Instruction, Mr. Hinman from Ely. Luckily, I had prepared a demonstration and presentation on buoyancy. It went well and he seemed to be impressed.

6th Grade Class, Pioche 1939

Justine and I stayed active during all my 30 years of teaching and beyond. It pains me to learn that Preston is hardly a wide place in the road anymore. In those days, Preston was known as the milk shed and potato basket of Ely. The large springs near Preston keep right on flowing, but the farmers don't reside in Preston anymore. Old timers there remembered the first anniversary celebration held in Preston. Everyone was primed for a good time and reunion, but it snowed all day and the celebration never could get off the ground. It was the Fourth of July!

17.4   Uncle Jeb and his Model T

Did you ever see Uncle Jeb in his Model T? If you haven't, I'll tell you about him. Uncle Jeb is a big, tall man with a long gray beard and long hair. He wears thick-rimmed eye glasses and an old black felt hat. Uncle Jeb isn't young anymore. One nice day not long ago, Uncle Jeb backed his old Model T out of the garage and decided he'd go for a ride. Now that Model T is one of those old, old cars with the

funny cloth top, and a crank hanging in front. It has the funniest sounding horn.
The horn is a big round rubber thing with two pipes sticking out in front of it. Oh!
It's a funny looking car, but Uncle Jeb thinks it's a beauty. "None of these crazy
newfangled autos for me," he says. Well, on this fine day Uncle Jeb cranked his
Model T and climbed in. He had to press on a pedal to start it out and he fed the
gas with a little lever up by the steering wheel. The thing on the other side is for
a spark. Anyway, he pressed on the pedal and gave er a lot of gas and down the
street they went. When it was roaring loud enough, Uncle Jeb let that foot pedal
out and the old car was in high. "Whackity whack, clackity clack, pop! Clackity
clack, whackity whack chug!" went the Model T and away they traveled. Now,
things might have been different if Uncle Jeb had decided to drive in the country.
But no, this fine day he decided to let the people in town have a look at a real car.
Pretty soon there were more and more cars on the streets and people were looking at
Uncle Jeb and his Model T, just like he wanted them to. He sat up straight with his
old black hat touching the top and his long, gray beard hanging almost to his belt.
"We'll show'em a thing or two," he said to his good old car. "Poppity pop, chugity
chug," answered the old car. "Poppity pop. Chugity chug," answered the old car.
But pretty soon they came to an intersection where there were traffic lights. The
light turned red and Uncle Jeb stepped on the other pedal, which was the brake,
and the Model T stopped. It purred along, "Whackity fut, whackity fut," and then
the light turned green. Uncle Jeb stepped on the low pedal and the old car crept
out into the intersection, but he forgot to pull down the gas and "Pop! Chug!' the
old car stopped. A lot of cars behind stopped too and then the light changed for
the other side to move, then a lot of cars came in from the sides and stopped. There
they wee, right smack dab in the center of a traffic jam.

"Ga rooga"' "Too Too Tee!" went some of the cars. Others went "Peep! Honk!"
and altogether there was a lot of noise. Then somebody began to shout and so did
somebody else. There sat Uncle Jeb and the old Model T right in the center of
it all. "Brrrr! Whooeeee!" A traffic policeman zoomed in on his motorcycle and
walked over to Uncle Jeb. Now he wasn't a mean policeman, but there was a big
traffic jam and the noise was getting simply awful. "Fweet!" went his whistle and
he put his face up close to Uncle Jeb and shouted, "Get this old wreck to heck out
of here, Grandpa." Now Uncle Jeb couldn't hear very well and all he heard was the
last word. "Grandpa?" he said, "I'm Jeb." "Get 'er going or I'll have a wrecker
yank ya' out of here!" he shouted and started moving away. "Crank," answered
Uncle Jeb, "Don't bother, I'll git out 'n crank 'er myself." And he did.

The policeman was walking back through the cars and waving his arms trying
to get some of the cars to back up, but they just sat there and honked. All at once
he got so mad that he blew his whistle read loud, "Fweeeet," and the cars stopped
honking just for a moment. By this time Uncle Jeb had the old Model T going again
and he was back in the seat. Just as all the cars stopped honking Uncle Jeb put his
hand on the old rubber horn and pressed it. "Squawk!" again he pressed it "Croak!"
and again, "Squawk, croak, groan." Well, all the drivers in those other cars listened
and stared with their mouths open and Uncle pressed it again "Croak!, Squawk."
Away back up one street the end car started to back away, then one backed away
on another street, then another and another. The policeman just stood and stared
at Uncle Jeb and the old Model T. The first thing he knew the cars had all backed
away and there wasn't anymore traffic jam. Uncle Jeb pressed on the low pedal and
gave her the gas. "Roar, bang!" and in a great cloud of smoke, away they went.
"I'll take ya back home by a better way," he said to his dear old Model T. "All those
new-fangled autos made me nervous too." The old Model T sang back, "Whackity

chug, poppity bang, clankity pop whackity, poppity, chug."

They had a lovely ride home. "Whackity, whackity, shackity, wh-a-ck-I-ity P O P!"

17.5 Thunderbabies

"Oh, John, let's take off our shoes!" cried Betty as she and John played in the hot summer sunshine. "Ok, Kay!" answered John, and their shoes and socks were off. Before long Betty moved into the shade of a nice big tree and started tending her dolls. "Whew it's hot!" complained John and he sat in the shade beside Betty. "Hey, Betty look at those cute little clouds up by Big Tree Mountain, They look just like pop corn, don't they?" "Oh yes!" answered Betty, "I'll bet they are thunderbabies." "I'll bet that's what they are," agreed John. "Gee, look at that great big thunderhead up by White Cliffs!" Just then Mamma Thunderhead, for the great big one was a Mamma, made a rumbling thunder, and it echoed in the two little thunderheads, for they were really her babies. "Gee the big one is thundering," said John as he and Betty kept on playing. Now those two Thunderbabies wanted to have some fun, so they crept closer and closer to Wild Rose Valley where John and Betty were playing. All at once two baby cloud shadows came stealing into the valley. The Thunderbabies wanted to play with John and Betty. "Look, they're coming close and see how big they're getting!" shouted John. Just then a drop of rain hit Betty's toe "Plink!" "Oh! They're going to sprinkle on us exclaimed Betty. Just then a bigger drop of rain struck John's ear "Twink!" "Boy! Did you see that?" yelled John. But then another drop hit Betty's nose "Tweek!" and both children ran out from under the tree. A patter of drops ran with them as they ran. "Plink, plunk, plink," the drops kicked up little puffs of dust all around the two children. "Pitter, patter, plink." "Whee!" cried Betty, as they ran and the drops ran with them. "Look up!" Shouted John, "You can see the drops coming down out of those little clouds." Betty looked up, and just then John fell flat on his stomach and Betty rolled over him. The little clouds were having so much fun that they laughed so very hard that they thundered just a little. Now Mamma Thundercloud wasn't rumbling just then and she heard her babies thunder. Oh! It made her angry. She thought they were playing in their own back yard. She left White Cliffs and started after the Thunderbabies who were having so much fun with John and Betty. She thunder-called quite loudly but they didn't hear her at all. Then she rushed up closer and thundered terribly loud. The Thunderbabies saw her too late and they were so scared that they shivered, and the rain drops came showering down upon John and Betty, who were both up again running. They both squealed and laughed when the little shower came down upon them. But Mamma Thunderhead was so out of patience that she took her Baby Thunderheads by their pop corn tops and shook them. "Oh, let's run to the house." Cried Betty as the drops started streaming off her hair. "Let's do," answered John and into the house they scampered. Mamma Thundercloud was so excited that she had come clear over Wild Rose Valley and the rain came pounding down with a great rush. The poor Thunderbabies were so frightened that they couldn't do a thing and Mamma Thunderhead gave them another hard shake with a great, crashing thundering roar. This time she shook the poor little clouds so hard that some big drops of hail came rattling down and rolled off the roof and bounced on the lawn. "I saw some hail!" shouted Betty. "I did too," yelled John. Both children stood with their noses flat against the window. Mamma Thunderhead shook her babies and sent one more cracking of hail down mixed with her great rush of rain. Then she left with her babies close behind and the rain stopped, just like that. The sun peeked from behind the Thunderbabies and out ran John and Betty. "Let's run in the puddles!" they shouted. "See this puddle!" shouted John. "This one is deep, clear up to my ankles." Said Betty. "Get a piece of hail under your toes," John yelled, "Gee it's cold!" Mamma Thunderhead went roaring away toward Piney Mountain to join Papa Thunderhead who was just showing his head and running up his rumbles. The poor little Thunderbabies went trailing along close behind. Gosh! They never did have so much fun! Why couldn't they stay longer and play with John and Betty? "Oh, aren't Thunderbabies fun?" cried John. "Yes, I just love a Thunderbaby shower," answered Betty, "I hope they come again tomorrow!"

17.6 End of the Coco Story

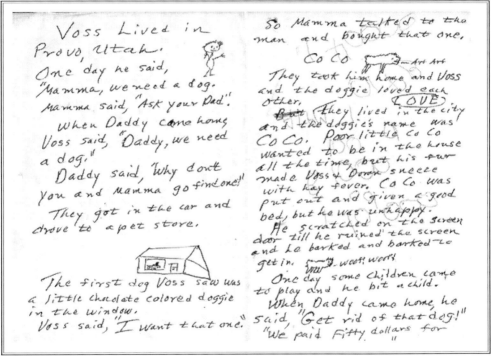

On February 4, 1990, at 7:30 in the evening, Coco stretched out on the throw rug in the living room and died, very quietly, with no struggle. About 10 years ago, Doran drove to our place in Rose Valley and left Coco. Eldon wouldn't keep him in Provo because he scratched their screen door to pieces and drew blood on the children. He didn't scratch our doors in Rose Valley because he lived in or out, mostly in, whichever he chose. Rula said that he was a pure strain poodle. He got pure strain treatment in Rose Valley and in Alamo. All he had to do was ask. He bossed any food given to him and the cats. One day we took him into the hills to trail a wounded deer. A pure waste of time, within 100 feet, he'd be following the wrong track. But he was a good dog. We liked him.

Doran was going to Rose Valley, so he took CoCo to Grandma & Grandpa. Voss thought that would be alright. Grandpa said, "I'll take him, Leave him here."

CoCo Loved Rose Valley. Grandpa & Grandma had cats but he liked cats. On a cold day, he and the cats slept together in his

CoCo got mad at big airplanes. He would run after them. Grandpa said, "One day he might catch a plane and drag it into the yard. Then we'll all be embarrassed."

CoCo got real excited during a thunder storm. He would chase the thunder and get all wet in the rain.

Grandma is not well and he stands guard for Grandma. He is a valuable dog!

Now he lives in Alamo and plays with John and Adam and Sam and Luke.

He still gets mad at airplanes, and he still guards Grandma.

Chapter 18

SO YA THINK YOU'D LIKE TO BE A COWBOY

Mama don't let your babies grow up to be cowboys
Don't let them pick guitars and drive in old trucks
Make 'em be doctors and lawyers and such
Mamas don't let your babies grow up to be cowboys
They'll never stay home and they're always alone
Even with someone they love …

-- Ed Bruce / Patsy Bruce

18.1   Some FreeHand Verse

Wayne's prose in the Red notebook occasionally slips into freehand verse, undoubtedly prompted either by deep emotion or humor enveloping the subject. The following sequence is extracted from his account of cowboy days with the West Side Cattle Company (Chapter 31).

So ya think you'd like to be a cowboy? I'm warnin ya — it's a job with lots a bumps and little joy. Did ya ever eat dust all day long under a sunburnt sky? Did ya ever try t' holler and couldn't, yer mouth was so dry? Did ya ever corral a bunch a beat up dogies without water er hay? Not for just one day, but two, three – 'til they looked like they'd blow away? Did ya ever try to keep a rack o' bones from holin' in the trees, While all the rest scattered like honeybees?

Did ya ever see a poor critter down in the snow, And all ya can do is shoot her ... though she's like a friend ya know? Did ya ever have ta rub the frost out a yer cheeks, While ya trailed a bunch o' dogies fer what seemed like weeks? Did ya ever see an old cow froze ta death with a new calf near by? Take it from me: It's a scene that'd make many a strong man cry.

Did ya ever trail a bunch o' skins that didn't look worth savin, A bunch that wouldn't make a meal fer one hungry raven? Did ya ever pull a cow out o' the mud with yer hard twist rope? Fer a critter that can't git up there's simply no hope. I'v seen sunken eyed dogies around a dried up sink hole, Tryin' ta suck up mud that's as tough as a shoe sole. I've seen cows tender from walkin' in the rough, That in every track they leave some o' that dirty red stuff. I've seen cows that staggered along with the wiggle. I've seen cancer eyes that would quiet any giggle.

Did ya ever fork a pony with a hump in his back on a cold morning? Some'll bounce ya off the frozin ground without any fair warnin'. Have ya had a pony break a leg and have to cut his throat? It's a thing that'll git most any man's goat. Then when ya look around and there's nothin' else ta straddle. It puts ya in camp bout midnight carryin' yer saddle.

Oh its great ta see a drugstore cowboy ridin' down the road, But take him ta the hills an he just adds ta yer load. Oh sometimes there's grass that makes yer cattle smile, But even then half o' em' ll go plumb wild. Sometimes it rains at just the right time. An' sometimes fer a minute ya even enjoy a lovely clime. But I've seen the country sa doggone dry I cl'd go on but there's no reason why. But say pard, I'm jist tellin' ya — if y're figerin' on bein' a cowpoke, Settle down fer a rugged life, it sure ain't no joke.

West Side Cowboys gather at chuck wagon circa 1917

West Side Cattle Company Cowboys
(Names cited from Left to Right)

Roy Lytle, Les Lytle, Jack Foliani (boy behind), Lewis Foliani,
Will Hollinger, John Francis, Garney Bennet, Will Flinspach, Will
Warren, Andy Devlin (on horse), Henry Hammond, Albert
Delmue, Joe Hollinger

West Side Cowboys at State Line. Government Peak in the background.

Chapter 19

THINGS KIDS SAY

I wish I was a little rock a sittin' on a hill;
Sittin', sittin', all day long;
Just a sittin' still ...
I wouldn't eat; I wouldn't drink; I wouldn't even wash!
I sit and sit a thousand years . . .
And rest myself, mygosh!

19.1 Sweet Memory

Our little four year old son kept talking to me with his head turned away. I asked, "Why do you turn your head, away son?" The answer, "I don't want to give Daddy my cold."

19.2 Overheard from a Six-Year Old

One day me 'n Doug were driving our ole Model D truck. Oh, she was no looker but she was a good truck. She had a good motor n' everything. One day we got in a mud hole bigger than the one you got in Daddy. Our ole truck just started chuggin an I shoved her into a bigger gear, now I remember — Low, Low, Low it was. The front wheels went deeper n deeper. Then the hind wheels went deeper n deeper. Then the radiator went out of sight an it just kept goin' deeper n deeper. We barely got out of the windows in time. Then the whole truck went clear out of sight. How'd we ever get it out? Oh we just got our shovels an dug an' dug fer days — fer weeks an' we finally got it out. It just went off as good as ever. Oh it was the bestest truck we ever had all right.

19.3 Overheard from a Seven-Year Old

How's I get this black eye daddy? Doug 'n I was just riding ole Buck one day. He wouldn't go fast enough so I got a big stick 'n hit 'im. Boy did he buck? I stayed on quite a long time, but I was on behind an' I fell off in a rock pile and bumped my eye. Doug stuck with him a lot longer — two —maybe three jumps but finally he went off, too. But he lit in a soft place 'n didn't hurt him any place. Boy! Did my eye swell up fast! Boy oh boy!

One day Doug 'n me was up on Ledge Hill 'n we saw an animal. He was a black one, a little black one, and boy did he wave his tail! He was a skunk! But soon's we smelt him we started ta run. We sure did run fast. We didn't even look back. The farther we went the farther we jumped. Boy! We was jumpin' twenty feet to a jump, 'fore we got to the bottom. That skunk jus' give up chasin' us, I think. We couldn't even smell 'im when we got down home. Boy! We sure did run fast!

19.4   Rose Valley School

Our school is a very small rural school and library books for my two second graders are much too scarce. Recently, I rented a half dozen good, well illustrated stories for my second graders. My own son is one of them. These six library books were at home the first Friday evening after I had rented them. Sonny started browsing and read avidly for more than an hour and for two whole books. Then he stopped. I asked, "Why don't you read another?" He replied, "That's enough now I'll save the rest till next week."

Chapter **20**

EARLY DAY REMEMBRANCES

I remember stopping at Prohibition Ranch on the way back. Everest had a house there where we slept one night. I remember that Everest had part of a quarter of beef hanging in that house. I have never tasted such rotten steaks!

20.1 Fear of the Dark

When we lived in Rose Valley and I was just 5 or 6 years old, fear of the darkness was one of my problems. One night, all by myself, I went clear out past the woodpile and returned, in total darkness. Just as I reached the kitchen door and the safety of the coal oil lamp, all hell broke loose. My mother had a broom beating a coyote to keep him from taking a hen out of a sitting hen's box. Dad was yelling, "Get the gun!" The hen was cackling and mother was really getting warmed up over the coyote. There I was. I had just covered that route and my fear of darkness returned. Needless to say, I didn't cover that course alone in the dark for a long time.

20.2 Grandma's Foot Warmers

Years ago, in 1919 or 1920, our family decided to go to a program in Eagle Valley, using a sled and team. We had a telephone, even a homemade one, and we had been told of the Christmas program that was going to be presented in the town hall in Eagle Valley. We got our warmest clothes, because the sled had 2 seats, but no cover. Much to our surprise, Mother had wrapped some good clean warm stones and warmed them in her oven in the kitchen. We made the trip successfully and were pleased again to find how warm the stones were even when we started home. The ride home was very comfortable and smooth. I had a special feeling towards Mother, who had made our excursion so comfortable. Did you ever ride a horse drawn sleigh under a bright moon? (Once I remember riding in that sleigh when I was very young (it was more like a skid) but the horses really pranced because it was so easy to pull. Farrel)

20.3   A Perfect Christmas

I am remembering Christmas, about 1920. Santa had brought a beautiful snow sleigh. I got a brown paper bag full of nuts and candy and other small presents. It was such a special Christmas that I gave Ring, a handful of candy and nuts. He enjoyed it immensely and wagged his tail and jumped on me. Then we went on to the "Clay Hill" and went sleigh riding in the new snow, which soon got trodden into a perfect sleigh trail. By noon time, the candy and nuts had been digested and we all settled at the table with roast chicken, dressing and pie, with milk to drink. We never had a blessing on the food. It was a perfect Christmas.

20.4   Hauling Hay

Once Mike and I, who were at about age ten, were helping Uncle Les haul hay, a mixture of alfalfa and wild hay. He had pitched it on the wagon, and Mike and I tromped it, so it would stay on. When finished he got on and took the reins for the two horse team, who were gentle and safe. Mike and I settled into the hay. We crossed the creek safely and went along fine until we came to the little grade by the Clay Hill. The backward bouncing of the hay was too strong and Mike and I and half the hay slipped to the ground. The hay covered us completely and Uncle Les drove on, none the wiser. We had to crawl out of the hay and run and stop him. He soon got it pitched back on the wagon and we all got it onto the stack without further mishap.

20.5   Aunt Maggie

Mike, Gladys and I had the luxury of staying with Aunt Maggie and Uncle Will Warren when it snowed too much to ride the bicycles or the horses to school in Eagle Valley. (25 years later Farrel and Eldon had the same luxury for the same reason — too much snow to drive.) Staying with Maggie and Will was a real treat. First of all, each meal including breakfast, was a banquet. Mike and I found our belts tighter after a week in Eagle Valley.

When bedtime was coming on, Uncle Will would doze in his big easy chair and as soon as he was asleep, Maggie would knock on the arm of her big chair. Uncle Will would rouse and say, "Somebody answer the door." Then he'd get up and stumble into the bedroom. Aunt Maggie would put all her house plants on a big, round table and cover them with quilts so they wouldn't freeze. Eventually the snow would melt and it was back to the horses or the bikes. I had to let my belt out a notch after a week with Maggie and Will. Their house has been changed, but it is still there with a *FOR SALE* on it. (*The house is now owned by Patty Crockett and has been restored to much of its original beauty. The yards and out buildings are also in good condition. Manetta*)

Aunt Maggie lived for may years after her husband died, managing the ranch herself. She relied on some good hired help and kept them on by feeding them like kings. A meal she prepared for them was a virtual buffet, with several main dishes and a variety of deserts. She annoyed her neighbors, however, by keeping hordes of cats. They easily subsisted on left-overs but crowded the town with their presence. Finally, one hired hand decided to solve the cat problem. While Maggie was away, he took a 22 rifle in hand and shot cats at over town. When she returned and inquired into the absence of her cats, he confessed. You guessed it --- Aunt Maggie fired him on the spot! She sorely missed the cats which zigged and zagged about her feet in the kitchen begging for a morsel. (Eldon)

KITTEN

Your motor, Kitty, generates the sparks That crackle in
your fur. Funny, when I rub them on by palms I
feel a sudden urge to purr!

Just what right, do you assume, permits The use of me,
your master, as a lowly lightning rod? You say, your
sinful master, In the face of stark disaster, even
Rubs with God!

Saucy Kitten! Can't you see I'm busy now? You're clawing
at my nerves. Skeedadle cat lest I tread those feline
toes ...Stop that nagging mew! ...Ah! Now it's
out. In emergency, Your motor runs a siren too!
(Eldon)

20.6 Battling Snow and Mud

During February of 1932, Everest Hackett stopped and told us that Alex Lloyd and another man were snowed in at the Little Buck Mine, up east of Deer Lodge. Mike and I agreed to bring one horse each and help go get them out. We managed to take a wagon to Deer Lodge, where Everest took his team of mules. We put some hay and water, some food and bedding on Everest's home made plow and headed for the Little Buck mine.

WE FOUND the snowbound men and they wanted us to plow the road to Modena. That's where we headed. Queen, my mare, had started out by pretending to flounder in the snow. After the mules hit her a time or two with the double trees, she made sure to never get down again. She wouldn't eat or drink the first night out, but soon got over that. It took us two days to get to Modena and two days back to Deer Lodge, but Alex and friend managed to get their pickup out and back. Two or three days after we got back, the weather turned warm and made everything a sea of mud, but they had made it out and back. I remember stopping at Prohibition Ranch on the way back. Everest had a house there and we slept there one night. **I remember that Everest had part of a quarter of beef hanging in that house. I have never tasted such rotten steaks!**

We were paid for part of the job by Lincoln County and for the other part by Iron County, Utah. I needed money badly. We were planning to be married when I could rustle enough money to do the job. I got a terrible sunburn out of it.

Chapter 21

DEER AND OTHER HUNTING STORIES

I soon dropped off, but awakened quite abruptly to a tapping on my chest. A little rattlesnake was trying to get a drink from a damp spot on my shirt. I gingerly grasped the tail with its one rattle and held the snake at a distance from me. We discovered that the snake had swallowed a small lizard, whole. I'm glad it was just a small snake!

Wayne downs a sizable buck

21.1 My First Deer

I was a grown, married man when I got my first deer. For years, we had a 44-40 with lifeless bullets, and if I hunted with it, somebody would "finish" shooting my deer. The 44-40 would not bring one down. After I was married, I bought a 30-06 [rebored Russian military rife] in Ely and I got my first deer at White Rock, a two point buck that wasn't heavy. I was above the buck on a ridge and shot him through the chest, but in spite of the place where hit, the buck took off down a canyon. I followed him on the run and the deer finally stood by a large brush. I shot at him, the shell missed and kicked up dust a quarter mile beyond the deer. I said to myself, "How did he get so far so fast. So I took after the dust. The deer had lain down and when I passed him he roused and took off beside me. For a time, we were running neck and neck. I got him with another shot and had my first deer. The ought-six did its job. After cleaning and hanging from a tree, the deer was ready to carry — four miles. Despite the work of carrying, I was happy that I had my first deer. My marksmanship improved and through the years I got many with the 30-06.

21.2   Scratchy Balks

During the fall season of 1950, Eldon, Don DaGrade, and I went hunting up in the Serviceberry area. I was riding Scratchy and the others were on foot. As we reached a point from which we could see, a large buck deer arose from his resting place, snorted and started leaving. As luck would have it, Eldon and Don walked into an open spot and their red shirts shone brightly in the sun light. The buck saw the bright color and stopped and stared. In the meantime, I was off Scratchy, tied her up, grabbed my rifle and flattened that deer right in his tracks. It was a nice buck, and after cleaning it out and hanging it up, I decided to load it on Scratchy. She would not let us drag that buck near to her. No way, was she going to carry it. I finally lost my patience, grabbed a handful of blood and gore and washed her face with it. That settled her down and she carried the deer the mile and a half to camp. Ike Orr came up that evening and said, "Wow! Where did you find that one?"

Emrys Jones with another big buck

21.3   Double Success

Emrys, Stanley and I went hunting to White Rock and on an early November Saturday, after getting about a mile out of camp, we saw a bunch of deer feeding in a canyon. The weather was cloudy and a stiff south wind was blowing and the deer didn't even see us as we slipped past them, with the wind in our favor. A buck was standing by a tree and I was going to shoot him but Emrys said, "Not yet." After sneaking 50 yards closer, Emrys said, "OK, now!" I shot and he shot. His deer went down, but mine struggled away, wounded. Emrys' deer had a 32 in spread, six or eight points on a side; all in all a beautiful deer. Mine turned out to be a common four pointer. We hanged each one in a tree and cleaned it, then went back to camp, ate and went to bed.

The next morning there was more than a foot of snow, but we went after the deer anyway. We cut the nice one in half, gave Stanley the head and started for camp. We could ride a half deer handily down a hill but had to carry it up the other side. Stanley wanted us to leave him, but Emrys dug out a candy bar and fed it to him. When we got to camp blue grouse were roosting in a tree nearby, a buck deer had walked right past and a cougar and kittens had passed by. The sun came out and I convinced Emrys that we could get my deer, so we went after it, leaving Stanley in camp. When we got my deer back and everything loaded Emrys had to walk ahead of me to mark the road. We got to Rose Valley before dark and had two nice deer.

21.4 Eldon's Big Buck

About 1950 we, Eldon, Don Dagrade, Emrys Jones and I were camped at Tobe and hunting back of Diefendorf's. We came to a heavily forested basin. I became tour director and gave directions. I said, "Eldon and Don, you go down into the trees and Emrys and I will take a couple of high rocks and shoot the deer you drive out." Eldon and Don were not too happy but did go into the trees while Emrys and I took a couple of high places. Everything was quiet for about a half hour, when there was one shot down in the trees. We hurried to find the shooter and came upon Eldon; He said, "Either it was a big buck or it had a branch on its head." The only sign I could find was a drop or two of blood. I said, "We can never track that, come on, let's go." But Eldon didn't go. He followed that track on his hands and knees. In about 20 minutes he said, "Come here." There he stood by a buck with a 33 inch spread and 12 points on one side and 8 points on the other. It was the most impressive buck any of us ever shot.

Don DaGrade's Recollection

IT WAS A BEAUTIFUL FALL DAY *in 1952 or 1953. Eldon and I were deer hunting together in the Ox Valley/Diefendorf area of Lincoln County. We hadn't seen many (or any) deer that day and were getting a little discouraged with our lack of excitement. So, we decided to split up for a while. He was to stay on one side of a hill, in a kind of "spiking" role, and I was to "haze" the area by moving slowly through some pinion and juniper trees across from Eldon on another hill and rolling rocks into the ravine. If deer were in the trees, I would spook them out and Eldon might possibly get a shot. I thought I had heard something two or three times as I crept through the trees but hadn't seen anything. All of a sudden there*

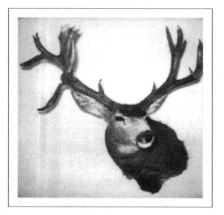

Figure 21.1: Eldon's massive mule-deer buck.

Figure 21.2: Tangled wilderness hideaway.

was a loud rifle crack and I dived for cover, as the shot seemed to be aimed in my direction. It was quiet for a few moments. I stayed put. Then, I heard a voice in the distance, "Don, I think I got one." Eldon had connected with a single snap shot as the buck had flashed through the trees near where I was standing. Bucks are very intelligent and sometimes try to avoid people by just remaining quiet while someone passes through their area. Evidently that buck had avoided me, but not Eldon's sharp-shooter vision. I'm sure it was the biggest animal either of us had ever shot, before or since. The rack was (and still is) spectacular.

21.5   Cougar Encounters

Figure 21.3: "I haven't lost any cougars!"

I was riding down Serviceberry Canyon one day on Scratchy. All at once, a large male cougar walked out of a bunch of trees and sat down, fully aware of me and

Scratchy, who raised her head high and snorted, then ignored the cat. My reaction was to go to camp and get the 30-06 rifle. It took two hours to get back there with the gun and the big cat was long gone. On another day, Noel and I were hunting deer, when a cougar started 'yawling.' We hurried to the sound and when we got there a deer bounded away.

> THERE WAS A SMALL GROVE OF PINE TREES there and I told Noel to go into the trees and see if anything would come out. Noel said, "I haven't lost any cougars." So I went in. The cougar was coming out and we passed each other at about ten feet distance. It was a young cougar and it had nothing in mind except getting away real fast.

21.6 Cougar Warning

Our families often got together and went deer hunting and pine nut picking in the fall. Once we went to Serviceberry to deer hunt. All of us had our bedrolls laid out side by side in a big row. I was near the end, and sometime in the night I was awakened by a high pitched scream. I thought it was a bird, so I was surprised to see my Uncle Wayne jump up, get his gun, and build up the fire. When the sound came again, I asked him what kind of a bird that was. He just told me to go back to sleep. In the morning he told us that a cougar had come within about fifty yards of our camp and screamed several times.(Karen)

21.7 Baby Rattle Snake Juice

One spring day in about 1950, Lin, Erma and children came to Rose Valley. We fixed a lunch, got some pillows, and went up to the bench, with adults and children. After eating a lovely picnic, drowsiness overtook me and went to sleep on some of the pillows, while everybody else went hiking. I soon dropped off, but awakened quite abruptly to a tapping on my chest. A little rattlesnake was trying to get a drink from a damp spot on my shirt. I gingerly grasped the tail with its one rattle and held the snake at a distance from me. We discovered that the snake had swallowed a small lizard, whole. I'm glad it was just a small snake! (Wayne)

21.8 Rushing in Where Wise Men Fear to Tread

...As active as I was in Church, the first morning of deer season, always a Sunday, found me out in the hills, with my boys who were big enough, right at my side. Emrys Jones, his boys and my boys and I usually hunted together. We had many good hunts. Then, the State of Nevada opened the season on Saturday, and I mostly stopped the Sunday hunting. Farrel, Eldon and Noel have no compunction against hunting on Sunday but Larry does. He grew up during the Saturday opening. (Wayne [25.50])

Deer Hunting was a ritual practiced by most healthy men on the in the area and no doubt monitored from the spirit domain with considerable interest by former devotees peeping up from under their headstones at the Lytle family cemetery. There was no greater 'burning in the bosom' than that occasioned by the sight of a mighty horns carving out a silhouette on the horizon or a sound more sacred to the hearts of the male population than the thunder of deer rifles at sunup on opening day!

THIS DEVOTION to what the majority of the female population looked upon as a 'primitive instinct,' however, was the source of considerable frustration and distress when it took possession of their soul mates some six weeks out of the year and forced all other matters relating to church and family to the status of a distant memory. At length a High Councilman from the Stake spent an hour in Sacrament Meeting addressing the topic. *"Why,"* said he, *"I'll site a personal example to make my point! Just this last Saturday I gathered my family together and we went hunting. The day turned out to be a glorious tribute to autumn weather, we had a wonderful picnic together under a shady pine with tables, shouldered our rifles and hiked up the mountain. How uplifting to stroll among the wonders of the Lord's handiwork as the colors of nature shifted with the downward course of the sun!"*

> I SAT ON THE EDGE OF MY SEAT expecting to hear how the Lord had sent them Old Blue (39.1) for their faithfulness, complete with all the exciting details of their hunting triumph, topped off the with actual real-life measurements of that legendary rack! ... But it was not to be. The truth was they had *not* reconnoitered the area, had no idea whether there were bucks to be had on the mountain, saw not a single track, and returned to their truck to pick pine nuts under an adjacent tree as Saturday slipped away into twilight and darkness with nary a tag filled.

I stared in utter amazement! My opinion had certainly not been altered: *"The Sabbath was created for man, not man for the Sabbath!"* Here was a man who had obviously never experienced buck fever nor tossed his toddler into a bush (21.12) and grabbed for his trusty rifle at the appearance of Old Blue. Here was a gatherer, to be sure, but a *hunter?* ... not in any sense of the word! Here stood 'half a man' who, from my admittedly slanted point of view, would do well to refrain from sermonizing on subjects he knew nothing about![1]

> But we had been ambushed and there was no remedy.[a] Deer hunting would never to be the same again! (Eldon)
>
> ---
> [a]As chance would have it there was a to be a 'remedy' of sorts. First, game officials shifted the opening day from Sunday to Saturday; second, local ranchers started cultivating alfalfa, which attracted deer to the valleys in large numbers. Ultimately, one didn't have to travel to White Rock or Reeses to find good deer hunting. Large herds of deer developed in and around the valleys themselves.

---

[1]Mom (Justine), perhaps, would have countered that commitment to any activity on *any* day of the week which would prompt a father to chuck his toddler into a bush and grab for a firearm was in some respect *ungodly*! Point taken.

Winter venison supply harvested in the Rose Valley area.

21.9 The Midnight Breakfast

Twelve O'clock and All Is Well!
– Rex Bently

Hunting Ox Valley and Ophir Basin

For a period of years, Wayne paired up with Emrys Jones, Lin Campbell, Rex Bentley and their sons to hunt Ox Valley and Ophir Basin, which lay west of State Line and Government Peak on the Nevada side. Wayne would normally heft into place Lurch's sturdy wrack (skillfully engineered by Mike [9.11]), load up Scratchy or Blaze, impose on Justine for a deer-hunting cake (a veritable work of art grounded in chocolate and spices with a cheese cake frosting), fill a gunny sack with late sweet corn, potatoes, tomatoes, carrots, and other garden vegetables, and strike out for State Line (11.1) via the Little and Big Summits situated along the old freight line from Modena to Rose Valley (11.13). Bales of hay would be stowed behind where the horse couldn't rip them apart and our bedrolls and tent (when we finally got a tent) was lashed atop the cab and secured to the wrack.

At Modena, a left turn put us on the rough road which climbed northwest up along the base of the range, past the Flinspach ranch at Little Meadows (11.8) and ultimately over the divide into the Great Basin with State Line still up the trail a mile or two. At State Line, we'd take the left-hand fork, shift Lurch into low or compound gear and creep up the remains of an old wagon road to Line Springs, which was a seep on the eastern slope of Government peak on the Utah side. The trickle of water there was skillfully channeled into a galvanized fifty-gallon tank, whereafter it filled up potholes in a grassy area where deer and cattle gathered for a drink.

A semi-level area in the close vicinity of the spring served as our base camp. Lin, Rex, and their wards would rendezvous with us there, complementing the food supply with substantial quantities of beef/venison steak, hamburger, bread, buns, soda pop, chocolate bars and what have you ... [2]

Rex was an old cowhand bred and raised on the Arizona Strip, where he had learned the fine art of campfire cuisine. He came supplied with a full complement of cast iron camping utensils — one customized for frying meats; another for potatoes, carrots, and onions; another for eggs, bacon, and sausage; another for mass producing hotcakes and bacon-power biscuits, and so on. When Rex was along, morning and evening meals worthy of homage and reverent remembrance.

Plan for the Hunt

It took a substantial chunk of time, obviously, for Rex to set up this outdoor kitchen with a careful selection of rocks able to collect and supply heat evenly to the cast iron utensils, build up a fire to just right to heat the various menu items. Charcoal briquettes, lighting fluid, and the like were yet to put in an appearance.

In order to meet morning deadlines for fielding a *proper* breakfast, Rex brought along an old-style alarm clock, wound it carefully, set it for about 4 am, and retired early. That would provide ample time to get breakfast out of the way, wash dishes, and dispatch the likes of Farrel, Eldon, and the other youngsters up the brushy reaches of Government Peak. If everything worked out as planned, the sun's first rays would be dawning about the time we topped out and began to 'dog' the canyons sloping downward into Ox Valley and Ophir Basin on the Nevada side. Meanwhile the older men would have circled around to take up positions overlooking the canyons where a plentiful supply of bucks were anticipated as we made our downward sweep.

Resetting the Alarm

Practical jokes were not deemed out of order, provided no one actually got hurt, and so on one memorable hunt, we put their heads together and decided to pull a 'fast one' on Rex. Once his head hit the pillow about 11pm Rex was fast asleep. Thereupon one of his boys tenderly lifted the alarm from its resting place and reset it for midnight.

Rex Springs into Action

Scarcely had Rex's snore settled into a steady pattern than the alarm sounded, whereupon he deftly unzipped his bag, pulled on his trousers and shirt, and slipped on his vintage hunting boots. When no one else stirred, he boomed out in his characteristic authoritative 'foreman' lingo, **"Time's awastin'. Let's get a move on, roudies!"** In a flash he struck a match and set his pre-arranged kindling ablaze.

Twelve O'clock and All Is Well!

Only then, with a quick glance at his watch, did Rex notice the muffled sounds of mirth emanating from the other tents. He enjoyed the situation as much or more than the rest of us, it seemed. **"Twelve o'clock and all is well!'** he **announced!"**, assuming the role of CAMP CRIER, whereupon he ground out the

---

[2] — but never ever beer or other alcoholic beverages.

Figure 21.4: Camp *Crier:* Twelve O'clock and all is well!

flame with his heal, removed his clothes, crawled back into the empty bag, and resumed a healthy snore.

21.10 An All-night Conversation

How perfectly fitting if those alien zombies had zeroed in on our camp that evening...

Wounded and Exhausted Hunters

Among the many memories of hunts in Ox Valley and Ophir Basin is one which stands out for its oddity. Not infrequently, the hunters arrived at the base camp late Friday night after the football game at Lincoln High had played itself out — for better or for worse. It was often the case that the younger set had invested their all in the carnage of the game and arrived for the hunt with not a few battle wounds of the usual vintage — nasty bruises bound up in analgesic balm, sprained ankles reenforced with plastic supports, and cracked ribs wrapped tightly in layer upon layer of locker-room tape.

On such nights there was little campfire conversation, especially when the game had been lost. Everyone quickly melted away into sleeping bags with a view to bigger and better things in store for the morrow — provided that enough healing occurred by sunrise to facilitate navigating the wilderness. A solemn silence then settled over the camp as the older hunters retired.

Something Strange Afoot

But one such night the pattern was broken. It was there at Line Springs in the environment of a dimming campfire and a huddle of tents where I witnessed something strange transpire. I had scarcely settled in myself, taking care to position my sprained ankle over a makeshift support, that an odd phenomenon occurred. Of a sudden, it seemed as though the sleepers in every tent had awakened to something worthy of continuing comment despite their general exhaustion. In the Jones tent I could distinctly here the tonality of Stanley's voice, only to be answered by Terry and Emrys. Then, simultaneously, as it were, I could hear the distinctive tonal patterns of Rex, to which his son Wayne responded. And so it continued, for an hour or more.

Finally, in my private pup tent, I had had enough! Didn't these gabbers have enough decency and presence of mind to let a guy get some sleep? My bag unzipped, I crawled out the flap into the frosty night prepared to give them a piece of my mind ...and then a light dawned. Outside the enclosure of canvass, the conversation shifted into a more audible form. No one at all was either talking or responding — they were simply *snoring*, each in turn and in a way which reflected the acoustic patterning of their natural voices. There was nothing to be done but crawl back into my own sack, plug my ears, and add my own tonality to the symphony!

THERE HAD BEEN MUCH TALK about UFOs and secret surveillance by aliens in a nefarious plot to scoop up our knowhow and apply it against us. Subsequently, in looking back upon that scenario, an intriguing thought occurred to me: How perfectly fitting if those alien zombies had zeroed in on our camp that evening, recorded our communications, and undertaken to decipher them! I could dimly envision their creepy crypo-analysts investing an eternity trying to expose the information hidden within the vacuous snoring of an exhausted encampment of humanoids wounded in a football game and afflicted with buck fever! (Eldon)

Just retribution!

21.11   Firefight in a Frying Pan

Miraculously, no one had been been drilled by an exploding shell. The only damage done, so far as we could tell as to the frying pan. It had been riddled like the helmet of a fallen hero in WWI!

Cartridge Management

Emrys Jones was an expert deer hunter. He seemed to get his buck — generally a sizable one — even when hunting conditions were poor. The key to his success was certainly not his rifle, which was an ancient 25-35 lever action with a bore worn essentially smooth by years of action. His success, rather, was anchored in subtlety and patience. While others were out scouring ridges far and wide, Emrys would take up a position opposite an active deer-crossing on a ridge, and simply sit glassing the area. In a word, rather than attempt to hike to the deer and flush them out, he would map deer movement and wait like a Paiute for the bucks to come him!

Figure 21.5: Like the helmet of a fallen hero.

Emrys normally carried extra cartridges in a waist belt, with a handful loose in his pocket for a speedy reload. You could hear him approaching as the loose cartridges made contact in his pocket. On one particular hunt at the old White Rock camp (21.1), he had already bagged a nice buck, dressed it out and hung it in a tree for transport to camp the next day. Meanwhile, he had emptied his pockets of rifle shells, returning them to the belt secured about his waist.

A Pocket Full of Pine Nuts

As he and this companions returned to camp, they came upon a pinion pine sporting a rich supply of very large, succulent nuts, many of which had loosened in their burs and fallen to the ground, as if pleading for someone like Emrys to pocket them — which he did. Upon returning to camp, he built a fire, positioned a frying pan over the flame, and emptied the pine nuts into the pan. Everyone gathered around, awaiting the pop of the pinenuts as steam within their shells expanded and burst the enclosing shell.

The Barrage

The first pop occurred within a matter of minutes as the pan became hot and the nuts began to sizzle. Pop! Pop! Pop! These were really active nuts! What a treat! But then there came a virtual volley of pops and branches on the surrounding trees began exhibiting signs of penetration by shrapnel. By this time, everyone was either bellied out, as flat against the ground as they could get, or taking cover behind the trunk of a tree.

Problem Analysis

Meanwhile, Emrys had figured out what the problem was. Earlier in the day, he and his boys had entertained themselves with their 22 rifle, competing with one another to see who could shoot the tightest pattern in a Carnation milk can. During this activity, Emrys had dumped a box of 22 shells into his pocket for ready access ... and subsequently forgotten to return the unused ones to their box.

There they had remained all day, bottomed out under his 25-35 cartridges. And there they had remained as he filled his pocket with pine nuts. And from thence had they been transferred with the pine nuts into the frying pan for cooking. Miraculously, no one had been been drilled by an exploding shell. The only damage done, so far as we could tell was to the frying pan. It had been riddled like the helmet of a fallen hero of WWI!

Emrys modified his protocol for cartridge management after that. Pant pockets were not longer used for storage. (Eldon)

21.12   The Family Hunt at Reeses

Eldon's recollection of a memorable family hunt which, after weathering a November windstorm, and close call with an injured buck's antlers, saw Wayne, Justine, Farrel, Eldon, and Noel return to Rose Valley with a trophy buck, cracked rear window, and a swarm of wood ticks to show for their efforts. (25.51)

For years, Wayne preferred to hunt White Rock Mountain, which loomed large to the northeast of Spring Valley. Its name derived from a sizable white ledge which stood out prominently on a southern slope. One could approach the mountain from the Spring Valley side to a long-standing base camp (32.5), or travel over the Reed Cabin summit into Hamblin Valley and approach it from the Utah side. A favorite hunting area from the Utah side was Reeses, an old dry farm long-since abandoned on its north western, Nevada slope.

A decision was made to spend a hunting weekend with Justine and the kids at Reeses. Given the nearly impassable condition of roads over the Reed Cabin Summit south of White Rock, we traveled around through Modena and thence up past the Flinspach ranch to State Line. At State Line, we continued up the valley to the base of White Rock and then up the bottom of the valley to the Reeses turnoff. Some five miles west up the ridge, we arrived at the old tumbledown Reese cabin on the Nevada side shortly after sundown.

A Wind-Swept Night

As we unloaded the car and found level spaces to accommodate our bed rolls (family tents had not as yet made their advent), a wind came up and clouds began drifting across the face of the mountain. By the time a campfire was blazing and supper was sizzling in the pan, a full moon arose to highlight the speed of the clouds as they came rolling in on a wind which continued to gather momentum.

Based on a life time of experience with weather in the area, Wayne predicted that we had until noon the next day to get a buck and get out! Meanwhile, he instructed us to gather sizable rocks and align them along the edges and bottom of our bed rolls. The reason for this was obvious. Lacking their weight, the onrushing wind would sweep our bedding away to an uncertain fate among the brush, cedars, and pines in its path!

Since we had implicit faith that Dad knew what he was doing, we didn't fret about the hurricane-force wind or the prospect of getting snowed in a zillion miles from nowhere. Local ranchers respected the weather, prepared for the worse, and didn't hesitate to face it head on if Mother Nature turned sour.

The Wind Dies Down

We all slept well, despite the wind. That experience looms in my mind (Eldon) as though it were yesterday, in particular the image of the wisps of nimbus cloud fleeting overhead in the moonlight and the wind exerting its all to rip the covers from under the stones which anchored them in place. By morning the wind had died down considerably, but the upper reaches of White Rock Mountain were concealed by the gathering clouds.

The Hunt Begins

After a quick breakfast, Justine shouldered a 22 rifle and positioned Noel[3] on a hip for the hike which lay ahead. Dad loaded and shouldered his re-chambered 30-06 Russian military buck-stopper, and we headed up the ridge which climbed steadily upward from the old cabin to a wide grazing area extending horizontally along the side of the mountain. A trickle of water bubbled among the stones of the meager meadow at the cabin and down the drainage in the canyon, which was obviously being used by both deer and cattle in goodly numbers for a daily drink.

We presently topped out in an open area from which a goodly stretch of the mountain side was in full view. Among the clumps of mountain flora moved a sizable herd of deer, some sporting racks which seemed large even at five hundred yards. At this juncture, Wayne and Justine settled us under the protective cover of a pinion pine with a clear view of the hunting zone, goodies to munch on, and a mandate to 'stay put.' Meanwhile, they crept on together towards the deer.

Shots are Fired

Within fifteen minutes we sprang to our feet as the thunder of Wayne's 30-06 shattered the morning silence. Justine too — not immune to the excitement of the moment — pinged away at the fleeing bucks with her 22! We half-dragged and half-carried Noel towards the location of the shooting. Presently Mom and Dad could be seen standing over a trophy-size buck. As we approached, the buck showed signs of life and Farrel pled for an opportunity to finish him off with the 22. Dad agreed, only to discover that Farrel knew less than sufficient about buck-skull anatomy to do the job properly. Farrel's shot only succeeded in bringing the animal to its feet with antlers ready to do deadly damage. Thereupon, Dad seized the 22 and put the animal down for good.

Buck Fever Again Manifests

Dad quickly dressed out the animal and fastened a hind leg to a nearby limb to facilitate the drainage of blood. He then shouldered Noel, passed the 30-06 to Mom, the 22 to Farrel, and we commenced an exploratory hike along the side of the mountain while the buck drained out and stiffened sufficiently to be divided into parts for transport to the car.

---

[3]Noel was old enough to walk well on level ground but was still a bit young for the rocks, brush and washes of deer-hunting.

WITHIN MINUTES, a massive rack of antlers materialized out of the brush in our path and the buck sporting them headed for lower territory in the trees below, bouncing over trees and rocks like a run-away wagon wheel. Wayne instinctively reacted to the inevitable attack of 'buck fever' by dumping Noel into a bush, grabbing the 30-06 from Justine, and banging away. Failing to accurately assess the steepness of the downward trajectory, Wayne's shot only managed to dislodge a tuft of hair from the animal's neck as it disappeared into the trees.

Meanwhile, Justine was retrieving her child from the bush, doing her best to quell a flood tears and deal with Noel's scratches as she lambasted Wayne with an uninhibited outpouring of exasperation and disgust. For his part, Dad was scolding himself for having misjudged the downward angle and missed Old Blue's (39.1) first cousin by a paltry inch or two.

The Carry

The squabble having played itself out, Wayne admitted that the miss had been a blessing. The first buck yet had to be lugged down to the car and we had no horse. A second buck would have delayed him until the storm arrived in full force.

Thereupon, we returned to the site of the kill and found the animal stiff and manageable. Dad first removed the neck and head, which he assigned to Farrel and I. Next he cut the body in half behind the third rib and split the brisket of the upper body in order to facilitate spreading the front feet. This done, he split the hind quarters through the pelvis to facilitate widening the spread of the hind legs enough to place one leg over each shoulder.

It would take two trips. On the first carry, Wayne shouldered the hinds and carried them out, with Farrel and I struggling to heft the head and neck by using the horns as handles. Justine shouldered the 30-06, and transported Noel on a hip. Luckily, the carry was downhill all the way to the car.

After a brief lunch, Dad, Farrel, and I retraced our path back up the mountain to what remained of the deer. Dad shouldered, the fronts, holding a foreleg on each side of his neck, while Farrel and I transported the liver and heart. It was late afternoon before we knew it, but the buck was now at the car, our beds rolled, lashed and stowed in the trunk along with our food stores, guns, and other equipment.

Getting Out

The final task was to crowd the bulky animal parts into the rear seat. This was no simple feat, owing to the size of the animal and the depth and spread of the rack. When the task was done, each half occupied a seat, while the head and neck with rack were jammed on top with one antler making heavy contact with the rear window and the roof of the car. With Dad in the driver's seat, and Justine in the middle holding Noel, there was scarcely room for Farrel and I to crowd in beside them ... but we did. As we pulled away, a snow flurry washed our windows clean for the drive out.

Post-Hunt Review

Dad managed to outpace the major snow storm and the trip home was largely uneventful. By the time of our arrival in Rose Valley, it was well past midnight, we were all dozy, and the weather was bad. Unloading the car would have to wait until morning.

UPON UNLOADING THE ANIMAL, Dad was ecstatic until he noticed that the antler pressed against the window had cracked it badly during the rough ride home and that a swarm of wood ticks had taken leave of the animal in its deceased state and now lurked inside the vehicle seeking either new victims or an exit. Still, Dad said it had been a remarkably successful hunt and family outing ... Justine said little, but may have held a somewhat different point of view!(21.8)

21.13 Reflections

We all took it for granted in those days that whatever might be required by the way of physical stamina presented no special problems. In looking back upon this hunt now, I am amazed that Dad had the strength to physically muscle that trophy buck off the mountain without the aid of horses, four-wheelers, or other men. Each half weighed in at more than one-hundred pounds and he made two carries of approximately four miles each. For him, it seemed like a rather casual undertaking — 'no worries!' One has to wonder whether Dad had his own supply of 'miracle snake medicine.' (Eldon)

Chapter 22

COW, HORSE, DOG, AND RABBIT STORIES

Blaze was child conscious! Children often rode him bareback. He'd walk slow with his head down, as though sleep walking. If a child fell off, however, he took great care with his feet, stepping either over or to the side of the fallen rider. You could trust Blaze not to injure the innocent. Kids were safe in his care.

22.1   Sheep and Flooding

When I was a child, sheep and cattle grazing was unrestricted on the open range. Every fall and winter Utah sheep would be driven into the area around Rose Valley, Eagle Valley, Dry Valley and Delmues. We knew they were there, because a half dozen coyote protection fires could be seen burning in the hills near our ranch. The range was depleted and every time we got a heavy summer thunder shower, down it would come in a huge flood, taking everything in its path. When we needed water, it was in the deep wash running past our place and long backbreaking work was required to dam the wash and turn water out. We broke our backs getting water out, only to see the dam wash away in the next flood.

When Roosevelt became President in 1932, a far reaching conservation law was passed, and the floods gradually diminished as grazing stopped. The ground had plants to hold it back. One day at about 5:30 PM, I met Mike driving five bedraggled milk cows. Mike was angry. He said, "When milking time came I went over to the creek to check on my cows and one by one they walked into that flood, which was rapidly rolling them down along with the logs, brush, and other debris. I had my lasso rope and started lassoing cows and dragging them out of the flood. If I had been fifty feet slower Old Jerse would have gone off your dam and I'd have lost her. Stupid old critters anyhow." Mike said shaking his head.

22.2   A Skittish Team

Our Dad usually had a team that was skittish, to say the least. One Sunday, Mother said, "Hook up your half broke team and let's visit the folks in Eagle Valley" and that is what we did. After a good visit, Dad, Mother and I headed back to Rose

Valley. A road had been dug with pick and shovel to make the crossing and climb up the hill at Serviceberry Wash. My sister, Gladys, Grace Devlin, Lena Lytle and Leah Lytle had ridden horses and they had gone on ahead of us. They didn't know it, but they had scared a poor cow and she had fallen down, rolling right to the bottom of the hand dug grade into the wash, where she lay with all four feet in the air. As we started down the grade into the wash, the cow kicked her feet, bawled and scared our team so badly that they tried to climb right up the side of the grade. They went a few feet straight up and wagon horses, people and all rolled into the wash. We fell headlong with our rolling team and wagon and all landed in the bottom, with the wagon upside down and the tongue sticking out the back end and the team still hitched. The team tried to run but Dad still had the lines in both hands and kept them from getting away.

It took quite a lot of work to get the wagon upright and the tongue sticking the right way. The seat and side boards had to be just thrown on. I think Mother and I walked the mile to our home, but Dad brought everything with him. Just as we left the scene of the tip over, Dad tailed up' the poor cow. She promptly got her bearings, took after me and went down again. Dad said, "Leave the old fool there." We arrived home a little shook and scraped, but none the worse after our experience.

22.3   Will's Black and White Team

On another occasion, Dad had Will Warren's black and white team. The black was a good, dependable horse, but the white acted like a fool when the occasion presented itself. We were driving down to the meadow about a mile from home and I had taken my 22 rifle along. About half way there, a rabbit hopped out and sat. I cocked the rifle, pointed it, and the old white horse threw a fit. He took us, wagon and all straight for the 15 foot high creek bank, without my ever getting the shot fired. To our great surprise, the black horse literally sat down on the head board of the wagon and the white couldn't move us. After getting off the wagon and settling the old white horse down, we were able to get back on the road and go do our work. Of course, I gave up shooting any rabbits. Thank the Lord for a sensible, dependable horse!

22.4   Queen's Triumph

My Dad was always proud of his horses. He knew how to train horses to work. One device in training a horse to pull was to stop the team at about the middle of a hill, to give them a chance to puff a bit, then attack the second half. Many teamsters didn't do that and wound up with balky horses and a balky horse is a pain. One day I took Queen and Ginger to the hills west of Rose Valley, hooked to our wagon. I got busy loading wood and when I had the wagon about loaded, I discovered that I was in the bottom of a quite deep canyon and would need a real pull to get out of there. I decided to stop a time or two in getting out of there, so I started up with that in mind. When we reached about halfway, I said "Whoa," but Queen didn't stop. She just lay on her belly and took the wagon me and Ginger out of there. When we reached the top, she stopped, held her head high and gave a whinny of triumph. One little old hill was not going to stop Queen.

22.5 An Ice Statue

During the winter of 1935, the snow was 18 inches deep and 30 below was quite common. One morning we drove to the meadow to feed the cattle. After we had scattered the hay, I went to the bed ground of the cattle. One quite small calf was standing leaning against a tree. I went to drive the calf to the feeding. I gave it a shove with my foot and it fell over, frozen solid. Thirty below was too cold for a calf.

22.6 Old Blaze

John Devlin and I rode our horses to the east and south of Rose Valley one time in March. I was riding Scratchy and John was riding one of his horses. We came to a bunch of wild horses and one of the mares had about an 8 month old male colt. John said, "Let's take the colt." We both got our ropes ready and took after them. When we threw a loop, the colt would simply jump through it. Finally, John made a loop and held it just ahead of the colt, finally getting it over the colt's head and catching him. The wild horses were somewhat weak as was the colt and we soon had him down and John made a make shift halter, putting it on the colt, who would promptly back away and fight the halter. We simply tied him to a safe tree and left him over night. The next day he was glad to see us and followed Scratchy willingly, with the halter on. We easily led him to Rose Valley. We named him "Blaze" and he grew large and strong, the best horse we ever owned. We even hitched him to the cultivator to plow rows in the potatoes. He would do anything for Julene.

> Blaze was 'child conscious.' Children often rode him bareback. He'd walk slow with his head down, as though sleep walking. If a child fell off, however, he took great care with his feet, stepping either over or to the side of the fallen rider. You could trust Blaze not to injure the innocent. Kids were safe in his care.

On one occasion, Wayne had used him to corral a herd of range cattle. One twisty-tailed old critter was as cranky and mean as a Hereford can get. As Wayne tended to feed and water, Blaze stood alone near the gate, head drooping, reins on the ground, and eyes closed in his customary manner. You'd never know that he knew he was in harm's way. That old cow snorted, put down her head and charged him with the intent of sinking a horn into his flank. Blaze stood motionless without lifting an eyebrow until an instant before impact and then suddenly shifted slightly, raised a rear hoof and planted it dead center between the charging cow's eyes. She when down like she'd been shot, knocked cold. Meanwhile, Blaze resumed his normal stance. The cow eventually struggled to her feet and staggered back to the herd. (As related to Eldon by Wayne)

He was a beautiful, dark chestnut sorrel with a blazed forehead and four white stocking feet, but when I rode him he would fall down in a level field. (Manetta)

22.7 Saving Lunch

Mike, Gladys and I got the assignment of taking about ten head of cattle including an old bull up to Serviceberry. One problem, three kids and just two horses but we had a lunch packed in a paper bag by Mother. When we got into the trees, we had to bend over for tree branches. Mike was riding behind me, carrying the lunch. The horse went under a tree limb. I leaned over to miss the limb, but Mike couldn't lean far because of me. A limb caught him under the chin and slid him off the bare back horse. He landed a little bit roughly but promptly jumped up yelling, "I've still got the lunch." We made it to the big tree and discovered that all three of us, with arms outstretched couldn't reach around the tree. We reached home at sundown. The old bull was back at the corral the next morning.

22.8   Old Snap

Gladys and I had the permanent job of getting the cows for milking time every afternoon. Snap, Dad's old plug, was our mount. We rode him bare back to make his frequent jump asides less painful. One late afternoon, Gladys and I were both on Snap at the lower end of the meadow looking for the cows. We rode near the edge of the meadow with about a ten foot bank, dropping into the large wash below us. All at once Snap's four feet slipped, dumping us onto the meadow and dropping Snap ten feet into the wash. We gathered ourselves and there was out horse, ten feet below us. Gladys climbed down and got hold of Snap's reins, but he balked and wouldn't budge. A wasp bit Gladys and she screamed. After a little screaming from Gladys, Snap decided to come out. We eventually found the cows in an unexpected place and drove them home. Dad said, "I'm glad to see you. Did you have any trouble?" Nope, nothing particular.

22.9   A Chemical Hazard

During April in 1921, Mike, John Devlin and I took an assignment from our fathers to get a horse each and roundup the cattle in Dry Valley and drive them north. There had been an ore processing mill in Dry Valley and the tailings contained Blue Vitriol, a chemical used in that ore milling process. (Farrel says what was used was cyanide. Blue vitriol is copper sulfate and not particularly poisonous.) The mining company had made a barbed wire fence to keep the cattle out of their tailing field, but any responsible people had long since left and the fence was coming apart in places, letting cattle in. The Blue Vitriol tasted salty, cattle would lick it and then would die a slow death. The only way to save them was to drive them away from there, thus the reason for our activity. The cattle just didn't want to go, but with a lot of hollering and galloping, we got them to moving, picking up more as we went north. By the time we were in the lower end of Eagle Valley, we had 250 head of cattle, every one of them resisting our efforts to make them go. We started the big herd up Serviceberry Canyon, when a white cloud appeared to the north of us. Before much longer, a strong wind with blowing snow enveloped all. We headed for home, wet cold and shivering. The cattle hunted protection in trees and brush and went right back to Dry Valley in a day or two.

22.10   Maud and Rocks

The year, 1936 to 1937 was very cold during the winter time with much snow. Our hay supply was very limited and no hay could be wasted. After my Dad's stroke managing the livestock and the hay supply fell upon me. After Dad's stroke Maude and Rocks, the big team, became unmanageable. During the big snow storm, Rocks got trapped in the deep snow away from home, and we left that as it was. But Maude couldn't survive, just eating with the cows and she came and leaned against the stockade fence and begged hour after hour. There was nothing to do but put a rope around her neck, get on Scratchy and lead Maude up into the brush and shoot her, a tough decision but absolutely necessary.

22.11   Katie

One winter while we were living in the "Superintendent's house" in Pioche, (That's the big, green house still up on the hill among the mine dumps south of Pioche.) I solved the milk problem by moving our milk cow Katie to Pioche, along with her calf that never sucked. He couldn't reach the teats that hung so low because of Katie's extremely sway back. She gave more milk than we could use, so I sold a gallon per day to the Don Peck family, who had several children. It was good rich milk. Katie was perfectly satisfied, so long as she had plenty to eat ...and me. We loved each other. All went well and I moved her back to Rose Valley when we moved back in the spring. She would willingly go where I went. I'll never know why I didn't take a snapshot of Katie.

Wayne, you did! The photo below is from your old Kodak box camera that jammed with a roll of film in it. When Farrel found it, he took it to a photo shop and they succeeded in opening it and developing that roll of film --- 40 years later. Here you are with beloved Katie the cow.(Manetta)

Wayne Milks Katie

22.12   A One-Man Cow

Katie fiercely resisted being milked by anyone but Wayne. I had to hobble her so tight that she'd fall down unless I leaned her against the fence until the milking was done and the hobbles removed. On one occasion Grandma Mary ended up with the milking chores when the men were away riding. She hobbled Katie, but not tightly enough. When the bucket was near full, Katie managed to free a foot lifted from a fresh 'cow pie' and promptly planted it in the bucket. Mary didn't often get angry enough to take action, but this time she did! You old "!@+ ," she, exclaimed and promptly dumped the 'manurized' milk on Katie's head. "Try some of your own medicine!" was Mary's advice for Katie. Luckily, the men were home for the next milking. (Eldon)

22.13   The Banyon Cow

A rider approaching State Line from the east makes tracks along a seemingly endless stretch of road extending from the north-south junction near the middle of Hamblin Valley. Stretching in the opposite direction to the east the road continues until it disappears into an old dry farm called Banyon situated on the ridges south of Indian Peak --- the site of the Reservation which served as a 'half-way house' for many of the original Natives of Eagle and Rose Valley on their homeward trek from the 'hell hole' which the Indian Agents had set aside for them on the Lower Muddy.

Indian Peak, Hamblin Valley, Utah

A spring of water at Banyon attracted range cattle, and the cowboys of the West Side Cattle company necessarily included it in the territory which they had to search at roundup time. Freel had one old cow that normally found her way there come fall. When included in a herd of other cattle, the Banyon Cow was manageable. Alone, she was as wild and slippery as an antelope. Her good point was that she invariably produced a calf.

In the fall of '53 or thereabouts, the Banyon Cow turned up missing in the roundup at Banyon, and there was concern for her survival come winter. One last swing through Ophir Basin during the drive up State Line Canyon and over the summit into Ox Valley and Serviceberry Canyon, I chanced to glimpse a cow and calf high on the ridge which tumbled off into Choke Cherry on the Utah Side.

Scratchy soon closed the gap between me and the cow — which it turned out was none other than the Banyon Cow! She clambered up a rock slide and slipped away over the ridge into the canyon providing drainage to the dry farm adjacent to State Line on the north. But Scratchy was not to be outdone and quickly put me side by side with the fleeting animal as it flashed through the mahogany on the downward sweep of the ridge.

Then, as always, the unexpected happened! Two trophy-side bucks with massive spreads happened to be bedded down in the brush in our path. The Banyon Caw slipped between them before the bucks took note of her presence and Scratchy sailed over them both in a mighty bound. One scrambled away to the right and the other to the left, with antlers rising on either side within arms's reach as I ducked and weaved through the mahogany trying to keep my head on my shoulders and my rump in the saddle.

> THE BUCKS BOUNDED AWAY IN TERROR and the Banyon Cow with calf in tow streaked downward through the tangle of rocks and trees to the base of the canyon. The pace of Scratchy and the cow had quickly bested race-track records, and within minutes the remains of fences flashed beneath their feet. The cow was wise to rusty wire and grounded fences and looked forward to seeing poor Scratchy helplessly snared and thrashing about in the barbed wire as she cut her feet to ribbons!

But Scratchy knew a thing or two herself and sailed over the tangles of wire as handily as she had the bucks. The Banyon Cow, however, had one last maneuver — she ditched her calf and high-tailed it for the bottom of the valley. At this juncture, there was no choice but to bring the chase to an end. Separated from its mother, the calf would inevitably die. Break off the chase now, and the cow would return for the calf and continue on her way alone . . . to Banyon and its watering hole no doubt.

With heavy snows in the offing and left to her own resources, the Banyon Cow's chances of surviving in Hamblin Valley were slim. But it had been her own choice. Scratchy and I had done our best to bring her home with the herd to a diet of rich broadleaf hay harvested from Rose Valley's meadows, but she had refused.

> Everest Hackett latter related his own frustrating experience with wild cattle. At the time when he had elected to sell off his herd and remove to greener pastures, it became necessary to hunt down a goodly percentage of them with a rifle, shoot them, dress and skin them on the spot, and transport them to market with pack horses. We would have come off better by 'harvesting' the Banyon Cow using similar techniques! (Eldon)

22.14   Horse-Cow Games

Old Blaze (22.6), our sorrel, former-mustang standby who served as part-time cow-pony and work horse, and Katie milk cow (22.11) used to regularly put on a human parody. Blaze would wait for Katie to approach the fence of the horse corral, where-upon he would reach over it and nip her with bared teeth at the top of her tail. Katie would then snort, stomp, and put on a fierce show threatening just retaliation. Blaze in the meantime would launch into a classic horselaugh and egg her on by taking up a position even closer to the fence. Katie would respond by approaching closer herself, only to get nipped on the rear end again with even more severity. Rather than move out of range, she would remain rooted in place stomping and snorting while Blaze would laugh with even more enthusiasm and prepare for his next assault. This game would go on and on and on until at length one or the other would get bored and move on to another pass time.(Eldon)

22.15   Cotton Tails and Owls

Once while my father was plowing, the plow dug up a nest of cottontail rabbits. They were blind and hairless, and he knew that the mother would abandon the nest after the plow had destroyed it. So he called me and put them in the pockets of my coat and told me to take them home to my mother. My mother fixed a box and lined it with cotton for them. And we feed them milk from my Betsy Wetsy doll's bottle. No one expected them to live But they grew and thrived, and soon we had rabbits everywhere. When something frigtenend them, they would all run and jump in their box. Soon they grew so big they wouldn't all fit in the box and amore. However, being in the house all the time wasn't good for them, and they started to lose their hair . . . and they were becoming a nuisance. So my father made a cage for them that could be put on the lawn, so they could eat the grass. We later turned them loose, but an owl got most of them. (Karen)

22.16   Jack Rabbits and Snakes

Once we found a nest of little jack rabbits. They had fur and their eyes were open, so they started to hop all over. We figured the mother would abandon them since we had disturbed them, so we caught them and took them and put them in Wayne's old chicken coop. I had the little cotton tails when I was a kid. So we thought it would be a fun experience to have some little rabbits. But these were never tame. It soon got so we couldn't catch them even in the confines of the coop. They could jump straight up in the air and change directions while still in the air. They would dig long tunnels under the walls and you could see their heads pop up out of holes at a considerable distance from the coop. So every day we would search for holes and cover them up with scraps of wood and discarded linoleum. I don't know what we would have done with them eventually. Then a huge snake got in and solved the problem. One day when we went to feed them, the rabbits couldn't be seen at all — just a big fat snake with five bumps along his body inside the coop! (Karen and Eldon)

22.17 Old Jack

For a while, Grandpa (Freel) had an old yellow, male, dog called Old Jack. He lived under an old table shoved up against the granary to the right of the door. Grandpa had tacked an old bedspread around the sides for protection with the bottom free, so either side served as a doggy door. He often went with us on our rambles. Especially, he liked it when we took him swimming down to the irrigation pond by the meadow. Two of us would grab him, one by the front feet and another by the hinds. We would then swing him back and forth until the momentum built up and then launch him out over the pool. Old Jack could turn any which way while in flight and always landed ready to swim back to shore, where he would go directly to our clothes and shake himself vigorously, drowning us and them with water. He would then rush to us and beg for another toss.

Old Jack was supposed to be a cow dog. And I guess he was some help with the cows, but most of the time he would stage a show instead. When you 'sikked' him on a cow, he would prance sprightly out towards the animal with his head high and peer in every direction, pretending that he couldn't see the critter. Having confirmed that it was a false alarm, Old Jack would trot back and give us a puzzled look.

But he was better at chasing cars. One day he ran out to chase a jeep that was going by. One of the guys in the jeep grabbed him by the tail and dumped him on his nose. He was a pretty sheepish looking dog when came back to the yard. I don't remember what happened to Old Jack. I guess he went the way of all dogs. But he was a part of our childhood. (Karen and Eldon)

22.18 Scamp

Scamp

Scamp came into Wayne and Justine's life shortly after the family moved to Las Vegas in 1959. One day, Larry (about 10 years old) happened to see some children giving away puppies. One cute puppy caught his eye and it was love a first sight. He picked up the puppy and walked to the store where his mom (Justine) was employed. Larry walked into the store with the puppy in his arms and found his mother. With tears in his eyes, he begged to keep the puppy. Justine's co-workers said, "Oh, let him keep it!" Finally, Justine relented and that's how Scamp came to be part of the family.

During his puppyhood, Scamp chewed up everything he could get his teeth on — including the neighbor's shoes. They accidentally left their door open and Scamp went exploring inside their house. They were paid for the ruined shoes.

But Scamp did have his redeeming qualities. He loved people (but he hated other dogs, which created an occasional sticky situation.)

He loved to go running with Wayne every night and they were both addicted to the nightly run. All neighbors for a mile around could predict about what time they would see Wayne and Scamp run by. If Wayne and Justine were out of town, Scamp would stand by the closet where his leash was hung and whimper and whine progressively louder until whoever was at home would relent and take him for his run. He was one spoiled dog!

There finally came a night when a concert kept Wayne up until after midnight. It made no difference to Scamp — he had to have his run ...and a long one at that. Then a patrol car pulled up by them and the officer requested to know what Wayne's business was in the area so late at night and so far from the address Wayne gave as 'home.' "Just walking my dog," officer. "In the middle of the night?"

Scamp and Wayne waited impatiently while the officer checked out his ID and called the office for reports of burglaries in the area. None had been reported. "Suggest you walk your dog closer to home and during daylight hours!"

When DeVon was sent to fight in the Vietnam war, Julene came home to Las Vegas. Shauna was born a few months later. Scamp was gentle and loving with the baby (Shauna) and when she learned to crawl, she crawled on top of Scamp and pulled on his fur. He would whimper, but never reacted in a threatening way. He was one sweet dog!

When everyone grew up and left home, scamp was definitely Wayne and Justine's dog and he returned with them to Rose Valley. He loved them and they loved him. He died at an old age when the lid of a trunk which he was investigating fell on his head. His absence left a big hole in their lives! (Julene and Eldon)

22.19   Pup Dog

Pup Dog was the answer to Voss Lytle's (Eldon and Rula's youngest son) dreams while he was yet a lad. He and his mother picked him out of a litter in Pioche. He was part australian sheep dog, not very large, but had a good nose, and was supersonic when he decided to transit distances. We left him behind once when we took off towards Deer Lodge in Lurch to hunt deer and were taken by surprise later when he appeared out of nowhere and chased a herd of deer over the ridge.

Pup Dog without his stogie and Stetson.

Pup Dog's favorite pass time was chasing rocks. You could pick up rocks of all sizes and throw them as far strength and skill allowed. Pup would follow them in the air, scoop them up, and retrieve them as though they were rubber balls. He also loved to play 'gloves.' You'd put on a pair of gloves and rough Pup Dog up good by pulling his tail and rolling him about on the ground. Then he'd growl ferociously and attack the gloves, gnawing on them and trying to pull them off. But Pup Dog was careful not to penetrate the gloves with his sharp teeth. It was just game and he avoided hurting anyone.

But Pup Dog became addicted to car chasing, and nearly got killed. So we assigned him 'deer duty' in the orchard with a tether that prevented him from chasing cars. For many years he kept the orchard free of deer, which would have otherwise killed young trees by eating both leaves and bark. His reward for this duty was all the goat's milk he could drink.

Pup Dog had surgery twice, once in Spanish Fork, Utah, where the family lived a year. The garbage can in the back yard attracted his attention and he ate plastic along with trashed food. When it didn't pass through, he became ill, and the vet had to make an incision and clear out his stomach. Later, in his old age, he got a cyst on his neck which had to be removed.

Eventually, when Pup Dog became a centenarian (in effect) he became deaf and nearly blind. Finally, he became confused and lay down in a pile of burning weeds. So, it was time to go. In the words of Wayne, "He was a good dog and we'll miss him!" (Eldon)

22.20 Scratchy and Whirlwind

Farrel and I were riding the range one day, he on Whirlwind and I on Scratchy. Up at the cabin at Serviceberry we came onto a cow of Farrel's with a big unbranded heifer calf. I said, "Get off and tighten up your cinch. We're going to rope that calf and mark it." Farrel said, "I won't tighten my cinch. I'm not roping anything." But he did let the loop on his rope hang down by his horse.

As I was chasing the calf through the brush, it ran past his horse and caught one front foot in his rope. That promptly turned the saddle under the belly of his horse and he stayed upside down in his saddle with his head stuck in a big wild rose bush. I yelled, "For heck sake get out of your saddle and help me." He got out of his saddle and by that time the calf was on top of me in another rose bush. I was trying to avoid breaking the calf's legs and succeeded at my own expense. Eventually, we got the calf down and I ear-marked it with my dull pocket knife, but couldn't manage to wattle it with that dull knife, so we let an ear-marked calf go with its mother. After about 2 months, the cow came home to Rose Valley. But she was dry and had no calf. It looked as if somebody stole it. Farrel lost his calf.

Branding a 'long ear.'

Dᴜʀɪɴɢ the *West Side Cattle Company* era, ranchers in the area applied three identifiers to their cattle. First, there was the registered brand burned into the hide familiar to most from western lore and movies. Second, was a distinctive pattern cut into the ears of the animal. In Freel's case, this consisted of a 'crop' (which lopped off the outer extension of the ear) and 'swallow-fork' (V-shaped notch) in the right ear, and an 'undercut' in the left (a V-shaped notch at the inward base of the ear). The third was the 'wattle,' consisting of a slice of hide severed at the top and left hanging downward (normally at some distinctive location on the neck, left or right side — under the right ear, in Freel's case). These markings healed quickly and seldom became infected if properly made. Any weaned, unmarked calf reaching a year of age was fair game for anyone to rope and mark for himself.

Chapter 23

IT

IT made a brief appearance at the wedding of each of our other children. It was very plain at Mother's funeral

I got a brief look at *It* when our youngest child, Larry was born in Dr. Fortier's Pioche Hospital on Friday, May 13, 1949. *It* appeared briefly, then hid in the shadows. *It* again showed itself briefly when Farrel and Manetta were married, then hid in the shadows.

I got a brief look at *It* at my father's funeral. *It* was almost riding in the saddle with me when Old "Jughead" bucked me off that evening and cracked a rib. It rode in the pickup with me when we moved to Las Vegas. *It* appeared briefly when I started my Las Vegas ten-year career of teaching at Nellis Elementary.

IT

It made a brief appearance at the wedding of each of our other children. It was very plain at Mother's funeral.

And again, when New York Life so carefully considered hiring a 58 year old [despite my education and professional experience working with people].

When we moved back to Rose Valley, *It* most definitely came along and helped me get stuck in the snow at the top of the hill.

It appeared more and more frequently and with more surety. Then after I turned 77, I went into a room, forgot why I was there and there *It* was.

OLD AGE then became my full time companion.

Chapter 24

WAYNE'S DIARY, 1986-1987

When children are born and grow up and leave home, they remain connected to us as parents, by a thin, sensitive, invisible cord. I presented the program for Family Home Evening at Larry's and Sandra's yesterday evening. I made the statement that Lehi and I might have been about the [same] age. Suzie said, ``Oh, he wasn't THAT old!"

24.1   Rose Valley

MATERIAL in *Wayne's Diary* was typed manually from Wayne's longhand by Gaylin Lytle, scanned, and now comprises this chapter of the book.

Dec. 19,'86

ON SUNDAY, Nov. 23rd Eldon, Gaylin and I went to Alamo and attended L.D.S. meetings. Larry was ordained Bishop and set apart as Bishop of the Alamo, Nevada Ward. It was a special occasion and an inspirational meeting. May the Lord be with Larry, Sandra and family through this busy and sometimes trying period. It is amazing how much Larry has grown spiritually and in leadership ability. We are proud of him. Sandra says he is a "people person." Hasier and Broadhead are his counselors.

Dec. 17,'86

GERALDINE LYTLE SOMMERVILLE comes in for about 4 hours four days a week to help with Justine and keeping the house, Suzanne Malan, R.N. comes in twice a week and gives Justine a bath. Geraldine, Gladys and I love to pick pinenuts. We have gone up the Deer Lodge way eight or ten times and have gotten some good pine nuts. I have sold $60 worth of them and have given and sent a lot. Connie McCall Hamber, her husband Ben and her mother Grace (my first cousin) particularly love pinenuts. I have given them pinenuts three or four times. We took Justine with us in the pickup.

Monday, Dec. 15,'86

GLADYS, GERALDINE AND I, with Justine along with us, went picking pinenuts. Along at about 3:00 P.M., without warning, a snow storm came up and we had to leave at once. Another inch would have stalled the '54 pick-up. But it wasn't snowing in Rose Valley and apparently soon stopped up there. Our winter is too dry and almost too mild. The deer check everything out every night, looking for a choice morsel of food. I wish those bucks would stop harming our trees. I played peek-a-boo with a four point buck around the shed out in the yard.

Dec. 26, 86

TODAY I WENT TO PANACA while Geraldine stayed with Justine. It was Voss's eighth birthday and he was baptized by his brother Wayne. Gaylin gave a talk about baptism and I gave a short talk about the Holy Ghost. Kaylene and Laura Prestwich sang a song, with Laura Wadsworth as accompanist.

Jan. 2, 87

TRINA CAME BY PLANE to Las Vegas and was met by her parents. While here, she went horse back riding with Yvonne Lister, fell off and sprained an ankle. She went back today to Logan, where she has a job in a root beer fast food place and where she also goes to college at Utah State. Among her studies is a heavy dose of Russian.

Jan. 17, 87

We HAVE HAD A FEW DAYS of extremely cold weather, with temperatures at or below zero and yesterday, Jan 16, a north wind of 30 to 40 miles per hr, making the wind chill way below zero. We have about 4 in. of snow on the ground. It's hard to keep the pipes from freezing. Lena Mathews has just been to a doctor in Las Vegas. She has had back trouble and is losing a lot of weight. Grace Devlin Cornelius had a stroke about three weeks ago and has been hospitalized. Connie reports that she is improving. Justine is about the same, requiring total care. Alzheimer's is a terrible disease to have.

In my last conversation with Julene, she related an amusing experience they had. Just after arriving in Colorado, they needed to move a refrigerator several miles to their home. Emily's MIA Maid teacher offered them the loan of their pick-up. She said, "We won't be home Saturday morning but we will leave it parked in our drive-way, with the keys in it." So, on Saturday morning, Julene and DeVon got in their car and went to get the pick-up. When they arrived in the neighborhood, DeVon said, "There's the pick-up there in that drive way." He stopped and checked it out. The keys were in the ignition. He had to put a few beer cans in the garbage, which seemed odd. Leaving their car parked, he and Julene took the pick-up, moved the frige, drove back, parked the pick-up, with keys in the ignition, got their car and went home. About three months later, Emily needed to see her MIA Maid teacher, so DeVon drove her over. He drove to the address where he had borrowed the pick-up and stopped. Emily said, "What are you stopping here for? She lives four or five blocks down the street from here."

Jan 30,87

We HAVE HAD A COLD JANUARY, including six in. of snow and a few nights of five below zero. We are lacking moisture, it is cloudy today - maybe well get more storm. Dan remembered of an incident that happened with the cowboys. A group of them were camping in the cabin on the lower Francis ranch. Roy Lytle shot a doe deer and hanged it in a tree near the cabin, for "camp meat." One day, while they were all out riding, Pete Delmue and a friend of his from Las Angeles, who was a fireman, stopped at the cabin. Upon seeing the deer, Pete had a plan. He and the fireman hid behind a tree as the cowboys returned that evening. When they were all back, Pete and friend stepped out. The fireman flashed his badge and said, "I'm going to have to take whoever shot that deer with me." Roy said they all failed him. He said, "I soon found out how loyal my friends were. They left me all alone to take the rap." As soon as Roy had suffered enough, Pete and his friend started laughing. Then everybody joined in the laughing and Roy heaved a sigh of relief.

Feb. 2,'87

IT HAS BEEN CLOUDY through this whole Ground Hog Day, so we'll have an early spring. Noel called this morning, mentioning that tomorrow he is going to Washington D.C. for a few days. Anita, Tracy and LeAnn just returned from there and reported having a special trip. I remember a story told about Ivan Decker, who had a hare lip and was hard to understand. He was teaching high school in Parowan and, near the first of the year, a period ended and he said to his class, "You're excused" in his usual sort of way. Nobody moved, so again he said "You're excused." Still nothing happened and finally he said in a loud voice, "Get the hell outa here!" They got [out].

Feb 6, 1987

DID YOU EVER HEAR of Aritho Thymia? Well, I have it! All my life I have striven to make counts come out even. Four, eight, sixteen, 32, 64, 128 - isn't that heavenly. Some infidel has stooped so low as to put thirteen spokes in a wagon wheel! And seven and eleven. Aren't those hideous? How heavenly it is to have stair steps come out even. Sometimes, its helpful to even ignore a step here and there. Of course, my strides in going anywhere come out even. Five and ten fingers and five and ten toes are a little hard to deal with, but of course we don't have to count thumbs or big toes. If you have it, get rid of it, or it will stay with you for life. How could we have ever had five children?

Feb 7, 1987

THESE OVERUSED SAYINGS of a few years ago have come back to me: FU-NEM? SIFM. FUNEX? SIFX. OK MNX. I saw a carton of an eskimo standing atop an iceberg with only his shorts on. Cool Man, Cool! I well remember Parley Dalley, who was Chemistry and math teacher at B.A.C. One summer he said, "When the first thunder storm of the summer comes up, watch it. It will establish a pattern and all the rest will follow in the same pattern. He had an analytical mind. It was Mr. Dalley who advised me to switch from Chemical engineering to an arts and literary major. I had failed to find the "unknown" from two different test tubes of liquid he had assigned me. He said, "Wayne, even though you get A's in Math and Chemistry, you'll be happier majoring in the fine arts. I followed his advise and did not become a scientist.

Feb. 9, 87

MICKEY ROONEY, who should be qualified, recently made a statement, "The key to a beautiful girl's heart usually fits a Cadillac."

Feb. 13, Friday

FULL MOON TONIGHT, also it started raining at about noon and seems settled in for considerable time. I hope February becomes known as the "Rainy Month." We had our first Feb. rain last Wed. evening of .36". Larry and part of his family were coming this evening, but Larry got called as Bishop to go to Las Vegas to visit Golden Hollingshead, who is in the Hospital, very seriously ill with an advanced leg infection. Anesthetic can not be administered because of a weak heart. If Larry survives this assignment as Bishop of the Alamo ward, he will have become one of the kindest members of our Family.

Feb. 21 - Saturday '87

WE HAVE HAD A COLD NIGHT, after all the miserable north wind ten above. I am reminded of an incident that happened when Mike was alive. I went over to his place one morning and his gate was in sad shape - badly broken. I said, "Mike did that old horse break your gate?" He said, "No a horses' butt broke it, Mary and I came from Eagle Valley in the jeep yesterday evening. We drove through the stream where the road crosses it and came down the back canyon. As we approached our gate, I stepped on the gas to give Mary a thrill. When I stepped on the brake pedal the brakes were frozen and we sailed right on though the gate at top speed. A horses' butt broke it."

Feb. 23, 87 - Monday

JULENE CALLED THIS MORNING and told me that De Von has lost his job. They are very worried about the house payment as well as all the other expenses attendant to raising a family. She can get about $1,100 out of her policy and I can get about $2,400 out of mine, so that should help a little. I sent a check for their house payment. I am reminded of the time Julene, and Dorothy Horlacher rode the old Blaze horse up on the hill near Rose Valley. They were gone for hours and Blaze patiently waited or them. If I had ridden up on the hill and gotten off, I would have walked home.

Feb. 24, '87

FARREL CALLED THIS MORNING to wish me a happy Birthday and to tell us that Drew is going to be married near the end of April. That is the last of their boys to leave home — their baby. I'll do my best to go to Idaho Falls and to Pocatello. Thinking of Farrel, I remember when Justine was trying to "potty" train him. He would sit in his little chair and Justine would grunt at him. He would grunt back, then laugh. He wasn't trained in a day. On another occasion, Justine was suffering morning sickness from being pregnant with Eldon. She was vomiting and straining and having a really rough time. Farrel would pretend to vomit and strain, then he'll laugh. We have had some nice, wet snow, yesterday and today - about 4 inches.

Feb. 25, '87

THIS HAS BEEN an uneventful but pleasant Birthday — about 4 in of snow on the ground. Julene called Monday, Farrel called yesterday, and Larry and Noel called today. Eldon is in New Jersey, but they plan some kind of an "event" when he returns. Two months after we had moved from Las Vegas, Justine planned a party that was really a surprise to me. Several local couples came and we had a pleasant evening. It was indeed a "Surprise."

Feb. 27, 1987

I VISITED BRIEFLY with Myrtle & Paul Bliss yesterday, immediately after making a Home Teaching visit to Bruce Condie, who lives across the street from them. Paul said, "They have put a season and a tag on cougars and they're trying to build up the deer herd. It's just like raising Bobcats and chickens in the same coop."

Sunday, March 1, '87

JULENE mentioned in her recent letter that Teresa is in demand as a babysitter. I am reminded of a large family in Las Vegas whose children, among other things, were babysitters. On one occasion, one of their boys went to baby sit. It turned out that the girl he was babysitting was older than he.

Monday, March 2, '87

I REMEMBER when Mike, Gladys and I were in Boston. We were visiting the Hill family, when Mike came out with this bit of information. "We come from Mormon country, but we're just Jack Mormons. Real Mormons have horns, but us Jack Mormons just have bumps. See, you can feel one of my bumps right here." Sure enough, Frankie Hill could feel a bump!

March 3, '87

I HAVE BEEN HAVING TROUBLE getting a cheap digital watch that will keep time. Years ago, Milt Damron said he was riding in the lower end of Eagle Valley and met Murray and Harry Devlin on their horse. Milt said, "What time is it, boys?" Murray got out his old beaten up dollar watch, looked at it, shook it and looked at the sun. Milt said, "Never mind, Murray I can quess as close as you can."

March 5, '87

I HAVE BEEN SO INCENSED by Bryant Gumble's TV news reporting that I refuse to listen to him. He leans way to the left. I have been turning to ABC and now that David Hartman has retired, away they go to the left! Joun Londen and Charlie Gibson The majority of the news reporters seem determined to trample down Reagan. I hope he survives. How did I believe ever believe in the Democratic party? As Nixon said about the news reporters, "Ninety five percent of 'em are commies."

March 6, 1987 Friday

I JUST SAW a brief TV showing of the Chicago Symphony orchestra. In 1929-30, playing in any large symphony was the ultimate ambition of Gladys and me; maybe of Mike also. Kare Myers and the New England Conservatory succeeded in making that an unattainable dream. The Great Depression and the 3 more years of conservatory training needed, made playing in any symphony impossible, but it was a great dream. Maybe some Grandchild or some Greatgrandchild . . .

Saturday, March 7, 87

WE HAVE HAD a few scattered thundershowers around this afternoon. I'm afraid the old saying may apply, "Thundershowers early, probably none later." I remember way back when I was about a teenager, mother had a turkey hen that laid a dozen eggs, then hatched most of them. The hen was out in the field near the house with her poults, when a red tailed hawk started circling over her. Of course, she made an awful fuss and Papa got his old double - barreled shot gun and shot the hawk out of the air. The hawk landed near the turkey hen and poults, with a broken wing. The turkey hen jumped on that hawk and really tore into him. Papa finished it off. When everything settled down, that turkey hen started strutting. She strutted for at least two days. As if to say, "Kids, look what mamma did!"

Monday March 9, '87

LARRY, SANDRA, Mrs. Hess, ShaRee, Sharlyn and Mike visited us Saturday evening. After we had eaten, Mike volunteered to do the dishes. He stood at the sink for a minute or two and said, "Grandpa, how do you put the stopper in this sink?" I went over, pulled a fruit jar ring out of the drain and put the stopper in. Then I pointed at my head with a forefinger and said, "Kidneys." I have never seen Mike so embarrassed. He is a special grandson.

Wed., March 11, 87

I AM REMINDED of when we had our first Model T, a used one, Papa and Mamma would sit in front and Gladys and I behind. He would drive, chew tobacco and spit. Gladys and I would get the full benefit of the juice in our faces. We would protest, but he'd forget. As soon as I was large enough I took over the driving and we'd seat him in the back if possible. Soon after they were married, my Grandmother said to my mother, "Mary, I want you to get Freel to break his tobacco habit." Mother said, "I married him to live with him, not to reform him.

Thurs., March 12,87

ON A TRIP to the Eagle Valley garbage dump, I met Myrtle and Paul. We talked about the recent deaths of Davenport and Gordon and others in the county and observed that we are all getting older. They are both 80, I am 76. Paul mentioned that his old blue jeep had made him walk home from the garbage dump twice. He said, "I usually give it a couple kicks and call it an old S. of a B. and it starts." He said, further, "Look at all the milk cartons and empty cans in that pit. We're supposed to be a bunch of farmers, but if we couldn't get to the store two or three times a week, we'd all starve to death."

March 16, 87

I HAVE BEEN cutting a little wood with a half inch of snow this morning and a little hail today, we may need a fire in the stove. While cutting wood, I remembered what my Dad said about Milt Hammond. Anybody who grabbed Milt axe and started using it would just about have a fight on his hands. Milt was very particular about his axe.

Mar 29, 87

DREW AND HIS FIANCEE, Paula Hancock, have been visiting this week end. She is a nice girl and I hope to get to the ceremony and the reception, which are in Idaho Falls Apr. 24 and Pocatello, respectively. I was surprised to learn that Drew did not take Paula to meet Eldon and Rula and their family. It is painful to see near relatives grow apart so rapidly with a little separation. We should do more living Genealogy.

Mar 30, 87

DURING THE NIGHT I remembered an incident that happened in 1947 — spring. We had gone to Enterprise with our with our then four children, to visit. Stanton and Viola invited us to go to Pine Valley with them to stay overnight. There was a large, roaring stream going through the campground. After sleeping the night, at about 10:00 A.M. Justine put Julene, age 7 or 8 months, to sleep on the seat of our pick-up, wrapped quite tightly in a blanket. After thirty or fourty minutes I checked to see how Julene was doing. I could hear nothing above the roar of the stream and reported that she must still be asleep. In a few minutes Justine checked on her, reached in the pick-up and grasped that child out of there. She had turned halfway, which put her face into the crack between seat and back rest. The poor little baby had been struggling to breathe and trying to cry and her face was swollen around her nose. That just sent a shudder through us, and we thanked the Lord that Justine had been more alert than I. Needless to say, we packed up and left. Beside a roaring stream is a poor place to be with a baby and small children.

4-2-87

LAST MONDAY NIGHT, Farrel and Manetta were here and Larry, Sandra, Michael, Suzette, Sha Lee, Sharlyn, John Wayne, Adam, Sam and Luke came to Rose Valley, as well as Summer Hes, their friend. Rula came with Gladys, Gaylin, Ayren, Kaylene and Voss. We had sandwiches, icecream cones and a splendidget-together. Eldon and Wayne had gone to Phoenix on business. Justine sat right in the middle of all in her wheelchair and seemed to enjoy every minute. It has been a real joy to have Farrel & Manetta here this week.

4-11-87

WE RECENTLY had a visit from Farrel and Manetta. I especially appreciated Farrel's getting my Roto tiller started. He learned to repair farm machinery as a teenager and still has the skill. The technical papers he puts out at work for Boeing are completely confusing to me. Eldon, Ayren and Voss came today and we hauled soil to the "old," place. I fixed dinner which was enjoyed by all. I never cease to marvel at Eldon's appetite. I hate to see them leave Lincoln County. Night before last, a number of deer were in quite early. Three were right near our gate, so I put Coco out after them. At his bark, every deer within sight took off at full speed. Within seconds, they were all gone. But about 20 minutes later they started filtering back again.

Figure 24.1: Coco, the Monster Dog

Figure 24.2: Bunny Mates

4-17-87

I REMEMBER when Mike, Gladys and I used to stay with Aunt Maggie and Uncle Will Warren. They had a large, pleasant house and right near it in the back yard was a stone cellar, which had been mouse-proofed, painted white inside, with shelves along the three walls. These shelves were packed with canned and boxed groceries of all kinds. When Maggie needed something from the celler she would send Will to get it, then she would open the kitchen window to give any directions needed. Invariably, Will couldn't find it, then he would come to the cellar door and tell Maggie, "It aint here." Maggie (in a plaintive tone) would reply, "Sure, it's there, right on the back shelf where I told you." Will would look again, then announce, "It just ain't here, you come look yourself." Maggie was heavy on her feet and wasn't about to go look. Will would try again and finally would find it. He would say, "It was back of other stuff and hard to find." This went on at every meal. When Bert Adair, a hired man, was there, he would slap his thighs and laugh.
Today, Doran Carolyn and Gaylin visited with us and had lunch. We enjoyed this Good Friday.

Apr. 27, '87

ON FRIDAY MORNING, April 24th we arose early and Noel, Anita, Larry, Sandra, Le Anne and I boarded Noel's plane and we flew to Idaho Falls. We were in time for the sealing, which was performed by Nelson Bleak in the Idaho Falls Temple. It was a very impressive ceremony. After the sealing, we all gathered at an Idaho Falls cafe, and Farrel hosted a dinner, with 100 present. It was very delicious and all had an enjoyable time. We hired a rent-a-car and drove to Anita's sister's and her husband's home the Leon Esplins. We stayed overnight there. That evening, we went to the reception in the Pocatello 23rd Ward Chapel. There was an especially large attendance for Drew & Paula. I took a few Polaroid pictures and especially enjoyed watching the Great grandchildren helping themselves to handsful of cake dugout of the wedding cake by the little guys. We flew over the main part of northern Utah on the return. So many, many roads, most of them oiled and we can't get even a small strip oiled in front of our home — just to help hold down the dust.

May 10, '87

TODAY IS MOTHER'S DAY. So far we have had calls from Noel and from Doran. Thinking back a couple of weeks I decided to trade for a new car, so Noel and Larry took the '83 Ford Escort to Las Vegas and traded it in on a new Ford Tempo. I'm sure they enjoyed the day and all I did was stay home and furnish the money. Anita and Sandra went along in Noel's new Mustang and also had an enjoyable time.

May 14, '87

WE ARE HAVING a couple of little thundershowers today. Our May weather is more like July weather. Hope it rains enough to give the range plants aboost. I was raised in the log house across the street, which has a tin roof. Every rainstorm could be heard so loudly that I was disappointed by the lack of noise when in a house with a shingle roof. In the house in which we live now, Larry made a porch shelter for us, with a plastic roof, so we get all the sound effects during a rain storm, in this house, also.

Billy McCrosky told of an incident while he was in "Boot Camp" in the navy. The "Sarge" gave stiff calisthenics every day. One day he noticed that the young men on the back row were only lifting their chins during push-ups. The "Sarge" went storming back there and chewed them out but good. One young logger from Oregon said, "Sarge I'll do push-ups with you." "You're on," yelled the Sarge, so they lined up side by side and the contest began. It went on and on and somewhere beyond a hundred the "Sarge" grew shaky and finally collapsed. The young logger put one hand behind his back and did ten more on one arm. Never again did they do push-ups during exercise period.

May, 16, '87 - Sunday

AT SIX A.M. FRIDAY MAY 14, Justine had a seizure! Her body what stiff, she went backwards, her eyes showed the whites and she foamed at the mouth. I was scared, but managed to get her flat on the floor. She gradually started coming to consciousness. I called Eldon and Rula, who came quickly in their station wagon. I called Dr. Wilkin and he said to take her straight to the hospital. She is doing better, and may come home tomorrow, Monday. The Doctor says that proper medication should stop any more seizures. I hope so. Her mother used to have them. Eldon and Rula have rented houses in Gardnerville and shouldn't stay here for our sakes. Doran & Carolyn will be here and we'll get along. If Justine gets hard to move about, I'll enroll her in a rest home in St. George. Saturday, while Eldon and I were in the hospital visiting Justine, Larry came. I anointed her and Eldon gave her a blessing. I was so proud that the two sons who were there were willing and able to do the administration — as would be the other two sons, if there. While I was in Caliente for most of the day Friday, a hard thunderstorm deposited 1.25 in. of rain and .20 in. more today, Sunday. "I ain't gotta water."

SOON AFTER WE WERE MARRIED, Justine and I were living in our present house in Rose Valley. Justine mother, Clarissa, came and stayed a few days with us. One evening, she had a seizure which Justine had seen her do before, but I had not. Justine got some oil, poured some on my hand and had me rub it on her mother's head, then she put my hands on her mother's head and made me bless her. My first experience of administering to the sick.

June 3, 87

ELDON, Rula, Gaylin, Ayren, Kaylene, Voss, Wayne Ray, Marianne, Joshua and Joseph moved Monday to Gardnerville, Nev. Eldon and Rula were forced to vacate the Robert Mathews home in Panaca and Eldon and Wayne needed to get nearer to "civilization" to carry on their business in the computer software. We'll miss them sorely. Poor RuLeena! They had just moved to Parowan from Albuquerque and were nearer to her parents. Now, away go her parents, quite far away.

In the Pioche Ward, I teach the High Priests' Group, lead the singing in Sacrament meeting and lead a choir, when we have one. But, in Priesthood meeting I am never asked to play the piano or lead the singing. This seems strange to me. We get some very lamentable leading from Owen and Paul Donahue of the Bishopric. For awhile, Jeff Fisher played the piano and his Dad did the leading, which was good. When they left, back to zero again. Now, Joshua Escobedo plays the piano and Paul usually leads, which is a step or two up. My opinion of this Bishopric has been seriously lessened by the way they use every device to bypass me in the presenting of music for the Priesthood.

June 6, 1987

SUZANNE MALAN has just been here. She is a Registered Nurse and gives Justine a bath, etc., twice a week. Justine, having Alzheimer's Disease, is unable to care for herself and I can't quite manage the bathing. During this time of graduations, I think back to the spring of 1928 when the Russell Brothers, whose mother taught school in Rose Valley, took their mother to Montana and invited me to go along, to make my fortune at .50 cents per hour, working with a bridge construction gang.

MY FATHER didn't want me to go, but I went any way. I was impressed by the beauty of Montana and wanted Billy to drive his oldsmobile down Main St. in every good-sized town we came to, but he wanted to avoid traffic and wouldn't do it. This was during Prohibition days, but Pat and Billy knew the location of every "Still" in Montana, I believe. I soon became convinced that Montana was peopled with drunkards. They were the class that the Russells knew. After running a wheel barrow loaded with cement up a ramp in a line of seven men, operating as "lead man" on a pile driver, in the hangover absence of the Russells, driving heavy nails into bridge decking for 10 hrs a day, forever camping in a tent and cooking outside, I finally got enough money together to return home by rail from Lewistown, Montana, to Modena, Utah, about mid-August. My parents met me at Modena. My mother was pale and thin, I'm sure from worrying about me, and I felt bad to have done this to her. The day of arriving back on the ranch, I was busy with the much work to be done and Gladys and I were fortunate enough to enroll in Junior College at the B.A.C. that fall.

June 17, 1987

DORAN AND CAROLYN finished the school year at S.U.S.C. in Cedar City and are here, living in "The old House," where I was raised. They are very helpful in helping care for Justine. Eldon, Rula, and family, Wayne, Marianne & family have moved to Gardnerville. Eldon hopes to find more contacts for his software business in a more populated location. Connie McCall and her husband Ben Hamber came to visit and eat dinner with us Sunday. They brought chicken and we had an enjoyable visit. On my recent trip to Las Vegas, Connie filled a tooth for me with a porcelain filling. Kathleen Bleak Clifton died just a few days ago, and many from Lincoln County went to Las Vegas for the services, which, I am told, were very impressive. It is sad that a relatively young woman should go so soon. Many will miss her outstanding talent as a soprano singer. Her parents, Frank and Kathryn Bleak and her daughter Joanne and husband Jeff Hybarger are survivors, as well as her husband, Jack Clifton.

June 23, 87

SUNDAY, JUNE 21, WAS FATHER'S DAY. Noel called Saturday, June 20, Farrel called Sunday morning, June 21, Eldon called a little later, Larry called that afternoon and Julene called that evening, from Halstead, Kansas. Teresa had been invited to visit her girlfriend in Halstead and Julene, upon invitation also, had gone with her. It was very kind of all our children to call, and made it a good Father's day.

6-25-87

THE WEATHER IS HOT AND DRY. I remember how my father used to watch for wild horses. Devlins had a half dozen mares that came in from the west to water. Occasionally, a wild stallion would follow the mares. When my dad spotted one, he would scatter a few "flakes" of hay up into the brush and leading into the corral. He would hide behind the opened gate and when the mares followed the hay into the corral, the stallion would eventually follow. Then, Dad, would shut the gate. He trapped a half dozen stallions that way. One summer he gave one to Aunt Maggie and one to Uncle Milt Damron. Milt made a really good horse out of his, but one of Maggie's cowboys let hers get away. We kept a "strawberry roan" that he trapped, altered and broke it to lead. We even rode him a little. Then when we moved to Las Vegas and after my Dad had died, the horse was turned out. He joined a white horse of John Devlin's and the two ranged near the road to Pioche for years.

July 4, 1987

TODAY BEING THE 4TH OF JULY, I remember when we used to buy firecrackers from the "Chinaman" in Pioche. He lived in a small, improvised house, near where the Lincoln County Telephone lot is today. It seemed like a mysterious place and when we would tell him we wanted firecrackers, he would disappear into a back room and bring firecrackers in bunches wrapped in paper with Chinese writing on it. Those were special to us. We would fire them one at a time and one or two in a bunch would always fail to explode. That "dud" could be made into a "fizzer" by breaking it half in two and lighting the exposed powder with a match. If it didn't fizz, I would invariably blow on it and would wind up with a blistered lip from a "fizzer."

July 23, '87

YESTERDAY, Doran and I took "Lurch" and went to Fay by way of the Big Summit and Gold Springs. There were at least three people "camped" in small trailer houses near Gold Springs. The steepness of the road between the Little Buck mine and Fay surprised us. We had to load in a few rocks to get Lurch up that climb. At Fay, my memory met George Moody and particularly his son Max who was born there, Uncle Milt Damron, Aunt Amy, Jay and Myrtle, Clarissa Adair, Milly Adair and many others, even some Chinese. Since you've been gone, your houses have all fallen down and have been moved. The Horse Shoe mine A-Frame has fallen into the shaft. You wouldn't believe it.

Aug 1,'87

I NOTICED that the crickets started chirping on July 26. July started off hot, then turned windy and cold for two weeks. We got 3/4 in. of rain here during July. Last night, I went to the Heritage plays in Pioche — three of them. It was well done and parts were learned well, but three plays in one evening are a little much. Noel called, reporting that he and Bill plan to motorcycle to the scenic parks in Canada during August. He thought that the Labor Day week end would be a good time for a Family reunion. I hope we can get most of us together. Larry called yesterday, saying that we can buy a trailer house for $7,500, which we intend to do. I can see the need to move to where immediate help will be available this winter. If Justine has another seizure, I need help.

Aug 14, '87

WE HAD SOME GOOD thundershowers around yesterday, but they mostly missed Rose Valley. Clear and windy today.I have been trying to organize a Family reunion for our immediate family and seem to have it lined up for Sunday, Sept 6 at 3:00 P.M. Julene and DeVon say they can't come. Hopefully, something will work out and all can be here. The group is getting larger every year.

Aug 24, '87

A WEEK AGO Doran and I went in Lurch, to Fay, where Doran scanned for coins and screened some dirt. He found an unbroken Bromo Seltzer bottle, but no coins. On the way back, we drove to the Iris shaft, which is still open. That's where my cousin Mike was killed years ago.(9.11) The pipe is still in place. Mike wanted to get that pipe to make strong corners for a fence around the Rose Valley transformers. Farrel and Howard went with him. He wired a pulley onto a cedar tree limb right above the shaft, threaded a heavy rope through the pulley, and went down the ladder. He was pulling the rope down with one hand and could easily have tied it around his waist. About half way down the 100 foot shaft, the ladder broke, the rope jerked out of his hand and he fell to the bottom. The boys went to Hachett's home. Everest went up to the mine and Helen came to Rose Valley. We summoned Dr. Gemmill and he called a rescue team from Castleton. Dr. Gemmill was afraid to go down the shaft, so waited for the rescuers. They did a good job in bringing him up on a special stretcher. On the way up he kept saying, "Start up the pump and let's have a drink." I was standing at the collar of the shaft, helping to guide the rope, and he died just as he reached the top. What a horrible day!(9.11)

Aug. 24

POOR GAYLIN has had to undergo heart surgery again. After a few days in Washoe Medical Center in Reno, he was taken to the University of Utah Medical Center, where he had a stroke. It was determined that the heart itself was sluffing the foreign material into his blood. The heart was removed and the faulty valve removed and replaced with a valve from a pig's heart. He is on the slow and painful road to recovery. I hope he makes a complete recovery and never has to go "under the knife" again. We are still aiming for a Family Reunion on Sep't 6th.

Sep't 8, '87

WE DID IT! The Reunion on Sunday, Sep't 6 was a marked success. Approximately 45 were there and we had a special, enjoyable time. Larry brought the Video tape recorder from Pahranagat Valley High School and the program was recorded in good quality. Tracy, LeAnn and Kristen and Shauna, Teresa and Emily hit it off exceptionally well. Ollie was able to come too, as were Gladys and the Prestwiches. Gladys and I successfully played "O Sole Mio" on the piano & violin. All disbanded quite rapidly, but at least we were together for a few hours.

Sep't 23, 87

DORAN & CAROLYN left today to go back to Cedar City and to college. We have enjoyed having them. Carolyn has done much watering and we have had a good garden. Doran is especially strong with his Grandmother. They plan to visit Gaylin at the Rehab center at Univ. of Utah Medical Center. Gaylin had a serious stroke and then had open heart surgery soon after. We are all pulling for him and praying for him. Trina is going to miss a quarter of college in order to help with the remaining members of the family, while her mother stays in Salt Lake City most of the time. Doran and I got three loads of wood in record time. Farrel is paying for new furnishings in our trailer house as we prepare to move to Alamo.

Sep't 30, 87

A GROUP OF US IN LINCOLN COUNTY are growing older quite rapidly, it seems I am getting so that I have difficulty picking Justine off the floor when she seems to insist on going down. So, we are moving to Alamo to be near Larry, Sandy, and family, and where Home Health care is well organized. Paul Bliss has had a stroke and isn't always rational. Myrtle can't see too well and walks with a cane, so they are moving to Idaho Falls to be near Gary and Judy. When we can't cope, we have to make a change. Once years ago I went with the cowboys on the circle through Hamblin Valley and we had been gone for at least a week. One day, someone said, "Paul, what time is it?" Paul answered, "Don't get technical. I don't even know what day it is."

Oct. 6, '87

THE DEER SEASON in this area opened Oct 3rd, I didn't get a tag, but Doran did. He and Carolyn got up early and went over onto the "Clay Hill." They saw 17 does and fawns, but no bucks. They came back to the house and Carolyn saw three deer come out of the creek, about 400 yards away. Doran tracked them with his scope and one was a buck! He shot at it 5 times and got it. When I got there, he said, "This deer was shot in the right foot and in the head. It's clean." Much to our surprise, when we opened it up, it was shot through the body three times. It was not so "clean" as he thought. He called Gaylin and told him. Gaylin's reply "Good! How big?" The liver is delicious! Justine and I ate it.

Oct 10,'87

WE, JIM LEES AND I, reclaimed quicksilver from abandoned mill sites during the summer of 1941. One of the most productive millsites was the "Grandelimeyer" right in Hamilton. Jim had an injured hip joint, so he did the picking and shoveling and I did the panning. One day I was panning, with my attention on my work, when the shovel came sailing through the air, with the pick right behind it. Jim came out, cursing until the air was blue. He said, with great emphasis, that he would not work in that slippinghole anymore. I sat him down, got him to light his pipe, and he became calmer. I took the pick and shovel and started leveling a place for him to stand, so he wouldn't slide down into the hole he was working. To my great surprise, I struck quicksilver muck richer than we had been working on. I said, "Jim come look." He took one look and said, "Get out of the way and let a man dig." On another occasion, we had Gladys and Karen, Justine, Farrel and Eldon, myself and Jim in my old Chevy sedan. We were taking an evening ride on the forest service road. Jim sat in the back seat with his 22 rifle. All at once, three large bucks jumped out and stood, not 30 yards from the car. Jim promptly rolled the window down and started aiming with the 22. Gladys cranked the window up. Jim cranked it down, and Justine cranked it up. Jim used some of his best cuss words, but he didn't get a shot at the deer. It was a time when female determination ruled.

Oct. 21, 1987 Rose Valley

WE HAD THE FIRST KILLING FROST last night. Foolishly, yesterday I took the coverings off the squashes, only to find myself covering them again, using a flashlight at 5 A.M. this morning. I am trying to get organized for the move to Alamo, and really miss having Justine to do all the detailed work in a move. As we are, if something should happen to me, we'd really be in a bind. In Alamo we'll have help nearby and more assistance from the program that is organized there.Wed.

Oct 21, 87

WE ARE STILL PLANNING THE MOVE. I just remembered the story of the farmer who had a horse. He experimented and fed the horse less and less each day until finally he fed it nothing. To his surprise, the horse just up and died.

Thurs Oct 22, 87

I HAD A CALL from Eva Boggs in Las Vegas telling me that Dorothy Thompson just died in Reno. Shortly after, I had a call from Don Thompson in Reno, giving the same news. Dorothy took piano lessons from me in Las Vegas. We started exchanging passages from the Old Testament or New testament, which was very educational to me. I gave her a Book of Mormon, but I'm sure she never read it. She was very anti-Mormon. I also gave lessons — Violin lessons to Charles, piano lessons to Dorothy and piano lessons to Jackie, who were her children.

24.2 Alamo

Oct. 27, '87 - Alamo

LARRY, SANDRA, JOHN, ADAM & SAM came to Rose Valley last Saturday, Oct. 24th and loaded our many boxes into the old pickup and to Alamo we came. Luke stayed home with Sharlyn. Larry and others had done much work on the hillside lot and Sandy and the kids had done a lot of cleaning inside the trailer house. It was very comfortable. After we got here, Sandy , ShaRee and Sharlyn unpacked many of the boxes and put the contents in cupboards and on shelves. Justine and I came in the new Ford Tempo and make it ok. We were able to get Coco and the old yellow cat, Maurice, into the car with us. When we got here, the cat took off, never to be seen again, but of course Coco stayed with us. The trailer house is comfortable. I can visualize spots for lawn and trees and a garden. Who knows, we might like it!

Nov. 1, 87

L AST THURSDAY, OCT 28TH the drought was broken! It rained "Cats and dogs" here in Alamo. A big thunderstorm came over from hurricane Selma in Baja. We went to Rose Valley yesterday and it had rained there and started again before we left. It is still raining here in Alamo this morning. It definitely has broken the drought! The temperature is quite mild.

T HE *"lights have gone out"* in our Rose Valley home; as they have also in the Bliss Eagle Valley home, and partially in the old Warren home, lived in by Billy McCrosky, and of course, the old Sam Hollinger home and the Joe Hollinger home. The same holds true of the occupants. Our "lights are slowly going out."

THE LAST TIME I WAS HOME

In solitude the farm house stands Against the autumn skies, Its shutters flailing at the wind As the summer dies. Its windows, shattered in their panes Lead me to surmise, It stares at me in darkness now With blindness in its eyes.

I pause the way a youth would pause Before a blind man's gaze, Lest a word or sigh offend His chosen right-of-way. Fences sprawl upon the ground, Slaughtered by the years. Tumble weeds upon Their graves Confirm a host of fears.

Locusts twist their drying limbs In desperate dismay, A hundred summers at their feet Breathe a slow decay. In solitude the farm house stands While its children roam, At least that's how the farm house stood The last time I was home . . . (Eldon)

Nov. 7, '87

SHAREE PLAYED BASKETBALL and Alamo won handily over Indian Springs. Mike played football on the Alamo 8 man team. They won quite handily over McDermott and in doing so won the State of Nevada high school Championship in the 8 man class. It is good to live where we can be spectators to our grandchildren's sports activity, as well as many other events.

Nov. 17, '87

WE ARE GETTING PRETTY WELL SETTLED IN. Had the first real cold snap Sunday and Mike and I went to Rose Valley and wrapped some taps and covered the carrots some more. If a deer can get hold of a carrot top, he'll pull the carrot and leave it lying on the ground. There are many deer, in spite of the large number of tags issued, of which I couldn't get one. I locked myself out this morning — got back in by cutting a screen and pushing the window in near the kitchen table. Justine seems happy, but does not improve.

Dec. 2, 1987

LARRY HAD TO GO TO LAS VEGAS on school business and Sandy wanted to go along. I agreed to have Adam, Sam and Luke stay here. They had a ball and almost ran out of things to do. As soon as lunch was over, they had to go down to their house for "nap time." Adam said he didn't go to sleep, but when I checked on them all three were "Sacked out." It is a joy to have them near. They love cookies and raw "hot dogs."

Dec 5, 1987

WE REMAINED AT HOME FOR MOST OF THE DAY. To my great surprise, at about 3:00 P.M. Larry, Mike, Sharlyn & John Wayne drove into our yard with a Christmas tree for this trailer house. It was a small tree. Sharlyn draped it with lights and we are in business! I had no intention of getting a tree, but it will help. Having children around at Christmas time will be a real thrill.

Dec. 24, 1987

WE ARE COMFORTABLY SETTLED in our trailer house in Alamo on this Christmas eve. Doran and Carolyn have come to visit for a day or two and Farrel & Manetta stopped by for a visit, on their way to Pioche, yesterday. Larry, Sandra & children have been in Utah for 3 days and expect to be home tonight. It is good to have children and Grandchildren around at Christmas time. It rained night before last, then snowed a skiff and turned cold, with a north wind. I remember a story told by Elbert Edwards Bishop Whitehead at verton received word that the Prophet Brigham Young and party were coming in about a month and would like to cross the Colorado River to visit to visit Saints in Arizona. The Bishop and other brethren went high into sheep Mountain, cut ponderosa pines, dragged them to Overton, ripped them and made planks for a raft big enough to support a team, wagon and occupants for river crossing. The raft was completed in time to do the job. The Prophet came as scheduled but became rather ill in the heat and decided not to go to Arizona, but to return to Salt Lake City. There sat the raft, unused. Bishop Whitehead wrote, "What a waste!"

Jan 8, 1988

JERRY PERKINS AND SALLY WALCH came and bathed Justine; Jerry on Monday & Wednesday and Sally on Friday. Sally has a lame back, so they both came today. They are pleasant and capable and work under Medicare program. We are lucky to have them. The weather has been cold, but not so cold as a little farther north. While Noel and Farrel were here we moved Larry's piano to Rose Valley and my piano down here. The banana squashes that we left in the old "milk cellar" were solid ice. We couldn't get a carrot out of the frozen ground. There were a couple inches of snow here, which melted right off, but there are six inches up there, which is staying for awhile.

MITTENS

When heaven in her sadness Broods in cold and winter storm Snowflakes spread a blanket On the earth to keep it warm Some trees in consternation Cast their wraps upon the ground Their barren shoulders lashed by wind --- You've heard their wailing sound ...But the oddest quirk of branch and limb That I have ever seen Is when Miss Prissy Pussy Willow pulls Her mittens on in Spring! (Eldon)

Sunday, Jan. 17

IT WAS A STORMY DAY. We had sleet and rain all day, then it turned to snow and snowed 6in. I tried tubing, but couldn't get up much speed. Sandy remember when I used to take Mike & Suzie sleigh riding when they lived in their trailer house near us in Rose Valley. People who live in Pioche, Rose Valley and Cedar city say they have had enough winter.

Feb 18, '88

ELDON CAME IN YESTERDAY EVENING, FROM GARDNERVILLE, VIA RENO. It was really good to visit with him. I'm sure his mother recognized him. We visited the kids down at Larry's and Sandy's for a little while and Eldon played the piano. I love to have him play. He puts feeling into his own music. Robert Hess came over this evening with her daughter June, and brought her violin. She is making good progress and has a good ear. She gets rattled when she plays for me and I get rattled when I play for her. This has given me a reason to practice on my violin. I had forgotten what a wealth of violin music I have. We sent my Stanley violin to Emily in Colorado. I am keeping the one which I think is a genuine Balastreiri.

Feb. 25, 1988

THIS HAS BEEN A PLEASANT BIRTHDAY. Eldon was here until yesterday morning. Farrel called yesterday, Julene called today. Larry, Sandy and most of the children came in at noon and we had venison steak, potatoes and cabbage salad, then the birthday cake, with 7 candles. I have the nicest collection of Birthday cards I can remember receiving. Then, this evening, Sister Hatch, one of Justine's Relief Society teachers, brought an apple pie! It has indeed been a special day! I plan to give myself a present tomorrow in the form of a trip to the St. George Temple.

March 15, '88

JUST GOT BACK FROM CHOIR PRACTICE. Alamo Ward has a fine choir — about 12 women and 6 men, with Bonnie Poulsen as director. She is good. We have been singing Mother's Day songs. One time, John Devlin, Mike Lytle and I went to Enterprise to a dance. The dance closed at midnight and all action stopped. We went on to Cedar City and finished off the night. I got home just in time to change clothes and milk the cows. Mother said, "That's enough of that kind of carryin' on ole boy." I took her at her word and didn't stay out all night again.

March 29, '88

I PRESENTED THE PROGRAM FOR FAMILY HOME EVENING at Larry's and Sandra's yesterday evening. I made the statement that Lehi and I might have been about the [same] age. Suzie said, "Oh he wasn't that old!"

April 6, 88 - Tuesday

ADAM AND SAM came up for the usual treat of cookies. It seemed that they were eating quite a number, so I asked them how many their mother said they could have. They reported she said "Three of each." She no doubt meant 3 each, but three of each kind added up to 9 cookies each!

April 23, 88 Saturday

WE HAVE BEEN HAVING DAMP WEATHER for almost two weeks. The wind blew my rain gauge down and broke it, but we must have received near 3 in. of rain during this storm - one gutter buster of a thunderstorm. My rain gauge in Rose Valley had 3 1/4 inches in it and it must have rained 1/4 in. while I was still there, after taking the gauge down. Besides, there has been considerably more, since I came back to Alamo. Tonight, it is clearing up and turning cold. The peas, radishes, lettuce and carrot are up, but I fear for the potatoes and corn, planted about 2 weeks ago. Our lawn is doing well.

May 2, '88

WE HAD .13 IN. OF RAIN NIGHT BEFORE LAST — with a north wind you wouldn't believe. It didn't freeze the corn & potatoes, however. I left Justine alone in the house with the door open while gave piano lessons at Larry's. Sharlyn came up to check, and their dog buck, was sitting on the couch with Justine.

May 27, '88 - Friday

JUSTINE HAD ANOTHER SEIZURE Wed-morning at 6:00 A.M. Her body stiffens, her teeth clench, her eyes turn with whites out and she breathes with difficulty. I got her stretched out on the bathroom floor and called Larry within an hour, she was returning to normal and at eight was able to be bathed by Geri Perkins. But, as she lies in bed she looks so very frail.

Friday June 3, '88

THE CHILDREN HAD A "PEA PARTY" TODAY. It is a tradition that when they get the first of Grandpa's peas in the spring, a party is held, during which peas are eaten and games are played. Luke came in while we were eating supper and wanted "one more pea." I said, "I'm eating supper I can't ran down just to get a pea for you." He said, "Luke will get."

June 20, '88

I WAS FORTUNATE in being able to go to Sacrament meeting in Panaca yesterday. It was the "farewell" meeting for John Prestwich as he prepares to go an a mission to New York City. It was a very special meeting. Clare, Erik, Karen, Clarence and John gave very uplifting talks. Karen and her three daughters sang very well. Jeff Chesley and Grandon Brewer gave the prayers. Karen and Clarence are truly blessed with children of intelligence and the ability to express themselves. I got a call from Eldon and a call from Julene on Father's day, also a nice book and card from Larry's and Sandra's family. I told Eldon that while DeVon was out of work I helped them some. He said, "That's what you did for us. You've got yourself hooked up to a sorry bunch."

July 12, 1988

NOEL DROVE A BIG MOTORCYCLE over last week and we had a nice visit with him. He, Larry and I went to Las Vegas where he bought a new shed. Larry brought it home in his Ford diesel Van and they put the shed up in a day. Then they went to Rose Valley, brought two motorcycles down. Now there are three motorcycles in the new shed.

Figure 24.3: Motorcycle's in reserve.

Aug. 2, 1988

DORAN AND CAROLYN have left Rose Valley and have moved back to Cedar City, thus leaving the yards in Rose Valley unwatered. They slept on the couch in Rose Valley during the time they were there. A small blow snake was seen in the "Master Bedroom" by one of them, so they would not sleep in the room. We went to Rose Valley on July 27th, finding that the pump had quit working. Upon dragging it out of the well, we found that it had an "oil leak," which as bad news. Larry got a new 350 pump in Las Vegas on July 28th, so Larry, John, Adam, Sam, Luke and I went back on July 29th to install the new pump. Just as we had the 90ft. column half into, the well, three red ants attached themselves to Sam. Boy, did he scream, but we couldn't drop what we were doing and run to him. Eventually, Larry removed the auto, but Sam wouldn't stop screaming until he was put in water in the bathtub. The pump worked after some anxious moments, then they all went fishing while Grandpa watered. Rose Valley was very dry, but Howard told me they got a good rain, Sunday July 31st. Pioche has had 4 or 5 good rains. Maybe the Pine nuts will mature. I talked to Noel this morning. Larry and I both got deer tags for Area 22, so the White Rock deer hunt will have to be transferred in a westerly direction.

Aug 8, 88 - (8-8-88)

THIS DATE HAS AN ESPECIAL APPEAL for those thinking of marriage, so the wedding chapels were busy on Monday, August 8th. Larry and I went to St. George, where I visited Dr. Snow, the Oculist. I had been told by Dr. Robinson of Ely and by Dr. Stewart of Las Vegas that my weakening eyesight covered be remedied only by a cataract operation. After extensive testing and examination Dr. Snow assures me that updating my eyeglasses prescription will improve my sight and surgery is not now necessary. What a good piece of news for 8-8-88!

Aug 14, 88 - Sunday Alamo

YESTERDAY WAS GLADYS' BIRTHDAY, HER 79TH. I visited with, her for a few minutes, Friday, and she was "headed for 80." This morning at 4:00 A.M., my car horn honked. I thought somebody was trying to steal it, so I got up and went out. When I opened the car door, out came the white cat, with the black and white close behind. I had left my window open just enough to admit a cat and they both got on the roof and squeezed in, of course, with no idea of how to get back out. That's the first time I've been honked awake by a cat.

Sep't 15, 88 - Alamo

SAM, LUKE, ADAM AND SOMETIMES JOHN, drop by real often, to read and play and have cookies and a drink. Yesterday, Sam got a neat idea. He said, "We'll lick the spoons off real good and put them back in the drawer." Obviously, it would save washing them. We had two or three cool days, but now it's hot again.

Sep't 14, '88

ROBERTA HESS, SUMMER HESS, JOHN WAYNE & I went north to find pine-nuts. On the way we stopped at Preston, the first time I had been there since the closing of school in 1938. Memories came flooding back. I remembered the Whitlocks, the Jensens, the Modsen, the Petersons, the Gardners the Hermansens, the Arnoldsens, the Allreeds, the Jones, the Nillsens. The "Team hall" where Sister Whitlocks organized so many activities, is gone. The school is there, but used for some other purpose. The Church is there, but unused and falling apart. I remember giving kids turns in ringing the bell. Alice Spencer taught the lower grades. I wonder what happened to her? We marched in Las Vegas. We don't take time enough to call back these memories of 50 years ago.

Nov. 2, 88

SAM AND LUKE came up to have a snack or two. As they were leaving, Sam wanted to take his yogurt with him. I said, "Okay, but leave the spoon here." Sam said, "I already licked it off real good and put it back in the drawer."

Dec. 16, 88

I CAN'T GET USED TO THE GENEROSITY of people in Alamo. Sandy is always giving me soup, bread, etc. Today, Sister Chapel and Hatch brought a jar of jam and a loaf of banana bread. Just at dark Sister Hardy, another Sister and about 15 children brought a fruit basket. It keeps me busy returning empty dishes, and containers, besides the layer of fat around my waist.

Dec. 20, '88

A COLD SOUTH WIND HAS BEEN BLOWING TODAY, with a hint of snow in the air. I am reminded of the time I caught a ride with Sylva Jones from Cedar City to Enterprise during the first part of February , 1930. There had been a lot of snow and it was melting. I was going to Enterprise to visit Justine's family as soon as I could after her brother Boyd's death. We got about a mile out of Newcastle, when Sylva's Model A Ford mired in deep ruts, high-centered all around. I couldn't walk in the road, because of the deep ruts, so I walked out in the bush, in 3 to 5 inches of mud, all the way to Enterprise. I was just starting back, with Uncle Adair in his old Dodge, when Sylva drove into town in her car — a truck load of CCC Boys had lifted her car out of the mud. I had despaired of ever getting Sylva and her car to Enterprise, so I was immensely relieved to see her.

Seth, Clarissa, Alwyn, Justine and Stanton were living with "Grandma, Aunt Lucy Adair" and I have never seen, before or since, a family so overcome by grief. Seth acted like he had just plain given up, Clarissa cried much of the time, Alwyn just quit talking and Justine and Stanton were grieving. I quess my visit helped some, but time alone could help heal their grief. Of course, their faith in the Gospel gave them hope beyond any I would have had at that time. I was baptized in 1932.

Jan 18, 1989

WE HAD A NICE CHRISTMAS SEASON. Eldon, Rula and all their family came and Farrel, Manetta, Drew and Paula came. It is good to have visits from loved ones at Christmas time. Larry's & Sandy's teenagers and Eldon & Rula's teenagers had a ball getting reacquainted. I was especially impressed with Ayren's development. Farrel wanted to help me do something, so I suggested that we hall dirt onto the garden spot with the old pick-up. We managed to find time for one load of dirt. Farrel called Larry aside and told Larry to have dirt hauled and he would pay for it. Farrel has worked 30 years for Boeing and is seriously considering retiring. From my experience, 30 years is enough.

Feb. 15, 89

SISTER COX brought at least 2 dozen packages to Larry's and Sandra's as Valentine gifts for all. There were also a small bear and a large one. The family spent their Home Evening opening packages. It was literally a second Christmas. Our snow is gone, but it gets cold every night. I went to Panaca Dry Valley and Pioche a week ago. There was a foot of snow and had gone to 30 below the night before. I needed an extra pair of trousers. Boy, it was cold!

Mar. 3, '89

ONE BLOW that hit us all hard was news of Eldon's heart attack, about Feb. 15th. It hit him during the night and Rula called the next morning, telling us that Eldon was in St. Mary's Hospital in Reno. Larry drove over on the second day, visited Eldon and got Rula to go home and get some rest. I'm sure Eldon was glad to see him. After a few days, Eldon was transferred to Washoe Medical Center, where the clogged artery was opened, using the "balloon" procedure. I talked to him at home last Monday. He was tired, but mending. A person is never prepared for such calamities. We are hoping that adequate finance will come through from *WordMAP* that Eldon and Wayne have developed. We had a "beast" of wind yesterday and most of the night. At 2 A.M. this morning it hailed for five minutes and quieted down for awhile. But today were really catching it from the north. Cold too!

Mar 8, '1989

WHEN CHILDREN ARE BORN AND GROW UP AND LEAVE HOME, they remain connected to us as parents, by a thin, sensitive and invisible cord. When something goes wrong, we feel a pull and pain on the cord. Recently, when Eldon had a heart attack, the pull on the cord and the pain were plain to me. I wanted to be there and to do what I could to help, but, because of mother I couldn't go. I could petition the Lord to bless this precious child. Luckily, Larry was able to go and Eldon has assumed that we care, deeply.

Mar 9, '89

I WAS AT ROSE VALLEY on Tuesday, Mar. 7th. I took the keys off the deep freezer, opened the old house, threw the keys on the Kitchen table, put out some rat poison and locked the keys in the house. Lena stopped by to see me, but figured I was too busy crawling in a window to have time for her.

Chapter 25

SILVER STRANDS AMONG THE GOLD

Wayne Looks Back on Life, Telling Some Familiar Stories, and Some Altogether New Ones

25.1 Marginal Land

"Wayne, this is Utah." "But I don't see any saws." The date was June, 1915. My father, mother, Gladys and I had travelled by team and wagon from Rose Valley to Richfield, Utah. Aunt Teenie, her husband Milton Hammond and four children had come in another wagon, with team, on the same trip. I had always wanted a saw with which to saw boards and one was purchased in Richfield. It was a small coping saw and only recently disappeared. I should have become a carpenter, but that skill was reserved for Farrel and Larry, oldest and youngest sons.

Our destination in Utah was the Fayette bench. Uncle Paul Jensen had reported to Papa and Mama and Milt and Teenie that some good new land had just been put under irrigation and was open for Homestead in 160 acre plots. He had judged that Nevada was not too hospitable to his sisters and their husbands and thought this would be an opportunity for them to better their lot. Uncle Paul was at that time an itinerant cattle buyer and had visited Lincoln County, Nevada, where we lived.

As a result of the trip, Milton and Teenie decided to return to Nevada for their belongings and to move to Fayette, Utah and homestead. My parents, Freel and Mary, decided not to take the plunge. This decision undoubtedly molded our lives in a different direction from that of Milton and Teenie and their children. They were inextricably tied to that land and I and Gladys had to get off our parents' "marginal" land and seek a livelihood elsewhere. We were just about forced to go beyond high school to college, seeking employment in on-farm pursuits, while our cousins ended formal education after high school and stayed with the land. Their land was not "marginal". I just accidentally found out that our land was classed as "marginal" after I was a grown man and had been to college. During the 1930's, when our national government sent CCC boys and college bred supervisors in to try to prevent erosion on our land, I accidentally picked up a report and saw the classification "marginal" for our land. I was indignant and am glad my parents didn't know they were such a special case. They might have starved, which they definitely did not do, even during the great depression of the thirties.

Figure 25.1: Lurch parked near remains of original Rose Valley Elementary (Chapter 16).

25.2   An 'onery' Team

I have another early and vivid memory. Mother, Papa and I had gone by team and "buggy" to Eagle Valley on a Sunday to visit. Gladys, Leah, Lena and Grace Devlin had gone to Eagle Valley on horses. On the way back they had frightened a poor cow as they rode into a deep wash which had a makeshift grade into it. The cow had fallen and rolled feet up onto her back, obviously unknown to them. As we started down the grade, the cow bawled and kicked her feet. This frightened the team and they tried to climb straight up the side of the grade. The wagon rolled with us in it and the team still hitched to it. Luckily, we all fell free of the wagon and team, and when Mamma and I had regained our feet, the wagon was up-side down, the team still hooked to it and my father still holding the lines. The team were trying to run and were dragging Papa on his stomach, but he held them and they stopped. The buggy seat was broken off and boards were broken, but Papa got the wagon back on its wheels, after unhooking the team. After we were ready to go, sitting on the bare boards, he "tailed up" the cow. She promptly took after me as a "thank you" gesture, and fell down again. We left her that way. Mother said, "Freel always has an ornery team."

25.3   Rose Valley Elementary

I was sent to the first grade in the Rose Valley elementary school at the age of five, in order to keep the legal school enrollment count up, possibly. I have one clear memory of the first grade. Gladys reported to me that Miss Dalton, our teacher, was upset at me because I had not cleaned things off my desk before leaving at the end of the day. I worried for most of the night, but do not remember any negative treatment the next day. We went through eight grades in that little hastily built

Figure 25.2: UFO Thundercloud formation hovers over Montezuma's gold (35.5).

school house, through two years of high school in a one room "Town Hall" in Eagle Valley before going to Lincoln County High School in Panaca for a year, then on to Cedar City to the BAC for the fourth year of high school and on to Junior College.

Later, during World War Two, I taught for three years in that same little school building. One day I said, "The cracks are so big in these walls that a bull could walk through." Soon after, one of John Devlin's bulls came and stood right in front of the schoolhouse. The kids were glancing at each other, obviously waiting for the bull to come in. However, he moved away and didn't try it.

My pupils during those three years were Kent, Buddy and Marion Lytle, Jack's children; Farrel, Eldon and Noel Lytle, my children and Douglas Wilson, Geraldine's son. They were good workers and good "kids".

25.4 Thunderstorms

Getting back to my childhood; I always was captivated by thunderstorms and snow-storms. One time, when I was sick in bed with the measles during the summertime, a thundercloud came up and thundered and rained, with me lying in bed and watching it out the window. I'm sure it hastened my recovery. Another time, on the fifteenth of May we had fifteen inches of snow, while school was still in session. I could hardly wait for school to let out so I could sleigh ride. To my consternation, we sat in that schoolroom and had to watch all that beautiful snow sink into the ground. There was none left at four o'clock when school let out.

Much more recently, during this past summer of 1985, our wells both went dry during August. We came home from Church on Sunday and all my beloved plants were beginning to wilt, with not half enough water to water them. To my great joy, a beautiful cloud formed in the southwest and rained enough to save the plants for a couple of days. A new well was the only solution to the problem.

I have always loved the rain and snow and still do. In the summertime, I have taken my family and have driven miles to observe thunderstorms. Farrel said recently, "It never rains in Rose Valley." But once in awhile it does. I have a rain gauge to prove it!

25.5   Kid Horses

While we were young, Gladys, Mike and I were constant companions. We went sleigh riding together, ice skated together, went swimming whenever a flood dug a deep enough hole for swimming, rode horses together and went to school together.

Gladys and I had the permanent assignment of getting the milk cows from the pasture every evening. The cows would go to the field by themselves and Papa would let them in, but at night they had to be found in the fairly large field or willow grove and had to be driven to the corral. A suitable horse was hard to come by, because Papa rode the range for his mother's outfit the "CL" and would not let us ride one of his good horses. We rode bareback and would make sores on the horse and otherwise would generally "spoil" a good horse. We were given "Old Slim," one of Papa's horses that was growing too old. But Slim was too tall and we had a hard time getting on him. He wouldn't let us "shinny" up his leg. He was really not gentle enough for two small children.

25.6   Old Snap

Then somehow, Papa found "Snap." Snap was not enough of a horse to ride the range. Papa said, "You won't have to clean the rocks out of his trail. He makes his own trail as he goes." Obviously, Snap was clumsy and was also lazy. His great ambition was to jump sideways and "dump" us, which he did practically every evening. One particularly difficult spot was a salt rock (the cattle licked it). One evening, we determined that we would show him what that really was. We got a stick and pounded and kicked him until he was right near the salt rock. All at once, Snap gave a mighty leap backwards and dumped us both just about on top of the salt rock. On another evening, the cows were no place to be seen, so we rode Snap to the lower end of the meadow and were looking off the straight up-and-down bank into the wash at the end of the meadow. All at once, Snap stepped into a little slanting and hidden ditch with a trickle of water in it. It was so slick that he fell on his side, depositing us at the top of the bank and he slid into the ditch, about ten feet down.

We scrambled down into the wash to get him and he balked and wouldn't lead out. We were frantically trying to get him to move and a wasp bit Gladys. She screamed to high heaven and Snap finally came out of the wash. When the cows were finally found, they were being driven by a muddy horse with two sorry looking riders. We always rode him bareback. On another occasion, we had been swimming and Gladys had a wet towel. We stopped at uncle Les's and on the way to the corral, Gladys on Snap and Leah on another horse, decided to have a race. Gladys slapped Snap with the wet towel and he bucked her off. When she got to the house, she was still knocked out. Papa said that Snap was not able to do more than "crow hop," but that was too much for Gladys.

One day Papa came rushing up to the house and yelled, "Mary, give me the rifle." Mamma said, "What do you want the rifle for?" Papa said, "I'm going to shoot that old horse." She said, "You're not going to do any such thing," and wouldn't get the rifle. Come to find out, Papa had gotten a shovel and crow bar to fix a fence and had gotten on Snap bareback and Snap had bucked him off. Snap grew old, doing as little as possible and died of old age. He was a light bay in color, with a white spot on his forehead and white fetlocks.

25.7 Bully and Babe

Mike, Gladys and I attended high school in Eagle Valley, getting there on horses or on our bicycles, which we rode most often. It seemed that whether we were on horses or on bicycles, the north wind faced us in the morning and the south wind faced us at night. The wind was usually cold and required more effort when pumping the bicycle. One evening, we had only two horses for the ride home, so Uncle Milt Damron loaned me his horse, named "Bully." All went well until we started to gallop as we were going home on the west side of Eagle Valley. I found out where "Bully" got his name. He ran away with me. Instead of falling into the Sand Wash, he put on all fours and slid to a stop, throwing me over his head. When I landed, my left hip went out of the socket. I was suffering extreme pain, so Gladys held my shoulders and Mike stretched my left leg until the ball went back into the socket. We did no more galloping on the way home. Even to this day, I occasionally feel the tenderness in that hip.

Our next riding animal was "Babe" a black mare that was mild in manner and a good riding animal. We were allowed to ride Babe. Papa had other horses to use for his "string" of range horses.

25.8 Enter the Opposite Sex

As I grew a little older, I became aware of girls. Josephine McCormack came out to be with Gladys for a week. I was no good for anything for that week. All I could do was try to watch Josephine's every move. So far as I could tell, she was perfect in every way. Then a little later, Ruth Christian came out for a week. She also was perfect in every way. In order to break my spells, Ruth's brother Walter came out from Pioche and stayed with me for a week. We had much fun hunting with our 22 rifles. Especially did we invade the mourning dove flocks. Mother would cook them for us. We also trapped quail with figure-four traps. Papa wouldn't let us shoot the quail.

When I was a little older, there was Dora Fogliani. I thought she also was perfect. She did not reciprocate the feeling. It seems that she had little use for me. I do remember taking her and her sister Mary home from a dance during the wintertime. When I stepped out of the Model T the reality of the Spring Valley winter struck me. I have not felt colder in my lifetime. They lived with it every day.

25.9 Enter Justine

Then there was Justine Jones. The year Gladys, Mike and I went to the first year of high school in Eagle Valley, Seth Jones came to Rose Valley to teach and brought Clarissa, his wife and family with him. Nobody had told me that Seth Jones had a daughter. I first saw her crossing through uncle Les's corral. She was dressed in a mostly white dress and was beautiful. Of course, we became well acquainted, and had much fun playing tag. Our friendship grew, and after Seth and family moved back to Enterprise, I went to Enterprise at every opportunity to see Justine. She went with other boys, I went with other girls, but eventually we were married in the St. George Temple.

25.10   Range Management

While we were young, over a hundred thousand sheep were brought from Southern Utah after the first snowfall every fall and grazed in Lincoln County, Nevada. I can remember seeing fires at night north, south, east and west of Rose Valley. Fires helped keep the coyotes away from the sheep. The range became so overgrazed, that we had destructive floods every summer and sometimes during the winter. The *Taylor Grazing Act,* passed into law in the early 1930's, eliminated the overgrazing and most of the sheep disappeared. The range has slowly come back. Papa said, "When I was a young man, you could ride all day and the grass would touch the stirrups." It is gradually coming back to that again.

25.11   Husband Management

While we were in elementary school, my father, Uncle Pat Devlin and uncle Les were the school board. Teachers were hired through a Teachers' Agency. To find a teacher when I was in the third grade, a likely young lady applicant was selected who lived in San Bernardino, California. When the "School Board" met to fill out her contract, all the details were properly filled in then just before placing it in an envelope, Aunt Noma wrote on the bottom in pencil, "and Murray." Murray was about 20 years old, handsome and unattached. But Aunt Noma's plan kind of backfired. Laura Stephan came, taught us in an able manner, but fell in love with and eventually married Harry, Aunt Nome and Pat's seventeen year-old son. After one year in Nevada Laura Stephan Devlin took her husband Harry and moved back to California — mission accomplished. Harry became a successful cement contractor and they raised a family of three boys, I believe.

25.12   Wayne Meets Piano

While Laura was teaching, a piano was found someplace and Laura began giving piano lessons to Gladys and me. She was paid .50 cents per hour and taught us a full hour once a week. Gladys stayed with it but I gave it up. An hour lesson was too much for a third grader, unfortunately. Gladys always stayed ahead of me. uncle Les and Aunt Ellen ordered a "Wing" piano through the mail, the piano came by rail freight and was a good instrument. I believe Lena and Leah also took lessons.

Later, while Seth and family were here, a piano salesman came into the valley with two pianos in a Model T truck. My father bought the *Monarch* and Seth bought the *Ellington,* both Baldwin pianos and good instruments. Justine and I have the *Ellington* and Karen Prestwich has the *Monarch.* Both were player pianos, but the player actions rotted and have been removed. I remember particularly liking "Repazz Band" on the player piano.

25.13 Recess Activities

While at school in Rose Valley, the only ball game we could play was "Rounders," a ball game in which a runner could be taken out by rolling a ball in front of him as he ran. We didn't have the manpower to man the bases. Of course, "Hop Scotch" was a popular game, as was climbing hills and ledges.

While at high school in Eagle Valley, volleyball was our favorite game. In those days, volleyballs were covered with quality horsehide, and the ball was forever going into the irrigation ditch that ran past the Town Hall, where we went to school. On a cold morning, we would play catch with the volleyball inside the schoolroom, before Mr. Brinley got there. We gradually broke most of the chairs that the Eagle Valley Relief Society had spent hard-earned money to buy. One morning, Lydia Hollinger and I were playing catch in the building and just as Mr. Brinley walked in the door the ball hit a quart of ink and broke it all over the floor. Mr. Brinley always arrived about five minutes of nine, and scold as he would, never did succeed in getting there early enough to stop our rule breaking.

The Movie Set in Condor Canyon While he was there, we minded him. He was an excellent teacher. During our freshman year, we found out that a moving picture company was filming in Condor Canyon. All of us, Gladys, Mike and I, Lorraine Hollinger, Lydia Hollinger and Mabel Hammond, sluffed school, took a Model T Ford and drove to Delmue's Ranch. From there, we started walking down Condor Canyon, but soon came to a railroad handcar. It didn't take much effort for us boys to put it on the tracks and away we went. We had been smart enough to take some cedar posts as brakes, which we soon needed. We came barreling around a curve and there sat the big steam locomotive right in front of us. Using the cedar posts we braked to a stop and put the car off the track.

Luckily, filming was going on and we saw the first movie "fake" of our experience. A small canyon had been made of small lumber, cheesecloth and cement and a fifty-gallon tank was filled with water and placed above it. When the train reached the real railroad bridge, the train stopped, a beautiful actress came out and peered into the chasm just as the 50 gallons of water were released and washed out a tiny bridge in perfect alignment with the large bridge. We were amazed at the fakery. Afterwards we watched any movie we might be fortunate enough to see in Thompson's Opera House, looking for fake scenes. Of course, those movies were silent at that time, with "talking" films coming a bit later.

25.14 Specific Teachers

Now, getting back to Rose Valley, we had Mrs. Joe Delmue as a teacher, Miss Dalton, who later married George Adair, of course Laura Stephan, Miss Marjorie Cross, who was courted by Lawrence Laycook, but they were never married. Then came Miss West, who followed the practice of a story she told. It seems that the teacher sent a note home to a mother saying, "Mary needs a bath, bathe her." The answer came back, "Mary ain't no rose. Don't smell her, learn her." Phoebe West evidently followed that practice. Most of the young lady teachers boarded at our place until they found a husband. Miss West set her hat for Murray Devlin, but he wouldn't cooperate. She became so upset that she quit before the year was out and Amy Devlin finished the year teaching us. Amy was a good teacher, even if she was our cousin. I was an eighth grader.

25.15   Enter the Model T

The Model T Ford came into the country about 1920, as I remember. Pete Indian said to uncle Les one day, "What the matter with Billy Warren?" Les said, "I don't know, Pete, what is the matter with Billy?" Pete replied, "No pushie, no pullie, go like the dickens." Billy Warren had the first Model T in the valleys. Papa soon bought a used one, as did uncle Les and Pat Devlin. One morning, during our second year of high school in Eagle Valley, we were late getting off. Uncle Les said, "Go ahead and take the Ford." Never again did we ride a horse or bicycle to school. Uncle Les even let us take his Model T to Panaca a few times when we went to the third year of high school.

25.16   Doing 'Body Work"'

One night we had been to Caliente to a show. On the way back, Mike wanted me to drive so he could sit in the back with his girl friend, Mary Fogliani. As we entered Panaca, I was suffering from drowsiness and didn't see a young horse head straight for the Ford, landing a-straddle of the hood, then dropping off the other side. Mike was furious. He said, "You stupid idiot, I saw the horse coming fifty feet before he hit us." Needless to say, I was well awake by then. The next day I said, "How are we going to tell your father about this?" Mike said, "We're not." We took that hood off and bent and pounded all the rest of the week, and straightened a fender and Uncle Les never did notice anything different. Previously, he had run into a sheep wagon, when he forgot how to stop. Both Les and my Dad would pull back on the steering wheel and yell "Whoa." Sometimes they would remember the brake. My Dad pushed the back end of our garage south about a foot, but never did mention it to me.

25.17   Tragedy in Utah

After getting the first Ford, Papa took our family to Fayette and other points in Utah to see "Aunt Teenie and Milton" and other relatives. Teenie and Milton's daughter had been playing in a sandbank and the sand had caved and killed her. Soon after, little Henry found a match, went outside during a high wind, lighted some weeds in a pile of pickets, caught his foot between two pickets and did not get loose until his shoe and part of his clothes had burned off. Henry lived for a few months and then died. I admired Teenie and Milton. I don't know how they ever endured the grief. The Fayette Bench was not too kind to them.

When I was thirteen years old, Papa felt that he couldn't take the time to go on the usual visit to Utah, so Mother got me to drive and away Mother, Gladys and I went. Of course, I had already driven the Model T many miles. We had no trouble. While on the ranch at Rose Valley, everybody had to learn to carry his share of the load, as our own children found out later.

25.18   Under the Spreading Chestnut Tree

While we were still in the Rose Valley School, occasionally we would put on a Christmas program in conjunction with the Eagle Valley Town Hall. I well remember one Christmas program in which Edgar Hammond and I had each memorized "The Village Blacksmith" unknown to each other. Each of us launched into "Under the spreading chestnut tree the village smithy stands with great and hairy arms and large and sinewy hands." I had it memorized well then but it is obvious that now I have forgotten even the beginning. Mamma and Papa both said that I was the better of the two of us.

25.19 Twenty Below

At such occasions, it was customary to serve ice cream and cake. At one of the programs, Will Hollinger picked up Justine and sat her on the stage and told her to sing. She was frightened, but she sang beautifully. One evening, after the program was over, we went out and large snowflakes were floating down. It seemed a perfect ending to a special evening. On another occasion, ample snow had already fallen and we took the team and Pat Devlin's horse drawn sleigh. Mother heated large rocks and put them under the blankets for our feet. This helped. When we got back home, the thermometer registered twenty below zero.

25.20 Balancing Act

For a time, public dances were held in the old Eagle Valley Town Hall, with live orchestra and usually the drinking and carousing that followed such affairs. One evening as we went to such a dance in Uncle Les's Ford, Ezie was driving and every time we crossed a ditch, the lights would blink. Ezie said that he intended to borrow a flashlight and fix those lights. To our amazement a hen from Ellen's flock was roosting on the crossbar that held the lights and every time there was a bounce the hen would extend her wings in a balancing act. We left her right there and took her home after the dance in the same position.(See "Old Cluck," 33.1)[1]

As we neared the end of the eighth grade, Maude Frazier came as Deputy Superintendent from Las Vegas and tested us. Gladys tested 12th grate and Mike and I were not far behind. One important instruction we had received was in phonics. Mamma had Papa take us to Pioche and she bought tickets at the railroad station and we rode as train passengers from Pioche to Salt Lake City. Gladys was taken to a doctor for a medical check-up. It was a thrill both for me and Gladys to go to Salt Lake City.

25.21 Going on the Road

While we were under the tutelage of J. Harold Brinley, we accomplished much, including algebra, English, biology, history, short stories and drawings for the County Fair. Mr. Brinley also coached us in a play named "Betsy's Boarders." Lydia was Betsy and Mike was her principal boarder. She was supposed to fire a six shooter at a crisis point in the play. She held the gun, but Lorraine fired his dad's deer rifle out a back window at the exact time she pulled the trigger. We took scenery, the cast and all to Alamo, Nevada and put on Betsy's Boarders for those people. I remember that we traveled all night getting back from Alamo. Henry Hammond's Model T had a rash of flat tires on the way back. We ate breakfast in Wing's restaurant in

---

[1]One event and two versions or two similar events? Take your pick.

Pioche just at sun up. That was the first time I ever tasted ham that was not salty. At home we ate much home grown salt-cured pork and potatoes and gravy.

25.22   Other High Schools

We entered drawings, short stories, poems, the one act play and even public speaking in the Lincoln County Fairs and came away with many prizes. Mr. Brinley had a dislike for Lincoln County High School and claimed that the six of us won more prizes than the entire Lincoln County High. It may or may not be true.

I do remember that while we were in Lincoln County High, English under Miss Ohman was the first subject of the day. Clemens Walker coaxed her through the whole period to let him smoke on the back step. He always won and had his smoke.

Gladys and I were sent to the BAC High School in Cedar City for our senior year of high school and Mike went to West High School in Salt Lake City. Good education was had in both locations.

25.23   Venturing Forth

During the summer of 1928, after graduating from high school, Mrs. Russel's sons Bill and Pat persuaded me that I should go to Montana with them to "earn my fortune." Mrs. Russell had been teaching in Rose Valley. My father was against my going to Montana, but wild horses couldn't hold me back. Bill Russell had a used Oldsmobile that he claimed was the best car on the road. Our first stop in Montana was at Missoula, where the one daughter in the Russell family lived, Mrs. Olsen. I was impressed by the beauty of Montana, Idaho and northern Utah and by the cities passed on the way.

Bill would never drive down Main Street of any place if he could avoid it. He didn't like traffic. The Russel brothers had a job with the McGuire, Blakesly Construction Co., a company that built highway bridges. They got me a job as "flunky" at .50 an hour, a job that was mostly occasional. Before long, I was convinced that Montana was peopled by drunkards. That was the crowd the Russell brothers mixed with. This was during Prohibition, but obtaining liquor was no problem for them. I partook only once, shortly after arriving there. They found an old lady and man who make "homebrew" beer. We went fishing and drank beer. When I came to my senses, I was sitting in an ant bed trying to fish, wondering why it hurt so much. That was enough drinking for me.

Our first job was on a pile-driving rig in Helena, Montana. Telegraph poles were driven into the ground, small end down. The Russells could run and fix anything when they were sober.

The boss, Mr. Sigvaard, depended upon them quite heavily, but every two weeks he had to pay them, and the big drunk would always keep them disabled on the next Monday. On one occasion, Sigvaard put me to "snaking" in the poles, while his son ran the tractor. I almost hit the boss with a pole I was "booming in", but we drove pilings the whole day. On Tuesday, the bleary-eyed Russells showed up. Pat always said, "Son, you keep the tent in shape till we get back." The only time I really resented it was when we ran out of food because they had drunk up all the money. The next location was Great Falls, Montana, on another pile driving operation. Over the Fourth of July, I became so homesick that I was going to "jump a freight" and go home. The Russell brothers said, "If you can't buy a train ticket and go back as you should, you'll stay in Montana until you're an old man." Finally, I earned enough money, and bought a ticket home in August. While we were in Great Falls, the first place they hit was "Hobo Jungle". I had never seen so many derelicts in my life. They couldn't afford to buy "Moonshine Whiskey", so got canned heat, drained the alcohol off it and drank it. That was a sure way to shorten one's life. One of the bums called me "Sonny". I was glad when we left that place. While the boys were carousing, I started walking into Great Falls and attending shows and occasionally a dance. One girl at the dance hall particularly appealed to me. I danced with her often one evening and finally asked her for a date. She said, "I'll ask my husband; he plays in the orchestra." That ended any attempt at romance in Montana. Our last location was Lewiston, in central Montana. I was glad to get on the Milwaukee and St. Paul electric and head for home. I thought that Butte, Montana was especially beautiful as we approached it after dark. My parents picked me up in Modena Utah and I felt bad to see that Mother looked pale and worried. My Dad had just about written me off after I left against his will. But soon things were back to normal. He was glad to have my help on the ranch before they sent Gladys and me to junior college in Cedar City. While I was gone, I wrote Justine a letter or two telling her I was in the "North Country". She also doubted that she would ever see me again. My parents' ambition was to give opportunities to Gladys and me that they didn't have; thus the plan to send us to college. We were eager to go. Besides, Harold Brinley had always preached college to us.

25.24 Slim Sandwiches and a Drunken Beatuy

While yet in Montana, on the first job at Helena, we decided to take board at a small caf. We paid for each week in advance. During the first few days, meals, including lunch, were ample. Then the amount of food served began to diminish, and lunch became two slices of white bread with a slice of ham in between and maybe a piece of celery. I ate too slowly and couldn't keep up with the crowd at breakfast time. When I worked a ten-hour day, the food in me would run out at about nine and one-half hours. "Big Ole", the Swede, would say, "Set down kid, we'll finish." Just as an aside, I saw a beautiful girl in an evening gown "drunk as a skunk" at a dance in Helena. I wondered about her.

25.25 Upgrading to the Model A

I believe that the Model A Ford came out in 1928. Our Student Body President was employed at Thorley Motors and he announced it from the stage at an assembly program. We had to crank the Model T but the Model A had a battery and starter. The Model T had a low gear with the left pedal down and a high gear with the pedal up. The Model T had a reverse pedal in the middle; the Model A had three forward gears on the stick shift and reverse on the other corner. The Model T brake was the third pedal; the Model A brake was on a pedal separate from the gearshift. Henry Ford said that you could have a Model T in any color you wanted, just so it was black; the Model A came in colors other than black. The Model A had a solid steel and wooden body, with windows that rolled up and down. In starting the Model T, you had to take hold of the crank and spin the motor fast enough to generate a spark to fire the plugs. On cold mornings, we sometimes put a pan of hot coals under the oil pan, or sometimes drained the oil, heated it and put it back in.

I believe that antifreeze came into being about at the time of the Model A. Before that, we covered the hood with blankets, or just drained the radiator. Ethyl alcohol was tried as an antifreeze, but boiled away too rapidly. While cranking a Model T, you had better not straddle the crank handle with your thumb, or you would probably get a broken arm, especially if you forgot to retard the spark. T Model T throttle was a lever on a notched scale on the steering wheel, spark lever on the other side. The Model A had a foot feed, with automatic ignition adjustment. Just as an aside, before the Model A came out, somebody said that Jim Hollinger had purchased a Dodge car with battery and a self-starter. I commented, "It will never work." A man was crossing the street and a Dodge car ran into him. He said to the driver, "Why didn't you honk the horn?" The driver said, "I don't need to, I have a sign on the front of my car." The pedestrian said, "What sign?" The driver said, "Dodge, Brothers!"

While being raised on the ranch, we learned all the skills that go with ranching. Gladys and I could milk cows, tend chickens, tend pigs, feed calves, weed in the garden, irrigate and etc. I learned to drive a team, mow hay, rake hay, pitch hay onto a wagon, run a grain binder with team, haul and stack grain bundles, feed a threshing machine; the last requiring the most skill. We were forever working and struggling to keep an irrigation dam in the creek. In the early 1930's the CCC camps came in and built a cedar log crib dam for us, but it didn't hold. It was against regulations to build a concrete permanent dam for individuals.

25.26   Wayne and Justine

I kept going to see Justine at every opportunity. One time when I went over after a long lapse, I asked a local boy, Lamar Truman, what he was doing for the winter. He said, "Trying to take your girl away from you." Indeed, Justine had been on a date with him the night before. That cooled me off and I stayed away for at least a month, then one day I received a short note from Justine, saying that she had been very ill with the quinsy and would I please come to see her. It was March, and we had had rains and serious flooding everywhere and the road was washed crosswise and lengthwise, but I made it clear to the wash just before you reach Enterprise. I made it to the middle of the flood and drowned out. Within minutes, Mr. Pickering was there with a team. He had been given the job of pulling cars out of the wash. Well, we had a good reunion. Justine was very thin and peaked looking, but she had her spunk back. We got Alwyn and Melva and went to Veyo. We just soaked in the sun and Justine was very cross. She was mending. A few years after we were married she had to have those tonsils removed.

25.27   Working for Wages

Later, during the summer, I had returned from Enterprise rather late and was put to mowing hay. It was a warm day, the ride was smooth and I went to sleep on the mower. When I awoke, the team had mowed a diagonal right angling across the piece I was mowing. I came awake and really got to work. By the time Papa came down, practically all of the tell-tale sign had been mowed under.

Every summer, Mike, Jack Lytle and I figured on pitching hay for Billy Warren at $3.00 per day and board. Aunt Maggie never cut down on the quantity of food served. There was always more than enough of delicious food. One afternoon, we unloaded a load of hay and it was only four o'clock, so we went back to the field for another load. Just as we came out of the field, here came Billy in his car. He said, "Unhook em right there boys and tie them to the wagon." Dinner was ready and nobody had better be late at one of Aunt Maggie's meals. We unloaded the hay after supper.

On another day, we had a load of loose wild hay on the wagon and a thunderstorm came up, just west of Eagle Valley. It rained a few drops, the wind started to blowing and blew that load of hay right off the wagon.

On another day, we were hauling hay for Uncle Milt Damron. I had our team there and we had cleaned some hay and pitched it into a net on the wagon. I had the trip rope clear, but when Milt said "Giddap" to his team, my team took one step ahead. The wagon wheel pinned the trip rope, I fastened it to the net and immediately the taut rope tripped it, hitting me, blacking both eyes and giving me a nose bleed from both nostrils.

25.28 Attending BAC

The fall of 1928, after I had been to Montana, Gladys, Mike and I went to Cedar City to attend the BAC (Branch Agricultural College) Junior College. We rented a small apartment from Arthur Fife, Geology instructor at the college. I believe that I signed up for 18 quarter hours and planned to Major in Chemical Engineering. Having gone to the fourth year of high school there, I was surprised. One of the other seniors had told me that college was a cinch. "Just a rehash of what you had in high school", he said. How wrong he was! The studying was much heavier than anything we had ever had, but we were thrilled. Who would have ever thought that there was so much to be had so close to home! The instructors were outstanding in every class and the enrollment was small enough that one could get individual help from his instructors. I was captivated by the band and orchestra under the direction of Roy Halverson, and I played a baritone horn in the band. That was an available school instrument, so I played it. Gladys and I had taken piano lessons from Mr. Tollestrup during the senior high school year, so reading music was no trouble for me. Neither Mike nor I had any chance in sports. We had never had a chance to participate when we were younger. I believe that 1928 was the first year that BAC had a football team. It generated a lot of school spirit, as did the basketball team, which was excellent.

25.29 Debating and Other Activities

After we had acclimated, I tried out for the debating team and made it. The other debating members were Rex Harris, Zola Smith and Lavern Gentry. We defeated Dixie College and debated at Snow College, winning there also, I believe. I also tried out for a play, got a small part and got to travel into Southern Utah to a few towns to let people know what was being done at their college.

The college put on at least one Grand Opera every year during the spring quarter and I tried for Pa Manning's chorus and made it. The rehearsals were taking so much time that Mr. Manning said, "If any of you don't have enough time, just drop out." I dropped out, but didn't go to the office and do the necessary paper work. That is the only F I ever got in school.

Mr. Halverson used to get a group of us and go up Cedar Canyon in the evening. We would build a fire and roast marshmallows and he would play his violin. It was one of the most beautiful times we had ever had.

I was still going with Justine and it seemed that every girl that appealed to me at BAC was related to Justine. Mrs. Russell was still boarding at our house and every time I came home she would say, "Which Jones girl is it this time?"

25.30   Walking the Girls Home

Gladys came home after the first quarter, because of health reasons and mike moved in with Floyd Whicker and Jay Applegate, so I was left alone for two quarters. My parents were paying for most of my schooling, so I studied hard and allowed myself the recreation of an occasional show and the Friday night school dance, which was free. One night I set myself the goal of seeing how many girls I could walk home from the dance. At about 11:30, I was dancing with Mildred Farnsworth and she said, "I'm so tired." I said, "Would you like me to walk you home?" She said, "Yes", and away we went. I dropped her off on foot and ran back to the dance. Edith Warren made about the same comment, and I walked her home and ran back to the dance. I was dancing with Margaret Pryor, Justine's cousin, and they started to play "Home Sweet Home". Of course, I asked her if I could take her home. But she lived at least a mile away in the eastern part of town. It started snowing, but I had on a felt hat and overcoat. Somebody had hurt Margaret's feelings and she started to cry. She didn't dare to take a boy friend into the house, because her father wouldn't allow it. She leaned on my shoulder and cried in that snowstorm until my overcoat started to leak through. Finally, I got away and went home to dry out. I guess it served me right.

25.31   The Costs of Dating

On another occasion, I took Margaret to a basketball game, with the agreement that we would go to the town dance after the game. I had only fifty cents, which should get me into the dance, with the game to be on our student body cards. When I picked her up, Dorothy Dix was there to go with us. When we got to the game, the girls didn't produce their cards, so I charged it at the window. I knew the boy who was there. After we got into the gym, they both produced cards to show me. I was burning just a bit. After the game was over, the dance hadn't started, so they wanted some ice cream. They ordered ice cream and I ordered water. They said, "Aren't you hungry?" I truthfully said, "No". I knew the girl at the counter and charged that. When we got to the dance, they had a new ticket taker and he wanted a dollar. Luckily, I borrowed fifty cents from Mike and got into the dance, although my enthusiasm for dancing was pretty low. About an hour into the dance, the fellow brought fifty cents to me for a refund. The next time I saw Margaret she said, "Where have you been lately?" I said, "Oh, around." She didn't know what a difficult evening I had had making expenses with her and Dorothy. I worked hard and got good grades. I did have a job cleaning the creamery for an hour a day.

25.32   Potato-Picking Date

During the fall of 1928, I borrowed the "topless" Model T that Mike had over there for a week or two and went to Enterprise to see Justine. I took her for a ride in that car, with only a small piece of oily canvas for a lap robe. The ride didn't last long. We froze! The next day I volunteered to help dig potatoes. We dug potatoes all day in a snowstorm! We earned every spud we got.

25.33   Drag Racing

I had been invited to come to Enterprise and go deer hunting. I got a coat and stood by the road leading out of Cedar City toward Enterprise. A fellow came along in a one ton Chevy truck going into Cedar. He said, "Get in, I'm coming right back." On the way back, he started racing with some fellows in a Model A Ford. He beat them on the level, but they passed us on the hill near Iron Mountain. When we got to the top of the hill, he said, "Now watch me take them." He stepped it up to fifty miles an hour on that dirt road and gave them the horn. They wouldn't let us pass and he said, "I haven't got any brakes!" Rather than hit them, he left the road and we ran into a substantial cedar tree. We hit it head on and the truck flipped upside down, flew through the air and came straight down on the cab. All the glass broke straight down and the cab telescoped about six inches. We both climbed out the broken windshield. The fellows in the Model A, who had obviously been drinking, were too stunned to get out. They were dumbfounded when they saw us walking around. We waited for another car to come along, got plenty of help and tipped the truck back on its wheels. One front wheel was folded like cardboard. The guys offered us a ride on the running board of the Model A and I arrived in Enterprise pretty much on schedule. They would only believe I had been in a wreck when I showed them the bump on my head. We didn't get any deer.

25.34   An Update of Girl Friends

Then there was Lillis. Her father was Sam Jones, Seth's first cousin. I noticed that during some of the speech contests, in which I took part, Lillis was in the small audience. Rex said she didn't have any interest in him, so it must have been me. That was unusual, because she was a sophomore and I was a lowly freshman. At any rate, I got up courage enough to ask her for a date and she accepted. We hit it off well right from the start. Of course we would, she was a Jones. I was not LDS at the time, so that was against me. We were getting along so well that I brought her to Rose Valley on one of our trips home. At the first opportunity, my Dad got me off alone and said, "Good Lord, son, don't marry that one. If you had her you'd have to ask for permission to breathe." Lillis had one aggravating trick that really bothered me. She would wait until five or six students were talking together, then she would tell one some unpleasant thing that another person present in the group was supposed to have said about him. We gradually tapered off and when I got back from Boston, she was engaged to marry Leo Larsen. She majored in education, taught school in Cedar Valley, then in town and eventually became Superintendent of Schools in Iron County. She and Leo managed to raise a family, also. In the meantime, Justine was not letting grass grow under her feet there in Enterprise.

Then there was Wilma Bulloch. She was a beautiful girl and a good classic dancer. Miss Bastow had her classes dance on the lawn on good days. But Wilma was cross-eyed and obviously life for her was dull. I asked her to go to a dance with me and she accepted. She was as good at ballroom dancing as classical dancing, and soon became popular. In fact, after a few weeks, she had hardly a glance for me. Mission accomplished.

25.35   Heading for Boston

Mr. Myers urged our parents to send Mike, Gladys and me to the New England Conservatory in Boston, Mass. (we were all "Geniuses"). That conservatory was commonly called the "Boston Conservatory", and someone had indeed set up a "Boston Conservatory" in a couple of rooms in a flat on Huntington Ave and took the money of some of the uninformed. Fortunately, Mr. Myers knew of this and got us into the right school. We bought Billy Warren's 1924 four cylinder Buick, with cloth top. If Buick ever made a "lemon." that one was it.

Adventures of the Road

We traveled on muddy road from Rose Valley to Cedar City, then found that 91 was graveled to Salt Lake City. Mike revved it up to 35 miles an hour and we found that the boot in the right front tire made it "gallop." So, we had to put the tire with the boot on a back wheel. To change tires, the wheels were left on the car and the tire pried off with a tire iron. Of course, a hand pump was a must. On the way, to Salt Lake, we found that the wobbling hind wheel sheared off the "dog" that held the brakes over the drum, thus leaving us with no brakes. On the second day, we stopped in Salt Lake to have it repaired, and since we were then on the Lincoln Highway, we decided to travel after dark. The great Lincoln Highway was also a graveled road. We were going along, with no other traffic to be seen, and suddenly came to a washout that had not been flagged. We crashed into it with such impact that a pair of shoes Gladys had put on the back seat were thrown out and we never found them again. When we came out of the far side of the washout, our lights were knocked out. Having no light to find the trouble, we got in a deep mud rut on the great Lincoln Highway and went on and on the dark until we came to Rock Springs, Wyoming, after midnight.

After a short rest in a motel, we struck out again and found that about 40 miles of road were under construction, with cars obliged to fend for themselves out in the brush. After a half of a day of that, we finally came to our first oiled, at Laramie. Mike stepped the Buick up to 45 and promptly knocked out a connecting rod bearing. We had to have that repaired there in Laramie. Mike could fix most anything, but he didn't have the tools for that. After Laramie, we went along pretty well until we reached Omaha. The Bear River Cut Off had just been finished, so we took that in order to avoid traffic. The road was newly graded of wet soil, a road grader crowded us to the side and we tipped over gently on the Buick's side. Mike, whose face was practically in the mud, took and handful of soil and said, "Good old Nebraska mud." The road crew promptly pulled us back on the road and we were eastward bound again. In Iowa, we found that most of the roads were capped with brick, which made for a rough ride in high-pressure tires. We were going on a good two lane road when one "farmer" stopped in the line ahead of us to talk to a man in a car coming from the other direction. Mike went straight at the oncoming car, then threw the Buick through the gap between the two, hitting each one just a little. Our brake had failed again. We asked Mike to stop, but no way would he stop for those "stupid farmers." Next, we came to a family in an old Dodge runabout. They really looked poverty stricken. They stopped us and asked if we could give them a tow. We said, "Sure" and hooked onto them and towed them about 15 miles to the nearest town. They offered to pay but Mike said, "Charge it to the dust and let the rain settle it." They were very, very grateful. We avoided Chicago by going through Chicago Heights.

Car Problems

We were still on our way east when we came to Ohio. About midway in the state, Mike said, "Look out, I think we've got a flat tire." I looked out and the hind wheel passed us by and rolled into a farm yard. We carried it back and the farmer let us park the Buick and work on it in his yard. We needed a key for the hind wheel and the man took us into Van Wert to get it. To them, Van Wert was at the center of everything. We had never heard of it, but didn't say so to them.

As we went through Mansville, Ohio, we got off the main road into the avenues. We had to fix a flat tire in front of the most elegant spread we had ever seen. No one said a word to us. Then came Pittsburgh! There was a long, downhill grade into Pittsburgh, Gladys and I failed to direct Mike on the road around town, and we wound up right in the heart of downtown Pittsburgh, then the brake had sheared off again. Mike slammed into a new Buick with a chauffeur. He said, "You get out and argue, I'm driving." The man, who was very proper, but very upset, got out and said, "Why did you run into my car?" I said, "Our brakes failed." He said, "What are you doing in Pittsburgh with failed brakes?" I said, "We are trying to get out." He said, "You won't get out until we get these bumpers repaired." I said, "Lead out to the garage and we will fix it and pay for it." We followed him, with his chauffeur, for a few blocks, but he led us into the service entrance. We had to go around several blocks again. He had his chauffeur take a left turn on a "NO LEFT TURN" sign. He went that away and we went the other way. Mike said, "I won't break the law for nobody." The last time we saw him, he had his head about three feet out the window, watching us get away. We stopped to get it fixed again, and expected every motorcycle policeman to arrest us, but we remembered that the only cop that had spoken to us said, "Get in your cars so I can clear up this mess of traffic."

The man who fixed our car that time, got a road map and plotted a route for us away from Philadelphia and New York. Easton, Ogalla, Harrisburg, Hartford, Springfield and Worcester are all larger than Salt Lake City, but we made it. As you will notice, Mike was driving in all the "rough spots." I didn't have the courage to negotiate the big cities. We managed to come through New York City and Philadelphia on our way back with the Flint, a car with hydraulic brakes.

But the Buick was not yet through giving us trouble. We stopped in a "Tourist room" in a private home inn Western, MA, and found our battery dead the next morning. The family had a boy just about our age. We were struggling to push the car and get it rolling. The boy got in his car and drove on their lawn to get around us, with never an offer of help. We got it started, and finally reached Huntington Ave. in Boston. We had a picture of the Conservatory, thought we had reached it and stopped. To our dismay, it was the *Museum of Fine Arts*. The battery was dead again and we tried to push the car to get it going. Some of the attendants in the museum saw us, came out and helped us push, but to no avail. It was a sight to see those properly addressed attendants pushing on that old car with the bedraggled kids who were in trouble. The battery was dead beyond rejuvenation, so we rented a battery to get us to the Conservatory. I figure that we took nineteen days getting there. To store the Buick cost $6.00 a month, so after we had found an apartment, we sold it for $20.00.

25.36   The Conservatory

The Conservatory was and is a state-run college, with accredited courses in semester hours. They had apartments to rent listed, and we found one to our liking at 31 Elmore St. #3; a good two miles from the school, but Boston had a good public transportation system. We sub-rented from a Miss Allen, who had two bedrooms, a living room for us, plus use of the kitchen, which she didn't use. She also had a piano, which we could practice during the day while she was away. It was a satisfactory arrangement for the school year. The first night we were at the apartment we asked her how to get down town. She gave car numbers and transfers, which totally confused us, so we walked and walked.

Getting Accustomed to City Life

Finally, we reached downtown, which was larger and more confusing than we had anticipated. I remember watching a boy my age serve milk shakes by taking the full glass, pushing it with a twist of the wrist and having it stop right before the right customer.

It didn't take us long to get onto the ropes of the elevated and subway systems. Standard fare was a dime to any place in Boston, or Charleston and Cambridge on the other side of the "tube" under the Charles River. The great problem in Boston at that time was the lack of an escape route for cars after they went in town. About half the time there was a traffic jam down next to the bay that you wouldn't believe. There was a Rapid Transit system that ran out to Lexington and Concord, etc. and came in underground at great speed. The boast of the rail system was "two million a day."

Studies at the Conservatory

Enrolling at the conservatory was more expensive than we had anticipated. Their opening statement was, "What are you taking besides private piano instruction?" We had Mr. Mason of the great Mason family as a piano teacher, Mr. Reasoner as violin teacher, harmony class under Mr. Curry, Solfeggio under Mr. LeNome, who was French, used his own textbooks, which were in English, but kept us constantly confused because he would forget to speak English. We had English Literature under Dr. Smeath, and theory under a series of lecturers. Pianos could be rented for ten cents an hour in the basement, which was indeed a place of many, many sound, all out of tune, because the pianos would not stay n tune in the atmosphere of the basement. We thought Gladys was quite advanced on piano, but she tested "Elementary Beginner," along with Mike and me. We settled right in and studied and practiced quite hard.

The Hill Family

We were fortunate in having Billy Hill in harmony class with us. After getting acquainted, we were invited to his parents' home on Jamaica Plain. They were common folks, even if they did have a maid. Mr. Hill was a salesman for the Browning Sporting Arms Co., from which has since come the BAR and others. He was very amiable and so was Mrs. Hill. The children were Billy, about age nineteen, and a member of Les Brown's dance band, Kay about age eighteen and Frank, age seventeen. We were surprised upon visiting the Hills the first time, in seeing young Frank smoking a pipe right along with his father. His mother wanted him to quit and be a non-smoker like Mike and me, but he never did succeed while we were there. Kay and Mike promptly "hit it off," even though Kay was supposed to be practically engaged to a Putnam young man. She did marry Putnam later, he becoming vice president of the Cuticura Soap Co. Billy attended harmony class with us, and having played until late the night before, usually managed to copy the harmony assignment from Gladys. Billy had a steady girl friend, named Verer (Vera).

They boasted of their maid's ability to cook brown bread and Boston Baked Beans, but it seemed to me like an invitation to indigestion. Her clam chowder was better. We visited them quite often and Frank came to see us occasionally. He always wanted to play poker and devised a system for beating us quite regularly.

Meet the Sea

We went with them to Portland Maine and Casco Bay, to an island where their relatives lived, the head of the house making his living from fishing. He took us fishing — in a heavy fog, guiding by buoys, each with a bell. We asked him what would happen if he shut the motor off, so he did. The boat went parallel with the trough, dipping way over on each side. Gladys got very seasick. That was a life different from any we have seen before or since.

The Maine coastline is beautiful, but looks harsh. On the steamship ride back to Portland, Frank found a poker game in the ship's hold, promptly cut himself in and landed a few dollars richer than he had been. We were all sitting on the deck, enjoying the ride, when the steamship hit some open water. It gave some heavy pitches and knocked everybody off his chair. Mike said, "Don't look now, but a woman has got me by the leg!" She was holding on for dear life.

Great Performances

The winter went fast enough. I have on regret. Rachmaninoff was playing a concert in the Gainsborough Hall at the Conservatory, and I couldn't persuade the rest of the kids to go and wouldn't go alone. That was a chance of a lifetime.

There were fine musicians at the Conservatory. San Roma was "Pianist in Residence." There was a fine orchestra and a brass band beyond compare. The lead trumpeter was a girl. We met a thirteen-year-old boy who could play Mozart on the piano like a dream. Whenever Mr. Lenome was absent, Tucker, a senior boy, taught his class, and we learned on that day. Tests were administered in a large room, with a "testee" in every other seat, with monitors at every hand. Mike was almost thrown out for asking a kid the date, before the test had begun. One day I dropped into Gainsborough Hall to listen to a Russian woman violinist. She played

Mozart concerto and it sounded as if the music were coming from the heavens. The acoustics were excellent. Mr. Reasoner said, "You don't hear fiddling like that very often."

We made friends with Fernstein, a Jewish boy, who played Dvorak's Humoresque like a dream. Mike was so good at scales that Mr. Mason appointed him to teach scales to a Jewish girl. Our Sears Roebuck violins didn't last long. The Stanley Co. of Stanley Steamer fame, was offering good violins at $150.00 each. We (Mike and I) bought one each. One day, while standing in a hallway at the Conservatory, first came Lenome, trotting with his bow tie floating at each side. Next a professor with a blink, then Chadwick, staggering with cane at the front. A girl said, "They don't have to be crazy to work here, but it helps."

Sundry Details

The Conservatory professors preached against jazz and said it would ruin one's playing. They seemed not to know that in the very basement of the building there was a jazz band beyond compare. Those well-trained kids could play jazz like they breathed it.

We wen to Fenway Park once and saw Babe Ruth play with the Yankees. He got no hits that day.

Gladys seemed to be a bit confused with the Transit systems, but she could take $5.00 and go in town alone and get back with no trouble. One day she was supposed to meet Kay Hill at the Milk Station, but got off at the Water Station instead. After not seeing Kay at the station, she walked up to the street, and met Kay on the sidewalk; of course, naturally. There were only thousands of people there. One day Mike and I went with her to a sale in Filene's basement. Once we got in there, we could get out only by following the crowd to the opposite entrance. We had never seen so many screaming, shoving women. Once was enough for that.

The Boston cops were characters. Every afternoon one would carry his little box to the intersection near school. One day before Christmas, Gladys and I were laden with packages waiting on the sidewalk for him to change signals. He saw us and stopped all traffic, escorting us across, with a constant chatter about Santa Claus. If one need a lesson in use of profanity, he could get it from a Boston cop. Bert Dillion went with Gladys some. One day we were with him in his Uncle's car. We got in a hopeless traffic jam. Bert, Mike and I kept rocking the Model T sideways until we got it on the sidewalk. It was simple to drive on the sidewak out of the traffic jam. If Bert got a ticket, his uncle was in City Hall and would "fix" it for Bert. We went to watch the BAA Marathon with Kay in her car, she slammed into a car ahead of her, bloodying her nose on the windshield. Mike gave the guy $15.00 to "forget about it."

After we had been in Boston for awhile, Mike and Kay decided that I needed a date, so Kay arranged one for me with a girl she knew at school. We met on Huntington Avenue and had dinner at Child's. She smoked cigarettes on a long holder and we had nothing in common; she didn't care about hearing about the ranch; I was not interested in what she might be doing. After the dinner, she got on a car and went her way, I got an another car and went my way. Kay did have a girl friend who was twenty-nine years old and supposed to be engaged. She and I could have a good time together — odd for someone so "ancient" and someone so young. I was then eighteen.

25.37 No Horns

ONE TIME Mike and Gladys arrived at the Hill residence without me. Someone said, "Where's Wayne?" Mike said, "He broke his leg and we had to shoot him." Mike told the Hills that we were Jack Mormons; that's why our horns hadn't grown. In fact, up to this time in my life, religion played no part; the same with Mike and Gladys.

25.38 The Road Home

The end of the school year was fast coming to an end. We shopped around and found a Flint Automobile than was in good condition, and had hydraulic brakes. Mike and I were obviously not twenty-one, the age to buy a car, but we pretended that Gladys was and she signed for it. She was twenty-one the following August. We sent to Nevada and got license plates, so were able to get by without a driver's license. It was a good car and would run all day and all night if you wanted it to. We came back through New York city and Philadelphia. As we were driving into New York, Mike got confused and was heading the wrong way. He turned around and landed on the sidewalk on Broadway, with the float stuck. We unstuck it and stopped long enough to walk a little way on Fifth Avenue, just to say we had been there.

Kay was determined that she was coming back with us. Mike was confidentially not in favor of it. He knew there would be no maid in Rose Valley. She shed a bucket full of tears, but we left her in Boston. Twenty years later, she was going to a Church convention in Los Angeles and came here to see us all. She had married Putnam and had on son; and, I'm sure a maid. She was impressed about how capable Eldon was with the pickup and horse. She wished that her son could learn to do that. She ate dinner with us at Mother's and seemed as much at home as could be. She had learned to mix Royalty with commoners. She and Mike hit it off again as well as ever, but Mary didn't let that develop.

We were were coming home in the Flint, everything went well until we hit graveled road, then the tires went, one by one. Since they were an odd size, we had to work on tires all the way from Wyoming to Salt Lake City, where we could get the right size. We sold the Flint to a fellow in Pioche for more than we paid for it. He got the brilliant idea when winter came, of putting kerosene in the radiator and ruined the motor.

25.39 Home Again

Back to work on the ranch. We did display our knowledge of the instruments to our relatives, who weren't overly impressed, I'm sure. Three more years on Boston would have made good performers and well educated musicians of us, but the Great Depression hit, and we did well to get back to Cedar City that Fall. We found that Mr. Halverson was a better violin teacher than Mr. Reasoner had been.

25.40   Death of Boyd Jones

During the year of 1931, Justine's brother Boyd died on January ninth. I went from Cedar City as soon as I could, catching a ride with Sylva Jones, a teacher. The snow had been deep and was smelting. Sylva got stuck just outside of Newcastle and I had to walk to Enterprise. It was dark and I had to walk out in the brush, because I would fall in the deep ruts. When I got to Enterprise, the only car available was Uncle Dell's old Dodge. He wouldn't let me drive it, and he got stuck on the main street in Enterprise. Soon, here came Sylva in her car. Some CCC boys had come along and literally lifted her car out of the ruts, following to lift it out when she went again. I was very relieved to see her.

> The Seth Jones household were the saddest people I had every seen. Boyd had fallen off a load of wood and had ruptured a blood vessel in his abdomen. Being the quiet boy that he was, he didn't say anything until he couldn't stand the pain. They rushed him to St. George, but it was too late. He died soon after that. When I visited them at Grandma's (Aunt Lucy's) house, Clarissa and Justine could hardly stop crying, Alwyn had withdrawn into himself and Stanton, although younger, was very sad. Seth acted as if he had just given up and life wasn't worth living. I have never seen him like that, before or since. I stayed until Sylva went back, and hope that my visit helped some. The road had dried a little when we went back, and she didn't get stuck.

One often wonders who Boyd would have married, where he would have lived, and on and on.

25.41 The Great Depression

In the spring of 1931, Mike and I graduated from the BAC. I went back in the fall, but needed courses that weren't taught there, gave up after the fall quarter and went back to Rose Valley to try to make a living during the Depression.

The school year of 1930-31 had been a good one for me. I took many courses, debated, contested in speech contests and had a minor part in a play or two. I won one medal for being "outstanding in extemporaneous speaking."

25.42 Creeping towards Marriage

Justine and I kept seeing each other and I hinted that I would like to marry her. I was convincingly informed that such a step would be taken in the Temple only. I was baptized on April 1, 1932 in the Veyo swimming pool. The only Church meeting I attended were in Enterprise. The one I remember most clearly was when President Grant stopped in Enterprise for a Sunday and talked in Sacrament Meeting. He said, "People ask me for whom I'm going to vote. Mark this down. I'm going to vote for Herbert Hoover!" President Grant spoke his mind, even if newspaper reporters were there. I was impressed by his stand, but actually voted for Roosevelt. We all probably would be ahead today if the nation had taken his advice.

Papa had purchased a 1929 six-cylinder Chevrolet sedan in 1930, I believe, and it was transportation to all of us. On January 17, 1933 Rosella Bauer and LaVon Jones wanted to get married in the St. George Temple. The old green Chevy seemed to be the only solution, so Rosella and LaVon, Seth and Clarissa and Justine and I went to St. George to get the job done. Of course, Seth was the only one able to go into the Temple with them; Grandma Adair was already there. After it was all over, it started to rain. It looked as if a fog was hanging on the mountains. When we reached Cottonwood, the "fog" was snow. I made it to the lane leading into Enterprise, but stuck about halfway through. We had a real struggle wallowing through the drifts, but made it. I was snowed in for a whole week, much to the approval of Justine and me. During that week it warmed up to eighteen below one afternoon.

The Hoover administration arranged to have a lot of surplus wheat ground and distributed to the farmers. Billy Warren had to hire a truck to haul his three carloads, my dad got three tons, Seth got five bags. The old politics was rank, even during Hoover's administration.

25.43 Marriage at the Temple

I worked at every job that I could, saving a little money. In order to be married in the Temple, I had to be ordained an Elder and had to pay tithing. Bishop Joseph Terry was our Bishop in Enterprise. One day I gave some money to Durward Terry to give to his father as tithing from me. When I went in to be interviewed for a recommend, the Bishop had no record of tithing having been paid. We summoned Durward and there was the tithing money in his coat pocket where he had left it.

Our wedding date was set for November 15, 1933. My parents and Gladys went to St. George and waited for us to come out. When I was asked for our marriage certificate in the Temple, I had forgotten it. I went rushing to the Big Hand Motel where I had left it. When the ceremony was over and I was changing clothes, and old Temple worker said, "Marriage is like a piece of cake. There is a thick coating of frosting on it, but when that's gone, it isn't nearly as good." Another Temple worker apologized for his remark, but the memory has stuck.

I had raised 150 turkeys, had picked them, and we went with Papa and Mamma and Gladys to Los Angeles to get paid and to have a short honeymoon. When we got to Los Angeles, we found Myrtle Damron's friend Blondie and she drove the Chevy for us all over the area. I was always lost, as was my Dad. He would get me to stop, so he could talk to a cop, but when he came back, we were just as lost as before. While in Los Angeles, we bought Cane wallboard to put in the house where we live now. The house had been used as a granary and our work was cut out for us. The cook stove was one I had hauled form an old mine hear Deer Lodge, our heating stove was a $2.49 rolled metal Sears Roebuck heater. I had hauled some wood with team and wagon. There was no electricity. I was "bare bones" indeed, but we were happy! While we lived in Las Vegas, I received a call from "Sonny" Royce. He had been working for Pat Devlin when we were married and was not LDS. He said, "You should remember me. I worked for Pat Devlin when you were married and always wanted a marriage just like yours if I could. I moved to Salt Lake City and married a Mormon girl. She eventually got me into the church and into the Temple. We have five children and every one of them has had a Temple wedding in the Los Angeles Temple. Yours was a perfect example."

25.44   Raising Turkeys

During the spring of 1934 we ordered 800 turkey poults and went into raising turkeys. Seth was doing quite well at Enterprise. I made a brooder down near the meadow and built a little makeshift cabin for us to live in. We got a little Shepherd dog named Skippy. As the turkeys grew and were put outside, on roosts at night, coyotes were a problem. On a night or two, something would frighten the turkeys and they would fly in every direction, completely senseless. I would drag our mattress out among them and we would spend the rest of the night out there. I put out so many poison "baits" for coyotes that I finally poisoned the dog; a real blow to us. I would lead the flock out into the grain field and onto the meadow. On a hot day, a hawk would stampede them into the willow patch, with no feed being eaten. On a cloudy day, they would chase a hawk. One day they followed a hawk from post to post clear to Devlin's orchard. On another day, I got my violin out, started to play, and stampeded the whole bunch practically on top of me. One day my Father and I were loading hay near the grain field. Justine, who was pregnant, came and stood near us, not saying a word. When I got her to talking, she had shot a snake. She was sitting at the cabin window sewing and a Red Racer had reared up and looked her right in the eye. She grabbed the twenty-two , shot it through the body, it tried to get away, but she went out and finished it off through the head. She was a dead shot! So far as I know, I never lost a turkey to a coyote.

We raised the turkeys. I had borrowed money and had to buy feed to "top them off." I hired several local people to pick the turkeys and shipped them all to Los Angeles just before Thanksgiving. We came out enough ahead to pay the $45.00 for Farrel. The doctor was Dr. MacFarlane, who had a very good reputation. Justine's labor was about thirty-six hours and I was with her all the way. Farrel was a fairly large baby; only about seven pounds, nine ounces, but fairly large framed. He was finally born at four o'clock in the morning of November 10th. I was so elated that

I felt like climbing to the top of "Old Main" and announcing it to the world. He brought more joy to our home that only a child can bring. He didn't walk until he was fourteen months old, but seemed always able to "think things through." One day, after he was walking we had a couple of inches of snow and Justine put on his overshoes and he walked around the house saying, "Walk, walk, walk," all the while looking back at his tracks. His tracks would be rather hard to fill.

We sent to Washington D.C. and got pamphlets on how to raise children. We were very fussy about the food we fed any of them. I think it is unwise to feed a baby from the table while he is still young. During the winter of 1934-35, Justine had to nurse Farrel by the stove we had. I very bravely got up to make a fire for her for a few nights. Within a week I was practically ill from loss of sleep. It seemed that Justine had to get up and make her own fire. One night we were awakened by loud crashes in the area of the kitchen. Justine said, "I think there is a cow in there". I had caught a wood rat by the nose in a mousetrap. The pain was so great that he would jump very high, bringing bottles, jars and pans with him at every jump. I soon settled that.

We didn't raise turkeys in 1935, but the Federal Government came in and offered half-month employment to all who wanted work. Mike and I were timekeepers at $60.00 per half-month.

Income didn't flourish during this period. Gladys and Jim were married in January of 1934. Before long, Jim developed sciatic rheumatism, which made it impossible for him to work as a miner, which was his occupation. Some men named William Westmoreland, Ira Hall and Robert Hughes came into the area and built a makeshift cabin near the Big Summit, on the way to Modena. They didn't last too long there and rather split up. Mr. Hughes, who was a fine fellow, came to our place and he and I got a contract to build a house in Pioche. He was a good builder and I was helper. He was a veteran of the Canadian Army of World War I. He always said, "If you're going to steal any money, steal a lot, because they'll soak you just as hard for a little as for a lot". We had the house more than half finished, when one day a "bum" came by and talked to him. Mr. Hughes made some excuse to go up town, and I never saw him again. They said at the post office that the FBI came looking for him about two days later, but he was long gone. His informants must have been quite efficient. We felt badly to see him disappear that way. Needless to say, that ended my carpentering.

25.45   Eldon is Born

In the meantime, Eldon was born on June 6, 1936; a fine boy, also delivered by Dr. MacFarlane in Cedar city, (for $45.00). Justine got ten days off again, in the hospital, but that luxury ended by the next time, I believe. As I went, with Farrel, to get mother and child, a nurse's aid was helping me get them into the car. I put Farrel in and bumped his head doing it. He started crying. The nurse's aid said to herself, "Clumsy Ox."

Eldon was smaller than Farrel and active at an earlier age. He developed boils in the area of his diaper, which became quite bad. One night we were holding him down and working on the boils when all at once, from across the room, came a little buzz saw. Farrel wasn't going to let us hurt his little brother.

25.46   Off to Reno

The "Marginal Land" couldn't support all of us. I had developed a small "herd" of about twenty cows, some with calves. We decided to sell them, so I could go to school and qualify for a teacher's certificate. Paul Bliss bought the cows. On December 30, 1936, Stanton came to Rose Valley with his father's new 1936 Chevy pickup, we loaded our belongings into it, and started for Reno. Stanton got stuck on the snow in our yard and it got worse as we progressed. We reached Eureka after dark and to get into the hotel, had to climb up a snow bank and slide into the doorway. It snowed eight inches more during the night and the next morning we were the only outfit moving on the road. But we made it to Sparks, stayed New Year's Eve in a motel in which the heat was shut off at midnight, Stanton helped us get moved into an apartment at Mrs. Meffley's and left for home that day, January 1st. A few hours after he got into Enterprise, the town was snowed in tight for three weeks.

I registered and got started to school, but my family got sick from the exposure during the trip. Eldon was a baby and was wrapped in blankets, but poor little Farrel caught a light case of pneumonia. Justine caught cold tending them, and had an ear infection. I would skip one class one day and another the next. After of few times of this, Professor Harwood asked me to stay after school. When we were alone, he said, "Get in or get out". I felt like bawling. Nobody had asked me what my circumstances were. I had to cope with things as best I could and not miss Mr. Harwood's Creative Writing class anymore. I did finally get a B plus from him.

We had to get a doctor to come to our apartment a time or two. This was the terrible winter of 1937. Snow was only one and one-half feet in Reno and twenty below, but bad enough.

When the weather had moderated, and the family were better, I went to pay the Dr. I had a goatee, in honor of Homecoming, and looked a little rough, I'm sure. I said to the Dr., "Do you want to check me? I don't feel to well." He said, "There ain't nothing wrong with you," and pulled my beard, sending me on my way.

One day Justine said, "Watch that baby so he won't fall out of his crib." I watched Eldon climb right up, over the edge and out on his head. I got told!

I played in the University band, bass horn, and the band went to Winnemucca by train to play at some celebration. I had to baby sit that bass horn all the way to Winnemucca and back. Would that I had played piccolo. Justine said that she was coming to the station to meet me that evening, but I told her not to. Commercial Row has always been a haven for bums and thieves. Justine came anyway, getting our neighbor, Golda Pendleton, to watch the two boys for her. As she was approaching the station, a man came from behind, grabbed her arm in a vice grip and said, "Keep walking and keep your mouth shut." She was terrified and at a loss to know what to do, when George Pendleton, Golda's husband, walked out of a bar, saw Justine and said, "What on earth are you doing here?" The bum melted into the crowd. The Lord was with us that night. Pendletons were good neighbors. They had two children also, I believe.

25.47   Teaching in Preston

When the school year was over, I found a job in Preston, Nevada, south Ely and near Lund. I was to teach grades five, six, seven, eight and also teach band. Alice

Spencer, of Idaho, Taught the lower grades. I was green but not lazy and made it through one way or another. They day we moved to Preston, Mrs. Jomes, from across the street, came over and said, "Don't let them make you Bishop." They didn't but Preston was the first place in which we became active in Church. The roster read like Little Scandinavia; Christensen, Madsen, Arnoldsen, Jensen, Funk, Peterson, Gardner, Whitlock, Nielsen. They were fine people. Especially did we like Hi and Marilda Whitlock. The salary was a whopping $1,125.00 per year, but that was more than we had ever had. I taught for two years in Preston, then on to Pioche, where the salary was $1,340.00 per year. We stayed many years in Pioche, were active in the Pioche Ward, and made many good friends. During World War Two, I was supposed to work on the farm, and laid off from teaching for a year, but the need developed in Rose Valley and I taught for three years in a little old one room school house, the shell of which still stands; my alma mater. After the war, I went back to teaching in Pioche, teaching sixth grade most often and band on the side.

25.48   Justine Teaches Values to a Wino

While teaching in Pioche, each fall presented Wayne and Justine with a forced decision --- whether to brave the winter roads and commute to Pioche or move to Pioche. One winter found us living along the road just west of the ward chapel in a rather 'marginal' dwelling. A hike up the road took Farrel and I past several old miner shanties occupied by pensioners who subsisted on wine until their monthly check ran out, supplemented by lunch-style handouts panhandled from Pioche residents.

One fine day, Farrel and I happened upon a bright silver dollar lying at the side of the road. We picked it up and promptly showed it off to one of the old winos who happened along. 'That's a right lucky find,' he exclaimed, 'but I've found a coin even better! And because I like you boys, I'll swap you mine for yours.'

So we made the swap, which turned out to be our dollar for a quarter. We rushed home to share our good fortune with Mom (Justine). She sized up the situation, took the quarter in hand and headed for the old guy's shanty with us in tow. She pounded on his door until he appeared, gave him a tongue lashing which set him (and us) straight on the value of coins, and demanded that he return the dollar. Upon hearing mention of words like theft and sheriff, he readily complied, whereupon Justine flipped him his quarter and led *us home. I seldom saw my mother angry, but that day she did 'get her hackles up.' (Eldon)*

25.49   Noel is Born

Noel was born on August 27, 1941, and was a fine boy, but developed asthma and hay fever. Rose Valley produce many dusts that he could hardly handle. When he got big enough, he would take a pick-up and sleep out of the valley during the worst season. He is now the largest of our children, although he was the smallest graduate of the Pioche eighth grade class. He has learned to handle the allergies quite effectively, and has three fine girls of his own. Santa Rosa, California seems to be a good location for him.

25.50   The Insatiable Desire to Hunt Deer

Soon after starting to teach, I developed and insatiable desire to hunt dear. During my growing up years we had never had a rifle capable of killing a deer; the 44-40 was all we had, with old, lifeless shells. When I could buy a gun, I got a 30-06 that has stood me in good stead. As active as I was in Church, the first morning of deer season, always a Sunday, found me out in the hills, with my boys who were big enough, right at my side. Emrys Jones, his boys and my boys and I usually hunted together. We had many good hunts. Then, the State of Nevada opened the season on Saturday, and I mostly stopped the Sunday hunting. Farrel, Eldon and Noel have no compunction against hunting on Sunday but Larry does. He grew up during the Saturday opening.

Figure 25.3: Wayne warms his hands on cold deer-hunting opener above Rose Valley.

25.51 Reeses

I will relate some deer stories. (21.12) Justine, I and the three boys went to Reese's, on the other side of White Rock Mountain. While we were sleeping on Saturday night, deer came near the bed and snorted at us. The next morning, after some tiring walk, we left the boys, including Noel, the baby, in the shade of a tree. Justine and I walked a short distance, and there was a large buck grazing in the brush. Justine had the 22, and I had the 06. She said, "Don't shoot, it's a cow." It raised its head and it wasn't a cow. I shot it, it went down and a dozen more bucks jumped up all around it. Justine was shooting like crazy with the 22 and I shot a time or two, but had to concentrate on the one I had shot. After we got the boys, we all gathered around the deer. I let Farrel shoot it in the head and it got up right among us! It was too far gone to fight, lucky for us, and I got it with another shot. After it was cleaned out, we started to a little spring on the side of the mountainside, with Justine carrying the rifle and me carrying Noel, the baby.

ALL AT ONCE, a large buck jumped out right in front of us. I threw away the baby, grabbed the gun and started shooting. The baby was screaming, I was shooting and Justine was cursing. I didn't get that buck, although my second shot tore a small piece of hair from atop his neck, which really put him in motion.

25.52 Eldon's First Deer

Another time, Eldon was twelve and I promised him that he'd get the next good shot with the 06. We got "ledged" for two hours, finally got out and there stood a little buck looking around a tree at us. I said, "Eldon, that's not a good shot, I'll take it." I emptied the rifle, but didn't touch that deer. Then, four large bucks walked out and stood, looking at us. I gave the gun to Eldon and he tried to aim by hand, but I grabbed him and leaned him against a large boulder. He got the biggest buck the first shot. He has been a deer hunter ever since, and a good one, too. The next one was Farrel's, but he wasn't successful that year.

So far as Julene is concerned, a deer hunt that was not on Sunday and on which nothing was shot, would be successful.(21.8)

25.53 Missing Old Blue

I'll give one more deer story. Some of the Grandchildren asked for one and this is the one I told them.

``One day Eldon and I had been hunting up at the Tobe area all day long, and finally headed for camp, dead tired and unable to climb one more hill. Then something prompted me to climb one more ridge. We went to the top of the next ridge, paused, and looked across the next draw. The stood ``Old Blue," the largest buck in the hills (39.1), with a huge rack of horns and a large body. I carefully placed the bead of that sight right behind his front shoulder and squeezed the trigger." ``Grandpa, what happened?" ``I missed him."

Chapter 26

Still More Threads in the Fabric

We had sugar rationing, Gasoline rationing, ammunition rationing, tire rationing, etc. I was not drafted, because I had quite a large family and I was needed on the farm.

26.1 Power and Water

While we were at Preston, Boulder Power was brought to Lincoln County and to Rose Valley. One of the first things we got was a pump for the well at my parents' home. Clarence Lytle and I "rocked it up," by laying selected stones in cement, by hand, from the bottom to the top, making it stable. Up to that time, every time I went from our house to go to work in the fields, I always took two buckets with me and brought them back full. Once wash days, I had to carry a lot of water before going to work. With new babies, wash day came quite often. That water was pumped out of the well by hand pump. Papa had a windmill which filled a wooden tank sitting near the well, and Mother used that for running water to her plants. When water was needed most, of course, the wind did not blow. An electric pump remedied all that. We went way over toward White River and bought some 1 inch steel pipe to carry the water over to our house. That remained in service to both houses for years, but finally had to be replaced by plastic pipe when we moved back from Las Vegas. Having the water freeze in that steel pipe was the plague of my existence. The well over at "The Old House" went dry during the summer of 1985 and I had to get a new well drilled.

Speaking of Boulder Dam, we went to Las Vegas in April of 1936, to attend the dedication of Boulder Dam by President Franklin Roosevelt. At that time, Las Vegas was just a very small, ratty town, with a few tamarack trees and mesquite bushes for shade. People kept their houses bearable by spraying roof and walls with a garden hose. We saw the dedication ceremony from a distance. Farrel, being just one and a half years old, became very ill with dysentery. We gave him everything we could think of, but getting out of there was the best solution. As we left, Justine said, "I don't know where we might live during our lifetime, but I'll tell you one place where we won't live." Later, she ate those words.

26.2   Julene is 'born

Julene was born on September 15, 1946, in Caliente, with Dr. Fortier in charge. He told Justine, "You have a beautiful, red-haired baby girl." Justine said, "Don't tease me, Doctor. It's a boy, isn't it?" After three boys, a girl seemed unbelievable. But her hair was black when she was born; lots of it. The nurses didn't like Dr. Fortier, so one of them promptly told Justine she didn't belong there, when the bed might be needed by a soldier. I went to see Justine the next day and she was all packed to come home. The time of the ten day rest at the birth of a child was over. Julene was a good baby, was active and walked early. One day, while she was walking, she had wet on the floor in the hallway. She kept her mother locked out until she wiped it up. Julene loved animals, including deer, cows, cats, dogs and horses. Blaze would let her shinny up his leg, climb on a bank for get on any way she chose. She could ride him up into the hills, get off and he would wait for her for hours. If I did this, I would walk home. She was the most dedicated horseman we had; Eldon was a close second. We took Whirlwind to Las Vegas and kept him at the Welfare Farm, but it was hard to get together to ride him, he grew old and Julene's interests changed. She rode him less and less.

26.3   Larry is Born

Justine said, "I will not have a baby on Friday the thirteenth." Dr. Fortier said, "Suit yourself." But Friday, May thirteenth was Larry's birthday in the year 1949. He was born in Dr. Fortier's Pioche Hospital. He was a fine boy; little did we know that he would be last. In order to make it easy on his "aging" parents, he was little trouble. He became a help to his Grandfather, Freel. Grandpa had a hard time keeping a car on the right hand side of the road, so at age five, Larry sat between his knees and steered it right. The local police said little because they knew that Freel would be on the wrong side if he were alone with Grandma. From the pickup, it was a natural step to the tractor, and Larry followed the other boys in being enlisted in running the machinery at an early age. One day Eldon drove the pickup down the road, and Mike said, "I'll swear that pickup was all by itself."

26.4   Kids at the Wheel

One fall, John Devlin and I and Farrel went to Hamblin Valley to round up our cows. On the way back, I drove the pickup home and John and Farrel came over the mountain with the cows. Justine had a fit when she learned where Farrel was. The next year, we went riding in the same area with Eldon as helper. When it came time to come home I let Eldon drive the pickup home, and I helped John drive the cows. Justine had a fit again. There was just no pleasing her!

26.5   U.N.R.

Because I had a provisional certificate, I had to keep returning to U.N.R. to gain more credits. I think I made the trip during the summer time at least twelve times, sometimes alone, but with the family along if possible. In 1941, just after we reached Reno, on a very strict budget, Farrel broke his arm and that ruined the budget. I got a job working at Safeway eight hours a day, six days a week. Luckily, most of my classes depended upon reading. Justine read the books and filled me in while I was eating lunch. I got two B pluses out of the arrangement. She learned more than I.

I beat Farrel to the Bachelor's in 1953, I believe, but he beat me hands down to the Master's. While he was earning his Master's, he was employed at the U.S. Bureau of Mines, near U.N.R. I had been teaching for fifteen years, and he was making more salary than I. I happened to go to B.Y.U. for my last two summers, while in Las Vegas, and kicked myself for not having gone there years before. As a music teacher, B.Y.U. had what I needed.

26.6   Getting a Masters Degree

Going back a couple of years, when I was in Las Vegas, I finished the paper for my Master's. I went to Reno to take the oral. One of the first people I saw was Dr. Reed, my advisor. He said, "Lytle, you don't have a Chinaman's chance. Our new graduate Dean, Dr. Obrien, invites himself to sit on the committee for education graduates and flunks every one of you." After a night's rest, I studied in the library, incidentally, pulling out the very books I was tested on, went into a men's lavatory to have a prayer, and presented myself before the committee. Just as we started, somebody called Dr. Obrien out and he didn't come back. The rest was routine, and I left for home with a Master's degree under my belt. That was a good feeling.

I like to think that my always going to college may have influenced our children to do the same. All five have a Bachelor's, or more, and to a man are smarter than their old dad.

26.7   Getting a C-

Going back again, when I enrolled at U.N.R. in 1937, I had to take their entrance exam. There were a lot of young people there and they started leaving before time was half over. Finally, another man and I were the only ones left, but there was still time. I got embarrassed and left. A week or so later, the Psychologist called me in and told me I had no excuse for not getting straight A's. I promptly got a C- from Miss Reubsam, in teaching of elementary reading. She handed out papers to fill each day and never gathered them. Some of us quit filling them out. She did gather one and it was the test, so much for Miss Reubsam, but I needed the C-.

26.8   Battery Acid

After school was out in 1941, Emrys, Jim and I took my '37 Chevy sedan and went to Hamilton, looking for quicksilver. We heard that there had been a landslide someplace, but didn't let it worry us. We were driving along the Forest Service road, looking at deer and, as I was looking away from the road, I came to the landslide, drove into it and tipped the car upside down. Emrys didn't right himself at once, and the battery acid dripped on the seat of his pants, later eating the seat right out. Battery acid also leaked into the fabric in the ceiling of the car, and without warning a large piece of it would fall, usually right in Justine's lap, after we had gone back home. She was expecting Noel, and as we went to Cedar City, a piece of the ceiling dropped onto her maternity dress, leaving her with a frontless dress when we arrived in Cedar City. She insisted that I get rid of the car.

26.9   The Buy of the Day

I found a "Buy of the Day" in a '38 Ford, and agreed to buy it, but when we went back, the salesman said they wanted $45.00 or more. We argued and argued, and he finally seemed to relent, so I signed a contract at apparently the original offer, driving away in a Ford sedan in good condition. After getting home, I got the contract out and they had written in very, very small print on the bottom, "plus an additional $45.00." I immediately protested, but I got the classic runaround, with nothing to do but keep what I had. It turned out to be a lucky buy, because World War II broke out , and cars of any kind could not be had. I had two extra spare tires, and it was supposed to be unpatriotic to have more than one, so I sent them, later receiving .10 per tire. The old Chevy would not have weathered out the war.

26.10   Word War II

We had sugar rationing, Gasoline rationing, ammunition rationing, tire rationing, etc. I was not called, because I had quite a large family and I was needed on the farm.

During the late 1930's and into 1940, our nation had been increasingly supportive of England and France, against Germany. We had taken sides against Japan, in all her conquests, which seemed to be unstoppable, but we were all shocked beyond belief when Japan attacked Pearl Harbor. To show how far we were from preparedness, two soldiers were manning a crude radar system at Pearl Harbor, and each reported to his superior officer that there was a large incoming flight of planes they destroyed. Once commanding officer said they were navy, a navy man said they were air force, and no alarm was sounded. It was Sunday morning, and nobody disturbed an officer on Sunday morning. Two days later, at the Philippines, our planes came in from patrol, were lined up in neat rows, for lunch, and the Japanese got them all in about two strafing runs. Our much-touted B17 Bomber did not have a tail gun when it was first put into combat.

26.11   Setbacks

After we declared war on Japan and Germany, the news seemed to be all bad. The Japanese were winning on every front, and British lost in Greece and in Norway, against the Germans. We lost two battle cruisers in ten minutes, as they were unloading at Guadal Canal. Eventually, British General Montgomery succeeded in pushing German General Rommel out of North Africa. General Doolittle and a few other brave men bombed Tokyo, but we all knew they would be unable to return. Some of them finally did make it back home. When things gradually began to turn our way, General Patton became a hero by helping push the Germans out of Italy. He had to be severely reprimanded. He was visiting soldiers in a hospital in Italy and came to a soldier who was there for psychological reasons. General Patton said it was for reasons of gutlessness and slapped the soldier's face. The newspapers made much of it, but of course President Roosevelt had to leave General Patton right where he could do the most good.

26.12 Misrepresentation

Britain fared as poorly in Malaysia and at Singapore. One British naval commander was offered air support for his two new, fast battleships, the *Repulse* and the *Renown*, I believe. He said that his ships could put up a "curtain of fire" through which no plane could fly. The Japanese put him, his ships and the "curtain of fire" beneath the ocean in short order. At Singapore, the British had "invincible cannon" that could be conquered by nobody. The fact was, the cannon only pointed out to sea, and the Japanese captured them by not firing a shot. They simply approached through the "impenetrable jungle" behind the cannon. It seemed that our side could never win, but gradually, the tide turned our way. After the dramatic siege of Berlin and surrender of the Germans, an allied meeting was held at Potsdam. The new President Truman represented the U.S. there. He came home soon. He said, "Nobody's going to make a fool out of me again." He was not used to European diplomacy. When the Japanese war should be ending, the prospect of our solders having to invade the Japanese homeland loomed larger and larger. President Truman tried to get an audience with the Japanese Emperor. The Emperor declined on the grounds that deity could not talk to mortals. After and Atom Bomb at Horishima and at Nagasaki, the deity became mortal pretty fast. Truman did not seem to ever feel regret for his action. He saved thousands of American servicemen's lives, and that is what was most important to him.

26.13 Below-Par Merchandise

We bought a Ford pick-up right after the war ended, and the metal was so thin that Jim said he was afraid to take it out in a high wind, for fear the sides would collapse. The six-cylinder motor was of about equal quality. The armed services dumped hundreds of jeeps into the ocean to keep them off the market.

26.14 Band Teacher

While I was teaching at Pioche, it seemed that the elementary band was always my responsibility. I had bands in size from forty to fifty members, together with majorettes, flag carriers, etc. Some of the "kids" were really gifted musicians. I learned to finger every band instrument so that I could answer questions of fingering "on the spot." I took lessons on clarinet, drums, saxophone, trombone, and I went to school in Reno. The other instruments I could already finger. The big event of every year was the Band Festival at Ely, in which we marched, played in concert and furnished members for an "honor band." Clarence Sawhill was our most respected and appreciated adjucicator. When my band would play in the auditorium at Ely, I was always amazed at the sounds I had never heard. The stage in the Gym in Pioche was hardly the place for good acoustics. I also, on two or three occasions, took band members to band clinics, especially at Flagstaff, Arizona. During the first year at Nellis Elementary in Las Vegas, I also had a good band. On one occasion, my crack snare drummer, Bruce, a black kid, changed our drum pattern as we started marching. He had heard a pattern he liked better and it was no trouble for him to switch over. Alas, I had to stop him and get him back to our pattern. My poor majorettes were barely able to comprehend the pattern we had been using for weeks.

At a clinic at Pepperdine, Alwright suggested that majorettes should be placed on stools or on oil drums. He said they couldn't make any stupid mistakes in that location. Anyway, it was a high point in the lives of some of the kids. My children had accumulated many funny books. On one trip to Ely in the bus, I distributed comic books to all in the bus. It kept them quiet for awhile. Julene and Larry were both in some of my bands, before we moved to Las Vegas. At the Rancho High School Band, Julene was content to play second clarinet, rather than compete for first before a crowd.

26.15   A Rotten Ladder

One day Mike and I were driving in the hills up near Deer Lodge. We came to the Iris shaft and decided to go down by the ladder already in place. We lighted our carbide lamps, because sometimes the air at the bottom of a shaft is "bad", that is heavy with carbon dioxide. We climbed down a good hundred feet and found that there was no ladder for the last seven or eight feet. We caught hold of the bottom rung of the ladder and dropped to the bottom of the shaft. Then we noticed that our lights were burning very dimly, so he helped me up to the ladder, I reached down for him and we climbed out of there. It did not occur to us that through the years the lumber in that ladder was slowly rotting.

26.16   Mike Is Killed

Several years later, Mike decided that the fence around the Rose Valley transformation station needed to be replaced. His first thought was of the one hundred feet of good pipe in the Iris shaft. I didn't have time to go, but sent Farrel, Howard joined them and the three of them, with a strong rope and chain and a good pulley went to the Iris shaft. Mike fastened the pulley to a strong cedar limb above the shaft, threaded the rope through it, and with rope in one hand, started down the ladder. Not too many feet down, the ladder broke, dropping Mike to the bottom of the shaft. He had not bothered to tie the rope around his waist. A special rescue team was brought out from Pioche, and with Everest Hackett's help Mike was brought out of the shaft. I was right at the top and Mike died right at that point. A sad way to lose a bosom friend.

It was the end of an era. Nothing seemed the same with Mike gone. Mike and Mary had no children.

My father had urged Mike to cut good strong pickets, and make the fence that way. He had said, "Keep away from those old mines." We cut good strong pickets and the fence was made of them, with good quality fencing. If we could only go back and start over, sometimes mistakes would be rectified and lives would be saved.

Gladys and Jim Marry Gladys and Jim were married in January, 1934, I believe. Jim was working at the time, but quite soon developed sciatica and grew progressively worse. Soon, Karen came along and they had to move in with our parents. The arrangement was difficult for all concerned, but Jim worked on the ranch as much as possible, particularly having a hard time working our "half-broke" team. Jim said one day, "They'll run at the drop of a hat and drop the hat themselves." When the power came in, I was in Preston, but Jim was able to help a lot. He was good at such things.

26.17 Digging for Quicksilver

In 1940, just as I changed teaching jobs to Pioche, Jim and I got together during the summer and started prospecting for quicksilver. Jim and Jack Spencer had done quite well at Bristol wells, but decided to break up and Jim and I went to Hamilton. We found quicksilver quite soon and soon had two flasks to ship. We recovered seven or eight flasks during the summer, and felt good about it. Jim couldn't wash the dirt, but I could and he could dig with the shovel and pick. One day, someone came along and asked him how we were doing. He said, "Pretty darned good for one man and a school teacher." Another day, Jim was getting small dabs of quicksilver bearing gravel out of a crack that went down and down. All at once, the pick came sailing out, landing in the brush, with the shovel right behind it. Jim had had it. I got him to sit down and light his pipe, and started digging a shelf for him to stand on. Lo and behold, I found much more quicksilver than we had had. Jim took one look at it and said, "Get out of the way and let a man handle it."

We never lacked for sage hens to eat. Each evening, Jim would get one for them and one for us, without fail. One evening, we were all riding in the old black Chevy, Farrel, Eldon, Karen, Gladys, Justine, Jim and I. Jim had the inevitable twenty-two rifle. Three big bucks walked out and stopped beside the road, Jim cranked the window down, maneuvering his gun to position; Gladys cranked the window up, Jim cranked it down, Justine cranked it up, etc. and eventually the deer trotted away. The air was blue. On the first day of the deer season, after I was long gone, he took his deer rifle and got all three bucks.

While we were digging quicksilver in Hamilton, Jim said one day, "let's take a few hundred dollars of this money and go to Las Vegas and Homestead one hundred and sixty acres." I said, "I wouldn't go down there if they would give me the valley." Jim said, "You'll be sorry." It would have been an excellent investment, but I couldn't see it.

26.18 Jim Signs on at the Power Company

After Jim's sciatica healed, and he was working for the Lincoln County Power District, he joined the Pioche Rod and Gun Club. Almost overnight, he became a game law enforcer, almost taking John and me in one Thanksgiving Day. John said, "Whatever happened to him?" I hadn't been aware of the change till then.

26.19 Jim is Electrocuted

Jim and Gladys bought a lot and Jim built a house on it in Pioche. They got a new Ford car. Jim was going to treat his daughter right. Then a few years later, about 1950, Jim was working on a hot line at Castleton, Gene McCleod threw a supposedly cloth tape to him, the wind caught the tape, draping it over the power line and over Jim's upper body. His clothes promptly burned off from the waist up and he dropped to the ground. The tape had little copper strands in it. I visited Jim in the hospital that evening. He was black from his waist to the top of his head. He said, "I won't live till morning." Gladys said, "Don't say that." But he was right, he didn't live until morning. I had come to like Jim very much and thrilled to see him take hold in his family as soon as he was able. If we just had it to do over again ...

26.20   Freel Injury and Death

While Jim and Gladys were at the ranch, my Dad got Maude and Rocks, the big team he had raised, and of which he was very proud, and went down to mow hay on the grain patch. The mower had a patent coil spring on it, which allowed it to take shock and spring back as before. He hit a large clump of wheat grass, the mower buckled very strongly and threw Papa off on his shoulder, laming it and actually causing a light stroke. He was never able to handle that team again. Jim fought them, somebody else tried to handle them, but they were never worth the powder to "blow them" after that. Rocks died in the deep snow of '49 and I had to shoot Maude so we wouldn't have to feed her expensive hay, of which we didn't have enough to feed the cattle.

Papa never did get his full capacity back again. He did his best, but suffered from the paralysis in his right side. One summer, about the mid 1950's, while we were in Reno, he had a heart attack. McCrosky Brothers took him by stretcher to the hospital in Caliente. He told them as he left, "Don't worry boys, I'll be back." I rushed home from Reno, stopping at the hospital on the way in, but he had already died. He didn't make it back. He was eighty years old.

26.21   The Ranch is Sold

After he died, I kept trying to run the ranch and cattle and teach school at Pioche. It was a losing game. One night, about dark, I was chasing a cow and big calf through the brush above Devlin's. I had borrowed old "Jug Head" from Howard, because my horse had cut his foot the night before, chasing cows in the dark. Old "Jug Head" bucked me off, because he wasn't used to the extra cinch on my saddle. It broke a rib for me. When I got home, I told Mother, "Sell them." She did, and not too long after, sold the ranch to McCrosky Brothers. Before too long, she moved to Gladys' house in Pioche, being much more comfortable there and away from the worry of chickens and cows.

26.22   Teaching in Pioche

I taught school in Pioche for a total of fifteen years, including the time before I taught in Rose Valley and after. One big problem was, "Should we rent and live in Pioche, or should we commute?" The year we commuted would be a bad one and I would fight snow, ice and mud. The good year would almost invariably be the year we rented and stayed in town. One year, we actually started to buy a little house on "Batty Row." The neighbors proved so miserable that we had to give it up before the year was out.

26.23   Looking South

Finally, Justine said, "I will move once more, and that's it." At about the same time, two or three people told me that the teachers didn't need a raise; we were already over paid. It so happened that Harold Brinley from the personnel office in Las Vegas, offered me a contract in Las Vegas, with a beginning salary as good as that in Lincoln County, where I had been teaching for fifteen years. Mother was well situated in Pioche, attending Relief Society and Sacrament meetings, with some good, fast friends, so I took Mr. Brinley's offer, we went to Reno so that I could attend summer school for two sessions (always trying for that Master's), and we went from Reno to Las Vegas to buy a house. On a hot August day, we went all day with Jim Hogan, real estate agent, in his car, on which he couldn't turn off the heater! We became completely frazzled, but looked at one last prospect at 704 N. 16th St. in the greater Las Vegas area, like the cool house we were shown, and agreed to buy it. One reason we liked the house, was because it sat above the street. So many we looked at had been flooded during the summer rains. That's where the "die was cast" for the next fifteen years. I was given an assignment of teaching seventh grade for half a day and band at the Nellis Elementary School, with Miss Heard as principal. She was a strict disciplinarian, believing that was expected at a school attended by children of the Air Force. The very first day, I was busy going from place to place, getting band set up, when Mrs. Armentrout, assistance principal said, "Mr. Lytle, we never walk on the grass at this school." When those kids were taken out to the playground, they marched single file out to the yard and then back. But I had no further trouble.

26.24   Off to a Good Start

On the day school was to let out for Christmas vacation, as I got to school that morning, the kids were preparing to swing from the chandeliers all day, but I put a stop to that. I put them in their seats and put them to work, and promised there might not be any party at all. What a lucky decision! At about 11:00am, in walked Miss Heard., Dr. Gray, Steve Early and Miss Hanrahan, the latter three in high positions, Mr. Gray being Superintendent. Everything was in "apple pie order" in that classroom. They were good, intelligent kids. The band turned out quite well and I figured my first year in Las Vegas successful. I had one odd development. I started teaching accordion as well as band instruments and that really took off; I soon had a dozen. Mr. Bickhart, music supervisor, said, "Cease and desist. We didn't hire you to teach accordion." As soon as the semester ended, I stopped the accordion class.

26.25   Wayne Tells a "Flewsie" to Take a Hike

There was another unexpected event. I was hauling three lady teachers to school and back each day, two more elderly and one young, attractive blonde girl. One morning, only the blonde and I were going to school. As we drove along, I commented on the beautiful morning. Just before turning into the gate at Nellis, she said, "Keep going. Let's you and I spend the day in the desert." I turned at the gate. I hadn't come all the way to Las Vegas, with so much at stake, to blow it on a "flewsie." She soon stopped riding with me.

26.26   Traffic Problems

I taught at Nellis for two years. I soon started giving piano lessons after school hours, on base. One night on the way home, I was new to the road and signaled a left turn too soon, then didn't take it, a city bus clipped my front bumper, bending it forward a little bit. The bus driver insisted upon stopping and calling a North Las Vegas policeman. The policeman came, looked at things, I told him I had no charges, and he said, "Get in your vehicles and leave." The three of us were standing on a traffic island, and before we could move, a drunk came barreling along and plowed into the police car from the rear. He and his companion were both soused and beer cans rolled all over the road. One of them had bloodied his forehead and an ambulance came. Before long, the ambulance left and the police handcuffed the two together and led them away. A wrecker had to be called to move the police car and the drunk's car. The North Las Vegas policeman made me report it after that. He had to have some reason for being there, but he didn't give me a ticket. I also reported it to Farmer's Group Insurance. The girl who answered said, "We know all about it. We also insured the drunk." That was my first experience with D.U.I.

26.27   No Church Vacation

On the first Sunday we were in Las Vegas, Justine and I agreed that we would take a "vacation from Church work." We went to church and lo and behold, that very afternoon, the entire Bishopric, the Bishop being Samuel Davis, gave us a visit. Our holiday from Church work ended before it began. I was made Ward Chorister, Justine was made Mia Maid leader. I was soon also made Gospel Doctrine class teacher, the Church job I love above all others.

The Las Vegas Second Ward was a special ward and Noel, Julene and Larry also enjoyed it. Noel left on his mission from there.

Larry and Julene had to adjust to new school situations, but managed it. Individual attention from teachers was hard to come by I always resented it because Larry got an F in shop. He was too shy to get help that he needed. Now he teaches shop! Even then, he could fix almost anything. He also left on his mission from the Las Vegas Second Ward.

26.28   Larry's Mission and Marriage

When Larry left for his mission, he had one thousand dollars in the bank. Bishop Orthen had an unwritten rule that each missionary should have that much in the bank. Larry drove delivery truck for Brother Gustin's Nevada Laundry, worked at Bob Baskin's restaurant, etc., to earn this money. We didn't have to dip into it while he was gone, so when he got back, the money plus interest was there. After being home about one month, he went to the bank, drew the money out, bought a motor bike and a diamond ring, borrowed is mother's suitcase, and went to Fayette. A few days later he came back. He had slid on a wet road, tearing his mother's suitcase apart, but with no other damage. Sandy must have accepted, they now have eight children! While Larry was in Fayette, Lowell Hammond, who is my first cousin, checked him out. When Lowell found out just who Larry was, he said to John Bartholomew, "John, it's worse than I thought it was." Larry had one year of college at Cedar City, Julene was a year ahead of him, but they were both there during his first year. He and Sandy both finished off after he got back from his mission.

26.29 Educational Challenges

Farrel and Eldon missed out on the "Las Vegas experience." They had already grown up and married when we made the move. Neither seemed much impressed when they visited us in Las Vegas. Farrel got the four thousand, four-year Harold's Club Scholarship, when he graduated from high school, and never again asked his parents for money. He became adept at many jobs while in Reno. He and Manetta were married before finishing at Reno. We were privileged to attend their graduation exercises, holding Nelson Wayne, while they accepted their graduation certificates.

Eldon had just as high a grade average as Farrel during his Lincoln County High School career, but was passed over for any large scholarship, because one had been awarded the year before in our family. It seemed like an unfair decision, but Eldon earned most of his college money by working summers at Tempiute, etc.

Noel graduated from Lincoln County High School, also, but did not specialize in high grades. Nevertheless, he was number ten among the top ten and had to give a talk, which he wanted to avoid. Justine was fit to be tied when Pres Price told us that Noel tested above the top 95 percent in his class. Pres had thought Noel was a dumbbell, and treated him as such.

26.30 Experiences in Las Vegas

At Rancho High School in Las Vegas, Julene and Larry got no special treatment, for sure. They misspelled each of their names on the list of graduates and also mispronounced it as they came through. Julene missed a tuition scholarship to S.U.S.C. because she could never get in to talk to her counselor at Rancho. Mr. Brinley said one day, "If I had one thousand dollars more to spend on each teacher, I'd get all those smokers out of there." It's too bad he couldn't get that money.

During our first summer at Las Vegas, I worked full time on the Welfare Farm, at one dollar an hour. It was better than nothing , and I learned to run a swather, bailer, bale wagon, and combine, besides learning to endure real heat. One day, it seemed hot out there, but I was up on the swather, getting a little breeze. When I passed by the Huntridge thermometer on the way home, it was showing one hundred and nineteen degrees! The Welfare Farm was just below the Las Vegas sewer run-off and filed on that water. There wan an underground concrete pipeline and that hay grew like asparagus seven crops a summer if managed right. The farm manager, who was Lynn Duke, soon learned that the Priesthood Quorums could not get that hay in. They would come out, promptly get a truck stuck by a valve, and would haul no more than two hundred bales a night. A bale wagon solved the problem. I gave many piano lessons after school, a sort of "Postman's Holiday", reported it as income, and came out of the Las Vegas experience with Social Security credit enough and one hundred dollars more in monthly retirement.

Justine worked at Cornet's, at W.T. Grant's, at the Ideal Asphalt Co. and as receptionist for George Tate, architect. Julene worked at Nevada Laundry, at a dress shop, and at other places. We all pulled together.

I am going to name a few of my students who became outstanding musicians. From Pioche I can think of Dean Alexander, Stanley Jones, Buddy Walker, Marguerite Walker, Linda Campbell, Donna Somers, Tim Fogliani, Eldon. Among majorettes there was Virginia Cottino, Nora Ann Gerson, Dorothy Gray, Mary Sue Horlacher.

In Las Vegas I can think of Steve Hines, piano; Sharon Smith, violin, Tom Goldston, bass fiddle; Carol Borg, violin; Bruce, drums; Dave Good, trumpet; Brent, baritone; Brent Olenslager, piano; Ron Parraguirre, piano; Kathy Parraguirre, piano; Anne Bozart, flute; Kathy Lake, piano, John Lake, piano; Randy Anderson, piano; Karen Stewart, piano. While I was giving private piano lessons, about twice per year we would hold a recital at our home, with the living room and kitchen crowded. This series of recitals went on long enough that at the last recital, my students were flirting with each other at every opportunity. They were growing up.

After two years at Nellis, I was given an assignment of teaching Elementary band and Flutophone at five schools. I came to classes to teach Flutophone, where, many times, the teacher was having a nicotine fit, waiting for me to get there so she could leave. I had the unique experience of having a a regular elementary band, plus a Flutophone band in one Helldorado parade. While at the B.Y.U., I discovered that an inexpensive recorder is much more of a musical instrument than a Flutophone.

Mr. Iddings retired as string teacher and I was appointed as "itinerant string teacher" in the Las Vegas High School Zone, with orchestra practice at the High School everyday, and classes in ten elementary schools and two jr. high schools. Each fall, before I got really settled into my schedule, I would invariably be at the "wrong school at the wrong time" at least once.

Don Miller was appointed to the same position for the Rancho High School Zone, Mary McCurdy for the Western High School Zone.

One of my annual assignments was to provide an orchestra to play the march music as the High School seniors marched into the Convention Center for Baccalaureate Services. This event invariably occurred on Memorial Day weekend, making it impossible for me to get a vehicle and help setting up for the event. Justine and I would up in our old green pickup, with a load of drums, bass fiddles, cellos, etc. One evening as we were carting all this stuff back, Justine said, "Could you really retire?" I said, "Yes, I got confirmation just a few days ago." She said, "For heaven's sake do it!" I retired in 1968, after thirty years as a teacher.

26.31   An Agent for New York Life

Before the summer was over, I got a letter from Bob Rose asking me as a New York Life policy holder to nominate somebody as a prospective agent. I nominated myself, and after some special wire pulling, was accepted at age fifty-eight, took courses and passed the state tests, becoming a New York Life Field Underwriter. I have roughly figured out that New York Life hasn't made any money on me. Too many of my clients have died. One early case stands out. Mary L Rhude was a teacher of my acquaintance. She contacted me early in my insurance career to get Life Insurance for a small grandson. We filled out the App, but when the policy came back, it was $9.91 per month and had to be increased to $10.00 per month. I went to the baby's parent's home. The mother, the grandmother and the baby were there. I increased the amount and they signed it. Old Brilliant me said, "As long as we're at it, let's change the policy date to April 1st, that day being March 25. They said, "Fine." I changed the date and left. The baby died on March 27! It was a "crib death" and Dr. Ravenholt was two months getting out a death certificate. Then I could submit a claim. New York Life paid it because the original app was before the baby's death and there seemed to be no intent to defraud. That family has since purchased six more New York Life policies.

On another occasion, a teacher said, "Wayne, my husband needs an insurance policy." I said, "I'm glad you asked. I have just one left." She didn't think that was funny and they never did buy from me. On another occasion, I wrote an app For a nineteen-year old boy, with his father pressing the sale, paying the premium, with the only asked from the boy being his signature. We had a "suicide clause" allowing the Company to pay death claims from suicide after the policy has been in force one year. That boy committed suicide one year and twenty hours into the life of the policy, not intentionally, I'm sure. New York Life paid.

I was sent, with a group, to a training session in San Diego, which was well conducted and informative. I qualified for "club" the following year, and Herman Nelson and wife and Justine and I attended. I was astounded at the general stupidity of the whole group after an hour of free liquor. Club was not too informative.

I insured poor Kirk Adams, who was killed by lightning while fishing on Cedar Mountain. He and a daughter were together, and he was killed, she was spared, the Dr. saying that his pulse was on pause and his daughter's was on pump.

After five years in Las Vegas in the insurance business; incidentally, I had given up my piano pupils, getting Mrs. Clifton to take them from me; one day Justine said, "I am willing to move once more. Let's go home." I agreed, and the first part of 1973 found us stuck in the snow, pulling a trailer loaded wit household goods, on the hill leading into Rose Valley. We had come home again! We wanted to be here and Las Vegas never was home to the older kids.

During 1964, I debated about taking a job in HeadStart for the summer. Mother assured me that I should; in fact, she had a compulsion about earning money wherever possible. She thought that we might all go broke. It should have been a signal to me. During July, Mame Campbell went to visit her and she was dizzy and disoriented. She actually had had a light stroke. Gladys got her and took her to Carlin, but after a few weeks, Gladys couldn't hold her job and care for Mother, so Justine and I got her and took her to Caliente to the hospital. I had to go back to Las Vegas to continue in HeadStart, leaving Mother in the hospital, with Noel being the only family member here at that time. Of course, several of the good ladies in Pioche checked on her every day.

26.32 Mary Passes Away

I had made plans to visit her on a Friday night in August, but she died on Thursday night, with us being far away in Las Vegas. Of course, Noel was aware and helped all he could.

I have kicked myself for getting all tied up when she needed me most; her insistence on my working should have alerted me.

Her Grandchildren put on the entire service in the Pioche Ward. She would have been highly pleased by the quality of service they put on for their Grandmother.

If we could just go back and do some things over again, I wouldn't have been tied so tightly.

26.33 Church Assignments

About three years before we left Las Vegas, President Reed Whipple of the St. George Temple asked us to be Temple workers. We accepted at once and started working every other Friday and Saturday. I had to do a lot of memorizing, since at that time Live sessions were still being used. After a while, the assignment was changed to every other weekend. We were there the day the Temple was to be closed for change over to filmed sessions. Everybody came that day. We could get to our posts only by squeezing along the walls. We had various experiences. One night I forgot to set our alarm clock ahead, so we reached the Temple an hour late. President Earl had checked my post and I wasn't there. Later he came while I was there. Brother Waymire said, "He's here, just like he's supposed to be." Another morning, there were eight inches of snow and I got stuck. Justine took over and threw snow all over me and I pushed. We made it. Another evening, I became very ill and had to leave my assignment. The next morning, I called to be excused. At about 10:00 a.m., I felt well enough to drive to Las Vegas. A few miles beyond Mesquite, I started seeing more stars than highway, so pulled over and stopped. I got out to get some fresh air and passed out. The next thing I remember was Justine pulling on my arm, saying, "Please get up." I finally got back and she drove to the outskirts of Las Vegas, then I drove on in. I particularly enjoyed conducting Temple sessions.

After we moved back to Rose Valley, we went right on with our assignments, but with film being used. We worked a total of seven years and were released, after the shortened assignments were instituted. One day when we left Rose Valley, the road was snow covered, beginning in our front yard, and there were travelers' advisories for all of Southern Utah. Just before reaching Veyo, I stepped up the speed a little and did a 360-degree turn. Justine said, "What shall we do?" I said, "I'm still headed for St. George, and that's where I'm going."

During October of 1970, Julene and Devon came to Las Vegas. Julene was expecting soon and Devon was on the way to Vietnam. Three weeks before Shauna was born, Devon was on his way, so Julene stayed with us. I got as nervous as I had ever been with any of ours, when the time approached, but I survived and Julene had a beautiful baby girl, Shauna. Needless to say, she soon became the apple of my eye, and Shauna, Skamp and I spent much happy time together. Skamp would watch her carefully and would not let her toddle out to the street. He would eat every teething cracker she got, but she didn't care. Julene and Devon had brought their little dog, Tag, along and he lived with us, too. He would run along nearby as Skamp and I went on our nightly walk with Samp on a leash. Just after Devon got back, someone just plain stole Tag on one of our nightly walks. Devon was back about two weeks, when he was transferred to Kilene, Texas, and Shauna and her mother were gone, just like that. The army doesn't take Grandparents into consideration when soldiers are transferred all over the country. We have visited with Julene and Shauna since, but that close bond does not exist anymore.

26.34 Back to Rose Valley

When Larry remodeled our house in Rose Valley, we had Larry, Sandra and Mike and Suzette near us for a while. Suzie and Mike especially enjoyed planting and gathering garden vegetables. I think ShaRee came along about that time.

Recently, Eldon, Rula and family have lived "across the road" and in Panaca. We have enjoyed getting well acquainted with the children.

Life would be practically useless with no children, grandchildren or great grand children. People without them must be terribly lonely!

After getting back from Las Vegas, I took Justine to the Salt Lake Clinic for extensive tests. The tests started at the clinic, then she was hospitalized in the LDS Hospital for a complete battery of tests. After she was released, and we were preparing to leave, Dr. Wirthlin called me aside and said, "Your wife has Alzheimer's Disease." Then as an after thought he said, "May I express my sympathy?"

26.35 Wayne's Poetic Response

We love the Lord with heart and soul to serve him well. Complete obedience has become our goal. When you saw a soul in need did you forget every lust and greed? Obeying his commandments is hard to do.

The task falls upon thee and me and you. When we think of eternal reward the job becomes not quite so hard. Our God knows all that we think and do. In his great love nothing is really new.

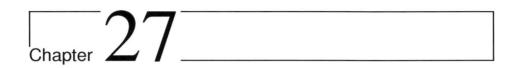

Chapter 27

CARS I HAVE KNOWN AND DRIVEN

Papa chewed tobacco and spit to his left. We got the full impact of the tobacco juice in the backseat. We complained loudly, but he'd often forget. -- Wayne

27.1 First Generation

First Model T

Our first family car was a Model T, purchased in about 1920, second hand, by our father, Freel Lytle from Spec Dolan in Pioche. It was a good car in that it ran and took us places far faster than a team ever could. My first distinct recollection is of Mother, Dad, Gladys and I all loaded into it and going to see Aunt Teenie and Uncle Milton in Fayette, UT. We were going up the long hill to the Clear Creek Summit and it wouldn't run in high. Papa was out with the hood up, trying to see what was wrong, when Bill Pitts came along, stopped and asked what was wrong. Papa said, "She won't take this hill in high, Bill." Bill said, "Freel, this country is a little bigger and a little steeper than you're used to. You'll have to take it in low." Take it in low we did. Of course, the Model T had only two forward gears, low and high. When we reached the Clear Creek Summit, Gladys and I were ecstatic. Mount Baldy greeted us in all its glory. That was the most beautiful and largest mountain we had seen.

Papa was captivated by the long, straight rows of corn and sugar beets in the Sevier River Valley. Gladys and I were going to go back home and brag about having seen the Sevier River, more water than we had ever seen. We had a nice visit with Aunt Teenie and Uncle Milton and even went on to Mt. Pleasant to see Cora, who had been married to Mother's half brother, Joe Madsen. Joe died with typhoid fever and Cora had remarried We were not prepared for the onslaught of mosquitoes. My legs and arms were one solid lump, and for years after that a mosquito bite wouldn't swell on me. I believe Gladys was the same.

GLADYS AND I WERE UNPREPARED FOR ONE DISCOMFORT. Papa chewed tobacco and spit to his left. We got the full impact of the tobacco juice in the backseat. We complained loudly, but he'd often forget. The last I remember of that first Model T is seeing it sit in the backyard with the top gone and our two pet sheep, Nanny and Ninny jumping into it, tearing leather off the seat and pulling the horse hair stuffing out. The sheep had to go.

Other Model Ts

Our second Model T was also second-hand, purchased from whom I don't remember. Water was the only coolant available and we had troubles during the wintertime. Even if we put hot water in the radiator, it would soon freeze, so horse blankets over the radiators were a common sight. Many times, the oil was drained and left sitting in the kitchen overnight then heated before pouring it in. Sometimes hot coals or even a little fire was placed under the oil pan to loosen it up.

There was no battery. Power came from the magneto, consisting of U-magnets placed in a circle around an armature. If the crank was used to turn the motor fast enough, spark would be generated to start the motor. The spark lever was retarded for starting then quickly advanced as the motor started. The cranker must not straddle the handle with his hand, or it might kick back and break his arm. We all learned to place the thumb so that the crank would kick out of the hand easily. There was no distributor.

When I was thirteen, mother wanted to "go see Teenie." Papa was too busy, so I took the Model T with Mother and Gladys and went to Fayette. I can remember a service station operator screaming at me because I was driving away without paying. I stopped and paid him.

Our first new Model T was purchased in early 1928 and was a good car. Gladys was driving by then and we literally "drove the wheels off it." We never did get a Model A, but Uncle Les did and it was a good car. It didn't have to be black and had a battery, distributor and starter in it.

Chevys

Chevrolet was advertising a new six-cylinder motor for its cars, so Papa bought one of those. It took us to college, served as transportation for Rosella Bauer and LaVon Jones to be married in the St. George Temple on January 17, 1932. I became snowed in at Enterprise as part of that trip and enjoyed every minute of it. That Chevy also got Justine and me married in the St. George Temple then took Momma, Papa, Gladys, Justine and me to Los Angeles for our honeymoon during the last of November, 1933.

While we were still driving a Model T, Pat Devlin, bought a 4 cylinder Chevy. Papa said, "Old Pat gets in that car, swells his old neck and goes out of here like he owns the world." The real test of a car was to climb the Rose Valley hill in high gear. Pat's Chevy could do just that, also our last Model T. Len Devlin was always tinkering with some old car. One day he got one started, drove south along their field and crashed head-on into his Dad in the Chevy. You could hear Pat cursing for miles.

Gladys and Wayne with Family Car

One evening, Mike and I went with John in Devlin's car to see a show in Pioche. While driving down Long Canyon, a coyote jumped in front of the headlights. John yelled "Ki Yi Yippee," tramped on it and ran over the coyote. The shock of hitting the coyote knocked out the headlights and John had to "feel his way" on to Pioche.

While still single I took the Chevy six and Gladys, Grace Devlin and Mary, Dora and Jo Fogliani to a show in Pioche. On the way, I had a flat tire on the rear and stopped to fix it. I got out the hydraulic jack, placed it by feel under a leaf of the spring and started jacking. I felt to see if the jack was still in place when it slipped and caught the webbing of my hand between jack and car spring. I screamed to high heaven and all five girls got out and lifted on the bumper. Lifting would ease the pain but wouldn't turn me loose. When they had to relax their lifting, I would scream again. After about five minutes of that, I thought to simply release the jack with my free hand and freed myself. I proceeded to change the tire with more caution.

I was quite enamored with Dora Fogliani in the first year of high school. However, she treated me so shabbily at times that I got over it. One day, while we had the new Model T, I asked a Miss Bowman, who had come to visit with her parents at Maggie and Will Warren's, to go to the show in Pioche with me. The word got out quickly and in no time I had a car full of kids. Dora jumped into the front seat between Miss Bowman and me. I didn't have the courage to ask Dora to change places. Her appeal to me became even less.

Still More Model Ts

When we were in the first year of college in Cedar City, Mike took their old topless Model T, leaving the Model A at home. The Model T leaked oil so badly that we took 5 gallons of "old Oil" and would add some every time the motor complained. Mike was driving as fast as possible, to conserve oil with greater distance. I was holding on for dear life. He hit a cross ditch so hard that it threw him above the steering wheel. He grabbed with a finger and managed to stay aboard. I borrowed the same Model T and went to Enterprise to see Justine. I took her for a ride and had only a piece of stiff canvas for a lap robe. She nearly froze to death.

Where's the top, Jack?

Dodges and Fords

While many of us were driving Model T's, Jim Hollinger bought a Dodge that had a battery and a "self starter." I predicted, "It'll never work." The Union Pacific Railroad wrecked a whole trainload of Ford cars. Ford sued for full value and collected $157 per car!

One evening in about 1927, Mike and I were in St. George with my dad's new 1928 Ford. Somehow, we ended up with 5 girls in that car with us. Mike whispered to me, "We've got too many." He went to the end of a street, found a huge tree with open space around it and circled around and around that tree. One by one, three girls asked to be let out, with Mike obliging. When we got down to two, Mike straightened the car out and away we went, each with a girlfriend.

Yep, that's Nina in the back seat. Tighten those nuts Wayne!

'Slob' Trouble

Nina Jacobson, weight 300 lbs., came from Salt Lake City to visit with Lena and Leah. When time came for her to go back, her ride back home was in Enterprise. Ezzie took their car with Nina seated on the right rear seat and the rest of us filling the other spaces. We had at least ten flat tires on that right rear side and just about worked ourselves to exhaustion, fixing and pumping. Those tires came off the wheel and the wheel stayed on the car. Then you patched the tube, stuck it back into the tire and worked it back onto the wheel. I believe the Ford V-8 came out with a dismountable wheel. After Nina was unloaded, Ezzie said to one side, "That's the last time I haul a slob like that."

Coverups

While we were going to high school in Panaca, we took the Les Lytle Model T to Caliente to a show. I was driving back to Panaca while Mike and Mary (Fogliani) occupied the rear seat. As we entered Panaca suddenly a young horse landed square on the hood of the Ford and fell off to one side. Honestly, I had been dozing off a bit. Mike said, "You damn fool, can't you even drive a car? I saw that horse coming long before he hit the car. You could have missed him." We took the car on home and the next morning I said, "What will we tell your folks?" Mike said, "We'll tell em nothing. Get your hammer and wrenches." We took the hood and radiator shell off and hammered and twisted Ford "tin" all week. No one ever noticed it. Maybe, because Uncle Les and Aunt Ellen had had the same Ford out on the range, where they met a sheep wagon on the road. Les yanked back on the steering wheel and yelled, "Whoa" and drove the car right between the horses, with the wagon tongue up over the roof of the car and a horse on each side. Our extra dent was never noticed. On one other occasion, I was driving the Ford while Mike and Mary occupied the back seat. It was snowing and I had to work the wiper by a little handle inside the windshield. I dozed a little and the snow really built up on the windshield. Suddenly, we landed in a ditch and had to work to get the Ford back on the road. Mike said, "You stupid idiot! Can't I even trust you to drive."

An Oldsmobile

During the summer of 1928, I went to Montana with Bill and Pat Russell to work on a bridge construction gang at the unbelievable high wage of 50 cents an hour. My parents didn't want me to go, but I went anyway, to "make my fortune." Bill had a fairly new Oldsmobile and sang its praises at every opportunity. One day we were going down a steep grade on a Montana mountain, when Bill looked down and the speedometer read 60 mph. He was about to jump but realized he had a speedometer malfunction. Both Bill and Pat hated Model T's, that by the way, had no speedometers.

Anything serious Pat? Nah, just lost a wheel.

A Dodge as Tractor

Sigvard, the boss, had a Dodge he used to haul his family as they moved from job to job. There was a thousand-pound hammer for the pile driver that had to be moved from job to job. They would try to drag it with the Ford tractor, but it would just bury itself. The Dodge car, even with its entire load, would drag that heavy hammer to the next job. Some of the places we drove pilings and put decking on top of them were Helena, Great Falls and Lewistown. During that summer I had the choice experience of driving a wheelbarrow up an incline, then dumping it in a cement form. I was one of seven in a line that seemed to never stop. I discovered that Pat and Bill worked two week shifts for Blakely.

Construction, then got their checks and stayed drunk as long as the money would last. About half the time they would take girls with them and would leave me in their tent, which they called home. I seldom had much money. Their work was erratic and work that I could do was even scarcer. I was going to "jump a freight train" and go home, but they wouldn't let me. Pat said, "You are going like a gentleman if you go at all; on a train in a passenger car. Needless to say, I stayed most of the summer and finally did get enough money to buy a ticket. When my parents picked me up at Modena, Mother was pale and didn't look well. My insistence on going had just about ruined her health. I was so glad to see her get better. She said my Dad had acted like I didn't exist. I deserved his treatment of my memory as if I didn't exist. We soon got smoothness going again.

A Chrysler

During the spring of 1925, Mr. Brinley and family made a trip to northern Utah. They came back with a Chrysler. Walter P. Chrysler had gone into the motorcar business and Mr. Brinley decided to support him. That car would take the Rose Valley hill in high gear. While going to school in Panaca, I had an opportunity to ride from Panaca to Pioche with Henry Lee in his new Studebaker. It would take the "long hill" between Panaca and Pioche in high gear. Henry Ford was getting competition. Ford challenged all automakers by paying his employees a starting wage of $5 a day. Chrysler Motor Co. eventually bought out Dodge Brothers Motor Co., and still produces Dodges today.

A pedestrian was hit by a car while crossing the street. He yelled at the driver, "Why didn't you blow your horn?" The driver replied, "I don't need to, my car has a sign." "What sign?" asked the pedestrian. "Dodge, Brothers" was the reply.

Ford V8

When the Ford V8 came out, Emrys and Ila Jones traveled all the way to Detroit by train, bought a new Ford V8, and drove it home. They got good service out of the Ford V8. We couldn't understand how it got about the same mileage as the four-cylinder car.

Model B Ford Pickup

Justine's and my first car was a Model B Ford pickup that we bought in Ely during the fall of 1937, as I started teaching in Preston. It was a good car, but leaked a good deal of oil out of the rear main bearing. I used it to haul wood for our stoves in the teachers' apartment at Preston and of course drove it wherever we went. On Christmas Day, 1937 we decided to go to Rose Valley and I decided to go down the valley and over the Silver King Summit. There were about six inches of snow in Preston. Brother Whitlock threw two pieces of rope and a canvas into the pickup just before we left. To our dismay, there were 18 inches of snow in the shadowed wash on the Silver King Summit. I got over by wrapping the ropes around the rear wheels and by driving onto the canvas. Then I stomped the snow in front of the car and drove onto the canvas. Then again and again. We had a real struggle, but finally reached summit thanks to the foresight of Hyrum Whitlock. As I was driving toward Bristol Wells, a Cedar City sheepherder stopped me, got off his horse and offered me a drink of wine to celebrate Christmas. I declined.

The Black Chevy Sedan

The next car we owned was a black Chevy sedan with the marvelous "knee action." I learned to carry a crow bar because the "knee action" would jump up above the wheel and it could be gotten back in place with a crowbar. We owned that car while

Jim, Gladys and Karen and Justine, Farrel, Eldon and I were living at Hamilton and digging quicksilver. I would go to Ely with two flasks of quicksilver on the rear floorboards and the car would "slop" along with the quicksilver shifting in the flasks. We were in that car the evening we went driving along the mountain road near Hamilton, with Jim and the kids on the back seat and Gladys, Justine and I in the front. All at once, three large buck deer jumped out and stopped. Jim cranked the window down and stuck his 22 rifle out. Gladys cranked the window up. Jim started cursing and cranking, then Justine got into the act and the deer trotted away.

> I was driving the same car the next summer, 1941, with Emrys Jones and Jim Lees along. All at once I hit a small landslide and tipped up side down. Jim [and fishing rods and gun mixed up together in the back, but Emrys remained upside down and the battery acid dripped on the seat of his pants. The seat of his pants fell apart the next day.

Justine was expecting Noel and on our next trip to Cedar City, the ceiling of the car dropped onto her lap. There was still enough acid so that her dress on her lap was eaten out by the time we got to Cedar City. She insisted that I trade the car that day. I went into the Ford agency and there was a '38 V8 Ford sedan on special sale. I agreed to trade the Chevy in on the Ford and we agreed on the price. When I went back to get the Ford, they had raised the price $45. I protested and wouldn't take it and drove off. Justine insisted that I trade the Chevy, so I went back again and they supposedly had lowered the price to match the original offer. I signed the contract and took the Ford home. The next day I looked at the contract and to my consternation they had written with a very small print "plus an additional $45." I called them and protested, but they claimed that the guy I dealt with no longer worked there and agreed that I had a splendid bargain. I grudgingly kept the car, and it was lucky I did. That was 1941 and when we got into World War II that fall everybody was stuck for the duration with whatever car he had. That was a good car, especially with no acid in the ceiling. I was teaching sixth grade and band in Pioche. I wound up with two extra used tires. All extra tires were to be sent to the US Government, which I did. They sent 10 cents each in payment for those tires.

The Chevy Half-Ton and Ford 'Lemon'

When World War II broke out, my Dad had a Chevy half-ton pickup, which barely lasted until 1946, when we bought one of the first new Ford six pickups that was built after the War. Since he was running a ranch he qualified. If there ever was a lemon, that Ford six was it. Jim, Papa and I drove it to Pioche one day and Roy Orr said, "How do you like the new pickup?" Jim said, "We should have left it in the garage today, Roy." Roy said, "Why?" Jim said, "The wind's blowin' pretty hard and I'm afraid the pickup will cave in."

After Jim got to working steady for the Power District, he ordered a new Ford sedan from Roy Orr. It came on a flat car on the train and everybody knew about it before Jim did. But they were happy to have a new car. It's too bad Jim didn't live to enjoy it for very long.

27.2   The Great Lincoln Highway

When our parents decided to send Gladys, Mike and me to school in Boston, we bought a 1924 Buick 4 cylinder, 4 door, cloth top from Billy Warren for $150. If Buick ever made a lemon, that was it. We left during the last week in August and traveled on muddy road from Rose Valley to Cedar City. After heading north from Cedar City on a graveled road, Mike stepped it up to 40 mph and a boot in the right front tire made it gallop. We had to change that to the rear and put a bootless tire from the rear on the front. Of course, the tires had to be deflated, pried off the rim and inflated60 lbs. pressure with tubes of course. Inflation was done by pumping mightily with both arms. By the time we reached Salt Lake City, we discovered that the wobbling rear wheel had cut the little stirrup that held the brake over the outside drum. This left us with no brakes and we had to have it brazed in Salt Lake. We were losing so much time that we decided to travel after dark. After all, this was now the famous Lincoln Highway; graveled, but nonetheless the best road so far. There had been some heavy rains and without warning we hit a washout in the Lincoln Highway that wasn't even flagged. We clambered out the far side of the washout with no lights and no flashlight to help us fix them. The mud ruts were so deep in the Lincoln Highway that we just got in them and drove on slowly in the dark. We got to Rock Springs, Wyoming after midnight, slept a few hours and headed eastward in the daylight. We had to dodge brush and boulders for 30 miles. New highway construction made no provision for motorists. At last, after reaching Laramie, we reached our first oiled road. Mike stepped it up to 45 and promptly threw a rod. We had to have it repaired in a garage.

Still running behind schedule we reached the outskirts of Omaha, Nebraska and took the new Bear River cutoff. A road grader forced the Buick too near the edge of the grade and the ground gave way and the Buick slowly tipped over. It tipped next to Mike's side, he being driver at the time. He took one hand, grabbed a gob of mud and said, "Good ole' Nebraska mud.'. The grader crew promptly pulled us back on the road, upright and we were on our way. In Iowa we came to brick road.

WE WERE BREEZING ALONG, when one motorist coming from the opposite direction stopped to talk to someone at the head of the line we were in. Mike pulled out of line, headed straight for the stopped car coming from the opposite direction, hit him and the other car just a little as he threw the Buick through the gap between the two. We said, "Mike, aren't you going to stop?" He said, "The heck with them. I won't stop for anyone that stupid." Later, I saw taxi drivers pull the same maneuver as they drove under the El in Boston, with steel uprights to dodge.

My mother had an aunt in Warsaw, Indiana and we detoured a few miles to visit her and her husband. Her husband was a Reverend Muldoon, I believe. They had a Danish girl about our age living with them and doing the housework. The girl wouldn't speak English and was no more then a slave. Our esteem for the Reverend, who was boss of everything, reached low ebb. We spent the night and drove on.

Troubles Pile Up

The next mishap occurred in Ohio. Mike said, "Look out, feels like a flat." As we looked out, the rear wheel passed us by. A steel square key on the axle had worked loose from the wobbling of the wheel and the nut dropped off followed by the wheel. We got the wheel back on and turned into a farmer's driveway. He was willing to help and took us into Van Wert to buy a new key. To them Van Wert was the center of everything. We didn't say so to the farmer, but we had never heard of it before. As we got off the main road through Mansfield, Ohio, we had a flat tire right in front of a huge mansion. We fixed the flat and no help was proffered. Next came Pittsburgh, PA. Mike said, "You two keep me on the shore road next to the river and let's keep out of downtown. We didn't do our job well and wound up in the most congested section of downtown. When the brakes failed, the Buick slammed into a Buick ahead of us. He had two bumpers, one on each side of his spare tire and we loosened both of those. Mike said, "I'm driving so you argue." Out I climbed and confronted a man of obvious importance, who had a Negro chauffeur. He said, "What's wrong with you?" I said, "Our brakes failed." He said, "Well you won't get out of Pittsburgh until this damage is repaired and you pay for it!" I said, "OK, lead off." Just then a cop stepped up. I said, "We're going to fix it and pay for it." He said, "OK, get movin,' all downtown Pittsburgh is bottled up because of you." He didn't ask for ID or a driver's license. It's a good thing. We didn't have drivers' licenses.

No Left Turn

We followed the man to a garage, but it was the service entrance and we had to go several blocks to a repair entrance. On the second time around the block, he had his chauffeur take a "No Left Turn." Mike took one look and said, "To heck with him. I won't break the law for nobody," and took a right turn. The man was leaning way out of his car watching us disappear, the last we saw of him. At the first opportunity, we stopped and had the brakes fixed. The mechanic got a map and charted a route away from Philadelphia, and New York City, through such "little" cities as Easton, Ogalala, and Harrisburg, PA, Hartford, CN, Springfield and Worcester, MA. Every time a motorcycle cop drove up, we would hide, but then it dawned on us that no cop had any dope on us, so we breathed easier.

Mike, Gladys, Wayne and Mr. Frink in Boston

The night before reaching Boston we stopped in a "room for tourists" in a private home. The next morning Mike, Gladys and I were straining to push our car out of the driveway in order to coast it on a dead battery. The boy in the home, about our age, came out, ignored us and drove his car on their lawn to get around us. When we reached Boston and Huntington Ave., we started looking at buildings. We saw one that looked like the Conservatory, stopped and found out that it was the Museum of Fine Arts. We started pushing the Buick to start it again and half a dozen white clad young men came out of the Museum and had a ball pushing the Buick, but it would not start. We had to rent a battery to get going and found the Conservatory on the second try. We discovered that it would cost $5 per week to park the Buick in a private garage, put our heads together and sold it for $20 to Bill, who owned a service station on Boylston Street. When he heard a big produce truck coming, he would stall the Buick square in the middle of the road, the truck would have to come to a screeching halt and many times the driver would want to fight. When Bill rolled up his sleeves, most drivers just told him to move his car and they would go on their way. Bill loved to fight. When we needed a car to get us back home, we found a Flint, with hydraulic brakes, no less. The only trouble we had with it was flat tires when we got to gravel roads. While we in Boston, we went to the annual auto show, which was impressive. I remember a Model A Ford with a glass engine block, all parts visibly working. The front wheel drive Cord was a special attraction at the show.

27.3   48 Ford 4-Door Sedan

After the 38 Ford and World War II, my next car was a 48 Ford, 4-door sedan, which was a good car. We took the 48 Ford deer hunting to Willow Creek and as we passed a pine tree, a stub of a branch hooked under the rear fender, pulling the car against the tree and bending the fender. We had forgotten an axe and had to take turns and cut down that tree with a hunting knife. Slow work! Forever after, that place has been "Bent Fender." Eldon got his first deer and when he showed it to his mother all three of us waited for her reaction, which we got. When I traded it, I learned that it could outrun any car in the county from Panaca to the Y [service station] or from the Y to Pioche up the big hill. (Should ask Farrel about this.) In the meantime, Farrel bought a Ford V8, which he carbureted with the help of a glass jar full of water, which was inhaled slowly through the carburetor. I may be wrong but I believe he ruined the motor on that one. He had another Ford that was mostly ruined through his driving it in heavy snow from Rose Valley to Reno via Warm Springs and Tonopah.

Eldon and the Silver Streak in Provo

27.4   The 'Silver Streak.'

Eldon bought the old *Silver Streak* Chevy pickup from Nelson Bleak in Pioche. (Eldon says he bought this pickup from Nelson Bleak for $50 and years later after his mission he sold it to Rip Richards for $50. It was a good deer hunting truck.[1]) Noel's first car was a Volvo, which he and Anita brought to Las Vegas before they were married. He repaired it while in Las Vegas, then blew the motor because of an oil leak on the way back to Provo.

WHILE AT BYU Noel figured out how to become a millionaire. Work a million hours for BYU!

When my Dad [Freel] wanted a new pickup, he and I boarded the train at Caliente during the last of March, and went to Salt Lake City. During the train ride, he said, "Let's check out the dining car." We did. All the tables bore white linen, shining silverware and white china, with a black waiter in white. He said, "This is class!"[2]

27.5   Lurch

This pickup has served well. It sits in my backyard today, nicknamed *Lurch*.[3] Farrel and I took "Scratchy" in that pickup and went to Hamblin Valley to get a stag (male

---

[1] Eldon painted the dash with stove-pipe black, accentuated that with a bright red, and applied two coats of Navy Silver to the body. An old Buick muffler scrounged up at the Pioche dump lined up perfectly with its bolt pattern on the block and worked like a charm. It was so effective, in fact, that you had to stop once in a while and raise the hood just to be sure engine was still running! It was striking enough upon its appearance in Provo that Rula didn't hesitate to climb aboard for their first date!

[2] Farrel remembers that this was a black, one ton pickup that was purchased between the 46 Ford and Lurch. The '54 Chevy one ton pickup, was bought in Pioche, Nevada from Von Morris. Manetta worked in the office at the time and typed the paperwork for it.

[3] Larry dubbed this truck 'Lurch' in an official ceremony, I'm told. Freel never did get the knack of driving cars with a foot clutch that was released slowly. He'd apply the old protocol,

cow born without testicles) of mine that was mis-branded. We found the stag with a cow and calf and a large, unbranded two-year-old bull. As I turned the pickup to unload, I ran out of gas. All I could do was put Farrel behind me on Scratchy and drive the cow and calf.

The stag and the bull would leave, but would come back. I couldn't chase them with Farrel behind which turned out to be our advantage If I could have chased them, I'd have lost the stag and bull. I successfully got them to the corral at the Jones Pond, sent word to Billy and Charley Flinspach that I needed gas and they brought some up. I recognized the bull as belonging to Maggie Warren so we put her brand on him. I got the stag and Scratchy into the pickup together and we made it home. Eventually, we got the gas gauge fixed.

My Dad, Larry (about six) and I, took that pickup "through the hills' to Cedar City to get a load of grain. There had been a hard thunderstorm and just beyond the State Line I got stuck in the mud. We shoveled and carried brush and rocks, I revved the motor and eventually, the pickup got unstuck. It was a high point in Larry's life. When we got home he got every toy he had stuck in the mud and made noises to match.

Wayne with Lurch and load of wood.[4]

When I decided to go to Reno for the second semester, beginning in January 1939, Stanton came to Rose Valley with Seth's new 1936 1/2 ton Chevy pickup and we headed for Reno on December 30, 1936. We got stuck in the snow in our yard as we left and made it to Eureka the first day. It stalled once between Ely and Eureka. The front wheel threw some snow on the distributor and shorted it out, but it dried quite soon and we were on our way again. To get into the Brown Hotel in Eureka, we had to climb a 4-foot snowdrift and slide into the doorway. It snowed 8 inches that night and we traveled almost all day in that much new snow. Everybody else was off the road, but we had that pickup loaded heavily enough so that it went like a veteran. Stanton helped us find an apartment on the morning of January 1, unloaded our stuff and headed for Enterprise, non-stop. Just a few hours after his arrival home, Enterprise was snowed in for a month. Since Farrel was a little older,

---

which required that you apply gas to the engine liberally and then release the hand lever. So, Freel would rev up the truck's motor and pop the clutch, resulting in a neck popping lurch forward and a hail of gravel to the rear.

[4]Note Larry's rebar reenforcing the fender!

he was exposed to the cold and wet more than Eldon and got pneumonia after we arrived in Reno.

We had to get a Doctor to come in. Justine got an ear infection and I had to skip half my classes every other day. After a week on that schedule, Professor Harwood, in Creative Writing said, "Remain after class, Lytle" I remained and he said, "Get in or get out." And walked out of the room. I could have bawled. Of course, I had to attend his class everyday after that.

Grandpa Jones' Big Truck

When we moved back home, Seth had a new 1 1/2 ton Chevy truck and came and got us in that. Eldon was just learning to talk and included "Grandpa Jones' big truck" in all his conversation. Eldon walked soon, was a year and three months old when we arrived in Preston. While we were getting settled, we looked at the schoolyard, and there was Eldon negotiating the biggest of the school slides! After all why waste time on the little ones? He called himself "Grandpa Jones" in his conversation to himself. Mr. Whitlock was so amused to hear Eldon say "Whoops, Grandpa Jones fell down."

Justine's mother, Clarissa, died in about the summer of '37. She had been work-ing in the yard at their homestead near Enterprise, developed a massive headache and became unconscious. When we got there she was unconscious and lay on the couch with labored breathing. Aunt Mame Holt, a practical nurse, was there.

Seth was talking to someone and was not noticing when Clarissa stopped breath-ing. Aunt Mame called to Seth and he immediately went to his wife's side. Aunt Mame said, "She died just as quiet and easy without upsetting anyone, just as she has always done."

'58 V8 Ford Sedan

I bought a new '56 V8 Ford Sedan, which was a good car. It got its supreme test when Noel borrowed it to take Larry up the hill road southeast of Rose Valley to look at deer. I told him to go no farther than we could see from the house, but seeing no deer, he went on, driving into Eagle Valley and came to the oiled road. He headed west on the oiled road, wound it up, sped over the hill into "dry wash" and plowed into a whole herd of deer, killing three outright, and breaking legs on others. Larry said all he could see were deer flying up over the windshield. The car was sitting at the very edge of the deep wash. After getting me with the pickup I pulled it back on the road and threw the dead deer into the pickup. The only damage to the car was a headlight ring that flipped out. I was in a bad mood and kept Noel out of cars for a few days.(32.4)

'58 4 Door Sedan

We bought a 1958 Ford 4 door sedan that also was a good car. We took it to Obregon, Mexico to see Eldon just as his mission was ending. We went to the New Year's Eve dance in the branch at Obregon and enjoyed watching them dance. Some of the older members had a whispered conversation with Eldon. They wanted to see Justine and me dance as a couple alone on the floor. We did and they applauded. One of the attractive girls tried to get Eldon or Elder Jay May to dance with them but of course that didn't happen. We found an adequate motel room. Mother was with us and shook her head in disbelief as we passed a Mexican woman about her age toiling along the road, apparently carrying all she owned on her back. We went to a meat market and everything was unacceptable except some shrimp in the shell that had just come in. We bought a quantity of that and Eldon and Elder May ate with us. The shrimp was delicious. We gave the two Elders what was left of some chocolate milk and told them to share it with their two companions. Elder May said, "If we drink it and dispose of the carton, they will never know."

It was interesting that the lights were supposed to blink at midnight. When midnight came, there were no blinking lights. Eldon said, "Give them time, they'll get around to it." At twenty after midnight the lights blinked. There were a lot of firecrackers and shooting sounds. The next day the 58 Ford had a 38 revolver slug sitting in a dent in the roof. On the way home we stopped at Guaymas while Noel, Larry, Julene and I went deep-sea fishing. I caught two nice sea mackerel and Noel didn't catch a thing. We were gone longer than we intended because we had to buck the tide on the way in with a 5 horsepower motor. Poor Julene got seasick and we were all crusted with salt. Justine and Mother were frantic when we were longer than we intended and they couldn't communicate with anyone. I was very happy with the two fish. Eldon also went fishing there as he was leaving Mexico, but didn't catch anything.

We were in the 58 Ford when we went to Lawton, Oklahoma at Christmas time in 1959 to see Farrel and Manetta at Ft. Sill where Farrel was filling his US Army obligation. We parked on the street in a small town and while we were parked, with Noel at the wheel, a colored man backed out next to us and bashed our front fender. He took off at full speed, with Noel in hot pursuit. As he came to a curve in the road, he didn't make it and landed in a drainage ditch full of water. Noel grabbed a tire iron and went for him, but ended up helping a policeman save him from drowning. I went to the office of Justice of the Peace in city hall and found the judge in bib overalls playing dominoes. I told him, "A colored man bashed in our fender." He said, " You mean a GD Nigger? You'll never git no satisfaction outa him." That ended it. The rest of the trip was pleasant and we had a nice visit. Eldon and Rula made the trip with us, also. They were married in May of 1959.

'Up' is 'Down' in the Great Basin

An experience I'll never forget happened in Hamlin Valley. We had the 1 ton Chevy pickup and Farrel, Eldon and I were riding in Hamlin Valley. We held our cattle at the Shearing Corrals and when we had covered the area we prepared to drive them home. I told Eldon to take the pickup and drive "up" Hamlin Valley and wait for us at State Line. As Eldon drove down the hill away from the Shearing Corrals, Farrel and I watched the pickup with Eldon in it, reach the Hamlin Valley road and turn north. We had forgotten to tell Eldon that "up" in Hamlin Valley was south. After a few hours, he turned around and came south. We were very glad to see him.

The Willys and Whippet

Jack and George Fogliani went into the garage business in Pioche during the early nineteen thirties. They bought the Amsden Garage on the most important corner in town, rebuilt the building, got the agency for the Willys and Whippet and took off like crazy. They had never had business training and ran the business "fast and loose" with the gas pumps untended, the parts bins untended and generally ignoring sound business practices. The Willys and Whippet were poorly made cars. I was riding with Jack up the Spring Valley Canyon when he got his Willys stuck in a ditch. After revving the motor a few times he "threw a rod." A Model T would have done better that that. After a couple of years, the business came crashing down around their heads and they went "belly up." After it was all over, Louie (their father) told my Dad "I can still writa da check." So he wasn't completely broke. Jack was elected Sheriff and George went to work for Pioche Mines.

'Power' Steering

One feature of the 54 Chevy (Lurch) was its "power steering" — the driver supplied the power. Noel discovered that when he took our bull up to Serviceberry, he could wind through the trees at a good speed and the bull, shifting his weight with the curves, would make steering much easier. We took that pickup to Las Vegas, loaded with our stuff, and kept it parked in our driveway a lot of the time. One day Justine and I went to the welfare farm and got an overflowing load of manure. On the way back, I stalled the pickup in the middle of a left-hand turn from Nellis to Bonanza. I expected to be ticketed any minute, when three or four "Hippies" in an old jalopy stopped and said, "What's the trouble Dad?" I said, "I'm stalled and can't start it." They said, "Have you got a chain?" I said, "Yes." They hooked the chain onto their car and onto the pickup and pulled me right onto Bonanza St. I started the motor as we moved and there I sat with motor running. They gave me back my chain, wouldn't accept any money and I was glad for at least one bunch of hippies.

The 58 Ford in Vegas

We had the 58 Ford in Las Vegas. The first year I taught at Nellis, I drove out there every morning with three or four lady teachers as passengers, then went back two or three evenings a week to teach piano. One night I was on my way home, signaled a left turn into the island above Bruce Street, realized my error and didn't turn. A city bus clipped my front bumper just enough to bend the end of it forward. The bus driver stopped and insisted that we get a policeman. The policeman came, saw no apparent damage and directed us to go on our way. The policeman, the bus driver and I were standing on the median preparing to leave when two drunks in an old car slammed into the rear end of the police car. The doors on the drunks' car flew open and beer cans rolled out onto the highway. One of the drunks bloodied his head on the dashboard and an ambulance came, as well as a wrecker. The ambulance drivers folded up their stretcher and turned the drunks over to the policeman for handcuffing. The policeman said to me, "You've got to go into police headquarters in the morning and report this. I've got to have a reason for getting this police car totaled." I said I would and did. My thought was, "Why didn't I stay in Rose Valley where I belong?" I also reported the accident to my insurance agency, *Farmers' Group Insurance.* The girl said, "I already know about it. We also insured the drunks."

A S WE DROVE to Nellis every morning, I picked up Ethel Adams first, so she sat by me in the front seat In fact, she sat by me so frequently, that one day I had Justine sitting by me when I picked up Ethel. Ethel obviously resented having Justine in "her" place. I managed to get someone in Ethel's place as often as possible, after that. Ethel was a widow and a few years my senior. She was from Twin Falls, Idaho, a good teacher and very lonely. She rented a room from my cousin, Grace Cornelius and one day she told Grace that I was "a perfect man." That is the only time I've been called "perfect" by anybody, before or since. I sometimes wonder about her judgment.

The '49 Dodge

Julene needed a car and we found an old '49 Dodge sedan for $65. Larry and Gerald Rich went to work on that and got it to running pretty well. One place it would almost invariably stall was right in the middle of downtown Fremont Street. Why Julene insisted on "dragging Fremont' I'll never know. Larry was not old enough to drive when he first got it going. They hauled so many kids to early morning Seminary, that one on the front seat was trained to "duck" if they passed a cop. One day Julene said, "I got a ticket for going 45 up Bonanza." Larry said, "That Dodge won't do 45 up Bonanza." Julene said, "Yes it will. I've got a ticket to prove it."

The '64 Ford

I believe that my next car was a '64 Ford. It ran well and got a continual work out, since I drove it as an "itinerant" teacher and turned right around and drove to many homes after school giving piano lessons. We had that car when Larry turned sixteen. I took him to the *Motor Vehicle Dept.* and for once they weren't busy. Larry filled out his exam papers and handed it to an officer. After a minute, the officer said, "Son, take this paper into a stall and go over it again." Larry was getting a second chance! He was successful the second time and soon passed the driving test. Guess who was taken for a ride that evening, Margaret!

The Pontiac 6

While in Las Vegas, we bought a Pontiac 6 with "overhead cam" and drove it for two or three years. On the way to Seattle, the water pump went out in an Oregon town and luckily, the service station where it went out had a young employee whose specialty was water pumps. He fixed it in record time. About the next year, we had the same Pontiac, returning from Seattle. The water pump went out on a Saturday afternoon in Boise. Garages were closed for the Labor Day weekend, but I found one car salesman at a garage in Boise. He determined that the only water pump was in Pocatello. He did call them and get an answer and they told him the price and agreed to send the pump by Greyhound bus, arriving in Boise early Sunday morning. I met the bus and sure enough, the part was on the bus and I paid $3 transportation charge. Believe it or not the *Seventh Day Adventists* had a garage open on Sunday! They put a young man on the Pontiac who worked very carefully, even labeling some parts. It took 8 hours for him to do the job and I was afraid the $50 I had wasn't enough, but the book rate for that job was $14 and that's what they charged. We went on to Salt Lake City and stayed with Noel and Anita for the balance of that evening. Back to Las Vegas on Monday and I reported for work at the School District Tuesday morning. By the way, I did put a check in the mail to Pocatello, to pay for the water pump.

The Oldsmobile 6

While we lived in Las Vegas, Bob Rose discovered that I was going to buy another car, so he sold me his used Oldsmobile 6. It had an automatic shift and used plenty of gasoline. It was not an outstanding vehicle, but we kept it for a couple of years and it did the job.

Ford Escort Doesn't Match to the Subaru

Just after we moved back to Rose Valley, I got a Subaru four door sedan. It was a very homely looker, but I believe it was the 'runningest' car I ever owned. I got another Subaru after it, but people ribbed me so much about buying Japanese that the next car was a Ford Escort. It was a fairly good car, but didn't measure up to a Subaru. I bought another Escort after that and that brings us to the Tempo, which I now drive. This Tempo was easy to buy. I just told Larry and Noel I needed a new car, gave them a blank check and the Escort. They left for Las Vegas, spent the day, and the next morning I had a new car. Just that easy!

Grandpa Jones' Really Big Truck

Seth Jones went into trucking as a business after Clarissa died. I think he had a 3 or 5 ton Chevrolet truck and, using Enterprise as a base, hauled mostly local produce to southern California. Our little Eldon was really impressed by "Grandpa Jones" great big truck." On one of those trips, he hauled Ollie and her mother to St. George in the cab of his truck. As he shifted gears, he touched Ollie's hand and she gave his hand a little squeeze. (That's all it took!) The romance developed into love and marriage. After they were married, he went into the turkey business. He would normally raise 4000 turkeys and said he made money out of it 3 of 4 years. He and Ollie lived in the house up at the ranch, but before long he hired Stanton to build a new house in Enterprise. I thought he was foolish, but he wanted Ollie to have a place to live in Enterprise after he was gone. That's just the way it has worked out.

27.6   Stanton and Alwyn

Stanton Jones went into trucking in a "big way." He bought the tractor and the trailer and spent most of the time on the road for several years. He would haul melons, lettuce, carrots, corn or anything else produced in California, into the northern

Utah market. He said it was "a sure way to be a stranger in your own home." Then he began working as a carpenter and construction worker, contracted on his own and became a construction superintendent before retiring.

Alwyn Jones worked in carpentry and construction also, and after retiring began making decorative and ornamental items of wood selling these at his home in St. George. He does attractive work. (Seth was Justine's father and Stanton and Alwyn were her brothers.)

27.7 Master List - Cars I've Driven or Owned Over the Years

Nash, Hudson, Overland, Willys, Whippet, Chevrolet, Citroen, Volvo, Subaru, Mitsubishi, Studebaker, Daimler, Stanley Steamer, Lasalle, Pearce Arrow, Flint, Cadillac, Buick, Honda, Oldsmobile, Chrysler, Dodge, Toyota, DeSoto, Edsel, Reo, Mack, Franklin, Hupmobile, Durrant, Tucker, Lincoln, Cord, Fords–Model T, Model A&B, Ford V8.

Chapter 28

LDS CHURCH ASSIGNMENTS HELD BY WAYNE LYTLE

Brother Kent Grant and I were Home Teaching companions in Las Vegas. One evening we visited Brother and Sister Robb (nee Thiriot). Out of a clear sky she said, ``I want you Brethren to heal this sore on my leg.'' She pointed to a spot about an inch across on her lower foreleg. We excused ourselves to go after consecrated oil and for prayer. I felt like leaving town, but we went right back. I anointed her and Brother Grant performed the administration. She had mentioned that she was going to a doctor in California and Brother Grant prayed that the Doctor would be guided to a proper treatment. When we went back about two weeks later, the sore was healed.

28.1   Early Music Assignments

In the fall of 1937, I received the assignment as ward chorister in the Preston, Nevada, Ward. Viola Peterson was organist (pianist). During the summer of 1939 we moved to Pioche, where I again became ward chorister, Mary Hansen was pianist, I believe Pioche Ward was in the Uvada Stake, with Marion K. Stewart of Alamo, President, with Brother Hansen and George Nesbitt as counselors. I became Gospel Doctrine teacher in Pioche and eventually became a member of the Stake Sunday School Superintendency, with Lorraine Hollinger as Superintendent. I enjoyed that position, which took us as visitors to Newcastle, Enterprise, Alamo, Caliente, Panaca and of course, Pioche. As time went along, I became Ward Clerk under Bishop Ridges, which job was not held for long. I became a High Councilor under Stake President Arthur Barlocker and especially enjoyed traveling with Lory Free and Clayton Farnsworth. Justine worked in the Ward and Stake Relief Society Presidencies and also was a Beehive teacher.

Our move to Las Vegas found me again as Ward Chorister and Gospel Doctrine teacher. I led a temporary choir on occasion in the Pioche Ward. In the Las Vegas Second Ward, a choir was a permanent organization. After being Ward Chorister under Bishop Samuel Davis and under Bishop Robert Linge, I was released by Bishop Richard Worthen. Again, I became involved in the Las Vegas Central Stake Sunday School Superintendency, with an assignment to pay special attention to the music in the Sunday Schools. I saw some fine music programs and some excellent teaching performances. My attempts to get the pianos in all the wards tuned according to a schedule, did not meet with Stake approval and I was released.

I became Assistant Ward Clerk, Historian in the Las Vegas Second Ward, and since I did not lead the music I became a member of the choir, preferably singing baritone, but many times obliged to sing tenor beside Frank Bleak, who had a true tenor voice, mine being mostly falsetto. Kay Reid led the choir, followed by her mother Nell, who is now Nell Foster, but who has been Las Vegas Second Ward chorister for nearly twenty years. I was appointed High Priests Group Leader under Bishop Worthen. He was an especially difficult Bishop for me to serve under, being very critical. I also served for many years as Teacher Trainer Director in the Las Vegas Second Ward. This job especially appealed to me. I remember one occasion when I was appointed to give the In-service Teacher Trainer lesson to the Priesthood. I had a neat little page of notes, but just as the lesson started, Brother Gustin grinned and said, "Brother Lytle never uses notes when he teaches." I did not use my notes and managed to present the material.

28.2   Priesthood Group Leader

As High Priests Group Leader I was required to take a once a week class in Genealogy under Sister Cummings from Boulder City. It was a weeknight, with a public school assignment the next morning. She always went from 1/2 to 1 hour overtime and I resented this so much that I didn't gain as much from the class as I should have. I am convinced that good teachers are the keys to a successful Ward and will increase Ward attendance. One of my last assignments in Las Vegas was leading a stake male chorus of fifty picked brethren. This was the best singing group I ever conducted. I cannot remember how often I held concurrent church assignments, but I believe that most of the time I had two.

28.3   Ward Chorister

After moving back to Pioche, I again became Ward Chorister and have had a choir when special occasion demanded it. I again taught Gospel Doctrine class and was given the assignment as Second Counselor in the Bishopric, with John Christian as Bishop and Tom Draper as first counselor. Of course the Ward Chorister position was dropped during those three years. I pushed quite hard for special teacher training while in the Bishopric and met with some success. After being released from the Bishopric, I was made High Priests Group Leader and on occasion taught my own class. Bishop Christian is now High Priest Group Leader and I am teacher of the High Priests class. Also I am Ward Chorister. As High Priest Group Leader I had Murray Fullerton and Emrys Jones as counselors. Of course, I have been a Home Teacher through all those years. After moving back to Pioche, Justine has been my Home Teaching companion, but she is no longer able to fill that assignment.

28.4   Temple Worker

We started working in the St. George Temple in about 1969; Friday evening and Saturday every other week for a time and then Friday evening and Saturday every week. While we lived in Las Vegas and while the Temple parts were rendered by the workers, I learned and performed two or three different parts. At about the time we moved back to Pioche, the Temple was remodeled and initiatory and veil assignments were the main jobs to be done. After seven years, we were released as temple workers. The Home Teaching assignment went right on as did our membership in the choir in Las Vegas. I am currently Pioche Ward chorister, High Priest group teacher and Home Teacher.

28.5   Home Teaching

Brother Kent Grant and I were Home Teaching companions in Las Vegas. One evening we visited Brother and Sister Robb (nee Thiriot). Out of a clear sky she said, "I want you Brethren to heal this sore on my leg." She pointed to a spot about an inch across on her lower foreleg. We excused ourselves to go after consecrated oil and for prayer. I felt like leaving town, but we went right back. I anointed her and Brother Grant performed the administration. She had mentioned that she was going to a doctor in California and Brother Grant prayed that the Doctor would be guided to a proper treatment. When we went back about two weeks later, the sore was healed. The Doctor had discovered that she was allergic to nylon.

28.6   Special Temple Experience

Larry and I were Home Teachers to Brother and Sister Schopman. Their goal was to be sealed in the temple, but Brother Schopman could not quit smoking. We made an arrangement with them wherein we would fast and pray if they would do the same at a certain time. When we went back two weeks later, Brother Schopman had quit smoking! After the fast and prayer they had gone to their Doctor, who told Brother Schopman that if he didn't quit smoking at once, emphysema would kill him quite soon. Since then, I have seen Brother and Sister Schopman in the temple many times. At one time in the St. George Temple, a man and his son were standing at the Recorder's desk waiting for their initiatory cards. After handing the cards to them, the Recorder said, "What happened to the other young man?" They weren't aware of another being there, but after the Recorder described him, the man realized that it was a son who had been dead for several years. He got busy and did the temple work for that departed son.

With this we exhaust the narrative of the present story trove — except for the contents of a small container embellished with Indian markings tucked away in one corner. A single glance reveals its contents — here we have a story line running parallel but intermeshed with that of our principle protagonists, namely, the Paiute players in the drama. We have already taken time to consider the legend of Tikapoo. Let us now turn aside to meet and learn something more about those who trod the Valleys before the pioneers arrived and gave Panaca its name. We must not minimize the influence of Native American oral traditions in shaping the interplay of imagination and fantasy in the story-telling of the Red Notebook *and the family presently in the spotlight.*

Part III

NATIVE AMERICAN TALES

Chapter 29

FIRST ENCOUNTER

The Paiute residents of Eagle Valley and the white settlers worked together in friendship and harmony for joint survival in a harsh environment. Later, when government agents suddenly appeared with horses and wagons to transport the entire Indian community of the valley to the Moapa reservation in the vicinity of Vegas Valley, women of both races wept openly as the wagons pulled away.
-- Martha Hollinger Bleak

29.1 Initial Encounter

Some of the first white explorers to come to Eagle Valley were a John (Milton) Lytle and Ira B. Hatch. Lytle was a brother to Charles Lytle who later settled in the Valley and Hatch was an Indian interpreter. They rode horseback through the hills, from St. George, Utah to Eagle Valley. (In 1863 boundary lines had not yet been established and the country was thought to be a part of Utah Territory.)

When these men first entered Eagle Valley they rode up on a knoll on the south east side of the valley to look around. When they looked down into the Valley they saw a tribe of Paiute Indians scattered about. Very soon the Indians discovered the two white men on the hill and at a signal from their chief, they quickly took cover under brush, and behind rocks and trees. The chief or leader of the tribe, whose name was "Old Hyena" remained in the open. The two men rode up to him and told him they were friends and had come in peace. Upon hearing this news, the old chief called to the others of the tribe. They came out of hiding and gathered around their chief and the two white men.

After some time spent in friendly conversation, the chief invited the two white men to stay in their camp that night. The men gladly went with the Indians and enjoyed a supper of rabbit stew and bread made of ground pinion pine nuts. The men said the food tasted good and they spent the night in the Indian camp. The site of this camp was the ground where John Lytle's brother, Charles Lytle, later built his corrals and cow sheds. This land was later owned by Mrs. Maggie L. Warren, Charles daughter.

"Old Hyena" was chief of the Paiutes for many years. When he died the other Indians of his tribe killed his horse and buried it with him. This was a custom often practiced among the Indians in the early days.[1]

29.2   Southern Paiutes

Southern Paiutes were native to the area in southeastern Nevada where Wayne Lytle's grandfather Charles settled as a Mormon pioneer. Arrow heads, pottery and other artifacts were visible on the surface where the first homes were built, and mounds of rocks[2] in specified areas in the valleys marked the sacred resting places of many natives of past generations. The family lore has a rich tradition of stories regarding relations and transactions between the settlers and the local Native Americans. The narrative of Tikapoo, yet to be related, is the stuff of legends which gather momentum with the passing of time. The following provides a glimpse of another interaction, ungarnished but by no means insignificant.

29.3   LaVan Becomes Paiute

The Adoption

LaVan Martineau, a Caucasian orphan, became an adoptive Indian following the death of his parents, when a local Paiute man[3] declared in a matter-of-fact way, "Come, be MY son."[4] Over the course of a lifetime, LaVan became thoroughly immersed in the culture and language of his adoptive people and eventually developed a sophisticated system for deciphering Indian petroglyphs. Contrary to the prevailing view in academia, LaVan boldly argued that there was more — *much* more to the strange figures that embellish the rocks and cliffs of Indian country than the artistic scribbling of ignorant savages. He eventually reported his work in a book entitled "The Rocks Begin to Speak."[5]

Farrel Lytle, having acquired and read the book, was so impressed — after applying its method to rock writings in the vicinity near his residence — that he wrote a fan letter c/o his publisher. When LaVan replied, he noted the Eagle Valley address[6] on the stationery. It turned out that his first wife, Doris Kanosh, had been a descendant of the original Paiute residents of Eagle Valley. This was about the time of LaVan's surgery for colon cancer and after some recovery time, LaVan accepted Farrel's invitation to bring his family to Eagle Valley to show them their roots. In September 1999 they came and stayed for most of a week. Farrel and LaVan were able to match the skyline in old tribal photos and show them precisely where the original Indian camps had been.

---

[1]The above story was told to Elizabeth B. Francis by Maggie L Warren, preserve by Mrs. Myrtle Bliss, and subsequently copied by Henry H. Lee, October 1, 1964.

[2]The rock mounds appeared to be for purpose of preventing predators from disturbing the graves.

[3]The man who took him in, Cedric Bushhead, was single and handicapped. He had suffered an accident that removed one arm at the shoulder. He barely scraped by through small jobs and lived in an 8x10' sheep wagon. Yet, he invited LaVan to live with him and LaVan readily accepted. Bushhead remained a father figure to LaVan all his life.

[4]There are reputedly NO orphans among the Paiutes because of such generosity among members of the tribe.

[5]LaVan Martineau, *The Rocks Begin to Speak.* (Las Vegas, NV: KC Publications, 1973).

[6]Eagle Valley is situated five miles north of Rose Valley, the rural setting where Wayne raised his family.

Figure 29.1: The man on the left is Eagle Valley Pete, the maternal great, great grandfather of Doris Kanosh, La-Van's first wife.

Figure 29.2: Tappus and Maggie, Brother and Sister

Indians Removed to Moapa

During the pioneer period, the Paiute residents of Eagle Valley and the white settlers worked together in friendship and harmony for joint survival in a harsh environment. Later, when government agents suddenly appeared with horses and wagons to transport the entire Indian community of the valley to the Moapa reservation in the vicinity of Vegas Valley, women of both races wept openly as the wagons pulled away. Subsequently, when Eagle Valley Paiutes found the climate at the reservation to be insufferably hot,[7] most reportedly walked away to the north and took up residence on Indian reserves in the Cedar City (Utah) area. Ultimately, Eagle Valley Pete of the above photograph settled (and eventually died) at the Indian Peak reservation in Utah some twenty miles over the mountains to the east of Eagle Valley.

Such were the stories about family roots and history that LaVan and Farrel shared during their time together.[8]

At the time of LaVan's death (from the cancer), a *Sing* was held for him at the Shivwits tribal hall/school in Sham, UT a few miles west of St. George. The purpose of this event was to honor the man and his accomplishments and to sing him on his way to the next life. Farrel and his wife, Manetta, attended and were

---

[7] Visit Las Vegas in the summer time, pitch a tent for a dwelling, and you'll 'get the picture.'

[8] Farrel has since assembled a pedigree of the Pete family that dates back to their tepee residence in Eagle Valley.

profoundly impressed by the spiritual depth and sensitivity manifested by those in attendance.

The Integrity of Paiute Culture

Subsequent to the *Sing* conducted in his honor at the time of his death, Farrel offered the following overview of his impressions:

> My short acquaintance with LaVan has profoundly changed my view of the Indian culture. Too much of our image of Indians and their culture has been the result of movies. Archaeologists have unearthed and documented the lasting (stone and bone) artifacts of their long-ago culture and have had no way to reach the non-material aspects. Our western society is based so much on material objects that we can't imagine what a culture based mainly on religion, history and story would be like. No TV, no movies — not even any light at night. **And every year during those long winter evenings, the history and traditions of the tribe were taught by the elders in the form of songs and stories. Many of the petroglyphs tell the same stories.** I was moved by the persistent integrity of the Paiute culture as represented in their process of mourning. The tribe is healthy and vibrant. People work in the local economy and are prosperous. Some of the youth are learning the old songs and traditional ways.[9]

The only negative note detected was disappointment on the part of his surviving kin, who could not comprehend the vitriolic resistance of titled academics to LaVan's work. Predictably, not a few had cited LaVan's lack of formal credentials as disproof of his arguments rather than confronting them in the context of a lifetime of hands-on experience. LaVan, it turned out, had left behind him a large collection of unpublished materials documenting more recent work, but the family seemed determined to shield him from further criticism by preserving them privately.

29.4   The Snake Clan

According to LaVan, the Paiute Indians roaming this area were members of the Snake Clan, notorious for their use of rattle snakes to protect holy sites as also for their snake dances. Tribal members reportedly would dig a pit, capture rattle snakes, and deposit them in the pit covered with brush and branches for safe keeping. In one ceremony, a dance circling the snake pit would be performed during which the dancers would strike the materials covering the pit with their feet in rhythm, thereby enraging the entrapped snakes. At a crucial point, the cover would suddenly be removed, the participants would each capture a snake, and race away with it, eventually releasing it with instructions to carry their request for rain or some other favor to the gods.

Farrel, upon hearing LaVan speak of such things, asked whether in the case of the rain dance, rain would be forthcoming. "You'd better bring an umbrella!" came the response. Fiction or fantasy? You be the judge. Perhaps the Lytle family addiction to story-telling rests in part on listening to Indian tales.

---

[9]Personal correspondence

Figure 29.3: Lavan Martineau deciphers a panel of Indian rock writing in Camp Valley, Nevada. The site was abuzz with a den of rattlers.

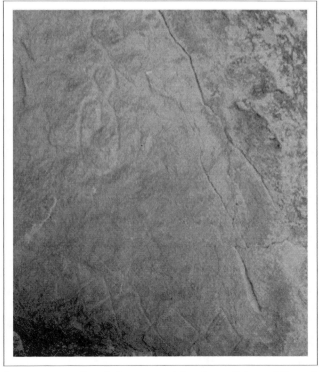

Figure 29.4: An onsite study of this ground-level rendition of Rose Valley's Snake God is a sobering experience.

Troubled by the prospect of LaVan's collection being unavailable to students of rock writing, Farrel suggested to me that I, as a linguist with credentials (Ph.D.), discourse on the significance of LaVan's work for posting on the internet. Being duly impressed by "'The Rocks Begin to Speak", I readily consented.[10]

29.5   Indian Artifacts

Rose Valley, Eagle Valley, and their environs were liberally sown with artifacts originating either with the Paiutes or earlier Native American inhabitants of the area. Farrel, Karen, and I routinely picked up shards of pottery, as well and arrow heads, with an occasional spear head. Obsidian flakes littered the ground here and there, as well as grindstones and rings of stone outlining the location of tepees now long gone together with their inhabitants. Down near Hoop Snake ridge there were abundant rock mounds, which we assumed represented a sacred burial ground(15.6).

At the head of the Valley, there were sophisticated rock-writing panels and, it would seem, a major campground atop a plateau overlooking the nearby creek. In this respect, the white man and his Indian counterparts had seen eye to eye — the layover area of the stage line from Modena was situated at the base of a tufa ledge within a stone's throw of the plateau formerly used by the local Natives. In either case, it was but a short distance to potable water and a variety of shrubs and grasses for grazing livestock.

Figure 29.5: Axle grease graffiti.

Figure 29.6: Solar Sensitive Paiute Panel.

29.6   Axle Grease or Craftmanship

A search of this area today reveals the clutter of both civilizations. Atop the plateau, after each heavy storm, one finds a smattering of pottery and obsidian. Nearby, at the base of the white ledges where the stages and freight wagons pulled aside for the night, is a junkyard of wagon parts and other refuse discarded by passengers and teamsters. The white man left his Kilroy Was Here daubed in axle grease at the base of the roadside cliff, while the Indian carved and painted arcane glyphs in more selective and sacred locations.

---

[10]See the composite article honoring LaVan posted at http://home.comcast.net/~carlbjork/ Marineau.html.

Figure 29.7: Plateau Indian camp area (center right) viewed from across the creek to the South.

Figure 29.8: A petroglyph resembling Freel's description of *hoop snake stubs* (1.1).

Petroglyphs etched in the cliffs at Rose Valley.

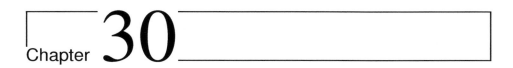

Chapter 30

PAUL MAMEGOENA

"Blow, blow winter wind --- thou art not so unkind as man's (in)gratitude."

30.1 Ottawa Indian Artist

Paul Mamegoena was a child of nature, a red man with a merry heart, a talented person of the Ottawas tribe of Michigan, a noble race which once owned and hunted the woods and glades along the Lake Michigan shore. His father, a great hunter of the tribe, recognized that Paul had the hand of an artist, sent him to a rough school where everything was strange to him. However he showed skill with pencil and chalk. On his slate he drew birds and ships that sailed Lake Michigan, and through the Straights of Mackinaw. He drew dogs and horses, also generally caricatured his teacher behind her back. His teacher did not like his distortion and exaggeration of her posture; so scolded and punished him.

30.2 Chicago

He left school and went to Chicago where he tried to put his art behind him as foolish thing of childhood, and unbecoming of a man. Chicago was not kind to him, so he left, restlessly wandering his way toward the west. He probably heard of the slogan "Go west young man". Finally he arrived at Pioche, Nevada about 1880. Roy E. Lytle writes that Paul stepped off the stage coach when Pioche was an exciting mining town. Artemus Millett, Roy's grandfather happened to be in town when the small boy got off the stage. Mr. Millett became interested when he noticed the lad was alone, so went and talked to the lad, who told Mr. Millett his story. Millett then prevailed upon the lad to come with him, and together they returned to the ranch in Spring Valley. He was welcomed by Gandma Millett and Paul became one of the family.

30.3 Paul Returns to Art

While there, the youngster got back to his pencil and paper, and drawing board. There was a large two story barn with a hay loft with two large doors. On these doors Paul painted a horse, rooster, goose and dog. Those of us who went to the rock school house near the Millett home remember well the paintings on the loft

Figure 30.1: Paul (lower center) attends school in Spring Valley, Nevada, with the other Millett children.

doors. He also painted the picture of George Washington on the large pink and white sandstone cliff across the valley east of the ranch home.

30.4   Attempts to Restore Paul's Work in Spring Valley

As the years wore on, the barn was torn down in 1933. The Washington picture had faded considerably, and could no longer be clearly seen from the road. In 1946, the people elected a new District Attorney, Jo. Martin, who was also an artist in his own right. He came from Arco, Idaho, where he had practiced law for some time. Jack Fogliani was Sheriff at the time and he mentioned that the Washington picture needed a touch-up to the new District Attorney, who immediately became interested. Later the two men went out to Spring Valley to look the situation over. Jo immediately saw the need of some action soon and suggested a scaffold had to be built and would require quite a bit of material — whoever painted the picture surely had some scaffolding.

At that time all we knew about the painting was that it was done by a person named Paul, whose name appeared below and to the right of the picture. Jo and Jack decided to ask the Board of County Commissioners to purchase the materials needed, and the District Attorney and Sheriff would put up the scaffold. The meeting was held but the Commissioners refused to purchase the materials . . . so the Washington picture kept fading away.

Figure 30.2: Paul's portrait of George Washington on a white tufa ledge in Spring Valley, Nevada, where he was taken in by the Millett family.

30.5 Current Status of Paul's George Washington Rock Art

In 1972, the Nevada State Park System purchased the Millett ranch and now has quarters there. Naturally these people want to preserve the painting, and are making every effort to select the best artist who can do a professional job in restoring the work of the Indian artist.

30.6 Word from Paul to the Milletts

Now back to Paul Mamegoena and Roy E. Lytle, who tells of Paul sending a picture of himself when Emily, the Millett's teenage daughter, was just sixteen years old — that would be the year of 1889. Paul (whose blooming relationship with Emily — some have speculated — had not been viewed favorably) had left the Millett family and gone to San Francisco, California, where the picture was taken. On the back of the picture he scrawled "Emily Millet Spring Valley. Regards of Paul the Artist. U.S.A". Before leaving, Paul had made a pencil sketch of Roy's Great Grandmother and Grandfather, which is presently displayed at the Lincoln County Museum, Pioche, Nevada.

30.7 Paul Becomes a 'Bohemian' Artist of Fame

A mining man from San Francisco by the name of Tom Magee had heard about the Indian Artist and came to Spring Valley to meet the young man. Magee saw the artist's work and was much impressed. He encouraged Paul to return to San Francisco with him where he could learn more about being an artist. When they arrived in the big city, Magee turned Paul over to Jules Travernier and Virgil Williams of the Art Association there. Magee felt that Paul's native talent might be directed in the proper channels by the Art Association. It was here that he met Harrison, Peters, Stanton, Dickman, Rodgiguez and the rest of the artists. Paul became the companion of Tavernier's erratic life.

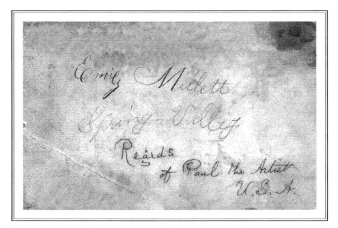

Figure 30.3: A Short Note to Emily from "Paul the Artist"

Figure 30.4: Portrait of Paul During the Zenith of his Career as a 'Bohemian' Artist in San Francisco

He roamed with Dan O'Connell and taught to the genial poet much of his won-drous wood-craft. The Bohemians of the day welcomed him as a 'heart fellow,' and he became a club character.[1] He blossomed in the cheery atmosphere. His laugh was of the gayest, his wants the fewest, his brush and pencil the readiest. Boalt and Behr, Bromley and Tilden, and all who gave the Club its fame, were his familiars.

---

[1]Bohemian Grove is a 2,700-acre (1,100 ha) campground located at 20601 Bohemian Avenue, in Monte Rio, California, belonging to a private San Francisco-based men's art club known as the Bohemian Club. In mid-July each year, Bohemian Grove hosts a three-week encampment of some of the most powerful men in the world.http://en.wikipedia.org/wiki/Bohemian_Grove

30.8 Paul Sketches a Famous Portrait

When Travernier went to Honolulu, there to linger and die, it was found that the Club which had so many of his matchless canvases had not his portrait. So, Paul Mamegoena sat down, and from his sketches and his memory, drew a wondrous likeness of his master and friend, and that portrait hangs upon the walls to this day, cherished and admired, while the man who sketched it wanders the town as an expressman's "lumper" and is stricken from the voting list because, living in the past, he gave his residence as the Bohemian Club.

30.9 Honors Won and Lessons Given

Paul Mamegoena won some fame in the art exhibits of the state. For years he was the assistant of Norton Bish in arranging the picture displays at the Sacramento State Fair. He was also made assistant at the Mid-winter Fair and Exhibition, as well as a similar capacity at the annual show of the Mechanic Institute where his judgment decided the hanging of the paintings, or award?ing the prizes. The Art Association doors were open to him, and he watched with critical eye the aspiration of the youngsters.

He gave some private instruction on his private account, and among his pupils was the beautiful Alice Edith Dickason , then companion of millionaire Thomas Blythe. And, altogether Paul Mamegoena of the Ottawas was a good deal of a figure in high society.

30.10 Humble Quarters

His home was the Bohemian Club, his quarters were modest, for he tucked himself away in a corner of the attic. He was always sure of three meals a day from the Club's larder, and at the Midsummer Jinks, he was the first in the groove, and the last to leave. Here he was on terms of joyous intimacy with the man who gave to the Jinks their world wide fame.

30.11 Paul Becomes an Outcast

The man he came to know and loved, drifted away and bustling business men came to take their places. The Indian artist's experience with the new cult is told in his brief wail which he gave forth in a publisher interview. "Travernier gave me one hundred good brushes. I had them at the Bohemian Club, and the plumbers stole every one of them." So, the time came when he was no longer welcome in his attic nook. There was no longer room for a man who merely painted pictures, but could not pay his own rent and dues. And, Paul Mamegoena of the Ottawas, friend of Travernier and O'Connell was thrust out upon the mercies of the world, so that even the Election Commissioners now knew that he no longer lived at the Bohemian Club. Consequently he could have no vote among the electors of San Francisco.

Roaming without a home, with age dulling the point of his pencil and brush, and necessity 'pinching at the elbow,' this talented child of nature, last of the Bohemians, may well say, "Blow, blow winter wind, thou art not so unkind as man's (in)gratitude."

Figure 30.5: Spring Valley, Nevada near the Millett ranch. Paul's portrait of George Washington is painted on the white ledge upper-right.

30.12   A Poem in Paul's Honor

Witter Byner, a member of the Club, wrote the following poem about Paul in 1912 and was published in the "Call" following his disappearance from the Grove that year. The date of the publication was 11-12-1912.

> I hear there is an Indian named Paul ... An aged Indian who every year
> Solemn as August, came to our festival Among the Redwoods.
> He would disappear — Eleven months, you say, and you recall
> His silent services; now always near The fire he brought new logs
> to raise the tall Gray Smoke Ghost of a redwood. But this year,
> I hear, there *WAS* an Indian named Paul.

30.13   Postlude

Tom Magee was a member of the Club from 1905-1908. Virgil Williams from 1873-1887. Jules Tavernier from 1874-1889. Tavernier went to Hawaii in the early 1880's and died there in 1889. So ends the trail of Paul Mamegoena who found shelter and love with the Millett family, early pioneers of Spring Valley, and fame and disappointment in San Francisco.

> Credit for the Mamegoena story: The San Francisco Examiner of 1911: Henry L. Perry, Historiographer and Roy E. Lytle. (Compiled by Jack Fogliani)

30.14   Tepee Lost

Interestingly, local verbal tradition (discounted by some as unreliable) has preserved a glimpse of the linguistic/conceptual divide between American intruders and the native Paiute. As the story goes, Pete was on one occasion wandering about among the junipers and pines, from one side of the ridge to the other, seemingly disoriented. A local cowhand who happened to ride by in search of stray cattle asked him if he was *lost*. Annoyed, Pete fired back that he was not *lost*; his TEPEE was *lost*. Pete, it seemed, could not conceive of having lost himself and did not know of anyone who had misplaced him? (Think about it.)

30.15 Sure Cure

Note: This story is somewhat 'gross,' but is apparently also included by Wayne to illustrate the difficulty Native Americans had in acquiring a working knowledge of English: Ike Mathes met Pete one morning and said, ``How are you Pete?'' Pete said, ``Not very good.'' Ike said, ``What's the matter?'' Pete said, ``Can't crap, for some reason.'' Ike said, ``Come over to my house with me.'' After reaching Ike's house, Ike went in and came back with a little bottle of pills. He said, ``Take one tonight and one in the morning.'' Pete left with the bottle and Ike went on his way. Upon seeing Pete a couple of days later, Ike said, ``Move yet, Pete.'' Pete said, ``no''. Ike said, ``Take two of those pills morning and evening and that should do it.'' Pete agreed to do that. Upon seeing Pete a couple of days later, Ike Said, ``Move yet, Pete?'' Pete said, ``Crap all over tent, all over squaw, all over papoose. Maybe so *move* tomorrow.''

Part IV

THE STORY-TELLING CONTINUES

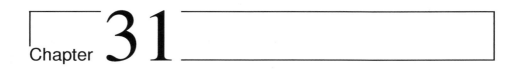

Chapter **31**

THE WEST-SIDE CATTLE COMPANY

Since Freel ranged some 150 head of cattle, and Charles as many as 500, it fell to Wayne, both as a youth and adult to participate in the activities of the West Side Cattle Company. *His grandsons, Farrel and Eldon later joined in.*

31.1 More Roots of the Red Notebook

Old timers say that when the original Mormon settlers first scouted the areas west of Cedar City to be colonized, they rode through an open range populated with native grasses as high as a horse's belly. It was prime cattle country and the local Paiute Indians were hospitable. And so, having dubbed it the *Meadow Valley* region, came and settled those valleys where water was sufficiently plentiful to sustain meadows, gardens, and orchards. Hereford cattle of a sturdy variety were soon thriving on the ridges and in the mountains of the area, where they pastured from April to September and were then herded southeast to lower elevations[1] or gathered into feedlots in the Valleys for the winter to subsist on wild hay which had been harvested when the sun was high.

Access to the railroad and shipping was first available at Milford, Utah, to the northeast and later, as the railroad evolved, in Modena, which lay opposite the Valleys on the Utah side of the adjacent mountain range. State Line, where the drama between Lou (Chapter 11) and her suitors played out, lay some twenty miles north on the southern tip of the Great Basin, and was connected by a rugged road to Modena. Freight wagons rivaling the size of modern 'big rigs' carved out a road up Serviceberry wash and over the 'little' and 'big' summits to Modena once the railroad had progressed southward to that point. Rose Valley with its flowing creek and ample camping area was a lay-over on the route and travelers intermingled their names, initials and dates of passage in wagon grease on its ledges at the head of the Valley.

Doran, Wayne's grandson passed over the former camping grounds in more recent times with a metal detector and, among the square-headed nails, horse shoes, wagon

---

[1]The famous purple sage of *Dry Lake* between Caliente and Pahranagat Valley provided winter range for many local ranchers.

parts, and other debris covered with layers of earth and animal droppings **managed to recover a gold coin which had been minted in France!**

TIME AND EROSION are slowly erasing their scribbles but many are still visible and legible . . . as are those of the Paiutes, one of which is solar sensitive and at the solstice is momentarily illuminated by a shaft of light which pierces the ledge atop the eastern rim of the Valley and strikes it dead center. Hollywood and Indiana Jones couldn't stage a more breathtaking archeological spectacle!

Subsequently, Pioche (1868-), a boom town populated by the usual meld of miners, bar keepers, prostitutes, and hired guns materialized in a canyon less than a day's ride away. This, town, reputed to have produced dozens of fatal shootings before the first natural death occurred, was sustained by lodes of rich silver ore. It lay some 12 miles to the west, where it was ultimately linked by a spur to the mainline of the Union Pacific, whose locomotives roared through Caliente some 40 miles to the south, stopping only for refueling or repair at its 'roundhouse' or to disgorge any freight and passengers destined for the area.

Local ranchers immediately exploited the opportunity to export beef by driving market-ready animals to Pioche for shipment, which was soon a target of cattle and hide buyers wielding hefty bank rolls. It was only natural, of course, that the ranchers should pull together for commercial advantage and common support in their management of the cattle. Given these developments, their ultimate response to the situation was *The West Side Cattle Company*, a confederation of ranchers having a common interest and range for their cattle.

West Side Ranchers

When the federal government had released its official survey of state lines in 1870, and the Mormon settlers were shaken to discover that they were in Nevada rather than Utah. Nevada immediately responded by sending out their tax collectors to the settlements to collect back taxes in gold and silver, while Utah, loathe to accept the validity of the survey, continued to levy its own taxes. Not a few pulled up stakes at that time and left for other climes where one didn't have to take up arms against tax collectors, but Charlie Lytle had decided to stay on and wait for things to sort themselves out. Besides he had an agenda of his own with respect to ranching and mining in the Pioche area.

Charlie later traded a mine east of the Valleys in the Deer Loge/Fay area for Rose Valley and the upper reaches of Dry Valley, which he subsequently parceled out three ways to Freel, Les, and Noma (two sons and a daughter), who set about establishing their own ranches. Given that his dad (Freel) ranged some 250 head of cattle, it fell to Wayne, both as a youth and adult to participate in the activities of the West Side Cattle Company. His older sons, Farrel and Eldon, joined him as soon as their developing cowboy skills permitted.

31.2   The Roundup

The yearly roundup was the major event of the Company. The ranchers would gather, cross the divide into Hamblin Valley with their cow ponies and dogs and then systematically gather any cattle in the Valley as far as end of White Rock Mountain to the north. In the early days, Hamblin Valley was patchwork of dry farms where hardy farmers struggled to plant varieties of grain which would mature and yield a crop after the spring rains and runoff. Slowly but surely, these sturdy but naive settlers were forced to abandon their holdings and move on.

The cedar posts of the barbed wire fences which had been constructed to keep range cattle out of the grain fields eventually rotted at the base, and their barbed wire lay strewn about Hamblin Valley, marking the boundaries of the original farms.

THERE IS NORTHING more hazardous to a cowboy and his horse than a tangle of barbed wire partly visible but largely concealed in the rabbit and sage brush which took over when farming ceased. But both horses and their riders became wise to the hazard, and by being constantly alert, serious wire incidents were minimized.

West Side Cowboys at State Line during the fall roundup.

31.3 Rat Splatter

Six Shooter Bill was the 'real MacCoy,' or something like that. He wore boots with spurs and an old baggy hat. Since he couldn't afford tobacco he chewed cactus, but he could spit juice with the pros just the same. His accuracy sure did need some work though. Most of all, what made him an **hombre** to be reckoned with was the iron on his hip. Yes, the real thing — a six gun, which he loved to practice with! He would practice on old cans every day and sleep with it on at night.

ONE NIGHT AT THE SHEERING PENS, an old rat ran back and forth on a ceiling rafter, raising a real ruckus. Finally old Bill, half asleep and half awake, drew his gun. The gun went off accidentally as he reached for iron. By then he was awake. Shots 2, 3, and 4 followed the rat across the ceiling. But shot 5 hit meat, and the rat disappeared for good, blown to smithereens and scattered in bits and pieces on every bed roll in the place! Shot six went off as he holstered his iron, just missing his foot. But he was back to sleep in an instant and everyone sighed with relief. Six shots and one rat ... A great shootout for Bill and all his toes still intact! (Doran Lytle)

An alternate version of this story certified by Farrel as an eye witness replaces Six-Shooter Bill with Don Wilson (36.1), who only required one shot to splatter the rat! Whether Doran and Farrel are describing or embellishing the same event, of course, has yet to be determined. For his part, Doran certifies that his version is every bit as true as Freel's tale of the *hoop snakes* or Wayne's account of the *magic snake medicine*. In either case, the rat comes out badly!

Come and Get It!

31.4   The Evening Watch

Cattle found during the day were corralled at the nearest dry farm for a day or so until the entire Valley had been searched. They were then driven to State Line, up the canyon en mass over the divide and into the Meadow Valley drainage. The principle camps during the roundup were at State Line and the Sheering pens on the south end of White Rock Mountain. At the conclusion of a day's ride, the cowboys approached camp carefully and stealthily. According to protocol, the first man in camp had the job of building a fire and getting supper on. Not infrequently, it was dark before any fire became visible in camp, not because of night work, but because the riders would approach to within striking distance, dismount and settle down under a tree to watch for a fire. Once one was visible, everyone mounted up and came riding in, ready for supper.

> THE RULE WAS that anyone who complained about the food was automatically chief cook and bottle washer for the following day. Six-shooter Bill figured he had a way to beat the system. When his turn to cook came around, he loaded the beans with salt. It almost worked. Bracken took a spoonful of beans and blurted out: "Good @! Those beans are salty! ...but's that's just the way I like em!"

Bill was finally relieved from cooking chores permanently for another reason. To make fresh coffee, he simply added new grounds to the pot, without first emptying out the old. Eventually, when the cooking fell to someone else who did empty and clean the pot, a dead mouse plopped out with the recycled grounds! Nobody trusted Bill to cook after that.

31.5   Rolling Your Own

The mark of a seasoned cowboy — excepting Mormons, of course — was to roll your own cigarettes. As a boy, it fascinated me (Eldon) to see a rider pull a pouch of tabacco from a pocket, shape a slice of paper like a trough, pour a stream of tobacco into it, lick the paper, roll it up into a home-fashioned cigarette, hang it from a lip, and light up — all without reigning in his horse or interrupting conversation with companion riders.

Farrel, Karen, and I learned for ourselves that this was no trivial feat, when we each snipped out paper which was sized appropriately, shaped it into a trough, and poured our own blend of tobacco (pulverized cedar bark), licked the paper, rolled up our own cigarettes, and applied a match. For one thing, the 'tobacco' dribbled out so fast it was difficult to get one lit, and when the light did take hold, the product immediately burst into flame. This was all done secretly up behind the Man's Head, but the attempt did't escape Freel's notice, who smiled wisely when we came in for a drink of water.

> "Not as easy as it looks is it?" "What?" "Rolling your own." "How did he find out?" we wondered. The answer became obvious when we washed up for supper and looked in the mirror. In place of eye brows were black mustaches of singed stubble.

31.6   Freel Forgoes 'Days O' Work'

Cowboys and teamsters, of which Freel was both, who didn't 'roll their own,' normally used chewing tobacco. As I witness the chewing and spitting of professional baseball players these days, I wonder seriously if they don't all descend from cowhands and teamsters.

When Mary tied the knot with Freel, he was a chewer and continued chewing and spitting until Mary became so exasperated with him missing the spittoon by the old wood stove, that she issued a cessation edict. Either the 'Days O' Work' had to go or he could resume life as a bachelor!

So Freel bowed to authority and gave it up. For many years thereafter, he would carefully select a pine chip when he left the house and chew on that. This practice came to and end too, however, when he developed a malignant sore on his lip in the chip area. The doctor told him that pine pitch was carcinogenic, removed the sore with minor surgery and advised him to chew gum. The image of a cowboy or teamster chewing gum, however, was so humiliating that he just couldn't manage it.

> BUT TIMES WERE CHANGING for Freel and the *West Side Cattle Company*, whether they liked it not, and 'old dogs' were struggling with it. It wasn't hard to detect the stress in Freel's face when they maneuvered his trusty wood stove out the door and replaced it with a fuel oil model. And when water was piped into the house, a bathroom installed, and the ol' two-holer demolished, he put it all in context with a single phrase: **"What's a man to do when they tell him he's got to crap in his own house!"** (Noel)

31.7 The Strawberry Roan

Mustangs figured among the natural wildlife of the area — not just domestic horses which had gotten away and became wild (like the ones managed and peddled now by the BLM) — but the variety first established when Native Americans had the area to themselves. A goodly number of these animals were built close to the ground, had hooves tough enough to navigate rocky terrain without being nailed to metal, and evinced more stamina than common domestic varieties. Last but not least, native mustangs tended to be remarkably nimble and sure-footed. Find a mustang of this vintage and you had a first-rate cow pony in the raw.

Mustangs on the Move

My dream as a teenager was to capture one particular mustang, a strawberry roan occasionally seen watering at an open-access trough fed by a pipe extending under the stretch of land between the windmill and the stockyard area. Grandpa Freel first drew my attention to this beautiful yearling with the comment, "Now there's a HORSE for you!" (See also 24.1)[2]

Once spotted, he was gone in a flash, but from time to time he dallied just long enough for me to form a fixation. I could just picture myself on that pony — appropriately decked out in boots, spurs, shaps, and a Stetson hat — heading some cantankerous old range cow in spite of her best efforts to vanish into a tangle of trees and rocks.

But the years came and went, and I with them, off to college without ever realizing my plans for the strawberry roan. The trough and windmill are long-since gone. But one never knows! That roan may linger still ... keeping company perhaps with Old Blue! (39.1)

MUSTANG

Majestic, as in years of old, The silent sentry stands, Loving from his crag of gold The sunset of our land.

Fingers of the twilight air Sift his flowing mane, Lifting sheaves of flaxen hair, Moist with desert rain ...

The marble stallion lingers still, Mane streaming, head held high, A silhouette of strength and will, Sculptured there against the sky.

A monument to sand and wind, To home ... to liberty ... And all that 'famous flight of years,' Engraved in memory. (Eldon)

---

[2]Whether the mustangs mentioned in this and the referenced story are the same or different is not known.

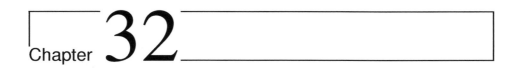

Chapter 32

THE ADVENT OF THE WILDLIFE POLICE

You Lytles are bound to have your venison one way or another another ...
-- Local game warden

32.1 Invasion from the South

Game wardens first made their appearance in our region in the late 40s and early 50s as the population in Vegas Valley exploded and a horde of *city-slickers* suddenly washed into the area every fall to hunt mule deer and fish its waters. They overran the area like an enemy force in trucks and jeeps every autumn, armed to the hilt and visualizing a trophy rack on their wall. At sunrise on the first day of the hunt, we ran for cover ...a horde of men crazed with buck fever were inclined to shoot at anything that moved! Thus, hunting regulations and their companion police force had become matter of necessity for safety of both the natives and the invaders.

Prior to the invasion, local ranchers harvested wildlife in the normal course of their labors. If the meat larder was low, and a fatted buck made the mistake of remaining visible when a rider happened by, out came the lever-action Winchester tucked under a stirrup flange, and the intoxicating aroma of fresh venison again filled the kitchen. Deer were harvested freely year round, without subterfuge or fear of reprisal from the law. Deer and rabbits were simply taken as a free offering of nature rather than another commodity to be taxed, regulated, abused, and bragged about in Vegas dens and bars.

32.2 Replenishing the Meat Supply

When Johnny Devlin drove Farrel and I (Eldon) up Rose Valley's Back Canyon and over the ridge into Eagle Valley in late fall or winter, deer were commonly seen along the way. Johnny loved to sing and stomp out the beat on the accelerator with his toe as he navigated the winding road up the canyon. More often than not, as we lurched along to the rhythm of his inimitable version of some western, bucks would spring out of the roadside wash or bolt from a resting place on the slope, and race for safer pastures.

If the animal looked right, Johnny would screech to a stop, leap out of his beat-up sedan, extract a 30-30 from under the seat, and use the hood as a rest for a sure shot. "@!, missed!" he would then grumble as he restored his rifle to its hiding place under the seat and resume his beat on the gas peddle. But we soon became wise to this maneuver. When he returned us to Rose Valley in the evening, a quick peek through the cracks of his garage revealed the target of his missed shot, neatly dressed and quartered, ready for his own table and distribution to meat-short neighbors.

But times were changing, and a number of men were employed by the County to police hunting and fishing. They even began requiring the purchase of hunting/fishing licenses and tags, and would set up check points to monitor compliance. We purchased our licenses and tags, and carefully tagged every buck we bagged during the season. I remember tagging three bucks one fall, all of them with the same tag. It wasn't hard to outflank check points with a vehicle like Lurch (27.5).

32.3   Atomic Survivor

One warden, who had learned all the tricks by working them himself — in short, a poacher 'par excellence' — was eventually cajoled into joining the wildlife police. To make things worse, they appointed a judge who would actually levy fines for violating the regulations. The Warden's name was soon a household word, people got fined for infractions, and scouts regularly reported his whereabouts so 'native' hunters could evade him.

But Steve was relentless. One Friday night, the Pioche theatre featured a film depicting an atomic shootout which left a sole and lonely Adam. As he wandered the scorched landscape calling hopefully for an answer from a surviving Eve, some wag in the balcony hollered out, "Shoot a deer, and Steve with be there!"

32.4   Restocking the County Larder

Some years later, when wardens had become a permanent fixture, Noel headed home from Eagle Valley in a new '56 V8 Ford Sedan after dark. For Noel at that age, a vehicle had two speeds— stopped or full throttle. As he rounded the turn in a cloud of rubber departing Eagle Valley for the climb to Long Canyon and the Rose Valley turnoff, he was suddenly confronted by a herd of deer smack-dab in the middle of the highway. The vehicle was a substantial hunk of iron and, given the momentum of the impact, the deer hadn't a chance. Within seconds, half the herd lay dead or wounded along a substantial stretch of asphalt.

At home, Noel related the misfortune to Wayne, who dutifully phoned the game warden. They agreed to meet at the impact zone. After dressing out and loading the unfortunate victims of the crash, the warden had only one comment: "You Lytles are bound to have your venison one way or another another, aren't you?"

32.5   Lurch Rescues the Warden

Wayne and Emrys preferred to hunt White Rock Mountain if the deer herd there looked promising and often scouted the area in advance of Opening Day. For this purpose, Lurch was called into service. With its ultra-long wheel base, oversized tires, and compound gear, Lurch could make roads for itself out in the rough. Larry had welded rebar along the fender flanges and its original wooden bed was replaced with heavy sheet metal. Jeeps were wimpish in comparison, despite their four-wheel drive and military medals. With a pile of heavy rocks loaded over its rear wheels, no other vehicle was equal to Lurch. Freel boasted that it could idle forward up an over-steep hill while sliding down backwards. (I tested out this claim and found it to be absolutely true! [Eldon])

The road to the old White Rock hunting camp was destroyed by BLM bull dozers when they chained the brush and trees in the area below, fenced it, and sowed crested wheat grass (a Russian import). To reach the old camp, you had to drive through the brush and washes flanking the field on the south and then make your way north through the trees and brush until you intercepted the old road. We routinely carried picks, shovels, and axes to build short stretches of road if necessary.

One weekend, just prior to the opening of the deer hunt, Wayne and Emrys climbed into Lurch's well-worn cab and headed for White Rock with a lunch but no guns. The game warden on duty in Spring Valley duly noted their passing and figured he'd bag two old poachers at once. He gave them an hour or two and then followed in his jeep, making his way along the path cleared by Lurch. Wayne and Emrys reached their intended hunting area in good time, scouted the area, saw some fine bucks, picked a few pine nuts, and headed for home.

A mile or so from the old camp, where a deep gash had been cut across the road by a passing thunderstorm, they come upon the warden, his jeep with its front end jammed in the bottom of the wash and its rear tires spinning aimlessly in the rear. Wayne drove Lurch across the wash effortlessly near the jeep and climbed out with Emrys to size up the situation.

"Might n't you best keep closer to home where you can walk out if that contraption get's you into trouble?"

No answer.

Wayne gathered up a chain tucked under the seat of Lurch, hitched onto the Jeep's bumper, backed Lurch around, and yanked him out.

"Suggest you follow us out so we can save your hide again if you get stuck . . . there's nothing up on White Rock that would interest you anyway?"

32.6 Treading the Line

A goodly number of the wardens that showed up during the deer season were obviously out of their element. The Utah-Nevada line runs north-south through mountains west of the valleys, a lesson learned the hard way by pioneer settlers. All of the locals knew exactly where the line was, and kept it in mind when hunting and riding.

The road from Spring Valley over the hump into Hamblin Valley crosses the state line at a spring hole just over the Reed Cabin summit. To the west was Nevada hunting territory; to the east was Utah territory. Local hunters commonly travelled into Utah and back into Nevada to reach their favorite hunting areas, and vice versa.

One bright fall day, Wayne and his boys stopped at the spring for lunch. Before long a very dusty but fancy warden vehicle with the Nevada shield pulled in from the road ascending to the watering hole from the Utah side. The warden promptly began to question us. He was hopelessly lost, it turned out, and had spent the entire day policing Utah territory. We suggested he'd better bone up on his geography before some Utah warden arrested him for unlawful intrusion.

32.7   Feeling Like a Paiute

An Alien Invasion from the South

As the invasion of hunters and vacationers from Vegas Valley gathered momentum, there were times when I felt a common bond with the Paiutes who had preceded us in the Valleys and had come to question whether this destructive race was 'human' or not. Nobody seemed to know how many there might be coming as times passed, but our fate seemed to be sealed. The wilderness of tall grasses and abundant game was being overrun by the White Man. The buffalo was gone, the sage hen was gone, the pine hen was virtually extinct, the suckers, minnows, and frogs in the creek were had been poisoned to make room for more popular species . . . — and the *hoop snake* was gone. A virtual tsunami of inhumanity was sweeping over Indian and Pioneer alike against which there was no defense.

How long would it be, I wondered, before the smog from Vegas Valley blotted out the stars and darkened the sun. One could already glimpse the cloud from Alamo and on occasion, if the wind was right, it seemed to creep into Rose Valley and envelop the surrounding mountains in a dirty mist.

One of my permanent memories of camping out with the cowboys at roundup time and rolling out our bedrolls under the stars on a deer hunt was the purity and pristine clarity of the atmosphere.

PINES

I love to contemplate at night The murmur of the pines, The wonder
    of that haunting flight Of metalogic rhymes, And raise toward
    the star-pierced dome My cacophonic cry, And hear the sighing
    branches drone Their hesitant reply:

"The harmony Of rushing sound That roars among the pines? 'Tis but
    the echoed flow profound Of thunder from your mind. Myriad
    voices rumble there, We merely correspond, Echoing the plural
    prayer Of gray monastic throngs Whose symphony of lives com-
    bined Subtend whom you call I"
Oh what silence in the pines, Should I chance to die . . .

Chapter 33

DOUBLE-BARREL POWER

A touch on one trigger was sufficient to get off two shots and, more often than not, when Wayne applied the touch, the hawk came tumbling back to earth in a mangled heap. (Eldon)

33.1 Freel's Weapon of Choice

Freel's weapon of choice was an ancient double-barreled, damascus-steel shotgun. One could easily surmise that in its prime it had been a work of art, what with the patterned steel and engraved stock. But time had worn it down. By the time we had occasion to use it, the barrels were pitted and it was a hair-triggered hazard which you could load up, thumb its butt against the ground, and both barrels would fire whether contact was made with a trigger or not. Just the same, if you knew its shortcomings and exercised due care, it could still get the job done.

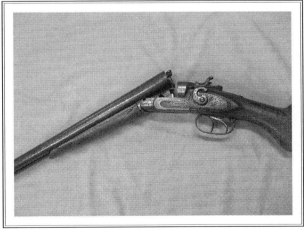

The celebrated Thomas Barker double barreled breech loading shot gun for $12.05.

Cooper Hawks

Cooper chicken hawks were a constant threat to Grandma Mary's chickens, and so Freel kept the old shotgun loaded and ready for action by the kitchen door. A

Cooper hawk has the speed of a jet fighter and the maneuverability of a bat. Their favorite tactic was to take up a position on top of a ledge within striking distance of the chicken yard and watch for a bird naive enough to venture from the cover of surrounding brush into the open. The hawk would then launch into a targeted dive for the chicken, picking up enough velocity that by the time it passed the house en route to the chicken yard, you could hear the rush of its wings but see nothing but a blur. The hawk would strike the chicken at top speed, sending it into a wounded tumble and instantly go straight up to size up the situation. The collision of the predator with a chicken, would make a distinctive noise which was recognizable for some distance. If no one happened to be around, the hawk would make a second pass to carry away its prey.

One's only chance to drill one of these deadly missiles was to get off a shot in the fraction of a second which separated its upward climb from its supersonic exit to a new perch. Wayne became an expert at besting these hawks. He would hear the rush of wings, grab up the shotgun, and close on the chicken yard just in time to bead the hawk at the zenith of its climb. A touch on one trigger was sufficient to get off two shots and, more often than not, when Wayne applied the touch, the Cooper came tumbling back to earth in a mangled heap.

Protecting Grandma's Current Bushes

Requiring less skill was the use of this fearsome weapon to clear uninvited black birds, robins, sparrows, etc. from Grandma Mary's dual row of current bushes. When Freel happened to approach the house while birds were feasting on Mary's currents, he would take the old firearm in hand and fire it into the bushes. The blast of the gun alone was enough to give birds pause within hearing range, and often managed to blast a few of them to smithereens.

One morning after breakfast Freel stepped out the kitchen door to see a swarm of birds in the currents. He stepped back inside, gingerly took the old shotgun in hand and exited the front room door. This placed him at the head of the berry batch. He raised the gun and fired both barrels down the rows of bushes.

The shot was a little low, resulting in a blizzard of shattered leaves, branches, berries and birds. In assessing the total damage, the count mounted up to some three black birds, several mangled bushes at the head of the rows, and three chickens! Freel declared victory, picked and dressed the chickens, and invited everyone to dinner. Discounting a bee-bee here and there in the chicken, it was a feast to remember!

The Stable Shot

When the meat larder ran low and deer were not to be had, a beef would be butchered. The hides of slaughtered animal were throw over rails in the stable to dry and later sold to hide buyers in the fall. One evening, while feeding the horses, Freel notice that some animal was gnawing holes in a beef hide hanging over the rail of the outer stall. When the transgressor did not put in an appearance during daylight hours, Freel decided to visit the stables with his shotgun after dark. Eldon was available and willing, so they headed for the stables in the dark.

Freel loaded up the shotgun and handed it to Eldon, wielding a flashlight himself. They crept silently through the horse corral and took up a position facing the beef hide in the stable. Sure enough, they could hearing the sound of some critter chewing on the hide. I'll put the light on it," Freel whispered "and, Eldon, you let 'im have it!

What appeared as large as life in the beam of the light was a large skunk. Eldon, did his job immediately by discharging one barrel. True to tradition, both barrels fired and the animal vanished in a flash. "God Lord," Eldon, "you missed him!"

Unfortunately, such was not the case. Upon closer examination, bits and pieces of skunk could be seen embedded by buckshot in the logs of both stalls. "I don't smell a thing." "Me neither."

But Grandma met them at the kitchen door. "Undress outside and I'll 'whomp up' a de-skunking compound," she ordered. It consisted of tomato juice and a combination of other odor eaters. Their clothes were hung over a limb in the yard as though they were beef hides and remained there until Mother Nature eventually worked her magic.

Solving the Beaver Problem

A day came when wildlife management decided that the Valleys needed beavers to 'round out' the wildlife in the area. Theoretically, it was beaver heaven. Pussy willows grew like weeds along entire stretches of the water course, offering a tender bark for food and a forest of sticks for dam building. The experiment went well until the beavers decided to seize full control of the water flow. At this juncture they plugged up the entrance to irrigation ditches with mud and sticks in order to channel all the water into their living areas.

One morning when Freel went down to the irrigation pond to turn the water onto an unwatered section of land, he found a sturdy beaver dam across the head of his ditch outlet, with all the water running down the creek channel. He promptly removed the beavers' handiwork, only to find it replaced by the following morning. Up removing it again, he called up the local warden, and suggested he remove the beavers promptly or he would.

When the warden failed to put in a prompt appearance and remove the beavers on his land, Freel devised a strategy of his own. 'Double-barrel power' formed the keystone of his solution. He cut a forked willow and configured his old shotgun to rest in the fork and point directly at the opening of the irrigation outlet. He then attached a string to a willow stick jammed in the mud at the opening of the ditch with its other end tied to a trigger of the gun. Lastly, Freel loaded both barrels. This trap was 'terminal.' Any beaver undertaking to move the stick attached to the string would be 'dead meat' in an instant.

As chance would have it, the warden showed up the very next morning prepared to trap the troublesome animals. Freel led the way in his pickup and they drove down to the pond. Upon approaching the pond, they looked upon an incredible scene of carnage. Beaver limbs and chunks cluttered the entire area. The old shotgun had been driven backwards by the force of its blast, but still remained propped up by the willow fork pointing at the entrance to the ditch. ``Good trap,'' managed the warden, ``but somewhat drastic! Hold off a day or too and I'll get them out of your hair.'' So Freel retrieved his gun, and the warden made good on his promise. Problem solved!

More Skunks

When Wayne took to raising a garden in the yard of his nearby log home, skunks singled out his corn as an irresistible delicacy. At one point, their constant visits to devour the ripening ears became so troublesome that he would take a position atop his tool shed with a spot light and kill skunks nightly. Wayne always prepared for the consequences of skunk warfare by digging holes in advance. He did not use the old shotgun, but would shoot them in the head with a 22 for an instant kill — thus preventing wounded animals from spraying — toss them into a hole and cover them up in a flash. When Doran and Carolyn stayed in Freel's house for a spell after the passing of Mary and Freel, Doran was frequently called assigned to 'skunk duty' atop the tool shed.

The Turkey Massacre

Skunks are not strictly vegetarian, but have a vampire streak in them as wide and long as their stripe topside. They thrive on the blood of birds, capturing them by the head and sucking their blood from the neck. On one occasion, a single skunk broke into Wayne's turkey roost and killed dozens of young birds.

The roosting facility had wall board covering the walls from ceiling to floor, with a narrow opening at the base of each panel. The skunk apparently took up a position within the wall and began thumping to draw attention to himself. The turkeys would stick their heads through the opening to check out the noise, whereupon the predator would seize them by the neck and suck them dry.

When Wayne opened the door next morning to release the turkeys for feeding, dead birds extruded from behind the panels on all four sides of the enclosure. It was all-out WAR between Wayne and the local skunk population from that day forward!

Turkeys

In general, chickens and turkeys make their mark on the world at table time rather winning recognition for their mental prowess. Wayne said that turkeys were so dumb that they'd drown while drinking if something didn't disrupt them at intervals to raise their heads.

Unwitting snakes would wander into the fenced area provided for the turkeys and inevitably perish. The turkeys were impervious to snake bite or hissing. They'd just stomp about making their warning cries and trample the poor reptiles until either miracle provided an opening for their escape or they gave up the ghost.

Wayne raised thousands of turkeys over the years, ordering the chicks in early spring and feeding them through the summer until Thanksgiving and Christmas. You could even visit Rose Valley, pick out your turkey, and help pick it if you wanted to. Not many took Wayne up on this offer!

Folks would have to add their names to the turkey list before Wayne ordered the chicks. There was no shortage of orders! Rose Valley turkeys were as fat, juicy, and tender as turkeys ever get.

Old Cluck

Only one chicken wins mention here. Wayne tells of the evening when everyone climbed aboard the Model T for a visit to Eagle Valley. It was just after sundown and the driver turned on the lights. The road was full of ruts and bumpy, and the riders soon noticed that with every significant bump, the lights dimmed! This aroused serious concern. Headlight failure meant negotiating that treacherous course in the dark under a cloudy, moonless sky.

The headlight problem continued but didn't seem to be developing into a crisis, and so the travelers persevered. Upon reaching Eagle Valley, Wayne walked around front to check for a loose connection, but found instead Old Cluck, one of Grandma Mary's Rhode Island reds roosting on the bumper. With each disturbance of her equilibrium, she would simply raise her wings, blocking the headlight beam momentarily and then settle back to her otherwise comfortable perch on the bumper!

"Get her off of there!" someone demanded. "Why?" came the response. She's in no danger and neither are we." Old Cluck made the trip both ways, apparently without raising an eyebrow. Grandma noticed only one minor deviation in her behavior . . . the next morning at feeding time, she seemed to eat a little more than usual.

Kid Stuff

Farrel, Eldon, and Karen were assigned the task of gathering the eggs. It wasn't like nowadays, when synthetic chickens lay synthetic eggs in contraptions which channel them into a chute for easy pickup. Coops *were* provided with nests, but being free to roam, some of the hens would do their very best to conceal them. We had to search all the bushes for new nests, search the stackyard thoroughly, and check out the stables. During the most productive egg months, we would gather a large bucketful of eggs and carry them to Grandma.

When egg gathering became routine, a competition was initiated to see who could gather the most eggs. Karen usually ended up with the bucket and brought up the rear with Farrel and Eldon scampering about and returning with eggs to the bucket carrier. But Karen was resourceful and overcame her disadvantage. She would streak ahead of the boys in spite of the bucket and beat them anyway! Trouble had laid a trap for us, but we didn't notice until the inevitable happened: Karen tripped and fell with the bucket full of eggs in the race for the last nest!

Grandma was furious, but the chickens and other animals were delighted. They all gathered in a flash for an 'omelet in the raw' and cleaned up the mess before you could say 'Old Cluck!' (Eldon)

Chapter 34

FISHING

Of a sudden, Eldon had a fierce bite which nearly broke his flimsy willow pole. Minutes later, the monster fish struck again! And again! But Eldon just couldn't manage to set the hook and heft the fish out on the bank. (Eldon)

Farrel, Eldon, and Karen — When just a willow would do.

34.1   The Fiercest Bite We Ever Had

At some point, the Nevada Fish and Game tanker began to show up and release trout fingerlings into the creek coursing through the Valleys. They thrived on the freshwater shrimp and other water bugs which populated the stream and, in time, many reached considerable size.

One dark, moonless night, the children were fishing with willow poles well after nightfall along the narrow but deep Spring Valley creek which wended its way through the meadows. They had stayed on because the fish were biting and could get by with the help of Wayne's flashlight whenever it was necessary to detach fish and rebait.

Of a sudden, Eldon had a fierce bite which nearly broke his flimsy willow pole. Minutes later, the monster fish struck again! And again! But Eldon just couldn't manage to set the hook and heft the fish out on the bank. Upon hearing the shouts of excitement, Wayne approached with his flashlight and shone it on Eldon and his gear, who, in the darkness, had managed to encircle one foot with his line. Whenever he shifted that foot or took a step, the monster trout would strike!

34.2   German Browns

Occasionally, among the fingerlings released into the creek by the Fish and Game tanker were German Browns. This hardy trout thrived, seeking out holes under banks deep enough to accommodate them. Years down the pike, Doran Lytle (Eldon's son) discovered the presence of Browns in the basin below Eagle Valley's cement dam and along the creek in the canyon above Rose Valley. Now Doran can catch fish in a bathtub, as it were, and managed to beach several browns measuring up to two-feet in length in waters which other fishermen routinely passed by as being to meager to support trout. Doran had discovered secrets about the feeding habits of diverse varieties of fish which he was reluctant to share with any one else and managed to fill his creel when no one else could get so much as a nibble.

German Brown taken by Doran up Rose Valley canyon.

34.3 Rose Valley's Fishing Bonanza

During the 50s a frightful thunderstorm smote the area with a down-pour of water which brought large flash floods down all the washes and canyons. These converged in the Valleys and promptly washed away the cedar-crib dams built by the CCC many years before. The weak point in each dam, it turned out, was lack of adequate re-enforcement on either side and under their spillways. The rushing waters gouged channels on the both sides of the dams and drilled pits so deep under their spillways that they eventually collapsed into the chasms, their cribs ripped apart and washed tumbling downstream with raging torrent of brush, trees, and sundry debris. A flood of this size has both and rumble and odor which jars the ears and nose for miles around.

The original crib dam in Rose Valley, once filled with sand and gravel, had raised the water level to a point where it could be readily diverted to adjoining fields and meadows for irrigation, but a deep channel reemerged after the flood. Where the crib structure had once been, it became necessary to manually construct a dam of sufficient size to create a pond from which water could drawn for irrigation. Each spring, if the runoff had washed out the dam, it would have to be rebuilt. The normal design was simple — haul rocks to fill up the channel, seal them with clay or manure, and create a pond large enough to feed our irrigation outlets.

Farrel and Eldon, discovering that rainbow trout routinely moved down stream and entered irrigation ditches at the head of the valley, weren't surprised to find them flopping about in the fields once the flow of water was diverted to another area. And so they were 'Johnny on on the spot' with buckets when the water was changed, to gather up surviving trout and manually transport them to the irrigation pond.

This pond was an extra-ordinarily rich feeding water for fish and a six-incher would routinely grow several inches over the summer. When things really became exciting was when the dam stayed in place for several years running, and those trout continued to put on size and weight. We discovered that the bugs and crickets hiding under cow pies in the adjoining field provided perfect bait. Needless to say, we frequently feasted on fat trout at dinner time! We even managed to beg a bucket of cut-throat fingerlings from the Fish and Game guys. Within a couple of years we had a fishing hole pretty much to ourselves which was unequalled anywhere.

> At its zenith, the pond produced fish more akin to salmon the trout. One afternoon while pitching hay in the field adjacent to the pond, we witnessed an amazing sight. Noel appeared on the road above the pond riding his full-size bicycle upgraded with peddle pads to compensate for a small boy. Speared through the gills by one handlebar was trout so large that its tail was dragging on the ground!

Chapter **35**

OTHER TALES OF THE RISING GENERATION

The impact knocked the wind out of her, and she came up gasping and thrashing wildly about, unable to swim to shore. She went down once and resurfaced, still unable to swim. Down she went a second time and managed to resurface but still couldn't swim ... (Eldon)

35.1   Karen Nearly Drowns

During the great depression, a contingent of CCC boys[1] were sent to the area. Their principle assignment was to bring erosion under control. To accomplish this, they cut cedars, trimmed them, and used the posts to construct dams across washes. These structures would slow down the rush of flash floods and eventually fill up with gravel and silt, which served to slow down the erosion process. Along the Muddy River itself, they built larger dams, some constructed with cedar cribs lashed together with wire, while others were more carefully engineered in cement. These served the same purpose in the valleys themselves.

The CCC constructed one cedar-crib dam about midway along the Rose Valley drainage and a larger cement dam at the foot of the valley to the south of Hoop Snake Ridge (1.1). Both dams slowed down the onrush of large floods through the Valley and eventually filled up with gravel and silt. Each dam had a spillway, at the bottom of which the floods carved out deep holes. When the creek was running calmly, these basins were great places to swim and fish.

---

[1] A racial meld of young men employed by the federal government and organized as the *Civilian Conservation Corps.)*

A flash flood renews the deep pool at the base of Rose Valley's cement dam.

Farrel, Eldon, and Karen — plus any visitors — routinely hiked down the Valley to the cement dam and swam in the deep pool below it. One bright, late-summer afternoon, during our swim, Karen dove from a large rock formation on the west side of the pool, but somehow messed up in her technique and struck the water in a resounding flop rather than a proper dive. The impact knocked the wind out of her, and she came up gasping and thrashing wildly about, unable to swim to shore. She went down once and resurfaced, still unable to swim. Down she went a second time and managed to resurface but still couldn't swim. Eldon was standing at the edge of the water, looking on helplessly. Farrel sized up the situation and concluded that the third time down would be her last, whereupon he shoved Eldon into the pool in Karen's direction, who promptly attached herself to Eldon. Farrel then managed to seize Eldon's flailing arm and pull them both to safety.

It was a close call and sobered us up considerably! Somehow, it had never occurred to us that our water games could be fatal if we became careless!

35.2 Blood and Hair

Farrel, Eldon, and Karen were inseparable during their childhood Rose Valley days, roving the ridges looking for Indian relics, rolling tires down the Sand Hill behind Wayne's log house, sailing planes from atop the Man's Head, climbing the ledges in canyons and so on. For the most part, their relation was non-conflictive, but from time there were disagreements.

Come springtime, Eldon had frequent nose bleeds — apparently a symptom of allergies kindled by the newly resurrected grasses and wild flowers. On one occasion, Karen and Eldon clashed over some issue which reached a climax when Karen unloaded a right on Eldon's nose. It promptly gushed blood, whereupon the bleeder forced Karen to the ground and let the blood run into Karen's hair until the bleeding clotted and stopped. Shortly thereafter, the incident was forgotten and the children returned to ordinary pass-times. The calm came to an abrupt end, however, when Justine and Gladys returned from a trip to Pioche. Gladys immediately noticed the state of her daughter's hair, matted with dirt and dried blood, whereupon Karen 'pointed a finger at Eldon,' who got his 'just deserts' from Justine.

35.3 On Throwing Stones

On another occasion, Farrel and Eldon had a disagreement and Farrel took action which sent Eldon into a rage. Sensing it would be wise to put distance between himself and Eldon until he 'cooled off,' Farrel struck out on a dead run across the rye patch bordering Freel's home on the west. Eldon response was instinctive. He snatched up a sizable rock, wound up, and hurled it at 'fast ball' speed after his fleeing brother. The stone clipped Farrel in the back of the head, who went down as though he had been shot! At that point, Eldon recovered his senses, and fearing that the blow had been fatal, rushed to Farrel's side. By the time Eldon reached him, however, he had shaken off the blow and was enjoying Eldon's repentance and tearful distress.

35.4 Age Gap

Noel was some five years younger than the other three, and for them a real 'pain in the rear.' He wanted to join in with them on everything they undertook, but was simply too little to keep up. So they mercilessly 'ditched' Noel, leaving him to unload his frustration and distress on Mom and Dad.

On one occasion, the older children engaged in a game of softball with some visitors. Noel was rejected when he requested to join the game. He couldn't throw and the bat was simply too large for him to manage. But he persisted and was finally conceded the add-on task of 'backing up the catcher.' Noel rushed behind the batter to reach his position without taking note of the fact the game was still in progress. Eldon took a healthy swing at the ball and followed through at the precise moment Noel's head intersected the arc of the swing. Pow! The bat struck Noel in the forehead, whereupon he collapsed in a heap. Wayne witnessed the misfortune, gathered up little Noel, and rushed him to the doctor. Luckily, there was no concussion, and within a day or two, normal activities resumed — despite the sizable knot in the middle of Noel's forehead.

Life has a way of leveling things *karma-style*. Of all the children, Noel grew up to be the most formidable physically, standing at some six-feet two inches — a virtual replica of the tall, slender build of his Grandpa Freel.

35.5 Recovering Montezuma's Gold

High on the cliffs of the canyon connecting Rose Valley and Eagle Valley there is a hole, roughly octagonal in shape, in the sheer up-sweep of the west-side ledge. This hole appeared to be encircled with a blackish ring of sorts with other curious gliffs etched in its vicinity ... non of which appeared to be of Paiute origin. Running lengthwise some twenty feet below is a traversable outcropping which angles downward and makes contact with the base of the canyon.

Figure 35.1: The Ledge hosting Montezuma's gold.

Having read in school about the conquest of the Aztecs by Hernan Cortez and the frantic efforts of the doomed natives there to secure their treasures of precious metal, this odd hole in the face of the ledge took on a special significance for us. A big article in Saturday Evening Post spoke of on particular treasure which had been smuggled out of Mexico by the Aztecs and buried in a cave over by Moab, Utah. Many had sought for it, but it vain. Freel suggested that they had just been looking in the wrong place — it was hidden in Rose Valley's west-side ledges, virtually within sight of the houses!

The immediate area did reveal traces of ancient Spanish activity. Could it possibly be that this apparently non-Paiute mining operation situated high on the ledge had been chiseled by Aztecs? ... that upon unsealing the entrance, one would enter a room laden with objects of gold and silver unmatched even by those discovered in Egypt?

It was there! We could feel it in our bones. Two long wooden ladders down at the stack yard seemed predestined for union. The spliced ladder plus a good waxed rope from the saddle shed, topped off with a sharp shovel, pick, and crowbar were there for the borrowing. And so we launched a project destined to recover whatever the Aztecs had stashed within sight of Wayne and Freel's ranching operation.

Establishing a 'Base Camp'

It was no small undertaking to transport the ladder and other equipment to the base of the ledge, and thence along the tumble of rocks and brush comprising the outcropping to a position perpendicular to the hole above. But in due course, thanks to the assistance of other 'interested' parties, everything was in place and a secure base for the ladder had been prepared.

The distance from the outcropping to the bottom of the canyon at that juncture was frightening to behold and it was with some trepidation that we peered down upon the ragged heaps of rock below from our 'base camp' on the ledge. But gold fever soon prevailed and we contemplated the task of raising one end of the ladder to a position just below the entrance to the treasure room which we visualized behind the hole.

Raising the Ladder

The slope of the ledge at that point was in our favor, so after knotting the rope to one end of the ladder, one of us held it while the others gradually raised its slope. At length the ladder was upright, lodged securely at the bottom with its top at the entrance. Eldon was elected to ascend the ladder while others pressed it firmly against the ledge.

Figure 35.2: Bat manure plugged the entrance.

Breaching the Plug

What confronted Eldon from the top of the ladder was a solid plug of bat's manure in the hole entrance. This dung material had dried and refused to be either hacked away or penetrated with the shovel. Swinging the pick from the top of the ladder was out of the question because the ladder twisted and turned in a dangerous fashion with the shovel activity and swinging a pick with one hand while clutching the ladder prong with the other didn't recommend itself as either a wise or effective technique.

A last-ditch effort with the crowbar managed to loosen some of the sludge, which showered down upon the party securing the ladder below. But Eldon simply could not drive the shaft of the crowbar from his eagle perch through the bat manure into the gold chamber within.

Aftermath

Finally, it became apparent that our approach wouldn't work. It would be necessary to lower scaffolding from above and apply mining knowhow and equipment to penetrate the barrier. But this was unquestionably out of our league, and none of the older folks able to execute such an operation were of the opinion that the hole harbored anything other than manure.

Figure 35.3: Rose Valley goats feared the Montezuma ledges.

Somewhat later, Eldon decided to do John Lytle's goats a favor by driving them up the outcropping, which was richly endowed with wild grasses, flowers, and shrubs. He had visions of goat herders in Switzerland with their animals serenely grazing the steep ledges of the Alps. But Rose Valley goats somehow lacked the ledge-grazing gene — they just stood frozen in place, bleating with fear until they were returned to level ground!

Rose Valley goats plus Rose Valley kids (Emily and Benjamin) and mother (Kaylene).

Looking back on this adventure from an adult standpoint, it was purely a miracle that we were not seriously injured or killed by a fall from the ledge! Rose Valley goats, it seems, had better judgment than Rose Valley kids! (Eldon)

And so it is that Montezuma's gold remains secure in its resting place until this very day in its ledge, stacked to the ceiling within a vault excavated by Aztecs and sealed by bats! (Eldon and Karen)

35.6   Rose Valley Playground

Karen writes about our Rose Valley Playground in her history:

> Grandma's yard was our favorite place to play. We made roads and houses and tunnels, using rocks for cars and houses and whatever else we needed. In those post depression years, we didn't have many toys. But our imaginations supplied what we lacked. Grandma put up with it until we started sabotaging her irrigation ditches and diverting the water away rom her flowers. Finally she had enough, and we were banished from her yard for a whole month.
>
> After that we moved to the sand hill back of Wayne and Justine's house. The sand hill was crowned with white rocks of volcanic tuff that were pitted with shallow caves. At the top of the hill was a large white rock that had been sculpted by wind and storm to resemble a man's head. Our parents before us had played on the sand hill and climbed on the Man's Head. But we discovered it anew. One large rock was a perfect playhouse with many rooms. What fun we had! We were cowboys and Indians that galloped and whooped and hollered and bit the dust dramatically, cops and robbers that stalked each other with rubber guns, or we were explorers discovering new and exciting territory ... (Karen)

Dugouts

Everyone did lots of digging in the Valleys. Post holes, trenches, cellars, irrigation ditches, digging for quicksilver at the old mill sites, mining ... you name it. And so Farrel, Eldon, and Karen decided to do some digging for themselves. The objective was to dig dugouts that were big enough to occupy. It was hard work, but with a pick and shovel, the right location and a few days of digging, you could have an underground room with a stairway of dirt steps roofed with old planks, branches, discarded panels of tin, or whatever. It was great to have a hideaway from the grownups that you crawl get into and they couldn't.

While there were potential hazards — such as cave-ins and roof failure — there were no serious accidents. The worst event that comes to memory was when Karen took her turn in the bottom digging while Farrel and Eldon when to the house for a drink. For one reason or another they were delayed and didn't return right away. Meanwhile, Karen excavated a remarkably deep hole, figured it was deep enough, and decided to show it off to her accomplices. But, when she tossed her shovel out and tried to follow it up and out of the hole, she couldn't. The hole was too deep to climb out of without an assist. Farrel and Eldon found her there, sitting dejectedly in one corner when then finally returned to the site of the dig. (Eldon)

Big Pharma

We also conceived of ourselves as important scientists developing medicines to cure dread diseases. After gathering up all kinds of old bottles and cans, we filled them with samplings of growth from trees and brush, including cedar berries, service berries, pine nuts and needles, wild flowers, moss, and so on. To each we added water and then boiled them up good over a brush fire so that everything in each container blended together into kind of a thin sirup. After pouring off the liquid into bottles with lids, we stored them in our dugouts for safe keeping in case of an epidemic of some kind.

The results were better than expected, owing the the rich chemistry of the flora growing in and around the Valleys. Some of the potions had remarkable odors and tastes, better than anything you could buy on the open market. We were forced to abandon our labs however, when storms filled them with water, and the potions sealed in their bottles fermented in the summer heat or froze in the winter and broke the bottles. Then, with the passing of time, it became apparent that these medications needed to be prescribed shortly after being prepared — their attractive tastes and odors were short-lived, rapidly transforming themselves into the most gagging and repugnant compounds imaginable!

It wasn't a totally futile effort, however . . . in their aged state, many of containers would explode like hand grenades when hurtled against the rocks on the Sand Hill. Lizards, horned toads, chip monks and snakes immediately evacuated when they sensed the stench of our concoctions in the air! (Eldon)

35.7 Desperado Country

Beyond the Man's Head (**Chapter** 1), which presides from atop the Sand Hill over the whole valley, is a topsy-turvy stretch of treacherous terrain which seems to harbor an unidentifiable presence. This geological jumble of ravines, rocks, and ridges is like history itself — one simply can't be certain what strange characters and events might await one there. Whether there may be desperados in hiding the likes of Six Shooter Bill, Billy the Kid, or the Mexican hit men who contemplated robbing Charley Lytle's place (4.12), together with other gunslingers imported by Pioche's mining companies and destined to push up weeds at Boot Hill, or simply the rattle snakes planted by the Paiutes (29.4) to protect panels of hieroglyphs, one can't be certain. At any rate, there is a mystery about it which attracts reptiles, ravens, eagles, bats, wildcats, coyotes, foxes, weasels, badgers, cougars, deer, skunks . . . and children.

Encounter with a Cougar

Gaylin Lytle tracked a buck along a game trail there and met a cougar face to face at a fresh deer kill. The cougar pounced up and away through the back door. Gaylin took the quick escape option.

Figure 35.4: Main entrance

Figure 35.5: Quick escape route

Figure 35.6: Inside

Figure 35.7: Backdoor

Running a Trap Line

Eldon decided to run a trap line in a tangle of ledges there in hopes of snaring a bobcat . . . but had to settle for a skunk. The family could smell the trapper en route home before he topped out on the Sand Hill above the houses!

Chapter 36

THE WAR IN THE PACIFIC COMES TO ROSE VALLEY

``What's the matter, Eldon? Horse too much for you.'' ``Naw! I managed to reply, ``as I spirited away the blood flowing from one nostril. ...just got off to get my hat!''

36.1 Meet Don Wilson

Don Wilson was an ex-marine from West Virginia who married Wayne's cousin Geraldine. Physically, he was a perfect specimen, not only strikingly handsome, but able to shoe horses without the help of tongs ... he simply held a shoe in his bare hands and muscled it to fit the horse's hoof being re-shod.

The War in the Pacific had left its mark on Don, he having personally lived the unspeakable horrors of that war. He had managed to survive the first wave at Tarawa and other bloody landings whose names I only became familiar with upon growing older. Don ridiculed us when we thought that thirty pull ups was an accomplishment and made his point by chinning himself some fifty times, first with the left arm and then with the right. So far as shooting firearms was concerned, Don simply didn't miss, whether the target was a bird in flight or a deer scrambling for safety hundreds of yards away.

Quick Draw

Don always "packed iron," as the saying goes. He was normally armed with a low caliber pistol and a knife of Marine vintage on his belt. Aunt Helen insisted that he hang his pistol on a hook by the door after an inside shooting incident. A cat had lept onto the table in the kitchen and proceeded to lap down his fill of the morning's milk yield. As Don entered the front door, the cat shot away from the table and headed in a blur for the back door. Don pulled his sidearm and killed it as it streaked for the exit.

Don's War Chest

Occasionally, he would give us pointers on marksmanship and self defense and I gathered from passing remarks that he had, in kill-or-be-killed situations, dispatched countless Japanese soldiers in hand-to-hand combat. That this was actually the case became crystal clear when Don showed me his 'war chest.' It was a travel trunk of considerable size stowed away in his bedroom with liberal brass re-enforcement along the edges and on the lid. Don kept his supply of 'Soldier of Fortune' magazine in it, plus a motley collection of artifacts taken for the bodies of the enemy. There were sabers and knives, pistols and cartridges, Japanese family and girl-friend photos, dog tags and a bag with a drawstring stuffed to overflowing with human teeth sporting gold crowns and other golden dental appliances.

A Potential for Trouble

My mother disapproved of my relationship with Don, not because he ever mistreated his wife or children or me, but simply because it discomforted her to contemplate our being influenced by his darker side. Don, did have his demons, to be sure, but normally kept company with them in local bars in the presence of other rough company. The challenge for the bar keepers was to keep Don reasonably sober and peaceable, because they had learned from experience that when he was angry and in a fighting mood, somebody was going to end up with a broken jaw or worse. The knuckles of both hands had been repeatedly broken from fist fighting, simply because the force of his blows was ample to crumple the bones in his own hands as well as those of the unfortunate individual on the receiving end. Local law enforcement was in quandary when Don decided to punch it out with someone. If officers tried to subdue him, he would toss them aside like mannequins, and to draw a weapon on him was suicide. The best policy was simply to give him a wide berth and warn 'tough guys' who happened to be present to humble themselves and do the same.

36.2   Punchin' Cows with Don

Don was a good cowboy (think of an Arnold Swartzeneger - Marlborough Man blend), and frequently stopped by with an invitation to accompany him when there was fishing, hunting, or cowpunching to do. On one occasion, he informed me that Joe Hollinger had horses in waiting for us . . . all we had to do was show up at his ranch at the high end of Spring Valley. Joe had seen cattle there with Freel's brand that needed to be gathered and corralled for transport to Rose Valley.

A Mustang in Training

Sure enough, Joe had horses — a weathered cow pony for himself and Don, and a mustang in training for me. They were ready to ride, with Don and Joe's horses duly saddled and bridled, while the mustang was bareback with a hackamore.[1]

The mustang seemed gentle enough, so I untied him, pulled myself aboard with a standard 'elbow-pump', and eased him north along Joe's outside fence with the other riders. Within a couple of miles, we spotted Freel's cows, circled them, and headed them south towards Joe's corrals.

---

[1] A rope or rawhide halter with a wide band that can be lowered over a horse's eyes, used in breaking horses to a bridle.

Figure 36.1: Spring Valley at race site.

The Horse Race

By this time the ride had become boring, so Don challenged Joe to a horse race, leaving me to bring the cattle along. But my mustang had ideas of his own! Not to be outdone by what he apparently considered to be a couple of used-up domestic plugs, he took off on a dead run after them. Try as I might, I could not rein the animal in with the hackamore and, lacking a saddle, I soon found my self clinging on with my knees for dear life. Before either Joe or Don had taken notice of my plight, the mustang passed them at sonic speed as if they were standing still. They looked on in humble amazement as the pony continued to put distance between us. At such times, THINGS happen, usually to one's disadvantage. As my Triple-Crown contender cleared a large rabbit bush, a startled jack rabbit leaped frantically from under his belly, whereupon the horse simply cleared the next obstacle with some twenty feet to spare and put on the brakes with all four feet. My high school physics teacher had taken a full week to teach what I then learned in a fraction of a second, namely, that a body in motion remains in motion unless countered by an opposing force. The opposition in this case was the ground and the face-down skid into which I was launched.

Rites of Passage

By the time Joe and Don caught up, I had managed to regain my feet and composure, but just same, they took no pains to conceal their amusement. "What's the trouble, Eldon? Horse too much for you?" "Naw,' I replied, "just got off to get my hat." Thereupon, I retrieved by bronco, heaved myself aboard and we continued the drive.

I was a teenager by then and knew better than to manifest any sign of weakness among the 'boys.' Besides, I'd already been tested out for 'manhood,' which simply meant that by then I could cut and trim one hundred pickets (cedar fence posts) in a day given that there was a ready supply of them at hand.

Crows Have Armor

Noel tells about the day Don suddenly braked to a stop, grabbed his 22 rifle, and fired 15 shots at a flock of crows flying overhead. Five of them came tumbling down. "Out of form today?" Don. "Ten misses!" "Come take a look," sonny boy! There were NO misses. Crows have a heavy armor of feathers and each crow had required several 22 slugs at a distance to bring down.

36.3   Disappearance of Don Wilson

After Don had spent considerable time in Rose Valley jump-starting a family and providing backup labor for his in laws, he planned a trip to Idaho, most probably in search of a job with benefits and more security. But, when the time came for him to return from his trip, Don didn't appear. A search was initiated but produced no results. Don had simply vanished. Some speculated that he had been killed in an accident, or perhaps bushwhacked in a bar fight, but no word or report was ever received regarding his fate. His wife Geraldine eventually remarried Henry Sommerville, a man who proved to be a kind and reliable step father to the children.

Now, as I re-read Dad's Red Notebook with its account of Billy Jack and Nellie Flatnose, and recall the remarkable good looks and physical strength of Don Wilson, I regret not having asked him about his parents in West Virginia and the nature of his diet when growing up. To quote Wayne:

> If you see an unusually handsome, dark-eyed person nowadays, you'll know he's a descendant of Billy Jack and Nellie Flatnose. If you get a chance, ask them if they know about the "miracle snake medicine." If he's descended from Billy Jack, he'll know.

Chances are that Don knew.

36.4   War Again Comes to Rose Valley

No town, it seems, escaped the tragedy of Vietnam ... nor any Valley. It was a phase of sheer madness set in motion by ignorance and miscalculation, and ending in more bitter lessons than the country has yet been able to absorb. Shifting to verse after the manner of Wayne's writing, the whole affair comes out something like this:

QUEST

I chase The fleeting beast Across the void; Fatigue My reason In a skull consumes, Whilest devils, Wafted on a yellow wind, Prance about the caverns of my mind.

The steaming spoor In silent mockery retreats Upon the slender lines of space, Promising with faithless smile To meet at DEATH, Where MAN and TRUTH Embrace. (Eldon)

Meet Jerry Barber

Jerry Barber Wilson was Don's youngest son. He was light-complexioned and the summer sun routinely 'burned him to a frazzle.' I found him one day asleep, face up, along the trail between Freel's and Les's houses. When I saw him there, I expected him to burst into flame at any moment. Sensing a probable threat to his health, I nudged him awake. He sprang to his feet and took off on a dead run for home.

The Ultimate Sacrifice

Years later I read his obituary. It wasn't the sun, however, which did him in. It was Vietnam. He had grown into a muscle-bound youth and followed in his father's footsteps. After surviving much of the worst that the Viet Cong had to offer, he was finally wounded. Appearing to be on the road to recovery, the was loaded aboard a ship en route to the states.

SADLY, before he reached home, a blood clot took his life. Search the Vietnam Memorial in Washington and you'll find his name ... or simply visit the Lytle Family Cemetery in Eagle Valley, where he currently lies in the company of relatives and the meadowlarks which serenade that beautiful setting. (Eldon)

Chapter 37

THE OSHINSKYS

The Oshinskys' pickup suddenly took flame and burned into a heap of molten rubble. Thereupon, they looked up the canyon to a structure which, short of a Janet-Reno assault outfitted with helicopters and army tanks, seemed to promise a safe haven.[a]

---

[a]The names of the actual persons featured in this story have been altered to protect their privacy.

37.1 Living Apart

*Mr. and Mrs. Oshinsky pose beside their 'home,'
a tumble-down mining structure near Deer Lodge, Nevada.*

Having 'rubbed shoulders' with people from many walks of life and social strata, Wayne extended a helping hand to the Oshinskys whenever the opportunity presented itself. They were what the majority of Americans would now brand with the stigma of 'homeless' persons, although Mr. and Mrs. Oshinsky did not consider themselves to be such.

Mr. Oshinsky, to the best of my recollection, was a decorated veteran, who had become disaffected with the drift of American Society and chose to live apart. He was fed-up with mortgages, premiums, and the like and simply decided that enough was enough! He drifted from place to place, eking out sufficient to meet his needs as he perceived them to be — namely, clothes on his back, a hat on his head, shoes on his feet, and a coat for when the weather was bad. Wayne discovered his cash-flow problem and reportedly helped him apply for Social Security, both he and his wife being well-past sixty-five years of age.

He had married a woman for life, who was ordinary in every way but one — she was in incurable kleptomaniac. This affliction made it necessary to keep her out of town to prevent periodic stints in the local lockup, where ever that happened to be.

37.2   Place of Residence

To put walls and a roof between them and the weather, Mr. Oshinsky would search out an abandoned structure in an abandoned sector of the county, and set up house-keeping there. Scattered about in the ghost towns which lingered on in the mountains west of Rose Valley at Deer Lodge, Fay, and elsewhere there still stood crumbled houses and sheds which, with a reasonable amount of effort, could be upgraded to tent-like condition. One a month, Mr. Oshinsky would shoulder a pack, walk out of the wilderness and into town. There he would collect his check at the post office, stock up on groceries, and hike back into the wilderness. Wayne and a few others soon became familiar with the Oshinskys' itinerary, and would lend them a hand by giving Mr. Oshinsky and lift into town and dropping him off within a more reasonable hiking distance of their dwelling.[1]

Wayne worked out a schedule with them to ease their burdens. Whenever Mr. Oshinsky showed up in Rose Valley on his way to Pioche, Wayne would put them up for the night in the Freel's empty home across the street. There was running water there, a bathtub, a fully equipped kitchen, and a stock of food. The following morning, he would drive Mr. Oshinsky into town to visit the post office and grocery store. He would then transport Mr. Oshinsky with his purchases to Rose Valley, there to pick up his wife, and head for their residence in the wilderness. Wayne's ever ready and willing — though *Lurching* (27.5) — truck was able to extend the road somewhat and drop them off within striking distance of their destination.

37.3   The Oshinskys' Pickup

Mr. Oshinsky was frugal and before long had saved enough money to buy an old but still functional pickup truck. This vehicle was a godsend to both the Oshinskys

---

[1] Riding in the same car with either of them was less than a pleasant experience, not for lack of stimulating conversation, but simply because they stank to high heaven! Having no toilet facilities, shower or bathtub, their contact with water was by no means a frequent occurrence. To make things worse, their cooking and heating appliances were not 'up to code.' Both had the appearance and odor of just emerging from a fire stoked by railroad ties. Bill McCrosky, a local rancher who commonly drove about in his truck with two large, black, floppy-eared hounds, reported that whenever he gave the Oshinskys a ride, both dogs would crowd to the window on his side and hang their heads out in the clear breezes until their passengers were delivered!

Figure 37.1: *The Oshinskys visit Rose Valley in 1981.*

and their local friends. He was free to move about and search out better shelter if he could find it without inconveniencing anyone at all.

37.4 Nowhere to Call 'Home'

Some conjecture that at this juncture an IMB operative decided that it just wouldn't do to have vagrants living on BLM land which they didn't personally own.[2] Meanwhile, local officers allegedly initiated the policy of searching him out and evicting him from whatever facility he and his wife had happened to settle down in. Before long, the Oshinskys were living out of their truck at the end of the half-road-half-trail terminating at the mustang crossing which descends into Serviceberry Canyon as it exits the gorge some five miles below Diefendorf's old homestead (11.19).

This too, however, was apparently unacceptable. The Oshinskys pickup suddenly took flame and burned into a heap of molten rubble. Thereupon, they looked up the canyon to a structure which, short of a *Janet-Reno* assault outfitted with helicopters and army tanks, seemed to promise a safe haven.

---

[2]During this period, BLM personnel were chaining a large area of brush and trees on the ridges below Serviceberry.

Figure 37.2: *Oshinskys show off their pickup.*

37.5   Aged Tenants in an Ancient Cabin

IN SHORT, the Oshinskys now undertook the impossible, as it were. They struggled five miles up Serviceberry Canyon — despite the fact that the Canyon did not offer so much as a cow trail for passage along its meager stream — on past the snake den exploited by Billy Jack for his miracle snake medicine (1.2) until Henry Diefendorf's old Cabin (11.19) hove into view on the hill above its meadow of spring waters and a maze of tumbledown fences. The dirt roof was still intact and with a modicum of work the accumulation of debris blocking the door had been removed. The old cook stove, it seems, was serviceable, and once the rusty stove pipe had been re-engineered and reattached, the Oshinskys moved in whatever meager belongings they had managed to lug up the canyon.

37.6   Life at Diefendorf's

Every month, Mr. Oshinsky, despite his advancing age, would shoulder a backpack and navigate the five-mile trek to the mouth of the canyon to his burned-out truck and thence along the bench road down into Rose Valley. There Wayne would put him

Figure 37.3: *Voss Lytle atop Diefendorf's Cabin after the Oshinskys departure.*

up for the night and give him a ride to Pioche the next morning. With check collected and his backpack stuffed full, Wayne would then transport him back through Rose Valley and up to the Serviceberry canyon entrance. From there, Mr. Oshinsky would hike up the canyon to rejoin his anxiously awaiting wife at the old homestead.

37.7 History Repeats

Then came winter with heavy snows of the same vintage which had driven Henry out so many years before (11.26). Their chances of survival at the cabin were clearly nil, so before the snow deepened to above knee level, they packed up and with foreboding headed downstream to 'civilization.'

Figure 37.4: *Towards Henry's cabin up Serviceberry Canyon. The mower blade is a relic of the old homestead.*

Figure 37.5: *Underbrush so congested the Canyon below the homestead that passage was virtually blocked.*

THE LAST WAYNE SAW OF THE OSHINSKYS, they were living out of a mangled van at the edge of a field-sized rest area on Highway 93 outside of Caliente.

Given the past record of treatment by local authorities, they were likely ordered to start their engine, escorted to the county line, and invited to disappear into *Never-Never Land*. Wayne received no further word from them but they likely never forgot his kindness to them in harsh circumstances. (Eldon)

Chapter 38

DORAN AND CAROLYN'S KIDDY STORIES

Doran and Carolyn's kiddie stories borrow from Wayne's technique of illustrating his letters and stories to children with stick drawings. (17.6) . . .

38.1 BOUNCE

Bounce! Bounce! Bounce! My ball loves to bounce. It loves to bounce high, bounce, bounce, bounce. "Thanks for my ball," Grandpa. I love IT, and IT loves to bounce!

My ball is named two colors: It is a "Circle one" - "Hard-Soft." But the best thing about my ball is it almost never stops bouncing. Bounce, bounce, bounce. Draw a picture of your ball. Color, size and firmness.

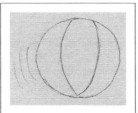

The Ball

I bounced it down stairs and I bounced it up stairs. Then I bounced it off the wall, and then it hit the ceiling and flew across the room. Oh no! no! no! Out the window it did go! Draw a picture showing the ball sailing out an open window.

Out the Window

Since grandpa took off the window screen to repair a torn hole, out the window did my ball go. And as it went out, off a tree limb it did bounce and shot down towards the ground. Draw your ball bouncing on a tree limb.

The Ball in Tree

But before it hit the ground the mail box it did find, and up and up it flew. Up and away it flew and bounced into the truck of the garbage crew. "Oh No!" I thought, and then out of the truck it flew. It came down in the street to bounce and by a policeman it next flew. Draw your ball with a mail box and truck and policeman in the picture.

Mail Box and Policeman

His eyes opened wide, as the ball sailed on by. The whistle he did blow but the ball it did go bouncing on full of fun. While the ball bounced with fun down the sidewalk, I began to run. And run and run and run. But soon it was out of sight. Draw you running after your ball on the next page.

Chasing the Ball

Long and far I did run and walk but my ball it did not stop, and after a long, long run and walk back to my home I began to roam. How sad I felt inside as a tear fell from my eye. Draw youself walking to your home.

Walking Home

As all the fun left my insides and the tears I did cry my thoughts turn to my grandpa. What would I say and what would I do. Only one choice of course, JUST TELL THE TRUTH! Towards home I did slowly roam heading back to my home. Swoosh! as a bicycle did race by as it raced up to each door with the daily paper. With speed it did race in and out of yards and gates. He is almost as fast as my bouncing ball I thought. Draw the boy on the bicycle.

Boy on Bicycle

Finally, after forever it seemed, I walked up into my yard and thought, "Well I better tell grandpa the truth." As I walked up to the door our newspaper lay near the floor so I stopped to pick it up. As I stood up with the paper, in my hands there in the doorway did my Grandpa stand. A tear started down my cheek. Draw a picture of the tear.

The Big Tear

Grandpa said, "Please don't be so sad, I love to see you glad. I saw your ball bounce away but someone saved our day." "What is grandpa saying," I thought to myself? I walked into the hall and to all my wonders there was my ball. In a box in the hall, WOW it's my bouncy, bouncy, bouncy ball. How? Where? I could not speak. Draw your ball in the ball box.

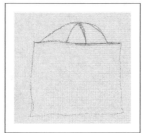

Ball in Box

The speedy newspaper boy's bike happened to fly just right under your bouncing ball. So as he rode by he happily said "H!" "I think I saw this here today. So I thought I might bring it back this way." "I Thank you paper boy for our ball." And into his hand did fall a quarter from my grandpa. Hey thanks the paper boy said and off on his paper route he sped. Draw the paper boy getting a quarter.

The Quarter Reward

"Thanks so much grandpa! I love you for being you, Grandpa! Even without the ball, I love you for being you!" Draw a picture of you and grandpa giving each other a hug.

The Big Hug

"I'm so glad you have fun, but after the all-day chase I no longer want to run." So with more care I shall bounce my ball. Bounce, bounce, bounce. Draw you and your bouncing ball.

You Bouncing Your Ball

38.2 MOUSE IN THE HOUSE

My House Has A Mouse

Written By Carolyn Lytle Illustrated By: (Write your name)

| CREATE ILLUSTRATIONS FOR THE STORY YOURSELF AS INSTRUCTED! |

One cold and rainy day I was stuck in my house and could not go out to play. So while stuck in the house I lay down on the couch and decided to read away the cold and rainy day. While I was reading away the cold rainy day I thought I heard a little vroom. Draw a man laying on the couch reading a book on the next page.

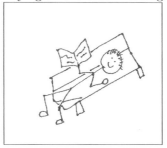

Then from the corner of my eye I thought I did spy back in a dark corner of the house. I saw a tiny shadow sneak about. It snuck from one room and then it flashed back. Bang and flop, oops, hmmm, how did the floor get up here? "Ouch" my head said.

Obviously, I was no longer on the couch. Slowly I picked up my book and blanket and laid back down on the couch. I must have been dreaming, I thought to myself. But if I was not? I sat up and dashed to my all-around junk drawer, shuffling throughout the drawer my eye caught the object of desire — My magnifying glass!

Draw a picture of the man looking through his junk drawer looking for and finding his magnifying glass.

Man searching for magnifying glass in junk drawer.

On went the room lights and down on my hands and knees I bent to look for any mouse that may have snuck into my house. Footprints I thought. I must look for footprints. So out I started in my search for footprints. On the next page draw a picture of the man looking for footprints with the magnifying glass.

Man uses magnifying glass to look for footprints.

In the meantime in a dim corner of the house a surprised little mouse scratched his head and said. "Are my eyes needing new glasses. Just now I went out to dinner and on my way back was it a person I could have passed? I'm not sure." "I doubt it," dear answered his wife. "As you know we have always lived in this house since the day it was so nicely built in our field." Draw a picture of mouse and his wife in the house.

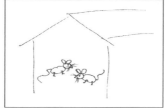

Man and his wife in the house.

"I mean no one would ever put a house in our field unless it was for us. And you know Ken and Gwen in the next field also were given a house and no people have taken it from them. Well none the less, help me find my magnifying glass and I will search and check the house." "Here it is," Ken. "But don't be too slow — our movie will soon start." Draw a picture of the mouse with his magnifying glass starting to check the house.

Man checking house with magnifying glass.

So we both found our mag glasses and put on our pest control hats and so out on a search of pests we both had sent. So Joe the mouse set out, looking for footprints he thought would be the best clue to see if they had people pests in their house, he said to himself. So as I continued my search at one end of the house Joe started his at the other end and off we both began to look. Draw both the man and the mouse with their pest control hats on.

Man and mouse with pest control hats on.

Just a week ago I thought to myself I moved into my new house. I sure should not have any mice I thought. It's too new and was just an empty field. Not a garbage dump or something I thought. As Joe began to search he thought, "This was my clean empty lot; no person would ever want my empty lot I thought." Draw a picture of the house in the empty lot.

The house in an empty lot.

So on with their searches they both did march thinking "It must just be my eyes." So they both thought about getting glasses. So very slowly and very quietly they both focused through their magnifying glasses and carefully examined the floor for clues. "Maybe if I found a dirty foot print," each one thought and so quietly and slowly they each began their search. Draw both the man and the mouse focused looking through their magnifying glass for clues.

Man and mouse search for clues.

I thoroughly searched the kitchen and then sneakily moved to the front room. In the mean time Joe had finished the front room but found no foot print signs. He removed his eyeglasses and rubbed his tire eyes and yawned. Then he thought he felt a breeze. He quickly replaced his eye glasses and grabbed his mag glass and turned to the kitchen. Draw the man in the kitchen and Joe in the front room.

Man in kitchen — Joe in front room.

This is a great place to look Joe thought and off like a blood hound he renewed his search. An hour later they both sat down and yawned. Hmmm all this hard looking each thought but with no success. So Joe wandered back to his miniature cubby hole behind the bathroom heater. And soon I went and had my dinner in the kitchen.

The man having dinner and Joe wandering back to his cubby hole.

Then tiredly we both staggered off to bed. And thought, "Well maybe I just need new glasses or it's just in my mind." Various memories passed through their minds as they slowly drifted off to visions and dreams of their beautiful new house being invaded by uninvited quests. On the next page draw each of them in their beds dreaming.

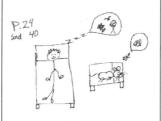

Each in bed dreaming.

During the night I had the urge to go visit Mother Nature so, I half awake stumbled out of bed. At the same time Joe got the feeling to also go see a man about a horse, or in other words to visit Mother Nature also. So half awake we each stumbled into the bathroom. I reached over and flipped on the ceiling light. Boy thought, "My candle sure just got bright."

Draw both of them stumbling into the bathroom, and Joe with a candle.

Now since we both had been too tired to put on our eye glasses, neither one of us could clearly see. So we each visited Mother Nature in our own private spots. But on the way out as we both let out a yawn into each other we bumped. My bare foot bumped Joe's head and into a turn Joe did spin. We both rubbed our eyes and stared.

But without our eye glasses we both did grope. Out went Joe's candle and against the light switch I did bump. "I don't believe in ghosts" we each thought. Our unclear eyes again began to picture invaders in our house. Quickly I stumbled back to get my eye glasses as Joe did the same.

Draw both of them going to get their glasses.

And again we both slowly snuck back to the bathroom. I had my large mag glass and Joe had his. And at the count of one, two, three we both turned on our lights. Looking and starring no one said a sound. We both looked up, down, and around. Then suddenly with great surprise I looked straight at Joe and he looked straight at me. Draw them looking straight at each other.

Draw them looking straight at each other.

Not realizing that I was a people person and he was a pest mouse we stared for a moment and then we both spoke. As our eyes began to slightly clear we both noticed that each other was wearing a *Pest Contro* hat. "Oh, what a relief," we both thought! Finally some help. "Hey I'm pleased to meet you," I said as I squinted hard through my mag glass. I'm sure glad he is a lot shorter than me I thought. Sure will help with finding any small pests. Meanwhile, Joe rubbed his eyes and squinted. "Pleased to meet you too; I'm Joe," and "I'm Pete I replied." I'm sure glad he is so big thought Joe. It sure will help if I get any large pests into the house.

Draw both of them squinting through glasses.

"Hey, where is Pest Control keeping you?" asked Joe. Feeling very relaxed now. Well I thought I'd stay in that front room. "How about you," I yawned. "In this back room across from here." "Well, that's great!" each one thought to themselves. "Now I will no longer need to run *Pest Control* in that part of the house," each one thought.

Draw Joe and Pete visiting with each other.

They both stretched and yawned and said "Hey it's great to have another *Pest Control* man as my neighbor," each one said as they started drifting back to their beds already half asleep. "Well I'll see ya tomorrow" each one said. "Sure happy to meet you." Each one with a smile slipped back into their bed to slumber. "Oh who was that?" asked Joe's wife as he started to doze off. "Oh, *Pest Control* was nice enough to send over a nice tall control man named Pete. He will be caring for the front of our house." Were his last words as he fell back to sleep. "That is just wonderful Joe," she said as she also dozed off to sleep. ZZZZZZZZZZzzzzzzzzzz A soft snoring was heard through the whole house. Now that it was entirely

PEST FREE! GOOD NIGHT EVERYONE!

Chapter 39

COWBOY VERSE INSPIRED BY THE NOTEBOOK

The stores of Tikapoo Indian and Old Blue Monster Buck are formatted and embellished for recitation as cowboy verse under the following headers.

39.1   Old Blue: A Hunter's Tale

In Nevada,
In the mountains,
Ere the summer long departs,
Cottonwoods
And quaking aspens
Fire the ridges and the valleys
In a blaze of autumn art.
An intoxicating freshness,
Wafted on the earth's exhaust,
Stirs the soul from boredom's slumber
And distills in morning's chalice
Cristal flakes of dewy frost.

Irresistible the pestilence of autumn!
Borne upon the sage and pine,
Contaminating springs and brooklets
With the steaming scent of bucks
Swollen with the lust
Of rutting time.

Then the ridges
Hump their shoulders
To delay the hunter's stride,
While the muleys in their sparring
Rip the canyons with their horns
And leave behind
The summer's velvet
On the cedar's

Flailing
Arms!

Have you ever had the fever?
When with flaming cheek
You pulled the 30-30
From the rack
Beside the door,
And deaf to hints and sharp reminders
Of the leaky roof
Or sagging door,
Dipped a rod
In Hoppe's potion for the ill
And pulled it gently
Through the rifle bore?

Oft
At night,
When moths of ash
And glowing cinder
Flutter o'r the shimm'ring flame,
Nostalgic thoughts of aging sorrow
Stir like eagles from my brain
And soaring,
Race upon the wings of longing
To the West,
Where they alight
Upon the crags of Ursine
On the canyon rim,
And breathe the freedom of my childhood,
Where my father
Spoke of Him ... Old Blue!

Dad the cowboy --
Dad the hunter --
With an ancient Springfield
Stained with horses' sweat
And blackened blood of stags
Whose antlers
Taped from beam to beam
Exceeded any spread
The Boone and Crocket boys
Have ever seen!

But he escaped ... Old Blue.
Phantom monster of the range,
Whose massive size
Dwarfed
Another famed and mighty stag whose horns
Swept out and down
In bovine-fashion
To the ground --

Also huge
But strange.

"A hunter's legend"
You may say,
"A fairy tale
To soothe the loss of those
That got away!"

Not Old Blue.
I saw him!
And not I alone:
Three seasoned members Of our clan
Met him face to face
And stunned with admiration and alarm
Lost our heads
And ran!

For his enormous chest
Of grayish blue
Rippled with intent
To tread us under razor hooves
Gore us through,
Hurl us
Gasping,
Disemboweled
Upon the ground
And stomp us out
Like pesky
Stinging
Ants!

We stared in disbelief,
Rifles silent, helpless
In our hands!
Betrayed by fright,
We ejected cartridges
Unfired
Upon the ground!

We
The imprint of his wide-pronged hooves
Had followed since the early dawn
Through canyons,
Ledges,
Clumps of tangled manzanita,
Oak,
Mahogany
And broken
Forest
Lawn.

But the blue jays
With their squawking
Gave our stealthy pace away.
Their raucous cries
Relayed a warning
To the Caesar of the ridges,
Whose heavy hooves in passing
Bruised the earth
And rocked the windfalls
Prone in homage there
Along the Monarch's way.

Alert, that crafty wizard of the wild,
Retracing carefully each step,
Paced backwards in his tracks
A hundred yards;
Then leaped aside,
Concealed in buckbrush
On a slope,
In ambush
For the loathsome fiends
Who with their fetid trash
Defiled the wind,
And with their dread machines
Defaced the land,
Impinging everywhere
Upon the solemn Monarch's pride.

Wheeling in the sky
With derisive cries of impudent delight,
A haughty crow
Beheld our brief encounter there,
Having from his heights
Observed Old Blue
Lay his cunning
Human Snare.

We fled in terror
From the mortal thrust
Of antler prongs
Which caught us unawares
To recompense
Atrocities
Committed
By
Our
Race!

A rifle cracked!
Flung clattering upon the rocks
In our headlong plunge for safety,
An abandoned rifle cracked!

He bolted
Sounding with the bellows
Of his lungs
A whistling snort
Of hot contempt!

He shocked the boulders
With his hooves,
Clearing cedars and ravines
In mighty bounds
Of umpteen yards
Or more,
Each exploding, soaring, jarring
Like a spring recoiling
From repeated sparring
With the ground!

Far below
We glimpsed his bluish hulk
Assume a trotter's pace
And passing through a thicket
Rattle with his awesome rack
Against the willows
Like a boy
Who races with his stick along a fence
To hear the sharp reverberating clatter
Of its trak-a-tak.

Another year,
And perched amid the pristine wonder
Of that wild habitation
Gazing o'r the vast expanse
Of boulders
Trees
And yawning canyons,
I saw a silhouette
Of tree-like antlers
Rise upon the dim horizon
In the twilight majesty of eve
To stand in silence
Watching.

Still he watches
Phantom monster of the range!

Twenty years,
And oft a hunter
In his roaming
Finds a fallen antler
By the storms of winter
Bleached an ashen hue --

An antler singular in structure,
Massive in dimension --
Unmistakably
A relic
Of Old Blue!

Oft at night
When moths of ash
And glowing cinder
Flutter from the dieing flame,
Nostalgic thoughts
Of aging sorrow
Stir like eagles from my brain
And soaring,
Race upon the wings of longing
To the West,
Where they alight
Upon the crags of Ursine,
On the canyon rim
And breathe the freedom
Of my childhood,
Where my father
Spoke of Him ...

Old Blue!

39.2 Tikapoo: A Campfire Story

And forever turned her steps away.

```
SCENE I:

Kailem, on a summer's eve
   The guests would entertain,
      Spinning yarns of suble weave --
         Of love,
            And gold,
               And death,
                  And fame.

Of Tikapoo,
  An ancient warrior,
    By tribesmen left behind to die,
      Bound in skins beneath a cedar,
        His sturdy mustang tethered nigh
          To speed the chieftan on his journey,
            To a land where game abounds,
               Where his fathers dwell in plenty,
                 In the happy hunting grounds.

Heaped hight with juniper and pine,
   Bonfires sear the autumn sky;
     Cloven tongues of smoke and flame
       Leap into the night,
                           and die.

Before the wizened sage, who prays,
   Grieved by visions of the morrow,
     Sits a sullen ring of braves,
       Chanting bitterness and sorrow
```

'Tis not cruelty, this deed ...
    (As Kailem hastens to explain)
        For Tikapoo, what further need?
            For Tikapoo is old,
                            and lame.

The pinions soon will droop with snow,
    Having shared their sheaves of nuts,
        And to the valleys far below
            Will bound the stately mule-deer buck.
                But those too weak to flee the storm
                    Increase the burden of the strong,
    Who sullen bind his legs and arms
        With yucca strands and rawhide thongs,
            And having scraped a shallow grave,
                They lay the silent chief to rest,
                    Abandoning the stolid brave
                        To fade like twilight in the West.

The lodges are dismantled now;
    Provision packs securely tied
        To make-shift pony-drags of poles,
            Bound and trussed from side to side.

This year,
    The vessels of the tribe are rife
        With squash and maize and venison,
            And pinion nuts, the staff of life!
                Nor do they ants, nor locusts shun.

  SCENE II:

Dawn upon the hills at last --
    To the south the clan departs --
        For Tikapoo, the die is cast --
            He views the train
                            with sinking
                                        heart.

Come!
    What childish tear is this
        Betrays the wrinkled face of stone?
            What senile whim this weakling wish
Not to --
    Not to --
        Die alone?

Her dusky eyes the mustang turns
    To search the Indian's misty gaze
        Voicing now at last concern,
            The pony nudges him and nays.

His dauntless squaw,
   To duty true,
      With water fills an urn of clay
         And placing it by Tikapoo,
            Forever
               Turns
                  Her
                     Steps
                        Away.

We shan't attempt to reconstruct,
   Or rhyme to reason here relate --
      Call it fickle chance or luck
         That rescued Tikapoo from fate.

But a trapper in his roaming
   Chanced to hear the mournful cries.
      Frightened, first he fled the moaning,
         A fact, of course, he now denies!

And when at length the pallid huntsman
   Loosed the chaffing rawhide bonds,
      In gratitude the aged Redman
         Forgave the Whiteman former wrongs
            And dwelt with him in placid sorrow
         For the space of many moons.

SCENE III:

Though a man may chance to borrow
   Days, or yet a year, or two,
      The eve will come when on the morrow
         Principal with tax is due.

A profecy?
  A mistic foresight?
     A fit of madness born of age?
        A dark presentiment at night
          Pierced the ancient
                  Indian
                     Sage!

The knarled warrior raised a finger
   To the crowded mountain sky ...
      "Yakway Tikapoo gozaftra,
         Tomorrow Tikapoo must die ..."

"Why, Tikapoo, you're strong and well;
   A match for any younger brave!
      Surely is a jest you tell ...
         You'll see ten years
               before

                              the
                                   grave."

But on the morrow,
    In his tepee,
        Tikapoo lay still and cold;
            In vain they sought the mustang pony!
                So goes the story;
                    So it's told ...

And if you ever ride the country
    Where the mustang bands run free,
        You'll glimpse them bearing on their journey
            Paiute braves you cannot see!

Listen now!
    You'll hear voices
        Echo on the restless breeze
            At night, especially,
                You'll hear voices
                    Whispering
                        Among
                            The trees!

And if you'll scan the deep horizons,
    Where the bat and nighthawk soar,
        You'll see blinking in the heavens
            That selfsame semaphore of stars,
                Flashing on the vital message

            To those souls whose time has sped,
                Summoning their spirits homeward,
                    When
                        The
                            Flesh
                            Is
                                Cold
                                And
                                    Dead.

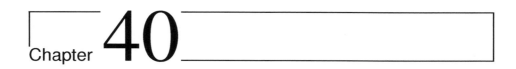

MELANCHOLY

Spit on the rose bush end all that melancrokery ... --Vladimir Majakovskij

The Valleys of the Meadow Valley Wash to the north of the Upper Muddy were essentially pristine wilderness when the Mormon pioneers settled them in 1864-65. Feed for grazing, arable land, and wildlife was plentiful and the Paiute who traversed the area seasonally to raise maize and squash — and to harvest its pine nuts — considered it to be an asset of Divine Providence, to be used with gratitude and respect for Nature's wisdom.

The White Man saw things differently. Native Americans could be uprooted and exiled if they presented an inconvenience, grazing could be multiplied until erosion washed the area into the Pacific, and the flora and fauna constituting the ecology of the region were respected only insofar as they could be converted to cash. Many species originally present in abundance are now extinct or on the 'endangered species' list.

> The RAPE of the land has been slowed down somewhat by insightful, dedicated conservationists, but it continues nonetheless. The most recent grave threat to the area comes from Clark County (Las Vegas in particular), whose water managers have determined to appropriate all of the underground waters in the region and pump them into the swimming pools and golf-course lakes of Vegas Valley. The only counter-forces holding run-away urban development in Vegas Valley at bay are the ecological studies forced by conservationist organizations to prevent the Mojave Desert from extending itself northward into Lincoln, Nye, and White Pine Counties when their waters have been pumped out from under them.

The following verses symbolize the conflict of interests and values represented by this scenario, which entails, as it were, a mystical worship of nature coupled with a tendency to simultaneously destroy it. *Rose Valley* derives its name from the profusion of wild roses growing along its water courses and fences. The wild rose is not remarkable for its aesthetic beauty and fragrance so much as for its key role in the ecology of the region. Its thorny tangle of limbs and leaves provide cover for rabbits, quail, squirrels, foxes, and a profusion of birds and insects. In the recent past, the entire east side of Rose Valley was divested of the roses which complemented the aging fence there. They had been demoted to the status of a nuisance requiring removal. A day or two with heavy equipment did the job.

While observing this downward stride, I seemed to sense a grin light up Rose Valley's Man's Head (Chapter 1). The ravages of values gone awry and disrespect for Nature's blessings seemed not to trouble him.

THE TRUTH — and HE knew it well — was that the revisionists would be 'pushing up daises' themselves in less time than it would take nature to restore itself along the eastern fringe of the Valley! Frustrating though it may be, the longevity of the wild rose far exceeds that of man. And so it is to the wild rose of Rose Valley that these closing verses are dedicated.

TO A WILD ROSE

O'r a brooklet's glacial spring Where dragonflies repose, A spider draped a wedding gown Around a wild rose.

The insect from his hour-glass Drew years of fibrous sheen, And dangling from a waxen leaf Plucked sun specs from the stream.

With petals raised in rustic grace She watched her suitor spin, Her image swelling with a sigh Demurely smiled on him.

I led my Cindy there to see Their poignant, sylvan pose, A spider with his dainty lace Array a wild rose ...

For raven hair--a scarlet wound! From stem and lover torn! The bridegroom flicked from petal-arms, Impaled upon her thorns!

Dusky lashes scatter whims On Cindy's hazel pools! Riffling lips return my kiss ...Oh, nemesis of fools!
(Eldon)

Part V

OTHER PERSONAL HISTORIES

Chapter 41

JOHN LYTLE

One day a mob, who were persecuting the Saints, notified the Lytle family if
they were still there the next morning, they would all be killed. In the night, the
Lytle family, with small packs on their backs, just what they could carry, walked
away from their comfortable home and fine farm, never to return.
-- Phoebe Lytle Esplin (December 1,1961)

Figure 41.1: John Lytle   Figure 41.2: Christina Wittner

Family Pioneer Roots

41.1 Youth and marriage

John Lytle was born August 18, 1803 in the town of Northumberland, Northumberland County, Pennsylvania.. His father was Andrew Lytle and his mother was Sarah
Davidson. His grandfather was Samuel, who was born in England. When Samuel
was a very young man, he served under General George Washington for seven years
during the Revolutionary War. When John was 15 years of age his father moved the
family from Pennsylvania to the State of Ohio and settled in Springfield, Portage

371

County, Ohio. When John was 17 years old he went to an adjoining town, Malbury, Ohio. Here he was apprenticed to a blacksmith. On February27, 1827, when he was 24 years old, he married Christina Wittner, of Talmadge, Ohio. Christina was the daughter of George and Mary Gregory Wittner, of Talmadge, Ohio. Christina and her family had come from Pennsylvania to Ohio and were Pennsylvania Dutch (German) People.

41.2   Farm at Far West Missouri

John and his wife had only been members of the Church eleven months when they took their family and journeyed to Far West, Missouri. They settled on a farm of 80 acres about 3 miles north of Far West on Steer Creek. On the farm he bred and raised live stock. Near the corral was the well with the old oaken bucket and the huge water trough where the live stock came to drink. Not far from the well stood the blacksmith shop. John Lytle was a trained, graduate blacksmith. Here the farm machinery was kept in repair and the horses had their shoes removed, or re-set, and renewed when needed.

41.3   Events at Far West

One of his daughters, Mary Jane Lytle Little, tells of the following incidents when they lived on this farm.

Caring for Joseph's Horse

It was not an unusual sight to see the Prophet Joseph Smith, riding his beautiful white horse, turn in at the farm gate as he was passing by. The Prophet and the Lytle family were very dear friends, and while the Prophet and her parents were visiting, Mary Jane led the white horse to the well, and lowering the old oaken bucket into the well, drew up the cool refreshing water for him to drink. It was customary when the white horse needed his shoes re-set or required new shoes for the Prophet to ride him in to the Lytle shop to have the work done.

Driven out by a Mob

These happy days did not last long. One day a mob, who were persecuting the Saints, notified the Lytle family if they were still there the next morning, they would all be killed. In the night, the Lytle family, with small packs on their backs — just what they could carry — walked away from their comfortable home and fine farm, never to return.

A group of Latter Day Saints with similar circumstances to those of the Lytles, had all gathered at one place and were waiting for things to be arranged for them to move on. They were all gathered in one extra large house. The men folks had all gone out to try to find some kind of work to get money to buy food with. The Lytle family joined them.

Late one afternoon when a mob arrived and made camp a short distance up the road, they found all of the men away looking for work and only the women and children were at home. Two of the mob came, walked into the house and notified the occupants that if they wished to be alive tomorrow they had better move on. The mothers with their children were panic stricken. Night was coming on and the fathers and husbands had not yet returned. After consultation, the mothers decided there was only one thing they could do, and that was to call on the Lord for protection.

Heavenly Cavalry

The sun was just setting, and they called the children and all assembled in one large room, there kneeling they called upon the Lord for help and protection. That prayer was heard and answered. Almost at once they heard a bugle blowing and they all rushed out into the yard. Imagine their surprise, there passing before them going down the road was a great armed cavalry. They could hear the horses hoofs strike the hard road bed and see the sparks fly from their shoes, while the bugles kept on blowing. There was no sign of the mob there the next morning. They had completely disappeared. The "Spiritual Troop of Cavalry" had accomplished what they had been called for. The mob had been frightened away and the prayers of the sisters and their children had been answered!

41.4   Removal to Commerce/Nauvoo

In 1837, John Lytle was ordained a Seventy by Brigham Young. At the expulsion of Saints from the state of Missouri, those who loved the Church were forced to move on. The following is a quote from John Lytle's diary:

> I started in the month of February 1839, with my family now consisting of my wife and four children, in a two horse wagon, to the Mississippi River. I also took another family with me. After a tiresome journey we arrived on the banks of the river, where I unloaded my wagon and my team immediately returned to bring out two other families. We crossed the river on the ice and stopped five miles east of Quincey, where my wife was confined. Our child, a son, dying and she barely escaping death. On the return of my team, it made another trip to Far West and brought two other families.

> I now took my team and moved to Commerce, afterward called Nauvoo. Here we suffered much from the Ague and Fever, so common among the Saints in that place.

41.5   Nauvoo Days

Great grandfather John now began to prosper in Nauvoo. He set up a shop and worked at the blacksmith trade. He relates the following:

> The apostates were persecuting the Saints, and were trying to take the life of the Prophet Joseph Smith. The apostates published a paper known as the Nauvoo Expositor. This paper was declared a nuisance by the Nauvoo City Council and the police. I was a member of the Police Force and was asked to do away with the press that was printing the libelous sheet. As we had no key to the door of the press room, I used

my sledge hammer to break the lock off the door. We then broke the press and threw it into a pond of water near by.

I was taken to jail, accompanied by the Prophet Joseph Smith, who was the Mayor of Nauvoo at that time. We were forced to give bonds for our appearance in court. The Prophet was retained on this and other charges. I, and the other police officers were afterward arraigned before the circuit court. The witness testified that it was Lytle the blacksmith who smashed the door of the press room, but in as much as my brother Andrew and I were both blacksmithswe were acquitted. They (the witnesses) could not prove which one of us was guilty. This confirmed the words of the Prophet as he had promised us that not a hair of our heads would be harmed.

At a more complete organization of the Seventies in 1845 in Nauvoo, John was appointed Senior President of the 15th Quorum of Seventies. He and his wife, Christina, received their endowments in the Nauvoo Temple.

41.6   Exodus to the Rocky Mountains

In February 1846, John Lytle started with his family in an exodus to the Rocky Mountains. They were in the first company with Brigham Young. John and his family remained at Winter Quarters the following winter (where Charles was born in 1846) and then crossed the plains to Salt Lake City in 1847.

Term as Bishop

Upon his arrival in the (Salt Lake) Valley he was ordained a High Priest in the L.DS Church. In February 1849, John Lytle was appointed to be the first Bishop of the Eleventh Ward. He established his family in Salt lake, but within 10 years he was called by Brigham Young to be a missionary to Carson Valley, Nevada.

Call to Carson Valley

In May 1855, he journeyed to Nevada to help pioneer that area and form another LDS settlement. In Carson Valley he became a good friend of the famous westerner, Kit Carson. Mr. Carson gave great grandfather a box made of lovely inlaid woods to keep his valuable papers and possessions in. This box, over 100 years old, is still beautiful. After two years (at the time of the Utah War), John was recalled to Salt lake.

41.7   The Call to Dixie

His next call came to go south and help with the Dixie Mission. He answered this call and came to St. George in December 1861, with the first settlers in this valley. He was now 58 years old and his wife Christina 54. Many years had passed and many wonderful pioneer experiences had come to them since he had taken the black-eyed Pennsylvania Dutch Christina as his bride. He worked at his trade as a blacksmith in St. George. He was appointed a counselor to President William Fawcett in the High Priests Quorum in 1862. He held this position until his death in 1892.

Building the St. George Temple

He helped to break ground for the St. George Temple. He also helped on the building of the Temple, and he and his wife were ordinance workers there. He worked from 1877, when the Temple first opened, until 1892 as an ordinance worker.

41.8 Summary

John Lytle was a successful pioneer who loved the Saints. He had the reputation of being especially kind and good to the poor and the needy. It was said of him that he would gladly, and often did, share the last pan of flour he had in the house. He and his wife were the parents of a fine family. Four sons and four daughters lived to maturity. They were John Milton, William, Mary (Little), Fannie, George, Charles, Cornelia (Snow), and Caroline (Whipple). His wife, Christina Wittner Lytle, died in 1881. John died October 12, 1892 in St. George, Utah.

Chapter 42

CHARLES LYTLE

Grandpa was always interested in mining and at one time owned the ``Home stake'' Mine at Deer Lodge, Nevada, a small mining camp (about 12 miles east of Eagle Valley). Also several other claims on down the canyon. He traded them for Rose Valley, where two of his sons, and one daughter lived and farmed for many years.— Karen Lees Prestwich

42.1   A Kindly Host

Grandfather Charles Lytle loved life. According to the stories about him. He liked to have people visit him, and always invited them to stay all night if they stopped at his place. He would welcome them with a hearty "Drive your team around thru' the gate, and put them up in the barn, and come on in!" Then, he would alert his two oldest girls, Noma and Amy, (who did most of the house work about that time). "But Pa," they would protest, "We just had supper". Some of the time one of the older boys, Ed or Les, would be sent out to the cellar to cut some beef steak to fix for the company. Then after the meal, everyone would sit around the big fireplace to visit.

Charles' Home as a Stage Stop

The Charlie Lytle home in Eagle Valley was a stop over for the "Stage" thru' to Milford. As Milford, Utah was as far as the train came during the 1880's and 1890's. Some years later it was built on through to the Coast. Also, Grandfather or some of the family kept the Post Office for many years.

A Boarding House for Teachers

Many of the school teachers boarded at their home–after the custom of each family keeping the teacher one week (taking turns) as part of the teacher's pay. All of the Lytle children went through "Readers", 1st to 8th as was in all schools then instead of grades. They were all beautiful penmen, and very good at figures and spelling. A small school house was built for the school where the "Town-hall" now stands.

42.2   Charles as a Father and Businessman

Grandpa was not a large man in stature, but sort of heavy set. Jovial, **a shrewd manager and business man,**[1] and a good provider for his family of four boys and three girls. Through the years he accumulated a large herd of cattle. A matched pair of dappled grey horses "Pat and Chief" were his pride and joy and he had a fringed white-top buggy to go with them. Many times we grand children would all play in the buggy when we would congregate at Grandma's for a Fourth of July picnic. (However, this was many years after Grandpa died.) Once in awhile Grandpa would take or send some of the children to Milford, where they boarded the train to go to see the "Jubilee" at Salt lake City. Mother (mine) said she went to see it once.

42.3   Mining Connections

Grandpa was always interested in mining and at one time owned the "Home stake" Mine at Deer Lodge, Nevada, a small mining camp (about 12 miles east of Eagle Valley). Also several other claims on down the canyon. He traded them for Rose Valley, where two of his sons, and one daughter lived and farmed for many years.

---

[1] Appendix: MANAGEMENT OF THE MATERIAL WORLD .Q

42.4 Food Storage Program

Every fall on the Lytle Ranch, 1000 pounds of flour was put up in the cellar loft, for their winter's use. Apples, plums, apricots and corn were dried and stored. Barrels of vinegar were made from the excess apples, and root cellars were built to keep potatoes, apples, etc. Grandpa could make wonderful corned beef. Hams and bacon were cured and smoked in the smokehouse (which is still on the old Lytle place, also the big rock cellar still stands).

When a beef was butchered old "Pete Indian" (who had a camp on the east side of the Valley) was always given the head of the beef. "Phoebe", his wife, came every week and did the family washing. Grandpa was good to the Indians, giving them food and money whenever they did some work.

There was a big log ice-house built on the Lytle Ranch. It had a thick covering of saw dust on the floor, and during January big blocks of ice were cut from ponds (built for that purpose) and stored in the saw dust for summer use. How good ice cream tasted when home made, then churned in a hand freezer and packed in the ice!

> **The above stories were told to Myrtle Damron Bliss — daughter of Amy Lytle and Milton Damron — Amy being the second daughter of Charles Lytle.**

Chapter 43

FREELAND H. LYTLE

One of his important assignments was to take the gold bars from Delamar to the rail station at Caliente whenever they were ready. He never knew more than an hour or two in advance when the gold was ready to be taken and would report at the assay office upon telephoned request, throw the small and the large bar into the buckboard, toss a saddle blanket or a bag of grain over them and drive to Caliente. The small bar, which was almost pure gold, was worth about $120,000, the large bar, which was not so pure, was worth about $90,000. -- Wayne Lytle

Mary and Freel's wedding picture.

43.1   Early Years

Freeland H. Lytle[1] was born May 23, 1878 in Eagle Valley, later named by the postal department *URSINE,* which is located in East Central Nevada in Lincoln County, the fifth child of Charles Lytle and Margaret Moody Lytle. Charles was engaged in ranching and in contracting with freighting teams, and of course all of the boys became involved at an early age.

Freel went to the earlier years of school in Eagle Valley, George Moody having been one of his teachers, then went to a higher grade in Cedar City, Utah, and part of one term in Logan, Utah. The boys worked on the ranch in Eagle Valley and learned at an early age to handle horses. It was interesting that Freel commented more than once, "Any man or boy who gets the habit of chasing wild horses ain't worth his salt." My father, Freel, mentioned that he and the other boys slept in the barn, at least during the summer time.

43.2   Working at Delamar

At the age of 18, Freel had a chance to go to work for the Delamar Mining Co. as teamster to the Superintendent. He had to give his age as 21 in order to get the job, so as he said, "I paid poll tax three years longer than I really was supposed to." He drove team for Mr. Swindler, Superintendent, for four years under the Delamar Co. and several times actually transported Captain Delamar himself. After a short return to Eagle Valley, he again drove team for the Bamberger Co. at Delamar for two more years.

One of his important assignments was to take the gold bars from Delamar to the rail station at Caliente whenever they were ready. He never knew more than an hour or two in advance when the gold was ready to be taken and would report at the assay office upon telephoned request, throw the small and the large bar into the buckboard, toss a saddle blanket or a bag of grain over them and drive to Caliente. The small bar, which was almost pure gold, was worth about $120,000, the large bar, which was not so pure, was worth about $90,000. He never was held up, went alone for four years, then under Bamberger was provided with a guard, Harry Turner, for two years. Harry stuttered badly. During one trip across the Delamar Flat, two horsemen appeared in the distance. When Harry spied them, he became very nervous. "D-d-d-do y-y-y-you th-th-th-think th-th-th-they'll h-h-hhold u-u-u-us u-u-up? Harry asked. Freel answered, "Only time will tell." Harry fidgeted, checked his lever action rifle, and was generally uneasy. At last they came abreast of the riders, both of whom were local cowboys. Harry, with great relief, waved and said, "G-g-good d-d-dday b-b-b-boys."

Freel estimated that he hauled some forty three million dollars in gold to the railroad station during those six years. Of course, he did many other things as part of his work assignment during those six years, especially driving Swindler, Captain Delamar and other important people to and from the railroad station at Caliente. However, he never did work in the mines or in the mill where so many became ill and died of the dreaded "Delamar Dust."

---

[1]The middle initial is not for 'Henry' (43.8) but for 'Henson' in memory of Harriet Henson, his polygamous Grandmother on the Moody side (46).

43.3 Mary and Tina Marry Cowboys

Mary Ann Jensen and her sister Teena Jensen came from Utah to Nevada to teach rural school; Mary in Clover Valley and Tenna in Eagle Valley. While Mary was visiting Teena in Eagle Valley, she met Freel, who was working as a cowboy after finishing his work in Delamar, and they fell in love. Mary said, "My gosh, he was almost thirty years old. All those cowboys were the same. They didn't have gumption enough to get out and find a woman. They would just sit and wait for a teacher to come in, then they'd try to marry her."

Teena married Milton Hammond and Mary married Freel (6.2), both of Eagle Valley. Freel and Mary went to Los Angeles on their honeymoon. While there, Freel visited "Nigger Johnson", whom he had known and liked in Delamar. Mr. Johnson was then a real estate agent and tried hard to sell a lot to Freel. When asked where the lot was located he said, "On Signal Hill," Freel. "That's a promising new area. The lot will cost you five hundred dollars." Freel decided to save his $500 for a later date. Of course, Signal Hill later became one of the best oil fields in Southern California.

Freel and Mary in Rose Valley

43.4 The Rose Valley Ranch

Freel and Mary settled in Rose Valley, on land that belonged to his mother, Margaret, who inherited the land that belonged to her husband, Charles. Freel and his youngest brother, Sam, bought a log house located at the Pope Mine near Deer Lodge, Nevada, hauled it by team and wagon to Rose Valley, ripped the logs lengthwise with a two-man saw, and built two four-room log houses, one of which still stands.

43.5   Gladys and Wayne Are Born

Two children were born to Freel and Mary in Rose Valley, Mary Gladys on August 13, 1909 and Freeland Wayne on February 25, 1911. During his early years of marriage, Freel managed the ranch and rode on the range for his brother Edwin, who ran the cattle from the Charles Lytle estate, branded with the C. L. Freel built a small herd of 135 head for himself and lost all but 15 head on the Dry Lake open range during the winter of 1915. It was interesting that he would never run his cattle on the open range after that. All that could be found came to the ranch for the winter. He would never trust a good cow horse with his children, Gladys and Wayne. He always rustled some "old plug" for us to spoil. Together, Freel and Mary made a good ranch, which he eventually inherited, and built the herd back to about 150 head. Freel was always working horses and raised some of his own. As they drove along in the buggy, Mary often commented, "If there is only one rock in the road, Freel will always hit it." Freel once replied, "Nance and Trill work well together, there is only one tongue between them."

43.6   Freel is Injured

It was ironic that in about 1945, he was mowing hay with a young team he had raised, named Rocks and Maude. The machine hit a clump of "wheat grass," threw Freel onto his shoulder and neck, causing a stroke, and he never did return to normal health. He had used chewing tobacco and a pipe for most of his life, and after the stroke, upon a doctor's advice, quit using tobacco completely. Gladys and I can well remember when he drove the model T and we sat in the back, getting second-hand tobacco juice in our faces as he drove along. Freel died on June 17, 1958, apparently of a heart attack, and was buried in Eagle Valley. One of his greatest pleasures was sitting in his big easy chair, reading to and singing to his grandchildren. One of his favorite songs ended, "that there dog got that there boy into many an ugly Muss." The tune wasn't important.

43.7   Wayne's Memories of Freel

I can remember my father for his kindness and patience and for his generosity. He spared no expense in sending Gladys and me to school — even to far away Boston to the New England Conservatory of Music for one year, and of course to the BAC Junior college in Cedar City. He had the ability to do much physical work, especially pitching wild hay and "punching" cattle. His philosophy was, "If you can't get it done in a normal day's work, it'll always be there tomorrow." He did not work into the night. He had a way of laughing at almost everything, even when it was not the best thing to do. I remember one day when his youngest sister, Maggie Warren and her husband Will rode horses to Rose Valley to visit. Maggie, who was quite heavy, had a beautiful padded saddle that Will had given her and rode a good looking bay horse. As they were leaving she led her horse to the wood pile and stepped on a log in order to mount more easily. After she mounted, the horse swung around and a limb from the wood pile hit him in the flank. He promptly started bucking and Maggie landed on her back with a heavy thud. Freel promptly started laughing and slapping his side. Maggie, who fortunately was not seriously injured, got up and Will helped her on again and as they left, Maggie was very indignant and my dad was laughing. My mother grabbed a log of wood and said, "If you don't shut up,

I'll hit you over the head with it."

Freel at his Rose Valley Ranch.

43.8 The Question of Freel's Middle Name

People in Pioche will well remember his sales pitch, "Would you like to buy some of
the best sweet corn in the county? I picked it fresh myself this morning." He signed

his name Freeland H. One day when we were kids we asked him what his name was. He said it was Freeland Henson. My mother said, "Who ever heard of a name like Henson? It's *Henry*." He said, "OK mother, Freeland *Henry* it is." And that's the way it stayed, even though Harriet *Henson* Moody was his grandmother.

Author's Note: A cursory reading of this account leaves one with the impression that the only issue involved was whether *Henson* or *Henry* somehow 'sounded' better. Actually, there was by all accounts an undercurrent of deeply entrenched emotion in Mary's insistence that *Henson* be displaced by *Henry*.

Mary and her mother had been abandoned to fend for themselves during the Edmunds-Tucker era(6.1), and her mother had instilled in her children a profound bitterness for polygamy and for the Church, which she perceived as having played the role of traitor. She had now married a man whose mother (Margaret) was the daughter of William Moody, a staunch polygamist, and whose grandmother, Harriet Henson (equally staunch), Mary had likely come to know after the fact[a] through Margaret and Charles, and, perhaps, from Freel's boyhood memories of her (47.5).

As their descendant, I feel compelled to ask whether Mary's compulsion to displace the *Henson* name embedded in that of her husband signals a transference of Mary's abhorrence for polygamy to the name? The point is that Mary was at this point not behaving rationally. Rather than avail herself of the opportunity to instill in her grandchildren an appreciation for their pioneer ancestor who had braved the hardships of both Dixie and Dry Valley, she actually robbed them of any awareness of the woman whom Charles and Margaret had honored when they named their infant son 'Freeland *Henson* Lytle.'[b]

Be that as it may, there is, in the author's opinion, A PLOT OF HOLY GROUND marked out by foundation stones some two miles south of the original Moodyville (47.5), opposite the site of the old Dry Valley mill along the eastern fringe of the field currently occupying that area. It would be appropriate to erect a marker there in Harriet's honor and for her descendants in Meadow Valley to visit it from time to time — lest we allow her role in our existence to be swallowed up in the Dry Valley Sink (2.1).[c]

[a]Harriet had died in 1884 when Freel was 6 years old.

[b]Harriet did not return to Eagle Valley after William's stint in Dry valley, but moved with three sons to Panguitch, Utah (45.7).

[c]All references to "Freeland *Henry*" are corrected to "Freeland *Henson*" in this book so as to conform to his birth certificate.

I will always remember my father planting corn with his grandchildren. He would "heel" it in with the shovel, while they placed the seeds in the "hill." All the while he kept a running story going, especially his experiences in Delamar. The grandchildren listened so carefully that they later received *A's* in highschool English classes by reproducing the stories he told them. Indeed, he was a master at reproducing his experiences in story form. Another one comes to mind:

> "Old Swindler stood right there where the road comes into Delamar, at nine o'clock at night. He didn't know that I had slipped through the trees and passed them on the Caliente Summit. He was sure that we didn't stand a chance with our old plugs matched up against that big team those two drummers had rented from Culverwell. You can't throw a gallon of oats into any horses and expect them to stand up on a long drive. They have got to have time to digest it. One of the drummers said, "Vy Mister Svindler, how did you get ahead of us?" Swindler said, "We just flew over you in the dark."

43.9   Addendum — The 'Religious' Heifer

Owing to Charles' clash with Church profiteers (5), Freel and the other children were neither baptized nor active in Mormon services. They apparently felt no inclination to get involved unless extended a specific request. Freel didn't belong to any church, and said he wasn't religious. But he was extremely honest and good willed. When the Church asked for donations of cattle for the Welfare Farm, he willingly donated a heifer. With a twinkle in his eye, he explained, "That there heifer just went and got religion."

Eldon personally recalls the day when the Bishop Harry Horlacher of the Pioche Ward first approached Grandpa Freel and asked him to donate a cow to the Ward's welfare farm in Panaca. Freel responded that he just happened to have a heifer that looked promising, and suggested he stop by that afternoon with his truck to pick her up. The bishop showed up at the appointed time, and Freel helped him load the animal. Within a week the heifer showed in Rose Valley — she had gotten away and returned 'home.' Freel promptly picked up the phone and told Harry to come get his 'religious heifer,' but to fix his fence first![2]

43.10   Brother!

Freel was seemingly quite proud of his religious heifer.' He donated a heifer to the Welfare farm every year for many years. But if anyone asked him what church he belonged to, he would jokingly tell them he was a *Holy Roller*. One day he was chatting with a lady as he peddled corn, and she asked him what church he

---

[2] Harry Horlacher was a dedicated father and bishop who reached out to help everyone regardless of faith. He labored long hours to support a burgeoning family of sons and daughters, often falling to sleep on the stand during church services. His wife Sue had a simple solution for this problem, however. She always arrived with the family in time to occupy the front row. Whenever Harry started nodding, she dispatched one of the younger children to ascend the stand and prod Harry back to life.

belonged to. Out came the standard reply, "Oh, I'm a Holy Roller." "Brother!""
she exclaimed as she threw her arms around him. He was a little sheepish about it
afterwards. (Karen)

Chapter 44

MARY GLADYS LYTLE — WAYNE'S SISTER

The years we spent in Pioche were good Years. I was active in the Church and community. My training on the piano was put to good use. For many wears I accompanied for everything in the Church and community. People would come five minutes before a funeral and say, "Can you play this song?" and I would do it.

44.1 Birth and Childhood

I was born at Rose Valley, Nevada. I arrived August 13, 1909 at 4 A.M. in the morning in the middle of a rain storm. My Parents were Freeland Henson Lytle and Mary Ann Jensen. They were living in a tent at the time while they built the log house that was to be their home for many years. My father and my Uncle Sam went up to a old mine in the Deer Lodge area and hauled down the huge logs from an old boarding house. They used a rip saw to split the logs so they could build Sam a house too. (See Chapter 3) That house belongs to my brother Wavne now. (April 1990) I was born several months early, so I weighed only 3 1/2 Pounds.

> MY MOTHER said I was so small that they lined a shoe box with cotton and put me in it and took me over to the neighbor's and put me in the warming oven. My parents never expected to raise me. But I always knew they would. My brother Wayne was born a year and a half later.

Stove Quarrel

Once when Wayne and I were little, we were sitting behind the stove quarreling. It was about Christmas time, and our mother told us that if we didn't be good, Santa Claus wouldn't come. But we kept on quarreling. So our mother went out and got the harness with the sleigh bells. We heard the bells come down the road, hesitate, and then pass on, gradually getting dimmer. We were very good from then on.

Gladys as a Child

Teachers

I was a very sickly child, so my mother let me stay out in the sunshiny and fresh air as much as Possible. We had a cousin "Mike" Leslie Lytle, and the three of us were inseparable. As we grew up our fathers built a one room school house and we went to school there until we graduated from the eighth grade. The Pupils were Wayne and I, our cousins Lena and Leah and Mike Lytle, and our cousin, John Devlin (see photo below). The teacher boarded with one of the families each sear. There were a succession of teachers, some good and some bad (Chapter 15). There was Miss Dalton, and Laura Stephen, and Mrs. Joe Delmue, and Phoebe West. Marjorie Cross was Just out of college and used to give us assignments like they give in college.

I was a way ahead of Wayne and Mike in school. But I wasn't good in math, and they were so I put myself back a year so I could be with them and they could help me with math. We thought we were average students, but when we went to other schools we found we were above average. One time they were having a fair in Las Vegas, and we were asked to contribute. The birds had just finished nesting, so I collected the nests and labeled each one. I even had a humming bird nest. I received a prize for originality, which was $5.00. The teacher took the money and bought a baseball and bat for the boss. I felt it was very unfair.

Self-Transport to School

We went to the first two years of high school at a temporary high school in Eagle Valley, five miles above Rose Valley. In good weather we rode horses or bicycles to school. I kept up with Wayne and Mike even though sometimes my heart would be racing when we got there. In the winter we boarded with my aunt and uncle, Maggie and Billy Warren, in Eagle Valley. Maggie never wanted to be called *aunt*, so we never called anyone 'aunt' or 'uncle.' Mr. Brinley was our teacher, and was very good. He was a vegetarian and wouldn't eat meat until he got burned and wouldn't heal.

Getting a Nickname

Mary and Dora "Dee" Fogliani were my best friends. They lived in Spring Valley. We usually had a feud going with the Eagle Valley girls. I vas always good friends with my cousin Mirtle Damoron though. One day Mary and I were riding double on the horse. I was lying across instead of sitting up, and Mary said, "Don't fall off, Gump." And then she said, "Hey! That's a good name for you." After that they always called me *Gump*. They still do. I had a nervous breakdown when I was a sophomore, but got back to school in time to take the tests, which I passed.

School Days in Rose Valley

44.2 Teen Years

We went to Lincoln County High School in Panaca for our Junior wear. We boarded with my cousin, Amy Devlin Mathews. I thought it would be great to be out on our own. We could stay out as late as we wanted to and do whatever we wanted to. But I found I didn't want to. One night we were out in the old Ford when we hit a horse. Wayne and Mike were worried about the car, but I was worried about the horse. They said, "Don't worry about the horse, worry about the car!" They got out and straightened it out and it still went. It didn't kill the horse either. Wayne and Mike had to do a lot of pounding to get the car straightened out (44.2).

Blacky and the Piano

When I was sixteen, my dad gave me a horse and a piano. I named the horse Blacky, and I loved her more than anything I ever had. The first time I got on her, she promptly bucked me off. Instead of being upset, our father picked me up and said, "Come on, I'll show you how to get back on." All the other kids were always wanting to borrow Blacky, so I taught her to take off as soon as I got on, so that no one else could ride her. My Dad taught us to ride bareback. so we wouldn't get our foot caught in the stirrup and get dragged. Once Vic Cottino came to get some cattle that were in the pasture, back under the willows. He was all decked out with his chaps and boots and fancy saddle. But he couldn't get the cattle. He kept getting everything caught on the willows. So I finally got on Blacky and slipped under the willows and brought the cattle out.

MY MOTHER was determined that I was going to play the piano. Wherever there was anyone who could teach piano, she sent me there.

44.3   The BAC Year

Our senior year we went to school in Cedar City, Utah, and graduated in 1928. The fellow that we boarded with in Cedar City used to say we couldn't be brother and sister --- we never fought.

Gladys and Wayne as Kids in Rose Valley

In the fall of 1928, Wayne and I and Mike enrolled in the BAC Junior College. I became good friends with Lydia Matheson. As always I took piano lessons. Mr. Halverson and Mr. Manning were over the music department and were very rood. But I got sick after the first quarter and had to drop out. I always had trouble with my stomach. The doctor finally put me on a milk diet — nothing but milk for a month. It was hard, but my skin was beautiful afterwards.

44.4   Off to Boston

The next wear (1929 and 1930) we went to the New England Conservatory of Music in Boston, Massachusetts (15.13). Mike wanted to go into aviation, but his folks thought it was too dangerous. So Maggie came down and consulted with them, and they decided he should go to Boston to the Conservatory with us. Billy Warren sold us a 1924 Buick, and we drove back to Boston. It took us two or three weeks. I remember when we went through Hershey Pennsylvania, it smelled just like a chocolate bar. We would be driving along and everyone would get crosser and crosser. Suddenly someone would say, "Time to eat!" and we would stop and eat and then everything would be fine. We rented an apartment about two miles from the school. Boston had a very good transit system and I got so I could go all over.

Gladys as a College Student

I thought I was fairly advanced on the piano, but when I got to the Conservatory, I was enrolled in basic courses. I took private piano and violin, and so did Wayne and Mike, but I wasn't cut out for the violin, and soon dropped it.

I DID WELL ON THE PIANO, though, and was especially good at runs. **They wanted me to study to be a concert pianist.** But I would have had to practice for eight hours a day and my nerves wouldn't take that. We would have had to stay several more years to become really proficient.

The Hill Family

We got acquainted with Billy Hill at the Conservatory. He took us home to meet the family, and we became friends with Frank and Kay Hill also. Their parents were wealthy, but they were just common people and we went there often. Kay used to take us around in her car. One day a guy came out of a side street and almost hit her. Everyone around leaned their heads out of the window and cussed him. On our way home, when we arrived in Salt Lake City, a guy came out of a side street and almost hit us. Mike said "Watch this!" and he leaned his head out the window and really cussed him. The guy just stood there with his mouth open.

Landlubers at Sea

We went with the Hills to Portland, Maine, and to an island where one of their relatives lived. He took us out on his boat. Frank insisted on holding me on his lap and I got very sea sick but he wouldn't let me up, which made it worse. Kay and Mike ran around together, even though she was practically engaged to a young man named Putnam. She wanted to come home with us when we left, but Mike was not enthusiastic. He wasn't ready to get married, and he knew Kay couldn't live in Rose Valley. She later married Putnam, who became Vice President of the Cuticara Soap Company. Billy had a steady girl friend, Vera Champus, but he had a crush on me, and Kay would have liked to have me take him away from her. But I wouldn't.

Mr. Frink lived near us and was a special friend. He was a lawyer and elderly and unmarried. Bert Dillion was a friend also. Bert worked full time to support his mother and brothers and sisters because his father had died. I went with Bert some. Mr. Frink used to lend him his car and he took us around, too.

44.5   Illness

A FTER WE RETURNED FROM BOSTON, Wayne and I went to college at the BAC in Cedar City. But I became ill in the spring of 1931 and wasn't able to continue in College. That summer I spent three months in Salt Lake City under a doctor's care. The doctors weren't able to operate, because I had a huge goiter that grew inward. So I went to Dr.Vincent in Salt Lake City, who was a friend of the family. He used a salve made from pine pitch to remove the goiter. Before I had the goiter removed, I had to add an inch to my necklaces. Afterwards I had to remove it.

After that I lived at the Ranch until I was twenty five. Mary Fogliani taught school in Rose Valley and stayed with us. There were always lizzards running around in our yard. I wouldn't let her kill them. If they stayed in the yard they were mine. But if they strayed outside, she would drop a rock on them. We had a good time running around the hills.

44.6   Marriage

On December 24, l934, I married James B. Lees. Myrtle and Paul Bliss went with us to Parowan, Utah so we could be married. He was from Provo, Utah, and had come south looking for work, having lost his job due to the depression. There was no work at Pioche either, so he ended up at Rose Valley working for my Uncle Pat Devlin on his ranch. He was shy and so was I, so when he came courting we just sat out on the hay wagon and talked. His brother, Red (George), worked in Eagle Valley and married Nelly Dwyer.[1]

---

[1]Red and Nelly had two daughters — Maxine and Faye. Farrel, Eldon, and Karen used to frequently visit and spend time with them in Eagle Valley. Billie Dwyer, their grandfather, owned a large orchard at the mouth of Spring Valley Canyon. The land was latter purchased by developers who converted it into the present *Eagle Valley Lodge* complex. (Eldon)

Gladys and Jim Courting Days

After we were married, we moved to the Little Buck Mine near State Line, where Jim was employed. Later we moved the tent house we lived in to Pioche, Nevada, where Jim was employed by the Pioche Mines. After Jim won the drilling contest at the Labor Day celebration, we used the prize money to hire his Uncle Charlie Scott from Provo to build a house for us.

44.7   Karen's Birth and Jim's Injury

On January 24 1936, our only child, Karen Lynne was born. Shortly after she was born, we moved into our new house. We didn't get to enjoy our house for long, because the Pioche Mines closed and we moved to Park City, Utah, where Jim was employed at the Silver King Mine. While he was working there, the mine caved in on him, and Jim's back was injured. The mine doctor refused to admit it caused by the cave-in, and called it *rheumatism* ...so he was denied compensation. So we moved to Rose Valley and lived with the folks awhile. It took about a year for Jim to recover.

When Karen was about four, we went to Los Angeles to Dr. Arthur Vincent, where Jim was treated for three months. My cousin, Adelle Burton (Cachonis), lived in Los Angeles, and she took us around to see things and showed us a good time.

When karen was about 5 years old, Wayne and Jim decided to recover quicksilver from the old mine dumps at Hamilton, Nevada (24.1). We spent an enjoyable and profitable summer there. Hamilton was a ghost town, so we lived in one of the abandoned houses. The sage hens were thick and Jim kept us all supplied. Emyrus Jones, Vern Stever, and the Joe Templeman were there also and sometimes the whole group would get together for a sage hen dinner. Once Jim accidentally tipped his dish in his lap. I think that was the only time I ever saw him embarrassed.

44.8   Hazards of Quicksilver

We had an old fellow, Bert Grosbeck, boarding with us, and he was always playing with the quicksilver. Sometimes it even got in the food. Jim and I both lost our teeth early, and I think this got salivated from the quicksilver. After we returned from Hamilton. Jim went to work for the Lincoln County Power District in Caselton, Nevada and we lived in our house in Pioche. Karen attended the Pioche Elementary in Pioche and the Lincoln Couty High School in Panaca where she graduated in 1954.

44.9   Community Service

The years we spent in Pioche were good Years. I was active in the Church and community. My training on the piano was put to good use. For many wears I accompanied for everything in the Church and community. People would come 5 minutes before a funeral and say, ``Can you play this song? '' and I would do it. I accompanied Mary Hansen and Lydia Werber and many others when they sang. Karen learned to sing, and I accompanied her also. I belonged to the Miriam Rebecca Lodge for many years, but gave it up when I moved. Jim was an Odd Fellow, and also active in the Volunteer Fire Company and the Rod and Gun Club. He used to poach as a way of life. But after he Joined the Rod and Gun Club, he was on the County Game Management Board, and he became very conscientious about poaching (see Chapter 32).

Gladys During Her Prime

44.10   Pionionette

I always had dry skin, and I never could find anything that did much good. So I began to experiment with various things to make my own. My first efforts were just mutton tallow and pitch, patterned after the mixture my Dad used on the cows' sore tits. I called it Karen's cream because Karen had such dry hands. But it was heavy and sticky so I got a book of formulas and began experimenting. The result was a hand cream I called *dry skin cream*. It incorporated the pine pitch, but was much lighter and nicer. Soon I was making it for all the family and even selling it to my friends. This inspired Justine, my brother's wife, to experiment. and she invented a cream lotion. And since both the dry skin cream, and the cream lotion were very popular, we decided we needed a trade mark. We first attempted to patent the name *Fragrant Pine*, but someone had already patented something similar. We were talking about it one day, and Justine said jokingly, "Let's call it *Pinionette*." I said, "That's it!" So it became *Pinionette*. Wayne and Justine even attempted to have it made commercially and sell it in a big way. But without money to advertise it didn't do very well.

44.11 Shooting

We went deer hunting every fall. One wear I killed the biggest deer in camp. I was standing there and it came right up to me. I was so proud that he and another guy packed it out whole so everyone could see how big it was. But some of the guys in came were really ashamed that a woman had shot the biggest deer. It was really good eating, too. It was as tender as beef.

I didn't know I was a good shot until I started going to turkey shoots. Once there weren't enough men to participate, so I said I would. They were shooting at targets with a bench rest, so I thought that would be easy. They didn't think it would be fair for a woman to shoot against the men. But I did better than most of them. After that they always put me up against the new comers. I won three turkeys, and they were live, so we took them out and let my Dad fatten them up. They were some of the best turkeys we ever ate.

44.12 Jim is Killed

Jim was killed June 13, 1952, while working on the power line to the Combined Metals Mill at Caselton, Nevada. My friend Kay Hill Putnam from Boston had come to visit us on her way to a church convention in California, and had only been there a day or two when Jim was killed.

After the funeral, Mike and Mary Lytle took us on a tour of Zion National Park. But it was many months before I could get over it. I attended church for many wears without ever becoming a member. But I was baptized into the LDS Church or August 3, 1952.

44.13   Dan Platt

After Jim's death I worked for Keith Frazier in the Pioche Pharmacy. In August of 1954 I married Dan (Dennis Marvin) Platt, and we lived at Tempiute, Nevada, where he was employed for a while. Karen stayed with us for a while in the summer, and then went to college at the College of Southern Utah in Cedar City, Utah. While he was working at Tempiute, Dan injured his back in a mine cave-in, and never worked very steady after that. He received a settlement from the mine but that was soon spent. After that we moved to Harrison Pass where Dan worked at a mine.

We also lived at Long Canyon for a while where Dan leased a mine. Karen stayed with us for a while the summer of 1955. He was always going to strike it rich, but he never got around to shipping much ore. Karen was married to Clarence Steele Prestwich May 28, 1956. They came to see us while we were still in Long Canyon. It was a beautiful place, but Dan didn't do much work on his own, so the lease finally fell through.

44.14   Working for a Living

Later we moved to Elko, Nevada, where I worked as a cashier at the Commercial Hotel. Mrs. Renton hired me on the 4th of July, the busiest day of the year. Someone asked her why she did that, and she said, "She can either take it or she can't. Now we know she can." I learned a lot cashiering. I was shy before I started working but I soon learned not to be. I worked there one and a half Years. While I was working there my father passed away June 17, 1955. After his death my mother moved to Pioche and lived in our house.

Dan got a Job at the Barium Mine in Carlin, so we moved to Carlin. Mrs. Renton didn't want me to leave, but I didn't want to drive to Elko every daw, so I went to work at Mac's Gear Jammer's Cafe in Carlin. I asked for a Job, and they said they needed a cook. I said I couldn't cook, and they said, "Good, we'll teach you." Mac and Ilene MacAchern who owned the Gear Jammer's Cafe became some of my best friends. When you work for someone for 6 years, you either love them or hate them. While I was working there I bought a small trailer. By then Dan had given up any pretense of working to support me. I wouldn't have minded supporting him if he had been nice to me, but he wasn't. And he was drinking more and more. So on May 22, 1962, I obtained a divorce from Dan.

44.15   Being a Grandmother

Karen and Clarence and four children went to Tonga for two years in June of 1962. I became very friendly with a truck driver named Red. He asked me to marry him, so I invited him to come with me to see Karen and Clarence off in San Francisco. But at the last minute he got cold feet and didn't show up. After that he didn't come around any more. So I continued to work at the O'er Jammers Cafe. Mrs. Renton told me I wouldn't like working there, that the truck drivers were awfully rough. But I found if you treat them nice, they treat you nice. I was known as the best hamburger cook along the route.

Clarence and Karen came back from Tonga in May of 1964, shortly before the birth of their 5th child. In 1969 my mother (Mary) had a stroke, and soon was too sick to live by herself so she came to live with me. But I couldn't work and take care of her So Wayne and Justine came up and got her and were taking her to Las Vegas, when she got so sick they put her in the hospital in Caliente. She died about a week later on June 24 1965.

44.16 Gladys and Pete Are Married

June I3, 1966, I married Pete (Hogar Adolph) Peterson. He was working on the mill for the Duval Mining Company out of Carlin, so we lived in Carlin, Nevada, for one year. Later we moved to Crescent Valley, Nevada, were Pete was Employed at Cortez Gold Mines. We lived there for six and a half wears. Our hobby was hunting bottles and artifacts at the ghost towns and mines around the area. We spent many hours digging for Chinese artifacts at the old Chinaman's camp on Mount Tenabo. Wherever I went I always had a garden. We had a beautiful yard at Crescent Valley. After we left, they Just let it die.

Gladys in Her Declining Years

When the mine at Crescent Valley closed, we moved to Battle Mountain for a short time. Then Pete obtained work at the mill for the Smokey Valley Mine at Round Mountain. We moved to Round Mountain on February 7, 1977, the day my youngest grandson, Kent, was born. Pete was made mill foreman, and was very well liked at the mill. We lived there 4 wears. Pete turned 65 on December 23, 1999, so he retired, and we moved to Elko, Nevada, on Mar. 16, 1981.

We bought a new trailer when we moved to Elko, and thought we would have time to pursue our hobby and enJoy life. Pete's sister, Agnes, and his brother, Harry, lived there also. But Pete had a massive heart attack and died April 17, 1983.

44.17   Move to Panaca

I continued to live in Elko for a year, and then decided to move to Panaca, Nevada, so I could be near my daughter, Karen. My brother, Wayne, was living in Rose Valley again, and many of my former friends still lived in the area, so it was like coming home. I bought a lot and moved my trailer down from Elko. Karen and Clarence helped me fix my yard. And soon I had a very pretty yard.

> ON NOVEMBER 15, 1996, I went to the Temple and received my endowments, and was sealed to my parents and also to my first husband, James B. Lees. Karen was sealed to us also. Karen and Clarence, and Wayne and some of his family were there also. It a very memorable day.

I lived in my trailer for 5 years, until I broke my leg. After that I wasn't able to take care of everything by myself. So I am living with my daughter, Karen, at the present time, April 1999.

45

WILLIAM CRESFIELD MOODY

The family was dismayed at the sacrifices they would have to make, but they obeyed the call to leave their pleasant valley for the deserts of Utah's Dixie. In October of 1863, he moved his families south to ``Dixie,'' one of the most difficult regions ever to be settled by families called to the task.

William Cresfield Moody

45.1   Early Years

Born to John Wyatt and Mary "Polly" Baldwin Moody, March 23 1819 in Coosa County, Alabama, William Cresfield Moody lived on slave-worked land. In 1835 when William was sixteen, the family moved themselves and their servants to Texas because of exceptional inducements offered by the Mexican government to new settlers, land being the primary appeal. William was strong and tall with a splendid physique. He was an excellent swimmer. He was also very practical and could do or make almost anything he desired. In 1835, immediately after "The Alamo," William joined the Texas army under general Sam Houston, but never had to fight because independence was won in March of 1836. However, William received a grant of a Spanish League, about 4,409 acres. He married Harriet Henson January 1, 1840. This marriage produced seven children.

45.2   Conversion to Mormonism

In 1850 missionaries of the Church of Jesus Christ of Latter-Day Saints taught his family. "The teaching of the elders had the ring of truth," he gave as his reason for joining with this unpopular religion. He was baptized in November of 1851 with his family. His sister Dorinda, his mother, and his brother John Monroe (two years later) also joined the Church. Although he was a wealthy man with large ranch holdings which would be lost unless he was in residence, William gave his slaves their freedom and left Texas for Salt Lake City in March 1853 along with his extended family. His brother John remained behind to settle family affairs, but sent his wife and family with the main company. William and John returned to Texas as missionaries, 1855-1857. They endured prejudice and hatred but baptized ten people including two Damron sisters who later were to become the brothers' plural wives.

45.3   Marriages and Missions

On 20 Dec 1857, in compliance with the Church's law of Celestial marriage, William took a second and third wife. Lola Eliza Bess became the mother of eleven children and Cynthia Elizabeth Damron bore five, making a total of twenty three children in all. Another mission took him to England in 1860. He returned two years later as leader of a company of immigrants, having sailed on the ship Antarctic to New York, by train to St. Joseph, Missouri, by steamer to Omaha, Nebraska, then by ox-team to Salt Lake City.

45.4   Called to Dixie

One day when William had been home only a few months, he was asked to attend a special meeting. When he returned, everyone could sense that he was troubled and he was very pale. He revealed his call to Dixie as a colonizer. The family was dismayed at the sacrifices they would have to make, but they obeyed the call to leave their pleasant valley for the deserts of Utah's Dixie,. In October of 1863, he moved his families south to "Dixie," one of the most difficult regions ever to be settled by families called to the task.

45.5 Service in Eagle Valley

From St. George he was sent to Eagle Valley, Nevada to preside over a small branch of the Church in 1866, the year he married his fourth wife, Louisa Gillard Williams. Spring and Eagle Valleys are twin settlements connected by a large canyon and fed by a lovely stream. William had been taught the trade of brick and stone masonry in his youth. He became a prosperous brick-layer in Salt Lake City, building one of the first permanent brick homes in the valley. But now, calls to barren lands forced him to become a farmer. Now he used his first trade mostly to build chimneys for his houses as he moved from place to place.

45.6 Dry Valley and Moodyville

Finally there came an opportunity to use his skills as a stone mason. A call to Dry Valley, where water had to be carted in and used very sparingly, seemed at first to be doomed to failure because of the lack of means to support his families. But he felt that his past service in the Church was rewarded when an opportunity came to make $15 a day constructing a quartz mill for the Pioche mining district. With his son George driving one wagon and a hired man another to haul the stone (Charles Lytle?), the family received a princely $21 a day, the money bringing unprecedented prosperity to the families. In Dry Valley they founded their own town of Moodyville.

Author's Note: We have spoken previously of the *Dry Valley Sink* and the author's near-death experience there (2.1). The preceding paragraph establishes a fact perhaps not generally known: Namely, that Moodyville first existed as a Church mission to Dry Valley which was on the brink of failure for lack of water for irrigation. Church authorities, apparently unaware of the sink situated at the exit of the creek from Rose Valley canyon, had likely assumed that an irrigation dam could be constructed to divert water to the rich farming lands in the Valley. Any dam constructed there by the settlers, of course, was doomed to empty out into the underlying sands and gravel (cf. the *Echo Dam* problem) before its waters rose to a point where they could be channeled out to water crops.

William Moody, however, rather than recommending that the Dry Valley mission be abandoned, took the initiative of developing an alternative to farming in Dry Valley which could provide a means of support for mission families. Being an experienced brick maker, mason, and builder, he submitted a bid to Meadow Valley Mining Company and won the contract to build the Pioche Dry-Valley mill. Thus, Moodyville continued to exist so long as the mill was active and then became a `ghost' mission.

Reports to the effect that Moodyville was just a `tent city' spawned by the mill are therefore incorrect --- Moodyville gave rise to the mill.[1] Also, there may have been tents pitched there at one point or another, but there were also dwellings with porches, windows, and doors. At least Margaret Moody makes mention of them in the structure were she and Charles were living (47.5).

---

[1] http://parks.nv.gov/ec.htm

45.7   Wood Cutter

After the mill was constructed, fuel was needed for its engine, so William became a wood cutter. He could chop into four-foot lengths four cords of wood in a day, 2 cords a day being good for most men. In 1871, the job of supplying wood for the steam mill having ended, they moved back to Eagle Valley. All William's family went with him except William's first wife Harriet, aged 51. She moved with three of her sons to Panguitch, Utah and did not again rejoin her husband. William married his fifth wife, Victoria Regina Rogers October 3, 1872, from which union there were no children.

45.8   Paiutes and Ranching at Deseret

Surrounded by Indian lands as they were, the family sometimes encountered Paiutes. One day William witnessed the beating of an Indian boy by his father. William rescued the boy by trading a horse for him. He named the boy John and set him to work herding cattle. William began to prosper as his farming and cattle and horse raising expanded. By the year 1881 several of the children by his second and third wives were of marriageable age, so he moved his families to Deseret, Utah where his children could meet other Mormon young people who had similar backgrounds and ideals.

45.9   Flight towards Mexico

An unwise herding of his cattle to bottomlands which were too bleak and inclement for survival caused his cattle business to fail, but he built up his resources by farming. He avoided arrest and persecution under the antipolygamy laws of the United states by fleeing towards Mexico in 1885. Two years later, when the persecution of "polygs" became very intense, Mormon men were generally advised to take their last wife (the others presumably would be well established with children old enough to help) and go to Arizona or Mexico. William was in the forefront of this resettlement.

He left his farms in Deseret to his second wife Eliza and family and took with him his childless fourth wife Louisa and his son William Alfred, age fifteen. (His first wife Harriet had moved away from him and his third, Cynthia Damron, had died. A fifth wife, Victoria Regina, a woman of 32 when he married her October 30, 1872, and subsequently childless, may have been merely under his protection, as sometimes happened, for we only know that she did not come with him.) He planned to move the rest of his family as soon as he could prepare a home for them.

45.10   Settling in Arizona

He was sixty-six years old in 1885, yet he hopefully began a new life in the Gila Valley where there were small colonies of Mormons, among them his brother John. He settled at Thatcher, Arizona and remained for the rest of his life, except for visits to his families in Utah for periods of time. He farmed a homestead with his son William, building the last of his brick homes.

45.11 Spiritual Gifts

Some of his remarkable experiences involved receiving the "Gift of Tongues" on occasion. He also received a number of spiritual manifestations, both in vision and revelation, in answer to questions he prayed about. He understood scriptures by praying and receiving answers.

45.12 Declining Years

But he was not always solemn. He enjoyed practical jokes. He loved to dance. Checkers was a favorite pastime as he grew older. He was a man of strong likes and dislikes. He hated lies, sham, and self-importance. He hated intoxicating liquor. He loved people, showing kindness to the poor, orphans, and widows. Especially, he loved children. When he was 87, he desired to visit his entire family for what he believed to be the last time. In June 4 of 1906 he began his journey to Utah, Nevada, then California where his son Thomas lived. There he died during the night of September 25, 1906, and his body was sent to Thatcher for burial.

46

HARRIET HENSON MOODY — FIRST WIFE OF WILLIAM AND MOTHER OF MARGARET

Then came the heart-wrenching call to leave all she had and go where poverty was the rule --- where starvation might occur. It took all the courage she had to go with the others to Dixie. In St. George they built a crude home, tilled the ground, and raised crops, working constantly to obtain a scant living.

No Photo Available

46.1 Marriage to William

Harriet Henson, the first wife of William Cresfield Moody was born in Miller, Arkansas December 22, 1820. A fond memory of her youth was the Saturday trips made into the nearby woods to gather wild pecan nuts and some of the beautiful leaves from the trees. There were used not only as a decoration in the home, but for a child's pattern to draw around. She met and married William Cresfield Moody in January of 1840, when she was nineteen years old, and they made their home in Grimes County, Texas. Their slaves helped with the work.

46.2 Conversion

Mormon missionaries visited the Moodys, whose home was one of the largest in the section. Services held there attracted Saints and investigators from miles around. The Moodys' southern hospitality led them to provide dinner for all. Harriet and her slaves spent the entire day cooking and preparing the house for church. They hauled white sand in and spread in areas to act as spittoons for the tobacco spitting crowd.

Five children were born in Texas: John Franklin, 1842; Margaret Josephine, 1844; Harriet, 1847; Nancy, 1850; and Henry, 1852.

Gathering to Zion

In the spring of 1853, the family felt the urge to gather to Zion. They left their affluent home in Texas and joined the pioneers. If they had known in advance the hardships in store, would they have had the courage to leave? They took a steamboat across the gulf of Mexico and up the Mississippi to Keokuk, Iowa, where they joined a group of saints crossing the plains by covered wagon. They arrived in Salt Lake City September 20, 1853, exactly six months after leaving their home in Texas.

Affluence

At first it looked as if the family would be affluent and continue the patterns followed in Texas. Harriet lived in a nice home. She gave birth to two more children: William, 1855; and Theodore, 1858. She believed so wholeheartedly in the gospel she had espoused that she willingly allowed her husband to take two more wives who came and lived in her home and shared her food and substance.

Call to Dixie

Then came the heart-wrenching call to leave all she had and go where poverty was the rule, where starvation might occur. It took all the courage she had to go with the others to Dixie. In St. George they built a crude home, tilled the ground, and raised crops, working constantly to obtain a scant living.

Call to Eagle Valley

She helped pioneer St. George and Eagle Valley [and Dry Valley]. While William served his two missions to Texas and to England, she, with the help of her older sons, provided for the family. Her life in the west held privation and hardship, but she accepted this as the price of serving in Zion. As she grew older, she moved with her three sons to Panguitch, Utah and then to Luna Valley, New Mexico, where she died at 64 years old in November 1884.

47

MARGARET JOSEPHINE MOODY LYTLE

It was in St. George, Utah that she met and became betrothed to Charles Lytle, who owned a freight outfit, and freighted out of salt lake City to the settlements in the southern part of the state. In order to be married in the endowment House, they took an ox team and wagon for the long trip to Salt Lake City, where they were married on May 10, 1869.

Margaret Josephine Moody

47.1   Conversion to Mormonism

The oldest daughter of William Crestfield and Harriet Henson Moody was Margaret Josephine, who was born in Anderson, Texas on December 2, 1844. In the spring of 1853 when she was eight years old, she, with her parents and brothers and sisters, left the state of Texas to join the Latter Day Saints on their trek to salt Lake City. She greeted with enthusiasm the idea of a boat trip across the Gulf of Mexico and up the river, but to her consternation the trip was ruined by the fact that she spent most of the time in bed suffering with the measles.

47.2   Trek to Salt Lake City

After six long, hard months of travel by boat and covered wagon, the family arrived in Utah on Sept. 20, 1853. Her father had had experience in making and laying brick, and the Moodys had one of the first permanent brick houses in the valley. This old brick house many years later became the home of the Salt Air ticket office. When Margaret visited it many years after having moved from Salt Lake City, she found the old spring that she remembered so well, still on the back of the lot.

Days of Hunger

The early days in Utah were fraught with hardship and many times even hunger. She remembered well how she and her brother John were often sent to the town square for their portion of flour, and once in particular she remembered how she hurried to get her share, but her brother John playing along the way, was too slow, and arrived after all the four had been apportioned to others. This was almost a major calamity in the family, for this was their only source of flour, and no one knew when they would be able to get more. She told also of another occasion when it was necessary to send to Ft. Harriman for flour. As they had no other means of transporting it, her brother Henry had to walk over and back in one day, returning with their portion on his back.

Financial Setback

While they were still in Salt lake City, Margaret's mother inherited some money, which was sent to her from Texas by a Mr. Hanks. After consultation they decided to buy teams and wagons and go to Sanpete County where grain was plentiful, buy up as much of the crop as possible and haul it to salt Lake City. This they did, storing the wheat in a storehouse to wait until the price was better before selling it. Soon after this, however, her father was called on a mission to Texas. The wheat was not sold at the proper time, and it spoiled, causing them to lose the investment.

47.3   Colonizing Dixie

Later the family was sent by President Brigham Young to help colonize St. George, Utah, and her father was given the mission of helping to build the Temple. It was necessary when they made this move for Margaret to ride a horse and help drive the cattle. The weather was extremely cold and her skirts got wet and froze. This terrible exposure resulted in an illness, which was characterized by a severe cough, which periodically returned throughout her life.

> Their first home in St. George was a dug-out which had been made in the red sandstone of the region. Margaret told of how she was often scoffed at by people living in houses.[a] This was particularly hard to bear as her father was one of the few builders in the settlement, and he, through his kindness, had built several other homes before he built one for his own family.
>
> ---
>
> [a]**This behavior defines the psychological divide between** *zionist* **and** *profiteer*, **the first consecrating his gain to the community, the second coveting his gain for himself and flaunting it as an emblem of superiority.** See Appendix: *MANAGEMENT OF THE MATERIAL WORLD* .I

47.4 Margaret Meets Charles Lytle

It was in St. George, Utah that she met and became betrothed to Charles ⟸ **Lytle, who owned a freight outfit, and freighted out of salt lake City to the settlements in the southern part of the state.** In order to be married in the endowment House, they took an ox team and wagon for the long trip to Salt Lake City, where they were married on May 10, 1869.

Margaret vs. Charles

They made the trip in company with another wagon, and Margaret often drove the slow, pokey oxen. On the return trip her new husband got in the habit of leaving her for a few hours each day, while he went back to talk with the man in the rear wagon. One day, her vanity rather piqued that he preferred other company, she came to a long downhill slope and whipped the oxen and got them to running. Her husband thought at once that they were running away, and came dashing down the hill, arriving just as she stopped them. After that he drove the oxen.

Author's Note: This anecdote, presented as a human interest item entailing a silent quarrel between newly weds, may well have more significance than meets the eye. Charles ran a freight line, which explains why the couple were riding a freight wagon pulled by oxen rather than availing themselves of transportation to their wedding by stage. The wagon had likely been loaded with cargo on their trip north. Very probably the man with whom he was spending time in the other wagon was involved in the freighting business himself and was therefore a valuable source of information regarding developments throughout the settlements which he had occasion to visit. As of their marriage data (1869), Brigham Young was expending settlers at a frightening rate against the powers of nature in Dixie and on the Muddy River for the upbuilding of his cotton kingdom and import highway linking to the Colorado which he had envisioned for that area . . . but was absorbing heavy casualties in the struggle and on the verge of abandoning agricultural development at the Muddy Mission while retaining plans for the import highway.[1] Charles may well have applied the information collected

---

[1]In 1871 over 600 colonists returned to Utah leaving behind 150 homes, irrigation canals and farms (See Appendix 47.6.)

from the man in question with respect to such particulars and applied them to decisions which he would be shortly required to make involving the young couple in ways she could scarcely imagine (**Chapter** 5).

47.5   Life in Dry Valley

Milk for the Baby

⟹   *Soon after their marriage they moved to Dry Valley, Nevada, and here her first son, Ed, was born in 1870. In order for her to get milk for her baby it was necessary for her to walk several miles each day down to the home of her mother, who had a cow.*

> **Author's Note: Harriet Henson** --- Margaret's mother and Freel's Grandmother[a] --- is by now 50 years old and apparently no longer living with William Moody, who had taken a younger wife and was living in Moodyville at the head of Dry Valley. John Mathews, however, current owner of lands south of the former Moodyville, reports the discovery of home foundations along the eastern edge of his fields in Dry Valley abutting the Mill. William Moody, unlike other polygamous husbands of the Edmunds-Tucker era, had apparently brought Harriet with him from St. George so that he could attend to her needs, but dared not put her under the same roof with his younger wife for fear of being arrested by federal marshals and thrown into prison. At any rate, here we find Harriet in Dry Valley with a milk cow, but living two miles away from her daughter and grandson in a separate dwelling. The foundations discovered by Mr. Mathews are within a short walk of the mill where William was working, which would have made it easy for him to look in on her every day before returning to Moodyville.
>
> ---
> [a]See the dispute between Freel and Mary as to what the letter 'H' represented as his middle name (43.8)

Finally as she expressed it, "she put her foot down" and demanded a cow. "Who'd milk her?" her husband asked. "I will, if necessary," she answered. "But I will not walk down there every day and leave my baby alone."

Her husband, Charley, went outside and sat down on the porch. Soon, as luck would have it, a man came by with a cow. "How much will you take for your cow?" asked Charley. "Fifty dollars," came the reply. "That's too much. I'll give you $47.50 for her."

And so Margaret had her cow. But as it turned out she did not have to milk it after all, for about this time Charley's brother, George, arrived to stay with them for a while, and he cheerfully took over the milking job.

Mexican Killers

Later the Lytles moved to Eagle Valley, while Charley still worked in the old Pioche Mill in Dry Valley. It was therefore necessary that she was alone part of the time. In those days Pioche was a rip-roaring mining camp. The rival factions were fighting for the ore deposited there, and history claims that each side imported gunmen and hoodlums to try and scare off the miners of the other. The only law was the law of the gun. Rough characters were very common, and fights, thefts, and killings were the usual morning news.

One night when Margaret was alone with her baby, she saw two Mexicans alight from their horses as she looked through the window of her darkened room into the moonlight without. Each, with knife in hand, began to creep slowly and stealthily toward her door. She was terrified! Dropping to her knees she called upon her Heavenly Father for protection. She said, "If I ever prayed in my life, I prayed that night, as I begged God to help us and save our lives." Her prayer was brief, but when she arose the Mexicans seemed to be in some sort of argument. They evidently could not agree on just what proceedings to follow, and soon they became angry and mounted their horses and rode away. She knew that God had heard and answered her prayer.

47.6   The Cattle Business

Mr. Lytle became interested in cattle, and eventually they owned a prosperous cattle ranch in Eagle Valley.

Margaret Lytle was the mother of seven children: Ed, John Leslie, Noma M. Lytle Devlin, Amy Lytle Damron, Freeland H., Samuel, and Margaret Leizette Lytle Warren.

Margaret Moody Lytle lived to be almost 79 years of age, passing away at her home in Eagle Valley on June 15, 1922.

Appendices

MORMONS OF THE MUDDY MISSION

Author's Note: For expansion of footnote references, see http://www.accessclarkcounty.com/depts/comprehensive_planning/post/Documents/MVTSCulturalResources.pdf.

.A Early Settlement

Mormon settlement of the Virgin Valley and the Muddy River area comprised the earliest Euro-American colonies in the region (Clark County, Nevada). Soon after the Mormons settled in Salt Lake City in 1847, pioneers and scouts ventured westward to explore the region[2]. A northern route and a southern route to the Pacific Ocean were scouted. The southern route was ascertained to be preferable as Native Americans in the south were perceived to be less hostile than those along the northern route[3]. In addition, due to the milder climate, the southern route was never blocked by snow, being passable at all times of the year. **A good wagon road, established along the southern route, remained a major transportation corridor to Los Angeles for freighters and emigrants for the next 20 years[4]. Brigham Young planned a continuous string of Mormon settlements along the 700 mile stretch from Salt Lake to San Bernardino to provide supply stations and way stops for the Church members[5]. By 1857 the Mormons had established 30 communities along the southern road.**

In 1855, Young began to explore the possibility of utilizing the Colorado river as a transportation corridor in order to reduce the overland mileage and cut transportation costs of bringing immigrants into the area[6]. Toward this end he sent a contingent of five men to explore the river to see if it was navigable by boat. In June of that year, the small party traveled to Las Vegas with the Bringhurst party which was to settle at the Las Vegas spring. From Las Vegas, the company headed for the Colorado River. **After five days, the party turned back due to the summer heat which made further exploration unendurable. They returned without answering Youngs questions about the navigability of the River and two years elapsed without further exploration by the Mormons[7].**

.B US Army Reconnaisance

In 1858, Youngs attention was again drawn to the Colorado River. Lieutenant Joseph Ives had been sent by the US Department of War to explore the possibility of using the river for transportation of troops and munitions into the Great Basin[8]. In a small steamship, the Ives party entered the mouth of the Colorado in the Gulf of California. Ives managed to navigate 275 miles upriver from Fort Yuma, and reported the mouth of Black Canyon was the practical head of navigation[9].

---

[2] Hunter, 1939

[3] Hunter 1939

[4] More likely, for the next 40 years. See .E below

[5] Hunter 1939

[6] Hunter, 1939

[7] Hunter 1939

[8] Hunter 1939

[9] Ives, pg 87 in Hunter 1939

Ives further concluded: **A reconnaissance, made from the foot of the Black Canyon towards the nearest point on the emigrant road to Utah, showed that a wagon-road might be opened between the trail and the head of navigation. For sixteen miles, while passing through the gravel hills and ravines that cover the eastern slope of the intervening range of mountains, the country is somewhat rough, and a little work would be required to make a good roadway, but, after reaching the summit, there would be no further difficulty. The distance from the river to the emigrant road is about 40 miles.**[10]

This expedition was brought to the attention of Brigham Young by Hamblin. In the aftermath of the 'Utah War in which the United States Government sent military forces to enforce Federal authority over the Mormons [11], Young was highly suspicious of the motives of the U.S. Government. Thales Haskell was sent to gather information on the Ives expedition[12]. Haskell reported that the steamer company was hostile to the Mormons and the ultimate goal of the expedition was to learn if the route could be used by a military force to enter southern Utah and subjugate the Mormons[13]. Fearing that the Ives expedition posed a threat, Young quickly sent another contingent of 20 men, headed by George Smith, to explore the Colorado River ostensibly for suitable locations for settlements.[14] The group followed the Santa Clara and Virgin Rivers to the Colorado River. Smiths report that there was no area suitable for settlement temporarily postponed further plans to develop shipping on the Colorado until the fall of 1864[15].

.C   Muddy Mission Founded

In 1864, Anson Call was dispatched to the Colorado River to establish a boat landing and colony. Young hoped that the Mormons would be able to enter Deseret by sailing up the river from the Gulf of California to the mouth of Black Canyon, described by Ives as marking the end of the navigable part of the river. Call established a church warehouse and landing on the north bank of the river approximately 15 miles up river from the present location of Hoover Dam[16]. Call, instructed to found a community near the landing, chose a site at the lower end of the Muddy River. **The Muddy Mission was founded in the fall of 1864 to provide support for Calls Landing (or Callville), and was part of Brigham Youngs plan to establish a continuous string of Mormon settlements and supply along the emigrant route**[17].

The Moapa Valley was a strategic location from which the Mormons could regulate extractive industries and provide a 'jumping off point' for exploitation and exploration of the little known western edge of 'Deseret'[18]. Young wanted to expand his empire westward in an attempt to discourage Gentile settlement of the area

---

[10]Ives 1859:42

[11]Blair et al. 1996

[12]McClellan et al. 1980; McClintock 1921

[13]McClintock 1921

[14]Brigham, of course, realized that potential military exploitation worked both ways. Arms running via the Colorado might just as well supply Mormon fighters as government forces.

[15]Hunter 1939

[16]Hunter 1939, Sterner and Ezzo 1996:94

[17]Hunter 1939

[18]Blair et al. 1996

he envisioned as a 'State of Deseret which included most of the Great Basin and extended to the coast of southern California. The mission was also to provide support for navigation of the Colorado River and be part of Youngs planned cotton-growing empire[19].

.D St. Thomas Founded

In January of 1865 the first colonists arrived, led by Thomas Smith, and within days the colony of St. Thomas was home to 45 families. Between 1865 and 1870, seven settlements were established along the Lower Virgin and the Muddy Rivers: Beaver Dams, St. Thomas, Overton, St. Joseph, West Point, Mill Point, and Simonsville. (McClintock 1921). St. Joseph (now Logandale, Nevada) was established in 1866 (12 miles upstream from St. Thomas) and the next year had 151 acres under cultivation. The primary crop was cotton but subsistence crops such as wheat, corn, orchards and vinyards were planted[20]. Simonsville was established in December of 1865 south of St. Joseph. By the spring of 1866 a grist mill used to grind wheat, corn and salt had been constructed at Simonsville [21]. **Steamers made regular runs from the mouth of the Colorado to Callville hauling freight bound for the Mormon settlements until at least December of 1866.**

.E Dangling Questions

The landing at Callville reportedly "ceased to exist by 1869 because navigation of the river was not possible during periods of low flow. In addition, the combination of the cost of building a road from Callville to St. George, and news of the transcontinental railroad [linkup at Promontory Point] made the landing obsolete."[22]

Author's Note: Either disinformation or confusion appear to be afloat on the Muddy at Callville. Periods of `low flow' were seasonal and sporadic, and had not prevented `regular runs' in the past. Moreover, the Ives report had estimated connection to the main artery by wagon road from this area to be a non-problem(.B). Secondly, the transcontinental railroad passed through Salt Lake westward over the Sierra Nevada at a vast distance to the north of the settlement areas to be serviced from Callville. Charles' Lytle personal history credits Eagle Valley as a stopover for traffic from the north. Milford, Utah was as far south as the train came during the 1880s and 1890s (42.1). More seriously, Indian insurgency compromised the railroad's reliability until the Wounded Knee Massacre of 1890 ended the Indian Wars. Thus, we find that Myron Angel, in his 1881 history of Nevada, lists Callville as still functioning, and as `the head of navigation on the Colorado.' Myron seems to have it right. Both colonization objectives represented by Brigham Young and corporate entities had a vital interest in maintaining an import/export link to the Colorado for many years after 1869. To stockpile military supplies as a hedge against further military intervention, imports via the Colorado were the only viable option. Ditto for the export of commodities to California markets. (See the discussion of *Appendix: MANAGING MATERIAL THINGS* (.Q)

---

[19]Gratton 1998

[20]Ezzo 1996

[21]Fleming 1967

[22]Ezzo 1996.

.F   West ·Point

West Point was the only settlement to be established in the upper part of the Muddy River Valley. In 1867, an abortive attempt at settling the upper valley was mounted by immigrants from the Beaver Dams area to the north. A town site was selected in the upper valley and 15 families moved from the fort. Later that December, it was determined that the settlers were susceptible to Indian attack as the Native Americans already living and farming in that part of the valley, were openly hostile about the new settlement. The small colony was ordered by Brigham Young to return to the fort at New St. Joseph. All but five families complied and either relocated at New St. Joseph or to went to their former homes in the north[23].

In the fall of 1868 a second town site, also to be known as West Point, was selected and surveyed in the upper valley and by June 1869, 20 families resided there with wheat and cotton under cultivation. The 1870 census enumerated 138 people at West Point (US Census 1870). The colony was short lived, lasting approximately two years as a flood occurring in 1870 destroyed many of the crops, forcing some settlers to abandon the site. There were, however, a few people still residing at West Point when the Muddy Mission was finally dissolved in 1871[24].

.G   New St. Joseph

Missionaries camping at the New St. Joseph Fort were instructed to build a city on the sandy bench above the river and adjacent to the fort (Its construction would be the first planned city in southern Nevada). After considerable hesitation, they began to dig seven miles of canal to provide water to St. Joseph City. **Terrible hardship was endured by all as seasonal winds destroyed each attempt to tame the shifting sands and provide water to the city plots. Temperatures were unrelenting and when there was water in the ditch for use, it caused great illness and sores to occur on all residents within the community.** Hauling water from the Muddy River most of the time, residents built their 24 small houses on the bench as they continued to farm the bottom lands[25].

.H   Muddy Mission Terminates

By 1870, the Muddy Mission as a whole was approaching destitution. In the fall of that year, Brigham Young made a long anticipated appearance to the distressed mission[26]. Upon observing the impossible living conditions, Young released the settlers from their mission and in December 1870, the people of the Muddy decided to abandon the location. The only dissenting voice was that of Daniel Bonelli who remained in the area with his family. In 1871 over 600 colonists returned to Utah leaving behind 150 homes, irrigation canals and farms[27].

---

[23] White 1990

[24] White 1990

[25] Blair and White 1999

[26] Blair et al. 1996, 1997; Blair. 2004

[27] Fleming 1967; McClintock 1921. For a more detailed account of Mormon expansion and the Muddy Mission see Blair et al ,1996, 1997; Blair, 2004; Gratton, 1982; McCarty, 1981; and White, 1990

.I The Muddy River Mission — Additional Detail

At the shoreline, looking north across the schoolhouse inset - the front steps and a water filled building

...not until Mormon settlers arrived in the 1850s did anyone seriously consider settling the area because the Vegas and Muddy Valleys were inundated with salts.

...A number of factors lay behind the Latter-day Saints' decision (to colonize broadly).[28] First was their general goal of achieving localized, economic self-sufficiency. Having fled from persecution in the Midwest, Mormon leaders hoped to completely cut ties with the gentile — as Mormons called non-Mormons — world. Yet when they discovered that the Salt Lake Valley was too arid to provide enough food and raw materials for a large and growing population, Church officials began looking to expand into the wider Great Basin, and south into the Mohave Desert.

To accomplish this, Church President Brigham Young established Mormon colonies across diverse ecological zones. Settlers in each area produced one or two resources and deposited surpluses in the form of tithing in central repositories, to be distributed as needed — for example, Cedar City, Utah, was the "iron mission," providing that ore to other Mormon communities. Apparently unaware of the salts and alkali permeating soils in the area, Mormon leaders viewed the Muddy River Valley as an ideal spot for growing and then sharing warm-climate crops.

Over time, Mormon leaders realized they would have to import some goods, at least for the short term. This, then, became the second (and decisive) factor driving them to settle the Muddy River Valley:

---

[28]This text is excerpted in part from www.onlinenevada.org/the_muddy_mission.

IT WAS AN IDEAL RESTING SPOT FOR TRAVELERS **hauling in merchandise**, and the confluence with the Virgin River connected the Muddy to a port site selected to receive commodities brought up the Colorado River by steamboat. Its importance in the commercial schemes of the times is witnessed openly by the railroad spur which was eventually extended to the site.

As of our times, the Lake Mead shoreline is the center of the old town of St. Thomas. The wide sandy beach seems to have been there in pre-flood times. What you see are several widely dispersed buildings. The chimneys that you see from the road are no longer the main landmark once you finally get to St. Thomas.

The hike from the lookout point is long and very hot. It makes you think about what the people who lived here experienced ... The Tamarisk is amazing here. It is thick and dangerous. You must wear long pants. There is no avoiding it. It will cut your skin because of the sharp branch spurs on them. One of the common names for this plant is `Salt Cedar' or `Salt Bush'. Salty excretions and a salty taste are two hallmarks of this intrusion plant. The cutting action of the spurs along the stems of this plant along with the obligatory dose of salt makes this a special kind of torment for those who have to cross it. If you come here, be wise, stay on the trails, cover your skin.[a]

---

[a]http://www.sunsetcities.com/lake-mead/stthomas.html

Mormons arrived at the Muddy in January 1865 and established St. Thomas; six months later a second group founded St. Joseph nine miles to the north. Both discovered ample evidence that local Paiutes were growing crops along the Muddy River, yet the settlers saw nothing wrong with expropriating the Native Americans' property. It was the Paiute practice to plant corn, beans, squash, and wheat before migrating to the cooler uplands for gathering and hunting. They returned every fall to harvest surviving crops. Needless to say, their 1865 return was an unhappy one. Not surprisingly, "Indian troubles" soon became a problem for the Muddy Valley settlements. Anger over losing their farm land as well as their belief in sharing resources prompted some Paiutes to appropriate Mormon animals and foodstuffs. Unwilling to admit they had pushed members of the tribe into food destitution, the Mormons called the Paiutes' behavior "theft" and "beggary," often responding by punishing "offenders." The Paiutes sometimes reciprocated with violence.

In addition to difficulties with Native Americans, the Muddy Valley Mormons faced severe environmental and climatic conditions. As the Muddy's source was a mineral spring, it was salty and unsuitable for large-scale irrigation agriculture. Searing heat in the summer and frequent bouts of drought tested the settlers. Man-made disasters also posed challenges. On August 18, 1868, the second St. Joseph burned down after two young boys lost control of a fire while roasting potatoes.

MANY Mormon families simply could not endure the Muddy Mission's extreme hardships and either perished or left. Note that THIS IS THE SAME 'GODFORSAKEN' AREA TO WHICH EAGLE VALLEY PAIUTES WERE TRANSPORTED AND SUBSEQUENTLY WALKED AWAY FROM TO RESERVATIONS IN UTAH AT INDIAN PEAK AND CEDAR CITY. (29.3)

Paiute usage of lands should have served as a pattern for the white intruders: Native Americans planted desert areas in the spring when the climate was reasonable, travelled north for the summer, only to return in the fall to harvest once the scorching temperatures abated. The White Man after *umpteem* generations has finally seen the light. We now see a flow of migrants headed north from Dixie and other desert areas in the spring, only to migrate south again when temperatures moderate.

> TO DETERMINE WHETHER THE SETTLEMENTS COULD SURVIVE, Brigham Young visited in March 1870. He was not hopeful. That fall, a flood wiped out the new Muddy village of West Point.

The final straw, however, came during a fight over taxes. In 1870, a new boundary survey confirmed that the Muddy settlements were in Nevada, not in Utah or Arizona. Both of those territories had accepted taxes in the form of goods, but Nevada officials wanted back taxes paid in gold or silver. Few settlers could afford this, so in early 1871 all but one Mormon family left the Muddy Mission for good. The community remained largely abandoned, and in the early 1930s the Boulder Canyon Project led to the creation of Lake Mead, which washed over the Muddy Mission.

> So far as the survivors of the Muddy Mission were concerned, they were called to settle Orderville (7.4), at which point we encounter Grandma Great, Justine's grandmother, a zionist heart and soul, living the *united order*.

MANAGEMENT OF MATERIAL THINGS

The Mormon pioneers were familiar with three modes of managing material things:

1. **The Order of Zion**, where all possessions were managed as stewardships consecrated to the upbuilding of God's Kingdom on the Earth.

2. **Competitive Capitalism,** where corporations and businesses seek to accumulate wealth through production and trade, the stock market, etc.

3. **Profiteering,** a corrupted form of Capitalism which attempts to dispossess people of their possessions through price manipulations, fraud or one kind or another, or — in the worst case — murder.

It goes without saying that modes (2) and (3) are of one kin and promote materialist behavior and thinking as opposed to the spiritual growth and material equality sought for in Mode (1). Mode (1) has been the declared objective of many religious societies, but few have successfully achieved it unless they had a way of separating themselves completely from materialists. As we have seen, the Mormon pioneers came west for the purpose of achieving such a separation, but were quickly overrun by profiteers and capitalists (4.1; 4.12).

.J 'Oxymormons'

The lineup of companies appended to the present discussion constitutes but a sampling of competitive capitalist entities (corporations) formed during the settlement period in Deseret. Financial studies[29] — comparable to those of our day which identify important names in the world of high finance and rank them as a hierarchy in terms of their comparative net worth — include the names of both Mormon and non-Mormon capitalists who had established themselves as millionaires during this era. Most likely, some Mormons in the listings consecrated their corporate gains to the 'upbuilding of Zion,' while others succumbed to the temptation of consecrating their gain to themselves.

.K Zion/Mammon Ambivalence

To cite an illustrative case, the holdings of just one prominent Mormon leader are rated at approximately $7.5 million net, amassed, of course, while simultaneously promoting the *Zion* emblem on the flip side of Deseret coinage.

Question pertinent to the subject at hand: Were the millions in question consecrated to the 'upbuilding of Zion,' or did they end up in personal bank accounts? Or perhaps an intermixture of both?

---

[29]Studies of this kind are freely available both in print and on the internet. The author omits identification of both publishers and subjects by name, since the purpose of the discussion is to illustrate a trend rather than to discuss individuals.

A 1860 $5 gold piece, with inscription "Holiness to the Lord" in the Deseret alphabet

The spiritual ambivalence between God and Mammon represented by material accumulation, which first manifested openly at the recall of settlers from the Carson Valley Mission (45.4), was not just a 'flash in the pan' of the gold rush years. Rather, it appeared to displace zionism at a rate proportionate to the realization of the church membership at large (leader and layman alike) that the United States Government, despite an all-out struggle for independence and freedom of religious expression, had forcibly wrested control of their lives from them again — that the Rocky Mountains had not and could not provide a refuge for the 'Zion' of Mormonism envisioned by its founder. The hope lingered that it might ultimately do so, no doubt, until the outcome of the War Between the States in 1865 certified the prospect of a permanent Union driven ever westward by *Manifest Destiny*, quashed Mexican claims to the territory, and undercut enthusiasm for the prospects of *Deseret*. Subsequent to that, Mormon pioneers no doubt harbored hopes that Custer's defeat at the Little Bighorn in 1876 signaled the prospect of evading complete dominance by the US government indefinitely. Brigham Young had certainly not surrendered his expectations for ultimate triumph when he died in 1877. However, such hopes dipped to new lows following passage of the Edmunds-Tucker Act of 1887 and the Wounded Knee Massacre of 1890, which effectively ended the Indian Wars.

'Manifest Destiny' Overshadows Deseret

.L   Promoting What Is 'Good for Business'

As noted above, a significant number of profiteers, concealed behind the mask of zionism, penetrated Mormonism at its inception and availed themselves at every opportunity to advance their selfish purposes by exploiting the commitment and innocence of unsuspecting zionists. Simultaneously, these 'tares' among the wheat were fostering changes in Church policy and doctrine calculated to close the gap between Mormonism and Christian society at large.[30] As in other forms of human interaction, the demonstration of shared interests and thinking substantially improves the chances of closing business deals. While a lengthy treatment of this subject is beyond the scope of this book[31], we identify and outline the essence of it because of its direct impact on the Lytle family story, especially with respect to marriage relations (Chapter 43.8) and Charles Lytle's U-Turn with respect to the Church (Chapter 5).

Potential for Abuse of Authority

> Unsuspecting zionist settlers who were `true believers' presented perfect targets for their counterparts, the latter knowing that Church covenants compelled the faithful to consecrate their all to the `upbuilding of the kingdom' --- even if their unquestioning response to Church calls for resettlement required abandonment of their properties to those remaining in place. Persons in authority, particularly, were beset with the temptation to form alliances with profiteering-minded individuals to divest settlers of coveted assets which they wished to incorporate into their own estates or to form business alliances destined to become profitable as plans for settlement advanced.

.M   Do As I Say, Not As I Do

For the Church member who remained a 'true believer' despite the unending series of setbacks, the trend from communal living to every-man-for-himself meant that — at least in some cases — difficult 'mission calls' requiring consecration of personal properties to the common cause represented cases of 'DO AS I SAY' not 'DO AS I DO.'

Needless to say, the melding of zionism and mammonism produced a number of notable *oxymormons*, i.e., terms reflecting a union of God and Mammon which were internally contradictory with respect to Mormon doctrine and zionist objectives, such as 'Zion's *Bank*,' and ZCMI ('Zion's *Commercial Mercantile* Institution').

---

[30] Joseph Smith had dealt with this problem from the outset as well, when his scribes and others closest to him accused him of being a "fallen prophet" and attempted to supplant his teachings (plural marriage and plural gods, in particular) with doctrines more 'friendly' to the sectarian community.

[31] For a comprehensive discussion, see Alexander, *Mormons in Transition* (University of Illinois Press; Rep Sub edition, 1996)

.N   Charles As an Eye-Witness To Change

How do these developments make contact with the Lytle family? As detailed in
Chapter 5, Charles Lytle found himself suddenly caught up in these cross-currents
at the Dry Valley and Eagle Valley missions. During his tenure there, he had witnessed a reversal of Church policy with respect to mining. Shortly before, Mormons
had been punished by excommunication for engaging in mining activities, which
were seen as an obstacle to the 'establishment of Zion.' Then — within the space
of several years — Church authorities had appeared on the scene in the vicinity of
Pioche[32] and organized a mining district representing Church interests. Next, in less
time than it takes a gnat to sneeze, Mormons transported a 5-stamp mill from Hiko
to Bullionville and put it into operation for one Pioche company (Raymond & Ely),
while Charles' father in law (William Moody) — technically on a Church mission
to settle Dry Valley — was providing jobs for its destitute settlers by placing the
winning bid to construct a large mill within a mile of their settlement at Moodyville
to process Pioche ore for Bullionville's competitor (Meadow Valley Mining Company). Reputedly, by this time, there were so many Mormons involved in digging
and milling in the area that not a few gentiles 'recoiled at the sight of their horns'
and fled the district!

.O   An Incongruous Mission 'Call'

To make matters worse, the local bishop approached Charles and issued what by
all appearances was a *bogus* DO-AS-I-SAY but NOT-AS-I-DO 'call' to the Muddy
Mission (Chapter 5), a *mission* which by then was in fact officially defunct[33] insofar
as legitimate zionist objectives were concerned, but leaving in its wake, apparently,

---

[32]The Pioche silver lodes were heralded by the press throughout the United States *and* Europe
as being even more lucrative and having more potential than the Comstock lode. Mining bonanzas
such as these in Deseret placed the Church leadership between the proverbial 'rock and a hard
place:' Either maintain the prohibition on mining and maintain an exclusive concentration on
agriculture while gentiles exploited the natural resources of Deseret for themselves — or get into
the game and garner as much of it as possible for their own purposes.

[33]See Appendix *MUDDY MISSION* Section .H

an amalgamation of corporate interests [34] intent on moving merchandise to and from the confluence of the Muddy with the Colorado or facilitating its transport.

.P   The Evidence

We adduce the included list of corporate titles as concrete evidence that there did exist in Charles day an expansive array of business entities whose vital interests made contact with the import and export of goods into Deseret, corporations of which Charles had perhaps become aware through personal experience in the freighting business from Salt Lake to Dixie. **Put differently, the suspicions evinced by him in rejecting the call in question were in no wise based on figments of his imagination.**

Brigham Young had spoken of shipping via the Colorado in 1864 from the perspective of emigration, with passing reference to import/export:

> *We shall want another path to bring home the Saints, and we want to prepare for it. The Colorado River is only a short way from St. George, and if I lived there I would soon have steamboats passing up the river, and it would serve as an island station for the other communities and outpost to furnish supplies to the immigrants bound for Salt Lake.*[35]

River imports (including, very likely, military supplies) had been envisioned from the outset as moving 'upland' in freight wagons from locations akin to Callville (`http://www.quehoposse.org/callville.html`) on the Colorado — where a warehouse had been constructed[36] — to settlements situated in selected regions of Deseret. In an apparently related move, the *ZCMI* chain of retail outlets was launched in 1869, despite opposition by the Council of Fifty .

Figure .1: River Steamer

Figure .2: Freight Wagons

Conversely, exports (e.g., cotton, silk, and other non-perishable goods) were apparently envisioned as moving from production sites 'within range' of the river and shipped to California markets. Bear in mind that Brigham Young had it firmly in mind to establish a self-sufficient Mormon empire incorporating vast areas of the western United States.

---

[34]POSSIBLY a consortium consisting of the likes of *R. G. Sneath of San Francisco, Hooper, Eldredge and Co.* (See Orson Ferguson Whitney, *History of Utah: Biographical.*) and others akin to those whose names are starred in the accompanying corporate lineup.

[35]Brigham Young, General Conference, 1864

[36]See Appendix *MUDDY MISSION* Section .C

A key motivational factor for merchants to develop a southern 'port' $\Longleftarrow$ was that transport to/from eastern sources from the north — even by railroad — had proven to be exceptionally difficult because of Indian insurgency, resulting in burned cargo and substantial financial loses for companies such as Hooper, Eldredge & Co.

.Q   Knowing When To Say NO!

So what? Simply business as usual, right? Hardly. Charles was NOT approached by a businessman making a business proposition but, rather, by a bishop who appears to have been issuing *a mission call* to service *a business plan*.[37]

Here indeed was a novel maximize-profits concept! An embellishment of profiteering methods which exploited consecration in zion mode for the advancement of corporate interests.[38] Charles — although so young as to be only in his mid twenties at the time of the attempted swindle[39] — was already thoroughly familiar with the methods and morals of the business environment in which he operated his freight line and had become a shrewd businessman himself (42.2), complete with his own network of informants (47.4).

I N A WORD, Charles was young but he was no fool! **More than that, he was the son of John Lytle and well-schooled in Mormonism.**[a] He saw through their corruption of gospel principles in a flash, perceived what that implied with respect to the spiritual state of 'Zion' in the vicinity[b] and respectfully declined to participate, both in the scheme to fleece him *and* the religious institution under the Bishop's jurisdiction — FOR THE REST OF HIS NATURAL LIFE! (Chapter 5)

---

[a] *And now I say unto you , all you that are desirous to follow the voice of the good shepherd, come ye out from the wicked, and be ye separate, and touch not their unclean things.* (cf. Alma 5:57-61)

[b] **Recall that Jacob Hamblin had refused to settle his family in Meadow Valley — despite the presence of three local Mormon settlements — due to the wickedness of the area(4.12).**

---

[37] A person, perhaps, who — the truth be known — actually knew more about *Mountain Meadows* than he did about *Meadow Valley*(5.5).

[38] **A variation on this theme personally familiar to the author is for profiteers to stand aside until a zionist undertaking nears completion, and then employ a combination of authority and legal maneuvering to hijack it for their own purposes.**

[39] It would appear that those targeting him had mistaken his youth for naiveté and seriously misjudged his intelligence, assuming that he would make an easy mark.

Representative Companies

1. Bank of Deseret (1871)

2. Big Cottonwood Lumber Co.

3. B(ig). K(anyon). Tannery

4. Brigham Young Bank

5. Brigham Young Blacksmith Shop

6. Brigham Young Carding Mill**

7. Brigham Young Cotton Factory**

8. Brigham Young Express Co.

9. Brigham Young Paper Mill

10. Brigham Young Silk Cocoonery**

11. Brigham Young Tannery

12. Brigham Young Woolen Factory

13. City Creek Foundry and Machine Shop

14. City Creek Sawmill

15. Cottonwood Canal Co.

16. Davis County Canal Co.

17. Deseret Bee, Stock and Fish Association

18. Deseret Currency Association

19. Deseret Dramatic Association

20. (Deseret Harness Co.)

21. (Deseret Iron Works Co.)

22. Deseret Irrigation and Navigation Canal Co.

23. Deseret Manufacturing Co.

24. Deseret Mint

25. Deseret National Bank

26. Deseret Store

27. Deseret Telegraph Co.

28. Deseret Woolen Mills

29. Eldredge and Clawson**

30. Empire Flour Mills

31. Excelsior Mill

32. Globe Bakery

33. Great Salt Lake City Water Works Association

34. H.C. Kimball Flour Mills

35. Hooper, Eldredge and Co. (1869)**

36. Howard Distillery

37. Jordan Irrigation Co.

38. Juab, Sanpete and Sevier Railroad Co.

39. LDS Bakery

40. Maid of Iowa (steamboat)

41. Millennial Star

42. Mutual Life and Savings Society of the United States

43. Nauvoo Water Power Co.

44. Perpetual Emigrating Fund Co.**

45. Provo Manufacturing Co.

46. Rush Valley Herd Co.

47. Salt Lake and Tooele Valley Railroad Co.

48. Salt Lake City Railroad Co.

49. Salt Lake House

50. Salt Lake Theatre

51. San Pete Coal Co.

52. Seventies' Hall Association

53. Timpanogos Manufacturing Co.

54. Union Academy

55. Union Pacific Railroad Co.

56. University of the City of Nauvoo

57. Utah Central Railroad Co.

58. Utah Southern Railroad Co.**

59. Utah Western Railway Co.

60. Wasatch Woolen Mills

61. Winsor Castle Stock Growing Co.

62. Young and Little Distillery**

63. ZCMI**

64. Zion's Savings Bank and Trust Co.

Proof

Made in the USA
Charleston, SC
23 June 2010